RELIGION IN THE EMERGENCE OF CIVILIZATION

This book presents an interdisciplinary study of the role of spirituality and religious ritual in the emergence of complex societies. With contributions by an eminent group of natural scientists, archaeologists, anthropologists, philosophers and theologians, this volume examines Çatalhöyük as a case study. A nine-thousand-year-old town in central Turkey, Çatalhöyük was first excavated in the 1960s and has since become integral to understanding the symbolic and ritual worlds of the early farmers and village dwellers in the Middle East. It is thus an ideal location for exploring theories about the role of religion in early settled life. This book provides a unique overview of current debates concerning religion and its historical variations. By exploring such themes as the integration of the spiritual and the material, the role of belief in religion, the cognitive bases for religion and religion's social roles, this book situates the results from Çatalhöyük within a broader understanding of the Neolithic in the Middle East.

Ian Hodder is Dunlevie Family Professor in the Department of Anthropology at Stanford University. He was recently awarded the Huxley Medal by the Royal Anthropological Institute and is the author of various books, including, most recently, *The Leopard's Tale: Revealing the Mysteries of Çatalhöyük* (2006).

John Templeton Foundation provided a grant in support of the project on which this book is based.

RELIGION IN THE EMERGENCE OF CIVILIZATION: ÇATALHÖYÜK AS A CASE STUDY

Edited by

IAN HODDER
Stanford University

CAMBRIDGE
UNIVERSITY PRESS

CAMBRIDGE UNIVERSITY PRESS
Cambridge, New York, Melbourne, Madrid, Cape Town, Singapore,
São Paulo, Delhi, Dubai, Tokyo, Mexico City

Cambridge University Press
32 Avenue of the Americas, New York, NY 10013-2473, USA

www.cambridge.org
Information on this title: www.cambridge.org/9780521150194

© Cambridge University Press 2010

First published 2010

Printed in the United States of America

A catalog record for this publication is available from the British Library.

Library of Congress Cataloging in Publication data

Religion in the emergence of civilization : Çatalhöyük as a case study / edited by
Ian Hodder.
  p.   cm.
Includes bibliographical references and index.
ISBN 978-0-521-19260-6 (hardback)
1. Çatal Mound (Turkey)   2. Neolithic period – Turkey – Konya Ili.   3. Religion,
Prehistoric – Turkey – Konya Ili.   4. Konya Ili (Turkey) – Antiquities.   I. Hodder,
Ian.   II. Title.
GN776.32.T9R45   2010
299′.9 – dc22   2010014060

ISBN 978-0-521-19260-6 Hardback
ISBN 978-0-521-15019-4 Paperback

Contents

List of Figures and Tables

Figures

Tables

Contributors

Maurice Bloch Department of Anthropology, London School of Economics (retired). Two relevant publications are *How We Think They Think: Anthropological Approaches to Cognition, Memory, Literacy* (1998) and *Prey into Hunter: The Politics of Religious Experience* (Cambridge University Press, 1992).

Ian Hodder Department of Anthropology, Stanford University, California. He was recently awarded the Huxley Medal by the Royal Anthropological Institute and is the author of *The Leopard's Tale: Revealing the Mysteries of Çatalhöyük* (2006).

Webb Keane Department of Anthropology, University of Michigan, Ann Arbor. He has been a Guggenheim Fellow, and his main books include *Signs of Recognition: Powers and Hazards of Representation in an Indonesian Society* (1997) and *Between Freedom and Fetish: Converting to Christian Modernity* (2006).

Lynn Meskell Department of Anthropology, Stanford University, California. She is editor of the *Journal of Social Archaeology* and has recently edited two volumes, *Cosmopolitan Archaeologies* (2009) and *Archaeologies of Materiality* (2005).

Carolyn Nakamura Archaeology Center, Stanford University, California. She obtained her Ph.D. at Columbia University on Neo-Assyrian figurine deposits and now works on the figurines at Çatalhöyük.

Peter Pels Department of Social and Behavioural Science, Leiden University, Holland. With Lynn Meskell he edited *Embedding Ethics* (2003). He is a specialist in the anthropology of sub-Saharan Africa and is currently the editor in chief of *Social Anthropology/Anthropologie sociale*, the journal of the European Association of Social Anthropologists.

LeRon Shults Institute for Religion, Philosophy and History, University of Agder, Kristiansand, Norway. He obtained his Ph.D. from Princeton

University and is the author of several books, including *The Postfounda-tionalist Task of Theology* (1999) and *Reforming Theological Anthropology: After the Philosophical Turn to Relationality* (2003).

J. Wentzel van Huyssteen Princeton Theological Seminary, Princeton University. Recently, he delivered the Gifford Lectures at the University of Edinburgh. His books include *Alone in the World? Human Uniqueness in Science and Theology* (2006).

Paul K. Wason John Templeton Foundation, West Conshohocken, Pennsylvania. His research on equality, social evolution and archaeological theory led him to write *The Archaeology of Rank* (Cambridge University Press, 1994), which includes an analysis of data from Çatalhöyük.

Harvey Whitehouse Department of Anthropology, Oxford University. A specialist in Melanesian religion, he is the founding director of Oxford University's Centre for Anthropology of Mind. His books include *Modes of Religiosity: A Cognitive Theory of Religious Transmission* (2004).

1

Probing religion at Çatalhöyük: An interdisciplinary experiment

Ian Hodder

The aim of this volume is to present an interdisciplinary study of the role of spirituality and religious ritual in the emergence of complex societies, involving natural scientists, archaeologists, anthropologists, philosophers and theologians in a novel, field-based context. Throughout the project, from 2006 to 2008, members convened at Çatalhöyük in central Turkey for a week each summer and also met in seminars at Stanford University. At the site they talked with the field team and spent time in the specialist laboratories discussing ways in which the data from the site could inform the main questions addressed by the project. Toward the end of the project, members undertook to write chapters for this volume, either singly or in collaboration. The volume presented here resulted from this experiment in bringing scholars from diverse backgrounds to work with archaeologists 'at the trowel's edge' at Çatalhöyük. During our discussions it became clear that many participants would prefer to place the terms 'religion' and 'civilization' in the book's title in quotation marks, as will be described later in this chapter and in Chapter 12. But whatever the difficulties with these terms and the lack of interdisciplinary agreement about their use, productive interactions took place that provided new insights into the interpretation of both Çatalhöyük and the Neolithic in Anatolia and the Middle East.

I am very grateful to the John Templeton Foundation for its support of the project on which this book is based, and to the participants in the project, who so willingly took on such an unusual task. I am also grateful to all the members of the Çatalhöyük Research Project, on whose long years of research this project was able to build, and in particular to Shahina Farid. Several anonymous reviewers provided helpful advice, and I am grateful to Lynn Meskell for her advice and guidance.

Introduction to the project

For about 140,000 years before the start of the Holocene, anatomically modern humans lived in small groups of relatively mobile hunter-
gatherers. Then in a relatively short time after 12,000 BC, human groups
began to settle down, adopt agriculture and take many of the steps that
we associate with 'civilization'. The reasons given for this shift have predominantly been climatic change, population increase and economic and
ecological factors, although social and cognitive factors have increasingly
been included (Bender 1978; Hayden 1990; Renfrew 1998). The aim
of the proposed study is to explore the extent to which spiritual life and
religious ritual played a role in this momentous shift.

The aims of the current excavations at Çatalhöyük in central Turkey
(7400–6000 BC) are to explore a site of great importance for our understanding of the first steps toward 'civilization' and to understand its art,
symbolism and ritual. The site occurs several thousand years after the
earliest domesticated plants and several thousand years before the cities
and states of Mesopotamia and Egypt, to which the term 'civilization'
is often applied. But its very large size (34 acres), its elaborate narrative
art, the occurrence of burials beneath house floors and its remarkable
preservation mean that it has taken its place as key to the understanding
of both early settled agricultural life (Cauvin 1994; Mithen 2003) and
the overall process that led from settled villages to urban agglomerations.

This foundational moment in the development of human society is
usually studied by archaeologists and natural scientists working in close
collaboration. In fact, this period of prehistory has been characterized by
the interaction of, for example, palaeoclimatologists, pollen analysts and
archaeologists. The emergence of settled life has remained the domain
of scientific and anthropological discussion. Recent work has increasingly
drawn attention to the importance of mind, meaning, symbol, ritual and
religion (e.g., Cauvin 1994; Donald 1991; Hodder 1990; Renfrew 1998;
Verhoeven 2002). But there has not been a wider discussion among
anthropologists of religion, philosophers and theologians. This volume
seeks to create such a dialogue, but in a concrete way, teasing apart the
evidence from one particular site.

History and background of the project

The focus of this study, Çatalhöyük East (7400–6000 BC) in central
Turkey, is one of the best-known Neolithic sites in Anatolia and the

Middle East, roughly contemporary with later Pre-Pottery and the following Pottery Neolithic in the Levant (Figures 1.1 and 1.2). It became well known because of its large size (34 acres and 3,500–8,000 people), with 18 levels inhabited over 1,400 years, and its dense concentration of 'art' in the form of wall paintings, wall reliefs, sculptures and installations. Within Anatolia, particularly central Anatolia, recent research has shown that there are local sequences that lead up to and prefigure Çatalhöyük (Baird 2007, 2008; Gérard and Thissen 2002; Özdoğan 2002). In southeast Turkey, the earlier villages of Çayönü (Özdoğan and Özdoğan 1998) and Göbekli Tepe (Schmidt 2001) already show substantial agglomeration and elaborate symbolism. In central Anatolia, Aşıklı Höyük (Esin and Harmankaya 1999) has densely packed housing through the millennium prior to Çatalhöyük. There are many other sites contemporary, or partly contemporary, with Çatalhöyük that are known in central Anatolia and the adjacent Burdur-Lakes region (Duru 1999; Gérard and Thissen 2002). Yet Çatalhöyük retains a special significance because of the complex narrative nature of its art, and many syntheses (e.g., by Cauvin 1994 or Mithen 2003) give it a special place. Much of the symbolism of the earlier Neolithic and later (into historic times) periods of the Middle East can be 'read' in terms of the evidence from Çatalhöyük, and the rich evidence from the site enables interpretation of the evidence from other sites.

The site was first excavated by James Mellaart (e.g., 1967) in the 1960s (Figures 1.3 and 1.4). After 1965 it was abandoned, until a new project began in 1993 (Hodder 1996, 2000, 2005a,b,c, 2006, 2007). Through both projects, only 5% of the mound has been excavated, but the whole mound has been sampled using surface survey, surface pickup, geophysical prospection and surface scraping (see reports in Hodder 1996). So far, 166 houses have been excavated by Mellaart in the current project. The main architectural components of the site are densely clustered houses, with areas of refuse or midden between them. The art and symbolism and burial all occur within houses. There is evidence of productive activities in all houses, in midden areas and on roofs of houses. None of the sampling shows evidence of large public buildings, ceremonial centers, specialized areas of production or cemeteries. The population of the settlement at any one time (between 3,500 and 8,000) has been conservatively estimated (Cessford 2005) using a variety of techniques and making a variety of assumptions about how many houses were inhabited at any one time.

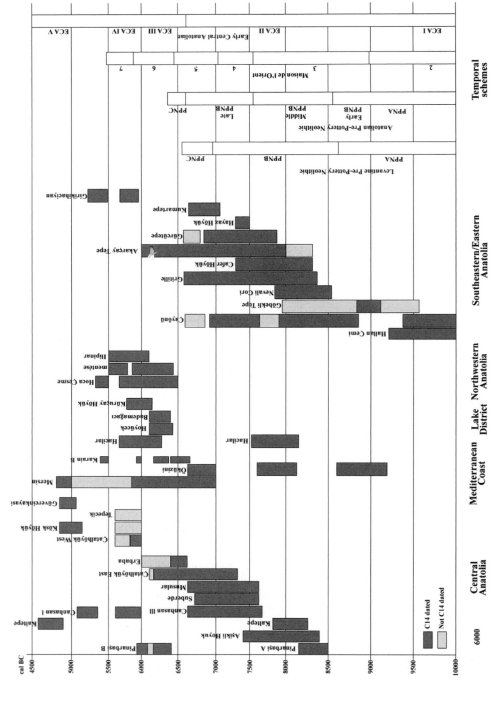

1.1. The dating of Çatalhöyük in relation to other sites in Anatolia and the Middle East. *Source:* Craig Cessford and Çatalhöyük Research Project.

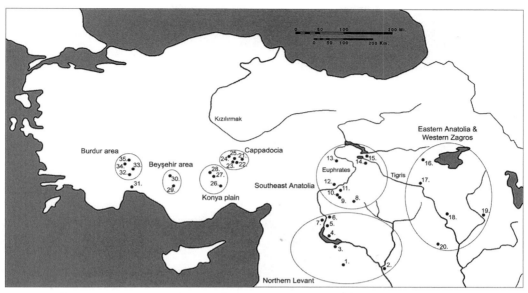

1.2. Map of Neolithic sites in Anatolia and adjacent regions. *Source:* Eleni Asouti. Map showing some of the main Neolithic and Epipalaeolithic sites in the main known regions in Anatolia and the Middle East. 1. El Kowm, 2. Bouqras, 3. Abu Hureyra, 4. Mureybet, 5. Jerf el Ahmar, 6. Dja'de, 7. Haloula, 8.Göbekli Tepe, 9. Biris Mezarlığı, 10. Söğüt Tarlası, 11. Nevali Çori, 12. Gritille, 13. Cafer Höyük, 14. Çayönü, 15. Boytepe, 16. Hallan Çemi, 17. Demirci, 18. Nemrik, 19. Zawi Chemi Shanidar (Palaeolithic-Epipalaeolithic), 20. Qermez Dere, 21. Gedikpaşa, 22. Aşıklı Höyük, 23. Musular, 24. Yellibelen Tepesi, 25. Kaletepe, 26. Can Hasan, 27. Pınarbaşı A & B, 28. Çatalhöyük, 29. Erbaba, 30. Suberde, 31. Öküzini (Epipalaeolithic), 32. Bademağacı, 33. Höyücek, 34. Hacılar, 35. Kuruçay (From Asouti 2005).

1.3. View of the Çatalhöyük excavations undertaken by James Mellaart in the 1960s. *Source:* Ian Todd and Çatalhöyük Research Project.

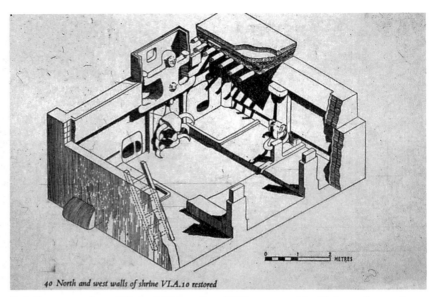

40 North and west walls of shrine VI.A.10 restored

1.4. Reconstruction of 'Shrine' 10 from Level VIB, excavated by Mellaart. *Source:* James Mellaart and Çatalhöyük Research Project.

Although 166 houses have been excavated at Çatalhöyük, only 18 buildings have been fully excavated in the present project using modern scientific techniques (Figure 1.5). Many other buildings have been partly excavated, but the buildings have been put on public display and so have not been completely excavated. All of the extensive excavation in the 1960s took place without screening, and with limited recording and no scientific analysis (except radiocarbon dating). It remains the case that only 5% of the mound has been excavated, and a very small proportion of that excavation using modern scientific techniques resulted in fully excavated houses.

In the earliest phase of the current project (1993–5), we concentrated on regional survey and on planning and studying the surface of the mounds, conducting surface pickup, drawing eroded profiles of the earlier excavation trenches and using geophysical prospection. We also undertook a reevaluation of the material in museums that had been excavated by Mellaart (Hodder 1996).

During the second phase of fieldwork and publication (1996–2002), the research aim focused on individual buildings. We excavated two main areas on the East Mound (Figure 1.6). In the northern area of the East Mound, we concentrated on excavating buildings (Buildings 1 and 5 and

1.5. Excavation in Building 5 by the current project. *Source:* Jason Quinlan and Çatalhöyük Research Project.

Building 3 in the BACH Area) in great detail in order to discern depositional processes and to understand how individual houses functioned. In the South Area, we continued the trenches that had been started by Mellaart in order to understand the overall sequence of the site and to see how individual houses were rebuilt and reused over time. Simultaneously, palaeoenvironmental work was conducted (Roberts et al. 1999), regional survey continued (Baird 2002) and excavations were undertaken on the later Chalcolithic mound at Çatalhöyük West (Figure 1.6). Publication of the monographs for this second phase of work was completed in 2007 (Hodder 2005a,b,c, 2006, 2007). The methods used by the project were published in an earlier volume (Hodder 2000).

The research aims for the third phase of the project (2003–12) turned from individual houses to the social geography of the settlement as a whole and larger community structure. Excavation took place from 2003 to 2008, with postexcavation from 2009 to 2012. Extensive excavation took place in a new area of the site, specifically the 4040 Area in the northern part of the mound (Figure 1.7), and in 2008 a shelter was

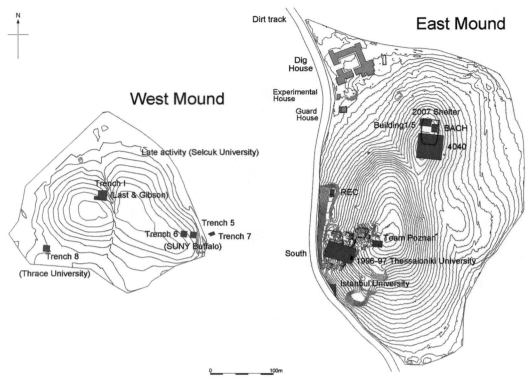

1.6. Excavation areas at Çatalhöyük. *Source:* Shahina Farid and Çatalhöyük Research Project.

erected over part of this area (Figure 1.8). Excavation also continued in the South shelter (Figure 1.9) so that we could explore the organization of architecture in the upper levels of the site and link our results to the work done by Mellaart in this area of the site. Excavations by other teams, especially the TP team led by Arek Marciniak of Poznan University and Lech Czerniak of the University of Gdansk in Poland, and by the IST team led by Mihriban Özbaşaran of Istanbul University, allowed further exploration of the upper levels. And on the following Chalcolithic West Mound, excavation by three teams (University of Thrace at Edirne led by Burçin Erdoğu, Selcuk University at Konya led by Ahmet Tırpan and Asuman Baldıran and Berlin University and SUNY Buffalo led by Peter Biehl and Eva Rosenstock) allowed an increased understanding of the developments in the 6th millennium BC.

In the 4040 Area the focus has been on understanding the variation among contemporary buildings. The new buildings and midden areas excavated here have allowed increased understanding of the social

1.7. Buildings in the 4040 Area. *Source:* Jason Quinlan and Çatalhöyük Research Project.

1.8. Shelter over the 4040 Area. *Source:* Jason Quinlan and Çatalhöyük Research Project.

makeup of the mound. In particular we now have clear evidence for the grouping of houses into small clusters that probably share ancestral burial houses, as well as larger-scale groupings into sectors of clustered houses bounded by midden areas and/or alleyways (as shown in Figure 1.7). In the South Area of the site our focus has been on a sequence of buildings in one 'column' of houses (from the base of the column these are Buildings 65, 56, 44 and 10). This sequence of houses (known as the Building 10 sequence) stacked one on top of the other over time has provided much clear evidence for strong micro-traditions and repetitive practices that almost certainly indicate long-term occupancy by the same group. The recirculation of human body parts is certainly part of this occupancy (as discussed later in the chapter).

Conducting the dialogues on religion and spirituality

Çatalhöyük is perhaps best known for its elaborate symbolism (e.g., Figure 2.1), which has often been interpreted in cultic, religious or spiritual terms (Cauvin 1994; Hodder 1990; Mellaart 1967). During the third

1.9. South shelter excavation. *Source:* Jason Quinlan and Çatalhöyük Research Project.

phase of the research described in the preceding section, targeted funding from the John Templeton Foundation allowed us to expand the scope of our work to consider the following four research questions regarding religion and spirituality: (1) How can archaeologists recognize the spiritual, religious and transcendent in early time periods? (2) Are changes in spiritual life and religious ritual a necessary prelude to the social and economic changes that lead to 'civilization'? (3) Do human forms take on a central role in the spirit world in the early Holocene, and, if so, does this centrality lead to new conceptions of human agency that themselves provide the possibility for the domestication of plants and animals? (4) Do violence and death act as the foci of transcendent religious experience during the transitions of the early Holocene in the Middle East, and are such themes central to the creation of social life in the first large agglomerations of people?

But how could one achieve answers to these questions that avoided the pitfalls so often associated with work on the interpretation of prehistoric symbolism and religion? The common approach has been to build cross-cultural models based on anthropology (e.g., Binford 1971; Lewis-Williams and Pearce 2005; Renfrew 1985) or on cognitive science (e.g., Knappett 2005; Mithen 1998; Wynn 2002). Alternatively, archaeologists have tried in-depth contextual readings, influenced by various anthropological perspectives from structuralism to phenomenology (e.g., Thomas 1996; Tilley 1997). The dangers of these approaches are insensitivity to the data context, on the one hand, and lack of broader comparison, on the other. In short, there is either insufficient knowledge of the archaeological data context or insufficient knowledge of the broader anthropological literature. It is difficult, given the depth of the specialisms involved, to master all the relevant archaeological and anthropological knowledge, never mind all the relevant theological and philosophical knowledge. How, then, could we bring the relevant knowledge to bear on Çatalhöyük, a site that, because of its mode of deposition and survival, has particularly rich contextual information?

I have argued that archaeology should focus on interpretation 'at the trowel's edge' (Hodder 1999, 2000, 2004a). What I mean by this is that the discipline has too readily accepted that data collection in the field and the interpretation of results are separate processes, carried out at different times and places. Since archaeology is destructive (it destroys the relationships between objects and contexts in the process of excavation), this separation of discovery from interpretation limits the potential for later reinterpretation and checking of data. Thus a better approach is to bring forward interpretation to the moment of discovery, as far as that is possible. The more that excavators are surrounded by interpretive possibilities as they dig, the more they are able to interpret what they find, and the more equipped they are to test alternatives. The approach also allows a wider range of interested groups to participate in the process of data interpretation at the critical and nonreversible moment of excavation.

The Çatalhöyük project has developed a number of ways of implementing this idea, in particular by instituting 'priority tours', whereby a wide range of analytical specialists discuss with the excavators in the trench. The building of specialist laboratories at the site has also facilitated such interchange. This idea of collaborative interpretation at the trowel's edge can be extended to a wider range of disciplines, including those dealing with spirituality and religion. For example, it is of value for archaeologists to draw on ethnographic and historical comparisons, especially regarding sacrifice, offerings, feasting and exchange. Thus the Sumba, where Webb Keane (1997) has conducted fieldwork, is virtually a locus classicus for the ritual slaughter of cattle and subsequent feasting, as well as of so-called ancestor worship. But rather than the archaeologist trying to draw out relevant information from Keane's account, would it not be far more productive to have Webb Keane in the trench, adding his background of ethnographic and anthropological knowledge to the debates about the interpretation of specific archaeological evidence?

For such an approach to be successful, the anthropologists, philosophers and theologians had to commit over a three-year period to engaging in discussions about Çatalhöyük – to really learning about the site in detail, as well as understanding something of the broader context of the Neolithic in the Middle East. I am forever grateful to the interdisciplinary group of scholars who were willing to take on this challenge with verve and good patience. The group consisted of Robert Bellah, Maurice Bloch, René Girard, Webb Keane, Peter Pels, LeRon Shults, Wentzel van Huyssteen, Harvey Whitehouse and Paul Wason. The discussions at the site and at Stanford were extremely successful and productive, if at times tense, and have led to important new developments in the way that the archaeological team understands the site. Throughout, the collaboration between the Templeton scholars and the archaeologists was seen as two-way and interactive. For example, the group of scholars suggested it would be important to see more of the Building 10 sequence, particularly so that we could see the start of the sequence and identify any special founding events. So in 2007 the archaeological team decided to continue excavating with important new results (see Chapter 7). With regard to analytical work, the group of scholars suggested that the faunal remains team focus on the issue of sacrifice. The team did so and reported back to the group in the following year. The group of scholars also asked that information be collated on the way in which some houses endured while others had shorter lives. Work by Jason Quinlan aimed at providing these data led to the results described in Chapter 7; when presented to the group of scholars at the site in 2007, the data led to the definition by Peter Pels of 'history houses' (see Chapter 7), which now frame much of the analytical work of the project as a whole.

This volume outlines the progress in providing answers to the four key questions enumerated earlier, which have been the central focus of the Templeton-funded project at Çatalhöyük. From the start a real tension emerged among the scholars regarding the use of and approaches toward the term 'religion'. Some participants were more willing to espouse universalist approaches that seemed to link theology and neuroscience in suggesting that the capacity for religion is a 'natural' component, while others saw 'religion' as a term covering a variety of phenomena tightly embedded within specific historical circumstances. At times these different positions seemed to come closer to each other – for example, when the contextualists accepted that there may be universal propensities that emerged in particular forms. And both sides came together in accepting that religion and the secular cannot easily be distinguished, especially in noncomplex societies. Yet there remained a difference in how they approached the data – from universal expectation of predicted patterns to critical inquiries of the specific. There was much debate about whether 'religion' occurred in all societies, whether it had universal forms and whether the baggage that came with the term impeded dialogue. There also remained disagreement among the authors of this volume as to whether one can make the universalist claim that religion always involves belief. All these issues have been widely discussed in the literatures on religion, but the discourse and terminology in each discipline vary, so that members of the group had to spend time trying to understand each other's positions. Difficulties of translation aside, there remained differences in perspective, particularly with regard to universalism.

Response to the validity and usefulness of the term 'religion' also colored the proposed answers to the four questions posed by the project. The different responses to the four questions are provided in the chapters that follow, and the debates are summarized in the concluding Chapter 12. In this chapter I will provide background and an introduction to the discussions regarding the four questions and related issues that were raised.

1. How can archaeologists recognize the spiritual, religious and transcendent in early time periods?

The rich symbolism at Çatalhöyük, widely recognized since its discovery by James Mellaart, provided an ideal context for exploring this question. There have long been debates within archaeology about the identification of ritual and the interpretation of meaning (e.g., Renfrew 1985), and a wide range of approaches have been applied, from the structuralist to the historical, cognitive and evolutionary (e.g., Donald 1991; Renfrew 1998; Tilley 1997). I have contributed to that debate (Hodder 1982, 1986, 1999), arguing for a contextual and interpretive approach in archaeology. Many archaeologists would now accept that a multistranded approach is needed. How can it be shown at Çatalhöyük that specific objects have 'aura' or transcendental qualities for certain groups of people? How is it possible to show that the art is ritual or spiritual in nature or that the houses partly functioned as 'shrines' or 'temples'? These questions can be approached by linking detailed contextual analysis of archaeological data to specialized natural science techniques within a wider framework provided by anthropology, history, philosophy and theology.

At the methodological level, it is clearly possible to note certain aspects of life that appear to us to have a religious or spiritual dimension. The kinds of information that can be interpreted in terms of religion at Çatalhöyük include burials, paintings and installations of parts of wild animals in walls and benches. Other examples include the passing down of human skulls from generation to generation within houses (Chapter 2), or the holding of feasts involving wild male cattle, or the obtaining of speleotherms (stalagmites and stalactites) from caves to put in graves, or the exchange of high-quality obsidian from distant sources when other, nearer sources would have worked equally well. There is no doubt that the rich elaboration of houses at Çatalhöyük and the paintings within them speak to a complex world of myths and meanings that transcend everyday practice. This point is particularly clear at the earlier, 9th millennium BC site of Göbekli Tepe in southeastern Turkey (Schmidt 2006), where much of the symbolism seen at Çatalhöyük occurs in clearly ritual contexts. A suite of meanings dealing with skulls and birds of prey, wild cattle and other dangerous animals circulated over enormous areas of the Middle East during the period in which people settled down into towns and adopted agriculture (see Chapter 2). This symbolism clearly had religious or ritual dimensions, but what was the relationship between the religious symbolism and daily life? Can contextual information and scientific analysis help to answer such a question?

As an example, the publication by Meskell et al. (2008) of detailed data on the figurines from the site has transformed our understanding of these objects. In much earlier work and writing on the site, including by Mellaart, these objects were seen as representational and as religious, relating to a cult of the mother goddess. The work of the figurine team has thoroughly undermined this interpretation. In fact, when properly quantified, few of the figurines are clearly female. In addition, examination of their context of deposition shows that the objects are not in 'special' locations, but were discarded, often in middens. A study of the fabric of the figurines by Chris Doherty (pers. comm.) has shown that they are made of local marls and that they are unfired or low fired. Many have survived only because they were accidentally burned in hearths and fires. Thus all the evidence suggests that these objects were not in a

separate religious sphere. Rather, it was the process of their daily production – not their contemplation as religious symbols – that was important.
They gave meaning, at the everyday, low-intensity level, to subjectivities
and to the social world that they helped imagine.

Much the same can be said of all our work at Çatalhöyük. In earlier phases of the project we had already found that Mellaart's division
of buildings into 'shrines' and 'houses' was incorrect. All buildings give
abundant evidence of both ritual and mundane activity. Indeed, it has
become impossible to separate these two spheres. Earlier (Hodder 2006),
I had argued that it was possible to distinguish a mundane domestic
southern part of houses from a northern part of houses in which art,
burial and ritual occur. Our recent excavation and analysis have shown the
inadequacies of this distinction. While it is still the case that there are differences between the activities and features in the southern (hearth) and
northern (burial) parts of houses, this is not a distinction between domestic and ritual. We have found burials, especially of children, routinely in
the southern parts of buildings. Hearths and ovens do sometimes occur
in the northern parts. But generally, every single act that we can observe
seems to blur the boundaries between the everyday and the sacred or
special. Thus the detailed micro-morphological and micro-residue work
being conducted by Wendy Matthews and Ana Spasojevic has shown
that even the dirtiest of 'domestic' floors may contain items that seem to
have been intentionally placed as foundation or abandonment behavior.
In making an oven, people used materials that created memories of past
events (e.g., crushed, painted plasters, or parts of figurines, that are so
distinctive that they must have been noted and intentionally included).
In placing obsidian below floors, people were not only caching useful
objects but perhaps also referring to the dead below the floors. In painting walls, people were using symbols but they may also have seen the
paintings as practical – as ways of interacting with the dead.

There are many examples in the following chapters that show the
interdigitation of religious and everyday life at Çatalhöyük. But in the
fieldwork and laboratory analysis, we have come increasingly to recognize
that certain events stand out. These events referred to broader mythical
themes, involved high-arousal experience and involved larger groupings.
The clearest example is the focus on teasing and baiting wild animals,
consuming them in feasts and remembering them in installations of their
skulls, teeth and claws on the walls of houses (see Chapter 2). Thus

we have found collections of wild animal bones in which there are high concentrations of large animal parts, not as broken up as with the domesticated sheep and goat bones, and in locations suggesting foundation or abandonment events. These events mark the change from one house to another, and they involve the types of symbolism seen at Göbekli and widely across the Middle East (especially the focus on wild, dangerous animals and animal parts; see Chapter 2). These events and objects thus refer to broader imaginings, focus attention, arouse interest. But they are also eminently practical ways of creating social community, distributing large amounts of meat and probably engaging in exchange and interaction. Thus the religious component of these events is part of a marking of those aspects of life to which the inhabitants at Çatalhöyük gave special meaning.

As another example, in Building 42 we found a burial in which a woman held the head of a man (Hodder 2004b). The man's head had been plastered to create the features of his face and had been painted red; indeed, it had been replastered several times, suggesting that the plastered skull had been retained for some time before burial with the woman. This was a highly charged event, as suggested by the fact that this is the only example of a plastered skull found at the site, and indeed there is only one other example from anywhere in Turkey. The burial was in fact a foundation burial: it had not been dug through the floors of the house, but the floors of the house had been built up above the burial. So this highly charged event had a social significance – the founding of a new house. The event had both practical and religious significance. The religious significance was heightened by the placing in the grave of another remarkable object – the claw of a leopard. I have written elsewhere (2006) of the complex mythic associations of the leopard for the inhabitants of Çatalhöyük. For the moment, it is clear that this burial is a marking event, and it can be called religious not because it is separate from everyday life, but because it focuses attention, arouses, refers to broader imaginings and deals with the relationship between self and community.

The houses at Çatalhöyük and all the activities that took place in them were seamlessly religious, social and practical. The lived-in houses were religious in the sense that they were about imagining, remembering and interacting with past houses and those who lived in them. The discussions and debates reported in the following chapters and summarized in Chapter 12 have led to a greater understanding of this connection between the religious and everyday life. They have allowed exploration of the ways in which religion is embedded in particular understandings of the world, marking out certain activities and dealing with the social relationships between self and community.

2. Are changes in spiritual life and religious ritual a necessary prelude to the social and economic changes that lead to 'civilization'?

Recent archaeological discoveries from southeastern Turkey, Syria and the Levant have identified large ceremonial structures that occur very early in the development of settled 'towns' and agricultural life. For example, Göbekli Tepe has produced clear evidence for public ritual and monumental sculpture beginning in the 9th millennium BC. Other sites include Jerf el-Ahmar, Çayönü and Nevalı Çori. Some of these are close to where recent biomolecular studies have suggested that the first domestication of einkorn wheat occurred somewhere near Karacadağ in southeastern Turkey, rather than in the Levant (Heun et al. 1997; Jones 2001). As Steve Mithen has suggested (2003: 67), the first domestication of wheat may have been connected with the nearby sites such as Göbekli Tepe. Indeed, it seems quite possible that people who had come together largely because of large ritual centers ended up 'accidentally' domesticating plants and animals (but see Wason, Chapter 10). The large agglomerations of people would have depended on a wide range of local resources that would increasingly have had to be more intensively collected (just because of the large number of people exploiting the same landscape). Part of that intensity would have involved keeping grains and replanting them. At Göbekli Tepe itself it is argued that there are still no domesticated plants or animals (Schmidt 2001). But the intensification would likely have produced the selective environment in which domestication could have occurred at some site in the region. Many now argue that the reason people started agglomerating and creating settled life may have been religious ritual (Cauvin 1994; Mithen 2003). Çatalhöyük is too late to contribute directly to this debate, except that our detailed studies of the location of the site have suggested that the search for the clays and plasters for symbolic installations may have been central to the site's location (Hodder 2006). In addition, the rich symbolism undoubtedly could have been a factor in attracting people to the site.

Discussions of the question of whether changes in religion and spiritual life were necessary for settled life and domestication have two components. The first concerns the evidence from the Middle East as a whole, and deals with the factors associated with the formation of settled villages from the 11th millennium BC and their association with fully domesticated plants and animals by the 9th millennium BC. The second concerns the factors associated with the domestication of cattle at Çatalhöyük itself in the 7th millennium BC.

In relation to the first, more general question, archaeologists have long argued that the shift to settled agricultural life was closely linked to climate change at the start of the Holocene and population increase (Flannery 1973). The greater availability of resources and the population pressure led to the adoption of agriculture and the formation of villages. More recently, a number of authors have argued that while these factors may have played a role, shifts in social structure are needed in order to create the long-term alliances that support an agricultural economy (Bender 1978; Kuijt 2000). It is also argued that the new social forms and the new relationships with the environment involved conceptual shifts, including changes in the way people interacted with ancestors and animal spirits (Cauvin 1994; Hodder 2006).

Pre-Neolithic ritual structures have been claimed in the southern Levant, such as the monoliths from Natufian contexts at Wadi Hammeh 27 and Rosh Zin (Goring-Morris and Belfer-Cohen 2002: 72). But key to the notion that fundamental social and economic changes were presaged in religious and spiritual dimensions of life is the site of Göbekli Tepe. This impressive site with its 4- to 6-m-high stele carved with a range of wild and dangerous animals provides strong support for the importance of religion and ritual. The subsistence evidence from the site indicates an economy based on the exploitation of wild resources. So this was a large, settled tell site, indicating agglomeration before domestication, although it may have functioned as a regional cult center rather than a permanent settlement (Schmidt 2006). Nevertheless, the collaborative endeavor that must have been involved in its construction and long-term use implies long-term social relationships and concentrations of population that would have been necessary for the formation of settled agricultural villages. In addition, the specific symbolism on the large stone pillars (see Chapter 2) indicates a centrality of the human form, dominating and dwarfing the world of wild animals. This central human agency was perhaps a necessary precursor to the relationship with animals that we term 'domestication' (see Question 4).

At Çatalhöyük we cannot observe the shift to agriculture and settled life, because the site is relatively late in the overall sequence in the Middle East. But the aim of the project was to ask a second question in relation to the more specific set of changes leading to dependence on domesticated cattle. As already noted, recent excavation at Çatalhöyük has focused on the upper levels of the Neolithic East Mound and on the ensuing West Mound (located on the opposite bank of the Neolithic–Chalcolithic river). Study of the faunal remains from the West Mound shows that by 6000 BC cattle had been domesticated. But we seem to see shifts in the symbolic use of cattle prior to this at the top of the Neolithic East Mound. In the upper levels of the East Mound, Mellaart had noted that there were fewer large wild bull installations and bucrania. We have found the same thing. On the other hand, we have found profound changes in the ways that animal bones were deposited. In the TP excavation area (the uppermost levels of the East Mound), for the first time, we have found human and animal bones deposited together. In the main sequence in the Neolithic East Mound, animal bones never occur with human bones in burials. There is an absolute separation of the human and the animal. As many have argued, the domestication of animals involves a new, closer relationship between humans and animals. It is thus of great interest that in the upper levels at Çatalhöyük East we start to see cattle and humans being associated together in burial deposits. Also in the upper levels of the East Mound, cattle and other animal heads begin to appear as handles on ceramic vessels used in serving food. At the time of writing we remain unsure at what point cattle began to show physical changes associated with domestication, and it remains possible that domesticated cattle were introduced from elsewhere. The change may have happened in the upper levels of the East Mound, before the clearer evidence we have for cattle domestication on the West Mound. For the moment it remains a possibility that the symbolic changes associated with cattle occurred before or contemporary with the physical evidence of domestication.

3. Do human forms take on a central role in the spirit world in the early Holocene, and, if so, does this centrality lead to new conceptions of human agency that themselves provide the possibility for the domestication of plants and animals?

For 140,000 years modern humans had lived as hunter-gatherers, and ethnographic evidence suggests that they would have seen the environment as giving and reciprocating, and that their spirit worlds would have consisted largely of animals and natural features with which shaman-like figures may have mediated (Chapter 2). While human figures do appear in the Palaeolithic paintings and in the 'Venus figurines' of France, Spain and elsewhere, these human representations are not shown dominating animals. There are images that suggest humans may have mediated with the spirit world, but there is no evidence of a central human divinity over animals.

Then suddenly in the 9th millennium BC at Göbekli Tepe and then at Nevalı Çori in southeastern Turkey there are monumental monoliths within ceremonial structures and/or communal houses. On these huge stones are the carvings of an array of wild animals. The huge stones have human arms. The symbolic world of animal spirits is here dominated by human figures. In the art of Çatalhöyük humans are shown teasing, baiting and dominating oversized bulls and other wild animals, in stark contrast to Palaeolithic art (Figure 2.1). Cauvin (1994) discussed this increased importance of humans as relevant to the domination of animals necessary in animal domestication, and Helms (2003) provided a wider argument about the emergence of human divinities in relation to domestication.

Again, this question has two components. The first deals with the general evidence from Europe and the Middle East. The second component deals with the specific evidence from Çatalhöyük.

With regard to the first and more general component of this question, there is little doubt that the remarkable pillars at Göbekli represent humans. It seems plausible that the placing of human forms 'above' or 'dominating' wild animals was a necessary precursor to or concomitant of the domestication of animals. This newer, closer relationship between humans and animals has been discussed with respect to Question 2. But it is the dominating nature of the humans in the Çatalhöyük symbolism that is significant in terms of suggesting a new form of relationship with animals that is less about equivalence and exchange with animals and animal spirits than about interference and control.

With regard to the second and more specific component of this question, could the increased centrality of the human in the spirit world have come about through the increased importance of 'shamans' or mediators? Or did it come about through the increased importance of ancestors? There is much to suggest the latter interpretation, although there may also have been elders who interceded with the ancestors and had 'shamanic' powers. In Chapter 2 Hodder and Meskell discuss the possible role of a 'trickster' figure. With regard to the role of ancestors, recent excavations at Çatalhöyük have found more evidence for the special nature of the removal and circulation of heads. It is clear that both men and women had their heads removed after burial, although this was a rare event and associated with the more elaborate 'history houses' (as discussed later). We have found adult men and women with their heads removed after burial, as well as an instance of head removal from a woman with a full-term fetus in her birth canal. There is also a case in which not the head but the limbs were removed from an adult skeleton. We also continue to find examples of the special placing of skulls in foundation and abandonment contexts, and as already noted we have found a plastered male skull in the arms of an adult female. The association of the latter case with the unique leopard claw underlines the overall evidence that the people whose heads were removed had a special status and that the circulated and handed-down skulls had a particular significance.

The detailed study of the figurines at Çatalhöyük has shown that removable heads and dowel holes in torsos to contain heads were much more prevalent than had been thought. The paintings too show headless bodies associated with vultures. The art from Göbekli also shows a headless body with an erect penis associated with birds. Overall it is possible to argue that myths circulated in which heads were removed and carried upward by birds of prey (see Chapter 2). This process could be reenacted in the removal and replacement of heads on figurines. It seems possible that the process of removing and circulating human heads created ancestors that could communicate with the world of animal spirits (as seen in the artistic renderings of humans interacting with oversized animals at Çatalhöyük) as well as be communicated with by humans (in the caring for and replastering of skulls, and in the reenactment of head removal on figurines).

Those studying the figurines have increasingly noted the fascination with body parts, buttocks, breasts, navels and so on. Indeed, the more examples of art we have found, the more we see the focus on the human form. For example, it is clear that the so-called splayed figures identified by Mellaart (1967) as mother goddesses are actually bears (Hodder 2006), but they have a human form with protruding navel. This protruding navel motif is also seen in all the stamp seals that have been found at Çatalhöyük. On the latter the navel is associated with spiral meander motifs that are also found engraved or painted on walls. Seen from this perspective the human form is everywhere at the site. It has reached a new centrality that does indeed suggest a new conception of human agency, less reciprocal and more dominant in the world of symbols, meanings and myths.

4. Do violence and death act as the foci of transcendent religious experience during the transitions of the early Holocene in the Middle East, and are such themes central to the creation of social life in the first large agglomerations of people?

With regard to this question, it proved important to separate the discussion of violence from that of death.

(a) With regard to violence, it has long been assumed that the primary focus of symbolism at early village sites in the Middle East is a nurturing 'mother goddess' who embodies notions of birth and rebirth (see Chapter 2). But recent finds at both Göbekli and Çatalhöyük have suggested a link to death and violence as much as to birth and rebirth (Chapter 2). The focus of the Templeton discussions was to understand this very different symbolic emphasis in the first large agglomerations.

Recent finds at Çatalhöyük include a figurine that looks like a typical 'mother goddess' from the front, with full breasts and extended belly, but at the back she is a skeleton, with ribs, vertebrae, scapulae and pelvic bones clearly shown (see Figure 2.9). And in 2004 a grave was found in which a woman held a plastered skull of a man in her arms; she was also found with the only leopard bone we have ever found on-site, worn as a claw pendant. In fact, there is much imagery and symbolism of death and violence at Çatalhöyük. There are bulls' heads fixed to walls, and other installations on and in walls, including the tusks of wild boars, vulture skulls, the teeth of foxes and weasels. The new finds from the earlier sites of Göbekli Tepe and Nevalı Çori in southeastern Anatolia indicate that this focus on dangerous, wild animals is a central theme of the development of early villages and settled life.

As noted, a particular discussion took place with the members of the faunal archaeological team regarding the role of animal sacrifice. There are many difficulties using the term 'sacrifice' in relation to the archaeological evidence. Wild animals were killed and eaten and deposited in relation to foundations of buildings, but these dedicatory acts do not necessarily imply the giving of something 'owned' or the giving to a specific being, spirit or god. On the other hand, there was much evidence for the use of sharp and dangerous parts of wild animals in installations in houses. We must be wary of assuming these objects refer predominantly to violence, since the main symbolic focus may have been on the power or energy of wild animals, but the narrative scenes in the art undoubtedly show dangerous interactions between humans and animals.

(b) Whatever the debates about the role of violence, there has been more agreement in our discussions that death acted as a focus of transcendent religious experience during the transitions of the early Holocene in the Middle East and that it was central to the creation of social life in the first large agglomerations of people. This is because of the role of dead ancestors in the creation of 'houses'.

There has been discussion earlier in this chapter of the evidence for the circulation of human body parts taken from burials beneath the floors of houses. Plastered skulls of both humans and wild bulls circulated and were deposited on important occasions, such as the founding or abandoning of a house.

Certain houses at Çatalhöyük had many more complete skeletons than there were people who could have lived in those houses. For example, Building 1, which was inhabited for only 40 years by a family-sized group, had 62 burials beneath the floors. It was clear that people had been buried into this house from other houses. So while some houses have no burials in them, the average is 5–8. There appear to be a small number of houses that have 30–62 burials and that therefore seem to have a special nature.

Members of the Templeton group of scholars were very interested in these special houses. They also noted the cases in which people living at Çatalhöyük had dug down into earlier houses in order to retrieve sculpture such as bucrania (plastered bull heads). The special houses often seemed to have been rebuilt over longer periods than other houses and to have more elaborate symbolism (Düring 2006). The anthropologists in our group noted the way in which sometimes house was carefully built on abandoned house in long sequences. They suggested all the evidence indicated that we were dealing with a 'house society' in which rights and resources were passed down to members of the same 'house' through time (for more detailed discussions of 'house societies', see Chapters 6–9).

During the project the archaeologists were therefore asked to provide data on the longevity of houses. Did some houses start and fail, and why did some succeed in being rebuilt over hundreds of years while others lasted only one generation of building? The data presented in Chapter 7 were collected in order to answer such questions. The houses with many burials had evidence of being rebuilt many times – up to four or more rebuildings – that is, for hundreds of years. Some houses had very short lives. But some houses were reproduced over long periods. These houses were also the more elaborate in terms of art and internal architectural fittings. Some of the internal symbolic features had been retained from earlier houses. In looking through their material, the human remains team (Dr. Başak Boz) found cases in which teeth from earlier burials were taken and placed in jaws in later burials in rebuilds of the same house. It seemed possible to argue that these houses had built a history. Peter Pels coined the term 'history houses', and we have gone on to use this helpful term.

Thus history houses are defined as those with many burials and a history of at least four rebuilds. They also tend to have more internal art and elaboration (Düring 2006). Much work needs to be done on other aspects of the history houses. There is some evidence from the work on bricks and clays that these houses had privileged access to certain resources (S. Love, pers. comm.). But the history houses do not have more storage or production than other houses; indeed, they seem to have rather less. Their status seems to have been based on the control of history, religion and access to ancestors. They may also have been central to the provision of wild bull feasts that may have had mythical and spiritual components. But they did not control production or storage, as far as we can see. Thus it is reasonable to argue that social structure (the house society structure) and social dominance (by history houses) were created not through the control of production but through the performance of rituals, links to ancestors and the animal spirits and participation in the transcendent. Thus religion and spirituality at Çatalhöyük were closely linked to the house and to the circulation of dangerous parts of wild animals.

One additional theme that emerged during our discussions concerned change through time. It has become necessary to note that the 'classic' Çatalhöyük of the early and middle levels (from pre–Level XII to Level VI in Mellaart's terms), with its bull horn installations and elaborate internal fittings, changes toward the upper levels of the mound (Level V and above). In these upper levels there are fewer elaborate installations in houses, more use of decorated pottery, less plastering of walls, less burial in houses and so on. One possible interpretation, being explored in current work, is that during the upper levels a more integrated house-based economy gradually emerged. This focused more on domesticated animals (sheep and goats), and their secondary products, rather than wild cattle. In these upper levels, there are more representations of women in the figurine corpus. Social status early in the site seems to have focused on wild animals, associated feasts and male prowess, whereas in the upper levels the success of the house was represented by the size of the house, by the centrality of the hearth and by representations of women. Other interpretations are suggested by Pels in Chapter 9.

Conclusions

The chapters that follow describe the responses of an interdisciplinary group of scholars to the four questions outlined in this chapter. Some of the chapters are directed specifically to the four questions, but others overflow into broader or related themes that were raised in our discussions over three years. Because religion is not seen as a separate domain by the scholars involved in the project, there is much consideration of house societies, of households, of political and social economies, of change through time, of temporalities. Indeed, a distinctive aspect of the project was that it proved difficult to contain accounts of religion, and in fact many of the most important results of the dialogues between interdisciplinary scholars and archaeologists dealt with matters that are not obviously religious. Thus the identification of 'history houses' seems to be about categorizing the social processes at Çatalhöyük in terms of house societies, and yet this result was arrived at by the consideration of the special religious nature of certain houses that contained many burials. Religion, then, at Çatalhöyük seemed to lead us in many directions and to be broadly present.

In addition, the four research questions have been formulated in overly simplistic and stark ways. They provide useful starting points for a dialogue, but the first part of our discussions was always to critique the terms and put them in brackets or quotes. I have already noted the difficulties that surround the use of the terms 'religion' and 'civilization'. Debates concerning origins of 'civilization' or 'domestication' often assume a chain of causality that is never available for confirmation (or refutation) in either the historic or prehistoric past. It may be unhelpful to talk of changes in religion as 'a necessary prelude' to settled agglomerations of people with complex social forms dependent on domesticated plants because so much depends on how the terms are defined (are we talking of genetic change to plants or just intensive collecting and cultivating?). It may cloud the argument to talk of changes in human representation leading to new forms of agency over animals, since the linking variables are likely to have been closely intertwined. Do symbolism and ritual surrounding violence and death lead to new social forms? Perhaps, but a simple causal analysis is likely to be confounded by problems of definition, interpretation and interdependence. In Chapter 3 Shults sees religion as an emergent property of complex human systems. The four questions act as platforms for diving off into more complex and fuller understanding.

This book provides a unique overview of current debates concerning religion and its historical variations. The key themes discussed among theologians, anthropologists and archaeologists concern the integration of the spiritual and the material, the role of belief in religion, the cognitive bases for religion and its social roles. But the book is most distinctive in reporting on an unusual experiment – an experiment that has paid off. The dialogue between different specialists in religion in the context of grappling with the data from a particular archaeological site has opened up new lines of inquiry and new perspectives on religion and its origins. The data from the site have acted as a player in the dialogue, bringing different perspectives together and forcing engagement between them. The end result is a coherent overview incorporating new perspectives on the role of religion in the early development of complex societies.

I will return to outline the results and conclusions in Chapter 12. The chapters that follow are organized so as to provide in Chapter 2 a broader starting framework in the Neolithic of Anatolia and the Middle

East as a whole. The chapters by Shults and van Huyssteen then provide a broad perspective from philosophy and religious studies, dealing with issues such as the definition of religion and its long-term evolution and seeing religion as an emergent property of complex human systems. A more specific evolutionary trajectory for specific forms of religiosity is then outlined in Chapter 5, and Whitehouse's model is found to be applicable to Çatalhöyük.

These broad and introductory chapters are followed by a group of chapters by anthropologists: Bloch, Pels and Keane. These are introduced by Chapter 6, in which Bloch explores some of the issues involved in applying ethnographic understanding to archaeological data, before introducing the notion of 'house society', which these chapters apply in various ways to Çatalhöyük. Keane in Chapter 8 sees religion marking presence and pointing to absence, and this focus on markedness is taken up by Pels in Chapter 9, where he also explores scales of temporality in relation to religion.

In the following two chapters, Wason and Nakamura build on this anthropological understanding to explore cosmology at Çatalhöyük (Chapter 10) and the role of magic (Chapter 11), the latter defined in contrast to normative religious behavior. In Chapter 12 I return to the broader themes explored by the authors and to the four questions asked by the project. I attempt to summarize the results and to demonstrate their contribution to understanding Çatalhöyük and the wider Neolithic of Anatolia and the Middle East, as well as their impact on studies of religion in prehistory and in general terms. I also evaluate the impact of the experience of working at Çatalhöyük for the varied scholar participants and their disciplines.

REFERENCES

Baird, D. 2002. Early Holocene settlement in Central Anatolia: Problems and prospects as seen from the Konya Plain. In *The Neolithic of Central Anatolia: Internal Developments and External Relations during the 9th–6th Millennia cal BC – Proceedings of the International CANeW Round Table, Istanbul, November 23–24, 2001*, eds. F. Gérard and L. Thissen. Istanbul: Ege Yayınları, 139–52.

Baird, D. 2007. Pınarbaşı: From Epipalaeolithic camp site to sedentarising village in central Anatolia. In *The Neolithic in Turkey: New Excavations and New Discoveries*, eds. M. Özdoğan and N. Başgelen. Istanbul: Arkeoloji ve Sanat Yayınları, 285–311.

Baird, D. 2008. The Boncuklu project: The origins of sedentism, cultivation and herding in central Anatolia. *Anatolian Archaeology*, 14, 11–14.

Bender, B. 1978. Gatherer-hunter to farmer: A social perspective. *World Archaeology*, 10, 204–22.

Binford, L. R. 1971. Mortuary practices: Their study and their potential. In *Approaches to the Social Dimensions of Mortuary Practices*, ed. James A. Brown. Ann Arbor: University of Michigan, 6–29.

Cauvin, J. 1994. *Naissance des divinités, naissance de l'agriculture*, Paris: CNRS.

Cessford, C. 2005. Estimating the Neolithic population of Çatalhöyük. In *Inhabiting Çatalhöyük: Reports from the 1995–1999 Seasons*, ed. I. Hodder. Cambridge: McDonald Institute for Archaeological Research / British Institute of Archaeology at Ankara Monograph, 325–8.

Donald, M. 1991. *Origins of the Modern Mind*. Cambridge, Mass.: Harvard University Press.

Düring, B. S. 2006. *Constructing Communities: Clustered Neighbourhood Settlements of the Central Anatolian Neolithic, ca. 8500–5500 Cal. bc*. Leiden: Nederlands Instituut voor het Nabije Oosten.

Duru, R. 1999. The Neolithic of the Lake District. In *Neolithic in Turkey: The Cradle of Civilization – New Discoveries*, eds. M. Özdoğan and N. Başgelen. Istanbul: Arkeoloji ve Sanat Yayınları, 165–91.

Esin, U., and Harmanakaya, S. 1999. Aşıklı in the frame of Central Anatolian Neolithic. In *Neolithic in Turkey: The Cradle of Civilization – New Discoveries*, eds. M. Özdoğan and N. Başgelen. Istanbul: Arkeoloji ve Sanat Yayınları, 115–32.

Flannery, K. V. 1973. The origins of agriculture. *Annual Review of Anthropology*, 2, 271–310.

Gérard, F., and Thissen, L., eds. 2002. *The Neolithic of Central Anatolia: Internal Developments and External Relations during the 9th–6th Millennia cal BC – Proceedings of the International CANeW Round Table, Istanbul, November 23–24, 2001*. Istanbul: Ege Yayınları.

Goring-Morris, N., and Belfer-Cohen, A. 2002. Symbolic behavior from the Epipalaeolithic and Early Neolithic of the Near East: Preliminary observations on continuity and change. In *Magic Practices and Ritual in the Near Eastern Neolithic*, eds. H. G. K. Gebel, B. B. Hermansen and C. Hoffmann Jensen. Berlin: Ex Oriente, 67–79.

Hayden, B. 1990. Nimrods, piscators, pluckers, and planters: The emergence of food production. *Journal of Anthropological Archaeology*, 9(1), 31–69.

Helms, M. 2003. Tangible materiality and cosmological others in the development of sedentism. Paper presented at the conference "Rethinking Materiality" (McDonald Institute for Archaeological Research, Cambridge).

Heun, M., Schafer-Pregl, R., Klawan, D., Castagna, R., Accerbi, M., Borghi, B., and Salamini, F. 1997. Site of einkorn wheat domestication identified by DNA fingerprinting. *Science*, 278, 1312–14.

Hodder, I. 1982. *Symbols in Action*. Cambridge: Cambridge University Press.

Hodder, I. 1986. *Reading the Past*. Cambridge: Cambridge University Press.

Hodder, I. 1990. *The Domestication of Europe*. Oxford: Blackwell.

Hodder, I., ed. 1996. *On the Surface: Çatalhöyük 1993–95*. Cambridge: McDonald Institute for Archaeological Research / British Institute of Archaeology at Ankara Monograph.

Hodder, I. 1999. *The Archaeological Process: An introduction*. Oxford: Blackwell.

Hodder, I. ed. 2000. *Towards Reflexive Method in Archaeology: The Example at Çatalhöyük*. Cambridge: McDonald Institute for Archaeological Research / British Institute of Archaeology at Ankara Monograph.

Hodder, I. 2004a. *Archaeology beyond Dialogue*. Salt Lake City: University of Utah Press.

Hodder, I. 2004b. A season of great finds and new faces at Çatalhöyük. *Anatolian Archaeology*, 10, 7–10.

Hodder, I., ed. 2005a. *Inhabiting Çatalhöyük: Reports from the 1995–1999 Seasons*. Cambridge: McDonald Institute for Archaeological Research / British Institute of Archaeology at Ankara Monograph.

Hodder, I., ed. 2005b. *Changing Materialities at Çatalhöyük: Reports from the 1995–1999 Seasons*. Cambridge: McDonald Institute for Archaeological Research / British Institute of Archaeology at Ankara Monograph.

Hodder, I., ed. 2005c. *Çatalhöyük Perspectives: Themes from the 1995–1999 Seasons*. Cambridge: McDonald Institute for Archaeological Research / British Institute of Archaeology at Ankara Monograph.

Hodder, I. 2006. *The Leopard's Tale: Revealing the Mysteries of Çatalhöyük*. London: Thames and Hudson.

Hodder, I., ed. 2007. *Excavating Çatalhöyük: Reports from the 1995–1999 Seasons*. Cambridge: McDonald Institute for Archaeological Research / British Institute of Archaeology at Ankara Monograph.

Jones, M. 2001. *The Molecule Hunt: Archaeology and the Search for Ancient DNA*. London: Allen Lane.

Keane, W. 1997. *Signs of Recognition: Powers and Hazards of Representation in an Indonesian Society*. Berkeley: University of California Press.

Knappett, C. 2005. *Thinking through Material Culture: An Interdisciplinary Perspective*. Philadelphia: University of Pennsylvania Press.

Kuijt, I., ed. 2000. *Life in Neolithic Farming Communities: Social Organization, Identity, and Differentiation*. New York: Kluwer Academic / Plenum Publishers.

Lewis-Williams, D., and Pearce, D. 2005. *Inside the Neolithic Mind: Consciousness, Cosmos, and the Realm of the Gods*. London: Thames and Hudson.

Mellaart, J. 1967. *Çatal Hüyük: A Neolithic Town in Anatolia*. London: Thames and Hudson.

Meskell, L. M., Nakamura, C., King, R., and Farid, S. 2008. Figured lifeworlds and depositional practices at Çatalhöyük. *Cambridge Archaeological Journal*, 18(2), 139–61.

Mithen, S. 1998. *The Prehistory of the Mind: A Search for the Origins of Art, Religion and Science.* London: Phoenix.

Mithen, S. 2003. *After the Ice. A Global Human History, 20,000–5000 BC.* London: Weidenfeld and Nicolson.

Özdoğan, M. 2002. Defining the Neolithic of Central Anatolia. In *The Neolithic of Central Anatolia: Internal Developments and External Relations during the 9th–6th Millennia cal BC – Proceedings of the International CANeW Round Table, Istanbul November 23–24, 2001,* eds. F. Gérard and L. Thissen. Istanbul: Ege Yayınları, 253–61.

Özdoğan, M., and Özdoğan, A. 1998. Buildings of cult and the cult of buildings. In *Light on Top of the Black Hill: Studies Presented to Halet Cambel,* eds. G. Arsebük, M. Mellink and W. Schirmer. Istanbul: Ege Yayınları, 581–93.

Renfrew, C. 1985. *The Archaeology of Cult.* Los Angeles: University of California Press.

Renfrew, C. 1998. Mind and matter: Cognitive archaeology and external symbolic storage. In *Cognition and Material Culture: The Archaeology of Symbolic Storage,* eds. C. Renfrew and C. Scarre. Cambridge: McDonald Institute for Archaeological Research.

Roberts, N., Black, S., Boyer, P., Eastwood, W. J., Griffiths, H. I., Lamb, H. F., Leng, M. J., Parish, R., Reed, M. J., Twigg, D., and Yiğitbaşioğlu, H. 1999. Chronology and stratigraphy of Late Quaternary sediments in the Konya Basin, Turkey: Results from the KOPAL Project. *Quaternary Science Reviews,* 18, 611–30.

Schmidt, K. 2001. Göbekli Tepe, Southeastern Turkey: A preliminary report on the 1995–1999 excavations. *Paléorient,* 26(1), 45–54.

Schmidt, K. 2006. *Sie bauten die ersten Tempel.* Munich: Beck.

Thomas, J. 1996. *Time, Culture and Identity.* London: Routledge.

Tilley, C. 1997. *Phenomenology of Landscape.* London: Berg.

Verhoeven, M. 2002. Ritual and ideology in the Pre-Pottery Neolithic B of the Levant and southeast Anatolia. *Cambridge Archaeological Journal,* 12(2), 233–58.

Wynn, T. 2002. Archaeology and cognitive evolution. *Behavioral and Brain Sciences,* 25(3), 389–402.

2

The symbolism of Çatalhöyük in its regional context

Ian Hodder and Lynn Meskell

Introduction

The aim of this chapter is to situate the symbolism and ritual at Çatalhöyük in the wider context of eastern Turkey and the Middle East. The rich symbolism at the site has already incited a wide range of inter-pretations of the site and its earlier and contemporary parallels to the east (Mellaart 1967; Clark 1977; Gimbutas 1989; Cauvin 2000; Özdoğan 2002; Lewis-Williams 2004; Mithen 2004). There are a number of con-temporary and earlier sites with comparable art and symbolism (e.g., Jericho, Jerf el Ahmar, Nevalı Çori and Djade al-Mughara), and new discoveries are being made all the time. In particular, the site of Göbekli, excavated by Klaus Schmidt since 1994, has an equally or more remark-able concentration of symbolism, ritual and art starting in Pre-Pottery Neolithic A/B, the 9th millennium BC.

Çatalhöyük and Göbekli are very different in time and in place. They are 450 kilometers apart and in different regional traditions, in central and southeastern Turkey, respectively (Gérard & Thissen 2002). There are major differences in their economy and architecture. While the inhab-itants of Çatalhöyük depended on domesticated cereals and pulses, as well as domestic sheep and goat, but on wild cattle, boar, deer and equid, at Göbekli all the plant and animal food resources were wild species. The

We are very grateful to Klaus Schmidt for encouraging us to make these comparisons and for providing access to Göbekli and its imagery. We should emphasize that the interpretations we offer here, including those concerning the Göbekli material, are our own, and we do not mean to implicate the excavator of Göbekli in them. An article similar to this chapter is to be published (Hodder and Meskell, in press), and we are grateful to the reviewers of that article.

architecture at Çatalhöyük is agglomerated individual houses of mud brick, whereas at Göbekli the buildings are of stone, sometimes of monumental proportions. There are also major differences in the setting of ritual and symbolism at the two sites: at Çatalhöyük the art and symbolism occur in domestic houses, whereas at the earlier site of Göbekli the symbolism is focused in separate 'temples'. And yet in comparing Göbekli and other Neolithic sites in Turkey such as Nevalı Çori and Çatalhöyük, we have been struck by various similarities and contrasts that we would like to explore in this chapter (see also Hodder & Meskell, in press).

Older work on the symbolism of Çatalhöyük and the Neolithic of the Middle East was based on notions of the goddess and the bull (Cauvin 2000; Balter 2005) with its classical genealogy, but scholars such as Mithen (2004), Kuijt (2008), Özdoğan (2001, 2002) and Verhoeven (2002) have presented a series of new interpretations. We intend to offer a synthetic perspective that has new dimensions and addresses the questions raised in Chapter 1 and in the Templeton project at Çatalhöyük. This synthesis brings together some of the apparently disparate themes found at a diversity of sites over a long period of time. We recognize the marked variation in the symbolism of the Neolithic of the Middle East, and we do not aim to impose a unified account. Rather we want to draw out some productive themes that seem to recur across different media and across a vast swath of space and time.

We have organized our account by focusing on sets of themes, starting with maleness, as we believe that it is important at the outset to move away from the female-centered narratives that have dominated so much discussion of the symbolism of the Neolithic of Anatolia and the Middle East. We then turn to the themes of wild and dangerous animals, and of headless humans and birds, since these allow us gradually to build an alternative social account based on notions of continuity, passing down and duration. The manipulation of the human body was an important part of history making. But so too was the house, and it is to the symbolism and social role of the house that we finally turn.

Neolithic phallocentrism

A historically strong theme in many discussions of Neolithic symbolism has been the centrality of the female figure to the supposed concerns of early agriculturalists with fertility and fecundity (Rudebeck 2000). Such narratives stretch back to biblical accounts and pick up in 18th- and 19th-century European scholarship (Meskell 1995; Hutton 1997). Frazer's *The Golden Bough* was a key text and remains influential to this day. Notions of the goddess or mother goddess had a major influence on James Mellaart in his original (1967) account of Çatalhöyük. In recent times this emphasis has been continued by Cauvin (2000) in relation to the Middle East Neolithic generally (see comments by Rollefson 2008: 398, 403, 408). In a similar vein Verhoeven (2002: 251) imputes that 'both women and bulls do seem to be related to vitality, i.e. domestication, life-force and fecundity.' While we do not seek to replace one meta-narrative with another, we do suggest that the phallocentric elements of representational schemas, monumental statues and material culture have previously been downplayed, particularly in the Turkish Neolithic. By 'phallocentrism' we refer to the privileging of maleness as a prime cultural signifier and the centrality of masculinity (both human and animal) as a source of power and authority within the material and symbolic repertoire of the Turkish Neolithic.

Wall paintings discovered at Çatalhöyük in the 1960s showed images of raptors and wild animals. In two buildings in the upper levels (Levels V and III in Mellaart's levels, counted from I at the top to XII at the bottom of the site), wild animals were depicted in narrative scenes of hunting and teasing and baiting wild bulls, wild stags, wild boars, a bear and a stag. Many of these teased and baited animals are shown with erect penis, and the wild boars clearly have their hackles raised. In one scene (Figure 2.1) the humans interacting with a wild stag are bearded. In the figurine corpus, there are examples of phallic forms (e.g., Figure 2.2). Most of the figurines at Çatalhöyük are small, were quickly made, were discarded in middens and are either of animals or of abbreviated human form without sex characteristics (Meskell et al. 2008). The largest number of figurines are zoomorphic (896) and they extend throughout the history of the site, with the majority being represented by horns (504). Given the importance of bull and wild sheep and goat horn symbolism at the site, and given that feasting deposits at Çatalhöyük are dominated by wild bulls (Russell & Martin 2005), it is reasonable to suggest that the maleness of the figurine horns was an important feature of their use. It is clear, on the other hand, that the predominance of the female human form at Çatalhöyük has been exaggerated in much writing about the site.

2.1. Wall painting showing teasing and baiting of stag from Çatalhöyük. *Source:* J. Mellaart and Çatalhöyük Research Project.

The well-known image of a naked woman sitting on a pair of felines is an isolated find, and indeed the number of clearly female figurines is small (40 of 1,800 so far discovered) (Meskell 2007). Moreover, these examples are confined to the upper levels of the site. Such images do not occur in the early and middle levels, where the installations comprise primarily wild animals, bulls and raptors (see Mellaart 1967: 102–3).

2.2. Stone figure from Çatalhöyük. *Source:* J. Quinlan and Çatalhöyük Research Project.

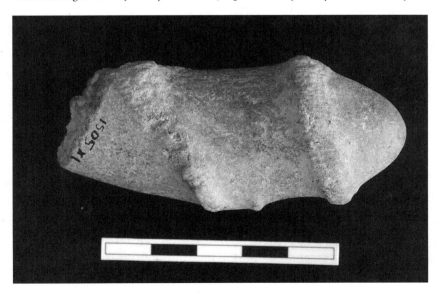

One of the most surprising and distinctive aspects of the Göbekli data
is the lack of female symbolism. As Hauptmann and Schmidt (2007: 72)
put it, 'In Nevalı Çori and Göbekli Tepe, the Great Goddess remains
invisible (cf. Gimbutas 1989)'. Female sculptures have not been found
at Göbekli Tepe. The most outstanding feature of the site is the T-pillars
that are occasionally identified as human forms with arms and hands, and
they sometimes have wild animals carved on their surfaces. These stone
pillar beings are arranged in approximately circular fashion around two of
their number, these central ones being distinctly larger than the others.
The two central pillars are freestanding, whereas the pillars in the circle
are connected by quarry stone walls and, inside the walls, stone benches
(Schmidt 2007: 74). The excavators interpret this as representing stylized
anthropomorphic beings of stone. These T-pillars, as well as representing
or being human forms, may themselves be evocations of the phallus with
an elongated shaft and a pronounced head. They are massive uprights
that themselves often have images of wild animals with penis depicted.
The T-pillar shape occurs frequently at Göbekli and at different scales,
including very small examples about 30 cm high, also carved in stone. It
is possible that some of the pillars with their long shaft and root resemble
teeth, a recurrent motif at the site, as described later in this chapter.

In the main the carvings on the T-shaped pillars depict wild and dangerous animals with bared teeth and exaggerated jowls. Some of the
Göbekli examples now in the Urfa Museum clearly show that these were
specifically male animals, some having delineated penises underneath their
large stone bodies, even though such surfaces may have been obscured.
Taken together there is a close association between human-like beings
(the T-pillars) and male animals, specifically in their phallic and aggressive aspects. As Verhoeven has noted, 'The basic relation expressed was
between humans and male wild animals' (2002: 252).

Near Göbekli at the site of Yeni Mahalle (Urfa), an ithyphallic larger
than life stone sculpture was discovered and reassembled from four large
pieces (Hauptmann & Schmidt 2007). This impressive male figure is
depicted naked, apart from a carved necklace or detail, with its splayed
fingers pressed outward from the genital area so that the viewer's attention is drawn immediately to the presence (or absence) of the erect penis.
One interpretation is that the splayed fingers effectively cover the upright
penis. Another interpretation would be that the penis is entirely missing
and present only when placed into the rather shallow depression below.

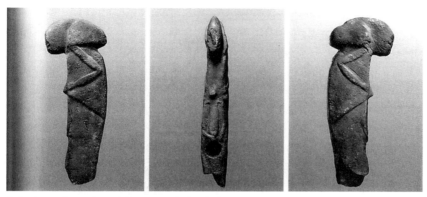

2.3. Stone figure from Adiyaman-Kilisik, Turkey. *Source:* Bettina Freytag-Loeringhoff.

Possibly red pigment, natural ochre staining or some form of discoloration marks the area. Testicles were also indicated.

While this impressive example is clearly anthropomorphic, it recalls a parallel stone figure from Adiyaman-Kilisik (found in 1965) that incorporates the T-pillar body shape with facial features, replete with two phallic bodies and two sets of hands (Figure 2.3). The large T-shaped body's arms extend to the head of the smaller phallic body inscribed on its front side, while the arms and hands reach to the genital area. The smaller body itself resembles a penis-shaped relief, and its hands are placed above the empty hole (where a penis could have been inserted). Moving a penis in and out of this slot could have enhanced the sexual element of this phallic being, mimicking masturbation. Other interpretations might be that this combination of penis and orifice symbolizes a hermaphroditic quality or instantiates the possibilities for bodily transformation and change. Whichever interpretation one chooses, the motif of the phallic body overlain by another is striking; moreover, this example substantiates the theory that the T-pillars themselves are anthropomorphic and perhaps also phallic. While the Yeni Mahalle and Adiyaman-Kilisik examples present a unique combination and accentuation, in many ways they recall the Egyptian Predynastic figures of the god Min (Kemp 2000; Bar-Yosef 2002), who holds his penis in one hand. We do not wish to argue for direct cultural links. Our comparison here is illustrative in purpose. In many representations Min holds one arm up as a sign of aggression, the overall effect being one of phallic intimidation. Originating in the Middle East in prehistoric times, according to Egyptian mythology, Min was popular over the millennia as a deity concerned with violence, sexuality and fertility (he was also associated with a deceased state and depicted in a mummiform shape). Large stone carvings from Coptos (although dating from the 4th millennium) look remarkably similar to the Yeni Mahalle sculpture in form and, like the Adiyaman-Kilisik, with regard to the prominent hole where the penis could be slotted in and out.

The bottom part of the Yeni Mahalle statue was left in the form of a pillar, which when partially buried resembled an upright stele like those at Göbekli (Hauptmann & Schmidt 2007). Hauptmann and Schmidt suggest that the Yeni Mahalle figure enables further reconstruction of other fragments from Göbekli and that a number of large stone phalluses probably originally belonged to large anthropomorphic sculptures similar to this one. Another stone sculpture from Göbekli, albeit smaller than life size, shows an ithyphallic male with the erect penis prominently connected (Schmidt 2006). Lending weight to the idea of phallic masculinity, this completed figure consists only of carved facial features and detailed penis, while the body is rendered simply as a block without arms or legs. Other finds from Göbekli include quite a number of stone pestles that Mithen, Finlayson and Shaffrey (2005) have convincingly argued have phallic associations in Levantine contexts (see also Garrod 1957; Weinstein-Evron & Belfer-Cohen 1993; Goring-Morris et al. 2008). Near Göbekli at a limestone quarry, three reliefs have been recorded, each depicting a 1-m-long phallus with scrotum; these have been plausibly considered contemporaneous with the main site (Rollefson 2008: 391).

Possibly linked to this concern with phallocentrism is the depiction of snakes at Göbekli and Nevalı Çori. One highly decorated T-pillar (Figure 2.4) has two sets of three snake bodies down the length of one front, and snake heads appear along the sides of the pillar's lower portion. If one accepts that this is a phallic pillar, then the writhing snake bodies could possibly have accentuated the phallicism. Schmidt (2007) describes another pillar decorated with a large fox, standing nearly upright. Schmidt interprets the snakes on this pillar as issuing from the stomach or from approximately the same position where one might expect male genitals. Some 266 T-pillars have been found at the related site of Karahan Tepe (MPPNB), some showing carved anthropomorphic arms on a pillar/ torso and animal legs, and another bears a snake relief like those from Göbekli (Çelik 2000: 7).

2.4. Stone pillar with engravings from Göbekli Tepe, Turkey. *Source:* Deutsches Archäologisches Institut.

The only clearly female image at Göbekli was incised on a stone slab on a low bench, which could have been sat upon, inside one of the stone circles from Level II, L. 10–71 (Figure 2.5). Compared with the well-executed carved sculptures and pillars, this is a crude and misshapen splayed figure with minimal facial features, small flabby breasts that hang

2.5. Stone engraving from Göbekli Tepe, Turkey. *Source:* Deutsches Archäologisches Institut.

to the side of the torso and scrawny arms and legs. Most striking, however, is the exposure of the body, the complete opening up of the naked form. Specifically, the explicit depiction of the genital region, previously unknown in the Turkish and Levantine Neolithic, is marked by an engraved hole that might be interpreted as being penetrated by a disconnected penis. On either side of the penis are incised areas that can be seen as accentuating the penis or perhaps representing emissions from the vagina. Since the splayed figure is the only female portrayal from Göbekli, was on a bench that people may have sat on and is a passively penetrated figure, one might interpret this as not being a particularly positive rendition of women and is perhaps unlikely to be associated with notions of fertility or matriarchy.

The phallocentric focus at Çatalhöyük and Göbekli is seen at other, closely related sites such as Nevalı Çori. The focus is found elsewhere in the Neolithic of Turkey, typically on a smaller scale, as demonstrated within the figurine corpus. At Mezraa Teleilat, Özdoğan (2003: 517) describes some 94 phallic figurines found in the transitional layers between the Pre-Pottery Neolithic and Pottery Neolithic levels. These limestone figurines greatly outnumber the standing or seated anthropomorphic figures from the same context and suggest a focus on male sexuality as denoted by the penis. Recent work in Turkey has attempted to catalog the many hundreds of phallic figurines for the Neolithic generally (Nergis 2008). Albeit to a lesser degree, early phallic objects and imagery have been found in the Levant in pre-Neolithic Natufian contexts. 'Natufian art also had an erotic element', seen, for example, in a calcite statuette from Ain Sakhri (Henry 1989: 206). The discussion by Mithen, Finlayson and Shaffrey of phallic imagery at Wadi Faynan (WF16) in the Pre-Pottery Neolithic has already been mentioned. Phallomorphic and male figurines have been noted in the Neolithic across a broad geographical region (Hansen 2007), including the Levant and Middle East (e.g., Ain Sakhri, Salibya, Dhra', El Wad, Tepe Guran, Nahal Oren, Nemrik, Ain Ghazal, Netiv Hagdud and Munhata) and Turkey (Göbekli, Nevalı Çori, Hallan Çemi, Cafer Höyük, Gritille Höyük, Mezraa Teleilat and Çatalhöyük). At Nevalı Çori more than 700 clay figures were excavated, with male examples slightly outnumbering female ones (Morsch 2002). The number of animal figurines, a mere 30, pales in comparison (Hauptmann 2007). Importantly, phallic or male figurines are typically outnumbered by geometric, ambiguous or zoomorphic examples in both Turkish and Levantine sites (see Kuijt and Chesson 2005: table 8.2; Meskell et al. 2008: tables 5 and 6). The same could be said for explicitly female figurines. Moreover, Rollefson suggests (2008: 408) that 'male figurines also occur in the central and southern Levant, but in some cases the lack of effort to represent male genitalia explicitly may be a reflection of technological problems (for example, in the fashioning of the plaster statues at 'Ain Ghazal).' Here we simply note an increasing documentation of Neolithic male and phallic imagery across both visual and material culture, even if much of the Levantine evidence partakes of a smaller scale than the paintings and sculptures of Çatalhöyük and Göbekli. It would be fair to say that the Turkish materials differ in style and intensity from those of the Levant, yet there are threads of common concern, as we suggest here.

The striking monumental imagery at Göbekli, Nevalı Çori, Çatalhöyük and other Turkish sites '(albeit on a reduced scale) appears in the central Levant at Jericho, 'Ain Ghazal, and Nahal Hemar, an area where the plastered skull cult was characteristic of the ritual arena' (Rollefson 2008: 404). In making sense of the Neolithic phallocentrism, at least in relation to Turkey, another stele from Göbekli is of considerable importance and will be discussed later in the chapter (see Figure 2.6). This stele shows an ithyphallic headless body in association with a bird. A focus on headless bodies and birds is also found at Çatalhöyük, where it is clearly linked to the removal and passing down of skulls. At Göbekli there seems to be a link between the phallus and the dead. As discussed later, links to the past will be one context in which to make sense of the phallocentrism.

So far we have focused on aspects of the symbolism of the Neolithic in Anatolia, and to some extent elsewhere in the Middle East, that give some insight into the role of human imagery (see Question 3, Chapter 1). We do not deny that there is female imagery, but at Çatalhöyük it is marginal and late in the sequence, and at Göbekli it is largely absent and, where present, seems unrelated to fertility and a nurturing mother. Elsewhere female imagery occurs but is often dominated by animal and phallocentric representations. We now wish to explore another set of linkages that help to contextualize the importance of the masculinity in general in these sites. These derive from the frequent associations already noted between the explicit display of penises and the portrayal of wild animals. What are the associations of wild animal depictions and installations at Çatalhöyük, Göbekli and related sites? This question takes us into the realms of violence, as discussed as a fourth theme in Chapter 1.

Dangerous, wild things

A distinctive and perhaps surprising aspect of the symbolism emerging from sites such as Göbekli is the focus on wild rather than domesticated animals. At some sites such as Göbekli we would not expect domestic animals in the symbolism, since the economies of the sites are based on wild animals only. Of course, there may have been increasingly close links between humans and animals well before genetic change was manifest (Mithen 2004). But at other sites the focus on wild animals continues in the context of the use of clearly domesticated plants and animals.

2.6. Stone pillar from Göbekli Tepe, Turkey. *Source:* Klaus Schmidt, Deutsches Archäologisches Institut.

Schmidt (2006, 2007) remarks that all of the beasts depicted at Göbekli were present (though not dominant) in the site's faunal assemblage rather than representing fantastic creatures.

We have seen that at Çatalhöyük the narrative paintings mainly show wild animals. Moreover, installations in the houses featured bucrania (wild bull or wild ram and goat skulls and horns with the heads plastered). The teeth of foxes and weasels, the tusks of wild boars, the claws of bears and the beaks of vultures were placed in protuberances on the walls. We have found a leopard claw and the talons of raptors in burials. So there is a focus on parts of animals that are dangerous or piercing; there is little symbolic emphasis on femurs, humeri, molar teeth and so on. Dangerous or flesh-eating wild animals and birds are also chosen for representation. The economy at Çatalhöyük is based on domestic sheep and goats, but these hardly appear in the symbolism. Wild cattle make up 54% of all animal bones in installations and special deposits, 46% of the animal reliefs but only 15% of the faunal remains from domestic, processing and consumption contexts. In contrast, domestic sheep constitute 56% of the faunal remains and thus the bulk of meat consumption and only 19% of reliefs and 13% of installations and deposits (Russell & Meece 2006: table 14.5). Bones of wild equids are found on the site and sometimes in special deposits (foundation or abandonment deposits in houses), and equids are depicted on the walls, but they are rare. Russell and Meece note that 6%, 0% and 1% of the paintings, reliefs and installations, respectively, at Çatalhöyük are equids. So it is not just that wild animals are being selected for symbolic representation. There are some deer paintings, and deer antlers are rarely used as installations but never as reliefs. There is a particular focus at Çatalhöyük both on wild, dangerous, flesh-eating animals and on their sharp, dangerous body parts. It is these that are predominantly brought into the site and installed or portrayed in the houses.

It can certainly be argued that in Turkey and the Middle East there was a general interest in the early Holocene in depicting everything that existed in the habitat (Mehmet Özdöğan, pers. comm.). Within this general frame there is a particular focus on dangerous wild animals or on the dangerous parts of wild animals from very early in the formation of settled villages. Already at Hallan Çemi in Turkey in the 11th millennium BC there is an aurochs skull on a wall of a 'public building', a row of three wild sheep skulls in a public space and a snake carved from bone (Rosenberg 2007). New findings from the 12,000-year-old Natufian cave site Hilazon Tachtit (Israel) have revealed the burial of an elderly woman with body parts of a range of dangerous and/or carnivorous animals, including wild boar, eagle, wild cattle, leopard, and marten, as well as a complete human foot (Grosman, Munro & Belfer-Cohen 2008). At the pre-Neolithic Natufian site of Nahal Oren in the Levant, Noy (1991) found carved stones with incised decoration, as well as animal heads carved on bone handles (e.g., of sickles). Carved bone, bone fragments and bone sickle hafts representing animals (deer, horse) were also found in Kebara Cave (Garrod 1957). The sickle shafts from El Wad and Kebara are in the form of deer and goat heads (Henry 1989). Fox (*Vulpes* sp.) teeth are widely used as raw materials for pendants (Goring-Morris & Belfer-Cohen 2002: 70). In the Natufian we see a marked rise in the number of raptor talons (Goring-Morris & Belfer-Cohen 2002: 71) and pendants of bone and canine teeth (Henry 1989).

In the following Pre-Pottery Neolithic A (PPNA from 9500 cal BC to 8500 cal BC), wild cattle imagery is found throughout the southeast Turkey–north Levantine region (Goring-Morris & Belfer-Cohen 2002). At Tell 'Abr 3 in Syria, a series of stone slabs line the bench around the walls (Yartah 2005) in Building B2. These are polished and decorated with wild animals – gazelles, panthers, aurochs – as well as with geometric designs. The panthers are spotted and highly stylized and look rather like lizards. Bucrania are deposited within a bench, but there are also bucrania on view in smaller buildings, interpreted as houses, at the site. Investigators at Jerf el Ahmar also found a building with four cattle bucrania, probably suspended on the interior walls (Stordeur 2000; Yartah 2005). Two impressive stelae some 2 m high in one building seem to represent birds, possibly raptors (Stordeur et al. 2000: 40). At Jerf el Ahmar there is also serpent decoration on the stone slabs of the benches of the large circular buildings (Stordeur 2000), along with a separate depiction of a vulture (for parallel symbolism at Hallan Çemi and Nemrik 9, see Kozlowski 1992; Rosenberg & Redding 2000). In the PPNB there continues to be a widespread symbolic focus on the fox, wild cattle, wild boar and birds of prey (Goring-Morris & Belfer-Cohen 2002: 70–1).

The depictions from Göbekli allow a fuller insight into some of the associations of these wild animals in the Neolithic. The animals shown overlap in great part with those found at Çatalhöyük, but there are differences in emphasis. Çatalhöyük has fewer scorpions and spiders and more cattle. This difference relates to the different subsistence strategies of the two sites, with the later site seeing the adoption of domestic cattle at least by the ensuing Chalcolithic West Mound. The cultural intensity of such motifs/genres at both sites is suggested by their appearance at multiple scales across the sites. At Çatalhöyük the images of wild animals occur both as large painted bulls and as full-sized bucrania as well as minute figurines. At Göbekli there are large and small T-pillars, from the monumental to the handheld limestone examples and miniatures less than 5 cm high (Badisches Landesmuseum Karlsruhe 2007: 273). To date no clay figurines have been discovered at Göbekli.

But the Göbekli data resonate with the data from Çatalhöyük in demonstrating not only the salience of wild animals but the hard, dangerous, pointed parts of wild animals. At Çatalhöyük 70% of the faunal remains are the bones of domesticated animals (sheep, goats, dogs) while the rest consist of wild cattle, equids, deer, boars and so on (Russell & Martin 2005), whereas in the paintings, reliefs and installations the percentage of domesticated animals averages 19% in the different media (Russell & Meece 2006). As already noted, at Çatalhöyük it is the tusks of wild boars, the horns of wild bulls, wild sheep and goats, the beaks and talons of vultures and raptors, the teeth of weasels and foxes and the claws of bears and leopards that are brought on-site and installed in walls in houses or worn as attachments on the body (Hodder 2006). The postcranial parts of some of these animals are rarely found on-site (Russell & Martin 2005). Where postcranial elements are brought on-site, as in the case of cattle, it is the skulls and horns that are used in installations. At Göbekli this same emphasis is seen in the sculptures showing bared teeth and fangs, and the snarling heads.

How can we make sense of all this? Verhoeven (2002: 252) suggested that PPNB human–animal linkages were an expression of the wild, dangerous, aggressive dimensions of the domain of nature. We can turn to wider, classic discussions of the role of violent male-centered imagery. For Bataille (1986) violence in ritual creates moments of transcendence. One returns from this 'other' world transformed and better able to cope with restraint in society. For Girard (1977) violent symbolic imagery is a way of managing and evacuating the violence generated inside the human community. Most archaic religions show a narrative that involves going through violence to resolution. While animals predate and fight, only humans have vengeance. There is no community unless there is something to prevent vengeance. Vengeance is overcome when a victim is found that all can fight against; then a solution has been found. The frightening god is thus good for community. The bull is made a scapegoat and society is reformed. Bloch (1992) discusses how, in ritual, things are turned inside out in some 'other' world 'beyond'. For him, the violence and symbolic killing take the initiate beyond the transience of daily life into permanent entities such as descent groups. By leaving this life, it is possible to see oneself and others as part of something permanent and life transcending (see Chapter 6).

We will return to an argument not dissimilar to Bloch's, but we are concerned about the imposition of terms like 'violence' and 'aggression' on the Neolithic imagery, and we are concerned about the relevance of off-the-shelf theoretical explanations of its social context. We would prefer to build more historically specific arguments for the Göbekli and Çatalhöyük material, and we believe that at least for the latter site there are now sufficient data to allow some progress in this direction.

We can start with the evidence already noted from Çatalhöyük of an association between 'feasting' deposits and the bones of wild bulls. Specifically, Russell and Martin (2005) noted that, of the cattle bones that could be sexed, female bones form roughly half the assemblage in daily consumption contexts, but only a third in 'feasting' and special deposits. It is, of course, possible that male cattle may have been selectively culled as part of an incipient herding/management strategy of the wild cattle population. But for much of the occupation at Çatalhöyük, there appear to be equal proportions of adult males and females deposited overall. The focus on wild bulls shows up only when 'feasting' deposits are considered, suggesting a consumption/deposition strategy rather than culling. Peters et al. (1999: 40) have demonstrated that at Neolithic sites in southeastern Turkey at which all the cattle bones are wild, such as PPNA Göbekli and EPPNB Nevalı Çori, a higher proportion of the remains are from bulls (>60%), whereas at sites with early domesticated cattle like Gürcütepe, the ratio of males to females is 1:5. Without contextual evidence we cannot say whether these data from Göbekli and Nevalı Çori represent culling or consumption.

At Çatalhöyük there is a shift in the upper levels (above Level VII) from roughly equal overall proportions of male and female adult cattle to an increase in adult females (Russell & Martin 2005). It is not possible to identify male and female in younger unfused bones, so the increase in adult females may have been the product of increased culling of younger males. Russell, Martin and Buitenhuis (2005) argued against this interpretation, as it seemed more plausible that the pattern resulted from targeting female + young groups. Male aurochsen tend to be more solitary. Their predominance in 'feasting' deposits and in the paintings and installations seems more likely to represent animals that were harder to hunt.

So bulls were preferentially selected for feasts and ceremonies at Çatalhöyük. We also see wild animals in large group activities in the paintings (in one case with all the human figures bearded; Figure 2.1). So there could be a social focus on male prestige and 'feast' providing, and the memorialization of this in the house and ritual symbolism. The heads, horns, teeth, claws and so on could be taken as long-term memories of these public events. They are the enduring hard bits as well as the distinctive elements of particular species. At Çatalhöyük we have evidence that after a house (Building 1) was abandoned, filled in with earth and rebuilt upon, a pit was dug down to retrieve a wall relief from the underlying room (Hodder 2006). It also seems likely that the bucrania stacked in houses (Mellaart's Shrine 10 and Building 52 in the 4040 Area; Twiss et al. 2008) were amassed over a considerable period of time. If a building is not burned on abandonment, the bull horns and other installations are often carefully removed, perhaps for reuse in later rebuildings of the house. The splayed 'bear' figures always had their heads and hands or paws removed at closure; evidence for this was bolstered by the discovery of bones from a bear paw encased in plaster (Hodder 2006). In the 7th-millennium levels at the nearby site of Pınarbaşı, Baird (2007) identified small collections of animal bones packaged in plaster that were presumably kept and were perhaps exchanged before deposition. But at Çatalhöyük, very specific or telling parts of animals were kept and passed down from generation to generation. They are the visible, aggressive, dangerous and ultimately durable parts.

Can the same be said of Göbekli? Here there is no published evidence of the role of animals in feasting or of the passing down of animal parts. The imagery may be associated with public gatherings in the circular 'temples' of monumental stones. Verhoeven (2002: 245) has warned that 'it seems that only a small portion of the entire [settlement] population could be assembled' in the public ritual buildings at 'Ain Ghazal, Nevalı Çori, Çayönü and Göbekli. For the latter site he estimates that up to 20–35 people were able to assemble in the buildings at any one time. In our view this estimate might easily be doubled or trebled given the size of some of the Göbekli 'temples' (the Double Pillar Building is 25 m by 5 m), but even if lower figures are preferred, some unit beyond a small family or group is indicated. As we shall see, there are claims that the Göbekli 'temples' were involved in links to the ancestral dead. But the Göbekli evidence complicates the notion that the durability of parts of animals involved in prowess and feasting was the central focus of the symbolic imagery, as this argument can hardly be put forward for snakes, spiders and scorpions. The latter are unlikely candidates for feasting or for memorials of public events, even if they had totemic or some other such marking significance.

While we argue that the symbolism at many sites focused on the dangerous, distinctive and durable elements of particular beasts, we also think that other factors may have been involved in the selection of the animals and body parts represented. At both Göbekli and Çatalhöyük, birds are depicted. At Çatalhöyük these are either raptors or cranelike. The overall assemblage of bird remains at the site is dominated by waterbirds, in particular ducks and geese, and ducklike birds such as grebes and coots (Russell & McGowan 2003). Herons and other waders are also well represented, but the art focuses on larger birds that eat animal, human or fish flesh. At Göbekli a wider range of birds is shown. They are at times difficult to identify, but again the focus seems to be on raptors, waterbirds and birds with hooked beaks.

Rather than, or in addition to, the focus on durability and memory construction, the focus on sharp pointed parts of animals may relate to piercing of the flesh. The role of equids in the symbolism at Çatalhöyük is interesting, as already noted. In the site's faunal assemblage, three types of equid have been identified (Russell & Martin 2005): the European wild ass (*Equus hydruntinus*), the onager (*E. hemionus*) and the horse (*E. ferus*). Although there are several equids in the paintings, they rarely occur in special deposits or installations. Herbivores like the wild goat, wild sheep and wild deer all have hard pointed parts that can penetrate the flesh, whereas equids do not. While a hoof can effectively be used to protect, it does not pierce. It is thus of interest that there is considerably less symbolism surrounding equids at Çatalhöyük than surrounding the other wild herbivores (Russell & Meece 2006).

In relation to Question 4a in Chapter 1, we have identified a theme of piercing and manipulating the flesh, associated with male prowess and the construction of memories. At Çatalhöyük these objects of memories were installed in and passed down in houses that we have come to term 'history houses' (see Chapters 6 and 7). In a relatively egalitarian society at Çatalhöyük, some houses became preferred locations for burial beneath the floors, and these houses were rebuilt over more generations than other houses (Hodder 2006). These history houses amassed objects of memory,

2.7. Wild bull horns on pedestals in northeast corner of Building 77 at Çatalhöyük. *Source:* J. Quinlan and Çatalhöyük Research Project.

such as human remains and the hard, durable, dangerous, pointed parts of wild animals. We wish now to expand on this notion of 'history houses' by arguing that they were closely linked to ritual knowledge about body manipulation and the piercing and remaking of human flesh. We thus move to Question 4b posed in Chapter 1.

Piercing and fleshing the body

So far we have outlined a set of possible connections between phallic masculinity, aggressive animality, danger and durability and the piercing and manipulation of flesh. Concerning the last-named, much of our account of the ways in which human fleshed bodies were treated stems from the more detailed evidence of within-house burial from Çatalhöyük. At present we lack complementary evidence for burial practices at Göbekli, but we will refer to some relevant imagery from the site, as well as to practices widely understood from the Middle Eastern Neolithic more generally.

In Building 77 at Çatalhöyük, wild bull horns set into pedestals seem to fence off or protect a burial platform in the northeast part of the main room (Figure 2.7). The platform was dug into during abandonment,

2.8. Pot with faces of humans at each end and heads of bulls on both sides, from 4040 Area midden at Çatalhöyük. *Source:* J. Quinlan and Çatalhöyük Research Project.

and traces of disturbed human bones were found; we assume that some attempt was made to retrieve human remains in the platform before the building was abandoned and then burned. Above the platform on the north wall of the room is a wild ram bucranium with a small niche beneath and with the horns no longer surviving. Much could be made of the specific association between bull horn pedestals and a burial platform. Perhaps the horns refer to an individual buried in the platform or to some ancestor of the individuals buried there. Perhaps the power of the pointed bull horns protects the dead. Perhaps both the buried humans and the bulls are ancestors. Whatever the specific interpretation, there are other examples at Çatalhöyük of a close link between humans and cattle, particularly in relation to the construction of histories and memories.

Recently, the most evocative materialization of this connection is demonstrated by one remarkable ceramic vessel that was assembled in 2007 from fragments recovered from a midden in the 4040 Area of the site (Figure 2.8). There is a human face at both ends of the pot and a bull head on both sides. The molded and incised human and cattle heads mutually constitute each other: the horns of the bull form the eyebrows or perhaps the hair of the human faces, while the human ears can also form those of the bull when the vessel is turned. Human and bull heads and to a lesser extent wild sheep and goat heads are treated in comparable ways in that they are removed from bodies and kept and sometimes plastered in order to symbolically reflesh the skull (Meskell 2008). We have already seen the plaster molding of bull skulls in order to create bucrania and other installations in houses. But what of human heads?

At Çatalhöyük there is evidence in the mortuary data for the intentional severing of heads, although the removal of human heads has been demonstrated to occur after death rather than being causal (Molleson, Andrews & Boz 2005). In the case of human bodies, only a few individuals were treated with head removal. Six out of 350 skeletons so far excavated during the current project beneath the floors of houses showed clear evidence of head removal, although the real proportion is probably considerably higher since most skeletons excavated have been disturbed by later additions into the same grave or platform. In two cases of headless bodies uncovered by the current excavations, cut marks were present and the heads were probably cut off some time after initial burial (Molleson et al. 2005). These bodies occur in Building 1 and Building 6, both good examples of 'history houses' as defined earlier – long-lived and rebuilt buildings with many burials (up to the 62 burials in Building 1). Other headless bodies were found in probable 'history houses'. In Building 60 a woman with a child in the birth canal was found without a head, and in Building 49 three individuals, including juveniles (L. Hager & B. Boz, pers. comm.), were found without heads. Individual skulls have also been found in abandonment contexts or in foundation deposits (e.g., placed at the base of a supporting house post in Building 17). The retention and deposition of human skulls can be argued to be involved in history building. Following removal, human skulls may well have circulated for some time before final interment in specific abandonment or foundation contexts. In 2004 the plastered skull of an adult man (sex based on cranial features) was discovered in the arms of a woman who had been buried in a pit as part of the foundation of a new building; it is the earliest example of a plastered skull recovered from Anatolia. The facial features, but not the eyes, had been plastered and painted red, perhaps several times (based on the appearance of multiple layers of red painted plaster in a broken cross section of the plaster). These particular treatments and actions of head removal and plastering appear to be directed at certain individuals – possibly deemed revered ancestors – not to collectivities of people, although social groups may have witnessed, or interacted with, curated or plastered skulls.

In addition to the example at Çatalhöyük, plastered skulls have been discovered at Kösk Höyük in Turkey and six Levantine sites (Verhoeven 2002; Bonogofsky 2005; Kuijt 2008), suggesting the possibility of a long-lived and shared set of bodily practices, although many regional and temporal gaps in our evidence remain to be filled. In the Levant, groups of skulls occur. Bonogofsky rules out plastered skulls as evidence for links to specific ancestors on the basis of the evidence for plastered children's skulls (e.g., at Kösk Höyük). The argument that children could not possibly be considered ancestors in the Neolithic does not take into account the many ritual contexts where children are revered individuals or embodiments of deities and spirits (see also Fletcher, Pearson & Ambers 2008). The tradition of strictly biological descent from adults is probably only one, very modern understanding of what constitutes the ancestral. Recent discoveries at PPNB Kfar HaHoresh in northern Israel have revealed the removal of both wild cattle and a human skull; the latter was retrieved some time after (Goring-Morris & Horwitz 2007).

At Çatalhöyük the removal of human heads is referred to in several wall paintings from different levels at the site that show vultures, in one case with human feet, associated with headless corpses. Cessford et al. (2006) have estimated that about 70% of those inhabiting the site were buried beneath house floors, and excavations off-site in the KOPAL trench uncovered disarticulated human remains mixed in with faunal remains. Although no evidence has been found in the bone remains on- or off-site of vulture disarticulation, it remains possible that some bodies were exposed. But the symbolic association between death and birds is widely found in the Neolithic of Turkey and the Middle East, and there appears to have been an important and long-lasting narrative in which head removal was associated with birds, especially raptors or waterbirds. A deposit of vulture, eagle and bustard wings at Zawi Chemi Shanidar (Solecki & McGovern 1980; Simmons & Nadel 1998) and stones engraved with vulture images like those at Çatalhöyük from Jerf el Ahmar (Stordeur et al. 2000) indicate that ideas about vultures belong to a set of practices and preoccupations with remarkable flexibility, endurance and sociospatial breadth.

On the Göbekli pillar in Figure 2.6, the two registers highlight the association of birds and a headless human. On the upper register we see the repeated and stylized motifs of possible structures and plants. Beneath these motifs were carved four birdlike creatures, some having the features of raptors, the others of waterbirds. Three of the four have human-like legs that extend out in front, making the creature appear to be in a sitting position. At both Çatalhöyük and Göbekli the birds that are associated with the headless bodies have human traits or adopt a hybrid human–animal form. The fourth bird image ends in a triangular, snakelike head instead of legs. Of particular interest is the raptor with the neck detail similar to the Yeni Mahalle sculpture that appears to be bouncing a sphere in its feathered wing. One interpretation is that this sphere or skull belongs to the headless male in the lower register, again reinforcing a connection between death, birds and a headless human state. On the lower register we see an array of dangerous animals, the scorpion, a snake, a toothy creature of unknown species and a waterbird that is paired with a decapitated phallic male. The male figure extends an outstretched arm as if to stroke the bird's neck while his penis is also extended toward the lower portion of the neck. While the pillar is damaged in this area and the decapitated man's legs are missing, it looks as if he were riding or directly positioned on top of the disproportionately large bird.

Another striking sculpture composed from four fragments uncovered in the Terrazzo building and other contexts at Nevalı Çori materializes a complex interrelationship between birds and human heads specifically. Described as a composite, freestanding 'totem pole', the three individuals are stacked one on top of the other, mutually constituting each other's forms. At the top a bird perches on two human heads whose hair is detailed in a cross-hatched pattern (Hauptmann & Schmidt 2007: 67–8). Associated with these heads, two opposing bodies are crouched with their backs toward each other. Hauptmann and Schmidt suggest that 'their swelled bellies and the depiction of their vulvae may represent pregnancy' and in one case 'the bird seems to grasp the human head by the cheeks with both feet.' The latter instance implies a form of violence, or threat of violence, that underwrites many of these monumental projects. Another stone statue of a 'bird-man' was found in an early phase of the Terrazzo building. The excavator interprets this as a hybrid being, a human dressed as a bird, or a bird with a human head in its mouth. In light of the prevalent skull cult documented at Nevalı Çori and other early Neolithic sites, this example – along with the human/bird pillar and the T-pillar with birds and the headless ithyphallic male – supports an interpretation that 'birds and human heads' are a central theme of Neolithic art (Hauptmann & Schmidt 2007).

The removal of heads is widely found in the Turkish and Middle Eastern Neolithic (seen at numerous sites, including Çayönü; Verhoeven 2002: table 3). It was perhaps at some times and places embedded in a narrative that involved birds, and perhaps birds taking away heads. In the Çatalhöyük wall paintings referred to earlier, griffon vultures (*Gyps fulvus*) have their beaks poised toward a number of decapitated, yet fleshed human bodies. A close examination of the composition reveals that each vulture's beak targets the area where the head once was rather than the limbs or fleshy parts of the body. This may lend support to the idea that vultures were associated with head removal and headless bodies, rather than with practices of excarnation per se. Moreover, the vultures were often painted red, and their talons were accentuated. The overall effect is of a pointy, bony and dangerous predator.

In Mellaart's Shrine VII.8, some seven vultures swoop upon six disproportionately small headless humans, although the burials below the paintings all retained their skulls. Mellaart also claimed that in Shrine E.VII.21 four skulls were positioned in direct association with plastered animal parts or paintings. Two skulls were 'perched on the corner platform below the vulture painting', another skull was in a basket below a bucranium on the west wall and the fourth skull was positioned below another bucranium on the east wall (Mellaart 1967: 84). Another fragmentary painting uncovered by Mellaart was interpreted by him as a human figure between two vultures 'swinging a sling in vigorous motion, presumably to ward off the two vultures from the small headless corpse which lies on its left side to his right' (Mellaart 1967: 166). Since all that remains of this panel is the artist's drawing rather than a photograph, we remain circumspect. Vulture skulls themselves were also inserted into the house walls at Çatalhöyük, plastered over into a lump with the beaks protruding (Russell & McGowan 2003: 445). Raptor claws were also curated and deposited in a grave in Building 75, and another three examples have been found in Building 77.

Besides the narrative art at Çatalhöyük the figurine corpus similarly reveals a connection to headlessness and may reveal resonances with bird imagery. There is an example of a carved stone figurine that may have represented a vulture or bird of prey (Mellaart 1967: 183). More generally, a subset of clay figurines that we label 'abbreviated' (Meskell et al. 2008) displays birdlike qualities (beaky, pinched heads) that sit atop stylized or truncated human torsos. Additionally, these figurines often have two legs that protrude out in a sitting position that resembles the vulture's human legs in the wall painting of Mellaart's Shrine VII.21. There are also visual similarities between these abbreviated, possibly hybrid figurine forms and the depiction of the seated birds (raptors and waterbirds) on the Göbekli T-pillar described earlier. Figurines from sites such as Nemrik display even more striking raptor imagery (Kozlowski 2002).

At Çatalhöyük many figurines are found without heads, and in one case there is evidence for the intentional severing of a stone figurine head (12102.X1) by cutting, probably using an obsidian blade. We have found numerous obsidian tools that show flattened and abraded edges from working stone surfaces (Karen Wright, pers. comm.). About a dozen clay figurines have dowel holes, suggesting that the process of removing and keeping heads could be played out in miniature. The ability to remove and replace certain heads might allow for multiple identities and potential narrativization (see Talalay 2004; Nanoglou 2006, 2008). Hamilton argued that detachable heads at Çatalhöyük 'were used to portray a range of emotions, attitudes or states of being' (1996: 221). In recent analyses Nakamura and Meskell (2006) have identified more bodies with dowel holes than heads made for attachment, which could suggest that the head is more determinative and the bodies are deemed more generic, although this may not imply a hierarchy. Among the figurines almost all of the examples with detachable heads are large female forms: 10 are

2.9. Clay figurine from IST Area at Çatalhöyük. *Source:* J. Quinlan and Çatalhöyük Research Project.

female and depict breasts, 2 are suggestive of the female form and 1 is androgynous. All but one of these examples are fleshed and corpulent.

One dramatic example (12401.X7, Figure 2.9) from Çatalhöyük plays on a possible tension between fleshed and unfleshed. The front portrays the typical robust female with large breasts and stomach, the navel protruding. From the arched shoulders very thin, almost skeletal arms with delineated fingers rest on the breasts. The back depicts an articulated skeleton with a modeled spinal column, a pelvis and scapulae that project above the shoulders. Individual ribs and vertebrae are depicted through horizontal and diagonal scoring. A dowel hole indicates that originally the piece had a separate, detachable head, and the circular depression around the dowel hole suggests that the head fit snugly into this curved space (Meskell & Nakamura 2005). It has previously been suggested that the heads of figurines themselves, especially detachable ones, came to represent real plastered skulls with their high foreheads and smoothed, minimal facial treatment, minus mouths and detailed features (Meskell 2007). There are interesting parallels at Göbekli, specifically in the carvings of beasts with bared fangs and claws attached to the large stone pillars described earlier. Several of these beasts, some still attached, others cut and removed in antiquity, have the same skeletal detail on the back, while retaining a fully fleshed belly and underside. Several examples show an erect penis underneath, even when it would have been difficult to view.

Like the Göbekli beasts, the Çatalhöyük figurine reveals the bony, skeletal part of the body that survives death (and interment) and explores a tension between embedded bony human parts and a shaped, fleshed, living body.

What we might be witnessing is a concern for the processes of bodily articulation or disarticulation across the Neolithic (see also Chapman 2000; Talalay 2004; Bailey 2005; Daems & Croucher 2007; Nanoglou 2008). As Kuijt and Chesson (2005: 177) have observed, the deliberate removal of figurine heads at 'Ain Ghazal coincides with the practice of skull removal in mortuary practices. The practice of removing, circulating and passing down heads at Çatalhöyük is something we have observed across media, from the wall paintings and burials to the figurine corpus, and is part of a repetitive suite of practices. For example, heads of animals in the forms of skulls (bulls, vultures, goats, wild boar jaws) were attached to walls and embedded and 'refleshed' with wall plaster, and there is one unclear example of a wall painting showing a headless animal in a hunting scene. N. Russell (pers. comm.) has noted instances of plastered animal skulls both with plastered horn cores (suggesting more decomposition) and nonplastered horn sheaths (less decomposition). These treatments might indicate different levels of enfleshment; horn sheaths would eventually deteriorate, and it is possible that after this happened, people would plaster and 'rebuild' the remaining horn core to achieve a similar effect (Nakamura & Meskell 2006).

At Çatalhöyük the context for the replastering is the house. Many of the bucrania were placed on structural pillars made of large timbers, themselves frequently replastered and embedded within the house walls. These wooden pillars too were usually retrieved at house abandonment and reused in later rebuildings of the house. They are not needed structurally as supporting beams, and so their inclusion in the house may have a more symbolic resonance, possibly harking back to an earlier time when they were necessary or suggesting an embodied element such as a skeleton for the house that was then plastered over.

The overall symbolic concern with flesh and its removal can be related to the practical knowledge of flesh and body part manipulation that must have been involved in the human burial process. In Building 49 a burial was found in a small grave adjacent to the painted northwestern platform. The head and torso were present but the arms and legs had been removed. The perfect anatomical position and articulation of the head and torso suggested that the arms and legs had been carefully removed while the bones were still partially fleshed. Lori Hager (pers. comm.) has noted the extreme care and bodily knowledge that must have been involved in removing the body parts. Not only the arms but also the scapulae and clavicles had been removed. And yet not a single cut mark could be identified, suggesting an almost surgical knowledge and care. While some secondary burials, as well as frequent disturbance of earlier burials, occurred at Çatalhöyük, most burials were of fleshed individuals. While some semidecomposition and drying of bones may have occurred prior to burial, the anatomical completeness of skeletons suggests that bodies were largely fleshed at burial and that heads and limbs were removed before extensive decomposition had set in.

We have already referred to the cut marks found in relation to two of the bodies from which heads had been removed at Çatalhöyük. As people dug below house platforms to make new interments, they came across earlier bodies, rearranged them and resorted them, and in Building 1 there is evidence of secondary reburial of body parts. Skulls were removed and sometimes painted in red ochre, and in the case noted earlier the facial features were remodeled in plaster. Daily practices at Çatalhöyük involved detailed knowledge of the human body and its flesh. But in particular, as we have seen, some houses became repositories for more burials than others, and all the cases of head removal so far found can be said to be from these 'history houses'. Groups of houses may have been associated with the houses in which people were preferentially buried and in which individuals had special knowledge of bodily manipulation. As already noted, we have little evidence for the role of burial in the 'temples' at Göbekli, but Schmidt has proposed a mortuary function on the basis of the evidence of mortuary associations for the buildings at Jerf el Ahmar and Nevalı Çori (Stordeur 2000; Hauptmann 2007).

The theme of bodily manipulation as a component of the social process of history making can be seen to link together many of the themes discussed in this chapter. Manipulating human bodies involved piercing, cutting and handling flesh. Birds are shown pecking the flesh from headless human corpses. In the symbolic repertoire of wild animals, the focus is on their claws, talons, horns, tusks, fangs and stings that pierce or tear flesh. The sharp body parts are kept and hidden in plaster on house walls. The wild animals are often male with erect penises, and in one case an erect penis is associated with a headless corpse and with the bird theme.

Clay figurines from Çatalhöyük also show the piercing or stabbing of animal bodies in a number of cases (Russell & Meece 2006; Meskell 2007), typically the fleshy parts of cattle, equids and boars.

It is of relevance to consider the tools involved in piercing the flesh. Many of the most finely flaked daggers from Çatalhöyük were made of flint. Two flint daggers have been found with bone handles, one depicting a boar's head (from Building 3; Stevanovic & Tringham 1998) and the other a snake (Mellaart 1967). The largest proportion of flaked stone points were made of obsidian (Carter, Conolly & Spasojević 2005). The elaborate, bifacially flaked projectile points occur in a wide range of contexts, including graves, and they may have functioned as arrowheads, spear points or knives/daggers. It is remarkable that in the Middle East as a whole, elaborate, large, bifacially flaked projectile points are not associated with late Palaeolithic and Epipalaeolithic sites. During these later stages of hunting and gathering the focus was on light arrowheads made with small microliths (Henry 1989) and on short blades in the PPNA (Bar-Yosef 1981; Gopher 1994). Bifacially flaked large points become more common in the PPNB (Goring-Morris & Belfer-Cohen 2001); that is the period in which there was a heavy dependence on domesticated sheep and goats and in which the symbolic elaborations involving dangerous wild animals, the dead and piercing the flesh reach their height. But large bifacial chipped tools are most common in the 7th millennium, for example, PPNC and Pottery Neolithic Levant, just as at Çatalhöyük. These points may well have played a role in protecting domesticated flocks from wild animals; they may be herders' tools. Some may have been used as knives to cut up domestic animals. But some points may have played a part in the confrontation of wild animals in social and ritual ceremonial and in the processing of human flesh. This may particularly be so of the more elaborate flint daggers with carved handles.

What, then, of the people who undertook the manipulation of the flesh? We have suggested that detailed knowledge of the biology of the body is implied by the careful and successful cutting and disarticulation of body parts. Is it possible that there were ritual specialists? We noted earlier that the Building 10 sequence has evidence that indicates the possibility of specialist wall painters, and the high quality of the paintings themselves could be used to make the same claim. While we wish to avoid the assumptions that often accompany the word 'shaman', it seems likely that specific individuals or elders specialized in ritual knowledge.

In his reconstruction of the vulture painting in his 'Shrine VII.21', Mellaart (1967) depicted two vultures with human feet standing over a headless corpse. Russell and McGowan (2003) have identified crane bones that suggest that crane wings may have been worn. It is possible that individuals dressed up as birds and vultures in the rituals surrounding death. As already noted, there are many hybrid bird–human depictions in the Neolithic of the region, and at Çatalhöyük itself the common abbreviated form of figurine can often be interpreted in this way. On the Göbekli pillar in Figure 2.6, the vulture-like bird seems to juggle a ball (or head?) and to have human characteristics. Hybrid human forms are not common overall at Çatalhöyük or elsewhere in the Neolithic of the Middle East. Apart from the birds and vultures, another possible example at Çatalhöyük is the bear: the splayed bear relief and bear stamp seal both have a prominent navel. One thinks too of the slit catlike eyes of the 'Ain Ghazal human statues. These species overlaps or, more often, anthropomorphizing of animal species might suggest an increasing belief in the overlapping fates of animals and ancestors or a stronger connection between the settled lifeworld and its broader landscape.

Levi-Strauss (1963: 224) describes the 'trickster' figure, in North America often a raven or coyote, as mediating between beasts of prey and herbivorous animals, hunting and agriculture, death and life. The trickster is an intermediary between opposed poles, and related forms appear very widely ethnographically. We do not wish here to make a specific analogy, but in conjunction with the new centrality of the human in the symbolism of Holocene societies in the Middle East (see Chapter 1, Question 3), perhaps a trickster-like figure may have mediated between life and death, acting as a ritual specialist involved in the manipulation of the human body at Çatalhöyük and elsewhere.

The house

As already noted, the context for the presencing of dangerous, wild things and the heads of humans and animals at Çatalhöyük is the house. The symbolic importance of the house has been widely noted for the Neolithic of the Middle East (e.g., Watkins 2006), and ideas and practices

surrounding the house, or 'domus', were central to the processes of
sedentism and domestication (Hodder 1990). The continuity of a house
in the same place over many generations, so clear at Çatalhöyük, occurred
very early in the late Pleistocene and Holocene. The house was used to
create long-term dependencies and relationships so central to intensive,
delayed-return economies. Already in the early Kebaran at Ohalo II about
21,500 years ago (Nadel 1990), the largest hut had three successive floors
(Nadel 2006). At Ein Gev 1 in the Jordan Valley, a 14th millennium BC
Kebaran site on the eastern side of the Sea of Galilee (Arensburg &
Bar-Yosef 1973) had a hut dug into the slope of a hill. 'The hut was periodically occupied as indicated by six successive layers which accumulated
within it' (Arensburg & Bar-Yosef 1973: 201). Similar evidence is found
at those Natufian sites with continuous occupation. According to the
reanalysis of the stratigraphy at 'Ain Mallaha by Boyd (1995), the 131–
51–62–73 sequence of buildings there started with 12 skeletons beneath
the floor of 131. Boyd draws attention to the continuity of activity in the
same place, starting with a set of burials. In the PPNA, Qermez Dere in
northern Iraq has good evidence of rebuilding in the same place (Watkins
2004, 2006), as does Jericho (Kenyon 1981), and there is much evidence
for such continuity in the PPNB at Jericho (Hodder 2007).

It is in such houses that elaborate symbolism involving the themes
identified in this chapter is increasingly found. In the Natufian at Hayonim Terrace, there is an association of burials with tortoise shell and
canid and gazelle bones (Valla, Le Mort & Plisson 1991). As already
noted, there are many associations of wild, dangerous things in houses
from the Natufian, PPNA and PPNB. As we have seen, the PPNA/PPNB
buildings at Göbekli are replete with symbolism of wild, dangerous
things. At Jerf el Ahmar and Göbekli there are larger, probably ritual, and
smaller domestic buildings, and certainly one of the differences between
southeastern and central Turkey is that the concentration of symbolism
in domestic houses is more common in the latter area. But the larger and
smaller buildings at Göbekli are very similar in form, and it is possible
that the line between communal ritual and domestic may not have been
clearly drawn, or that the 'temples' and 'houses' coreferred, or that the
'temples' were communal houses. Elaborate symbolism in houses and
communal buildings in the Middle East reaches its apogee in the PPNB.

Why was the symbolism of wild, dangerous things and death concentrated in houses and communal houselike buildings in the early Neolithic

of the Middle East? Can this association help us to understand the role of the symbolism? We have already argued that in Building 77 at Çatalhöyük the bull horns had a special relationship with the dead buried below the platform. Perhaps the curation and installation of the horns protected the ancestors. Or perhaps their main role was as memorials of hunting events. In some cases at Çatalhöyük wild, dangerous body parts were in the house but became hidden. Mellaart noted examples of the teeth of foxes and weasels, the tusks of wild boars, the claws of bears or the beaks of vultures in the walls of houses, but these were then plastered over numerous times, leaving a protuberance on the wall. So there is a pervasive presence of wild, dangerous things, some visible and some less so, perhaps having multiple roles.

Ethnographic evidence suggests that for most of the time that anatomically modern humans had lived as hunter-gatherers, they would have seen the environment as giving and reciprocating (Guenther 1999; Ingold 1999). Their spirit worlds would have consisted largely of animals and natural features with which shaman – or trickster-like – figures may have mediated. While human figures do appear in the Palaeolithic art of France, Spain and elsewhere, they do not dominate animals. The killing of an animal may have been accompanied by sacrifices of goods or food; the hunted animal may have been seen as 'given' in exchange for gifts in return, as is common in hunter-gatherer societies across southern Africa, Australia and South America (Fowler & Turner 1999; Politis 2007).

The process of domesticating different species of plants and animals was long and drawn out in the Middle East, but some genetic changes are visible in the PPNA, and by the mid-PPNB there is a full suite of domestic plants and domestic sheep, goats and dogs, with regional variation in terms of pig and finally cattle domestication (the latter in the 7th millennium BC). It thus seems that the increased concentration of wild, dangerous things in houses and buildings is coincident with the increased use of domestic animals, the increased stability and continuity of houses and the increased focus on the creation of histories. This is borne out by the figurine data, where cattle predominate, thus reinforcing this preference for depicting wild rather than domesticated animals. The same could be said of the subjects of the wall paintings.

One interpretation of this conjunction of processes is that animal heads, as well as human heads, were brought into the house or into communal buildings in order to create memories and histories. Bucrania (and perhaps paintings and engravings of wild bulls, etc.) may have memorialized feasts or the feats of hunters, tricksters and baiters. Handing down such items from generation to generation may have helped to create the histories of houses and the social groups entangled with them. But as already noted, not all the presencing of wild, dangerous things is very visible at Çatalhöyük. Another dimension of the symbolism may be that, by the PPNA and PPNB, wild animals came to be seen less as 'given' by animal spirits or the environment than as 'given' by the ancestors. At Çatalhöyük there is little evidence of any concentration of symbolism around storage bins and in food preparation areas of the house. The spatial associations of wild, dangerous things seem to be in the inner part of the main room of the house, where most burial occurs. As we noted earlier, there is much overlap in the treatment of specific cattle and human remains. There is also the striking example of the face pot where both human and cattle features mutually constitute each other. Mellaart also uncovered a number of stone figurines depicting bearded males either riding or birthing animals, and there are two examples showing humans and leopards together. This intense interaction between humans and powerful animals, rendered on a small and intimate scale, alongside the anthropomorphizing tendencies we have previously noted, might mark a proximal shift, an increasing intimacy and copresence in the ritual sphere.

If we turn to Göbekli, it is the large stone pillars with human form on which the imagery is placed. In the process of animal domestication, as people increasingly 'took' animals and kept them, rather than reciprocating with the environment, and as they increasingly 'owned' them in domestic or communal flocks, so too they may have come to see wild animals as provided by ancestors or human mythic figures. In teasing, killing and feasting on wild animals, people may have been interacting with ancestral entities as much as with animal spirits. Wild animal and human ancestral gods may have been closely linked, providing each other with authority and power. Just as, through burial, the ancestors were tied to the house or to communal buildings, so too were wild, dangerous things.

Conclusions

We do not wish to downplay the interesting differences in the symbolism of Çatalhöyük and Göbekli. For example, more herbivores (equids, cattle, deer) are shown in the symbolism at Çatalhöyük and fewer foxes, snakes, spiders and scorpions. This may relate to the different subsistence strategies of the sites and the different landscapes in which various forms of wild animal dominated. As noted at the start of this chapter, the two sites are far apart in time, and there are important social and economic changes that occurred between the two sites, particularly in relation to the increased dependence on domesticated plants and animals. Equally, there are important changes within the sites. For example, at Çatalhöyük the focus on animal installations in houses predominates in the earlier (pre–Level V) buildings, while the focus on fleshy figurines with removable heads predominates in later levels (Level V and above). There seems to be a breakdown in the centrality of the 'history house' themes and practices in the upper levels for reasons that are explored by Pels in Chapter 9, and the same may be true of other sites in the Neolithic of the Middle East, as the distinctive long-lived PPNB sites decline and transformation occurs into the Pottery Neolithic.

We do not wish to downplay these regional and temporal variations. The polycentric nature of the Neolithic in the Middle East has become abundantly clear in recent decades (Özdoğan & Başgelen 1999; Gérard & Thissen 2002; Mithen 2004). But it is apparent that a suite of themes involving skulls and birds of prey, wild cattle and other dangerous animals circulated through enormous areas of the Middle East during the period in which people settled down into large villages or 'towns' and adopted agriculture. The similarities between Çatalhöyük and Göbekli, and the similarities in material culture that we have drawn with other sites, suggest a very long term and very far flung set of myths, ideas and orientations, even if there were many local variations. These interconnections need to be set in the context of other similarities and interactions over the area in the Neolithic, especially in the PPNB – intramural burial, stone tool types and obsidian and shell exchange.

At one level we see the similar symbolic themes linked to the main preoccupation of the time – settling down and forming long-term villages, with all the dependencies on social structures that these villages imply. The long-termness involved delayed returns, and it was produced by the focus on constructing histories, as seen in the 'history houses' at Çatalhöyük and the repeatedly reused houses at other sites. As noted, the rebuilding of houses in place was a widespread theme of history making throughout the region from the Epipalaeolithic through the PPNB. At another level the focus on history making involved daily practices of living on and over human remains, the circulation of body parts and the cutting and remaking of flesh. There was some equivalence of human and animal heads, the latter perhaps as mementos of significant social events at which largesse and reputation were built around the killing and distributing of wild animals.

There is little evidence that all this was couched in terms of a nurturing female or a mothering goddess. Such imagery is absent from Göbekli, and it is all but absent from Çatalhöyük. While by the PPNB many sites were dependent on domesticated plants and animals, the symbolic imagery concentrated on wild, dangerous animals. We see a set of themes, including maleness, wild, dangerous animals, headless humans and birds. At Çatalhöyük and elsewhere these associations were linked by notions of continuity, passing down and duration, but also by the themes of piercing flesh and refleshing bodies. The manipulation of the human body was an important part of history making. The piercing of wild animal flesh was a key component in the building of reputation and in the protection of domestic animals and crops. Ancestors – human and animal – also protected the dead, the house and the inhabitants. Bodies, ancestors and skeletons could be refleshed to continue their roles in the creation of history and in the protection of the products of daily labor.

REFERENCES

Arensburg, B., & O. Bar-Yosef. 1973. Human remains from Ein Gev 1, Jordan Valley, Israel. *Paléorient*, 1, 201–6.

Badisches Landesmuseum Karlsruhe (ed.). 2007. *Die ältesten Monumente der Menschheit*. Karlsruhe: Badisches Landesmuseum.

Bailey, D. W. 2005. *Prehistoric Figurines: Representation and Corporeality in the Neolithic*. London: Routledge.

Baird, D. 2007. Pınarbaşı: From Epipalaeolithic camp site to sedentarising village in central Anatolia. In *The Neolithic in Turkey: New Excavations and New Discoveries*, eds. M. Özdoğan & N. Başgelen. Istanbul: Arkeoloji ve Snatat Yayinlari, 285–311.

Balter, M. 2005. *The Goddess and the Bull*. New York: Simon and Schuster.

Bar-Yosef, O. 1981. The "Pre-Pottery Neolithic" period in the southern Levant. In *Préhistoire du Levant*, eds. J. Cauvin & P. Sanlaville. Paris: CNRS, 551–70.

Bar-Yosef, O. 2002. Early Egypt and the agricultural dispersals. In *Magic Practices and Ritual in the Near Eastern Neolithic*, eds. H.-G. K. Gebel, B. D. Hermansen & C. Hoffmann Jensen. Berlin: Ex Oriente, 49–65.

Bataille, G. 1986. *Eroticism, Death and Sexuality.* San Francisco: City Lights Books.

Bloch, M. 1992. *Prey into Hunter: The Politics of Religious Experience.* Cambridge: Cambridge University Press.

Bonogofsky, M. 2005. A bioarchaeological study of plastered skulls from Anatolia: New discoveries and interpretations. *International Journal of Osteoarchaeology*, 15, 124–35.

Boyd, B. 1995. Houses and hearths, pits and burials: Natufian mortuary practices at Mallaha (Eynan), Upper Jordan Valley. In *The Archaeology of Death in the Ancient Near East*, eds. S. Campbell & A. Green. Oxford: Oxbow Monograph 51, 17–23.

Carter, T., J. Conolly, & A. Spasojević. 2005. The chipped stone. In *Changing Materialities at Çatalhöyük: Reports from the 1995–1999 Seasons*, ed. I. Hodder. Cambridge: McDonald Institute for Archaeological Research, 221–83, 467–533.

Cauvin, J. 2000. *The Birth of the Gods and the Origins of Agriculture.* Cambridge: Cambridge University Press.

Çelik, B. 2000. An early Neolithic settlement: Karahan Tepe. *Neo-Lithics*, 2–3, 6–8.

Cessford, C., M. W. Newton, P. I. Kuniholm, S. W. Manning, M. Özbakan, A. M. Özer, K. G. Akoğlu, T. Higham & P. Blumbach. 2006. Absolute dating at Çatalhöyük. In *Changing Materialities at Çatalhöyük: Reports from the 1995–99 Seasons*, ed. I. Hodder. Cambridge: McDonald Institute for Archaeological Research, 65–99.

Chapman, J. 2000. *Fragmentation in Archaeology: People, Places, and Broken Objects in the Prehistory of South-Eastern Europe.* London: Routledge.

Clark, G. 1977. *World Prehistory.* Cambridge: Cambridge University Press.

Daems, A., & K. Croucher 2007. Artificial cranial modification in prehistoric Iran: Evidence from crania and figurines. *Iranica Antiqua*, 42, 1–21.

Fletcher, A., J. Pearson & J. Ambers. 2008. The manipulation of social and physical identity in the Pre-Pottery Neolithic. *Cambridge Archaeological Journal*, 18, 309–25.

Fowler, C. S., & N. J. Turner. 1999. Ecological/cosmological knowledge and land management among hunter-gatherers. In *The Cambridge Encyclopedia of Hunters and Gatherers*, eds. R. B. Lee & R. Daly. Cambridge: Cambridge University Press, 419–25.

Garrod, D. E. 1957. The Natufian culture: The life and economy of a Mesolithic people in the Near East. *Proceedings of the British Academy*, 43, 211–22.

Gérard, F., & L. Thissen, eds. 2002. *The Neolithic of Central Anatolia: Internal Developments and External Relations during the 9th–6th Millennia cal BC – Proceedings of the International CANeW Round Table, Istanbul, November 23–24, 2001.* Istanbul: Ege Yayınları, 181–92.

Gimbutas, M. 1989. *The Language of the Goddess: Unearthing Hidden Symbols of Western Civilisation*. London: Thames and Hudson.

Girard, R. 1977. *Violence and the Sacred*. Baltimore: Johns Hopkins University Press.

Gopher, A. 1994. *Arrowheads of the Neolithic Levant*. Winona Lake, Ind.: Eisenbrauns.

Goring-Morris, N., H. Ashkenazi, M. Barzilai, O. M. Birkenfeld, V. Eshed, Y. Goren, L. K. Horwitz, M. Oron & J. Williams. 2008. The 2007–8 excavation seasons at Pre-Pottery Neolithic B Kfar HaHoresh, Israel. *Antiquity*, 82(318).

Goring-Morris, N., & A. Belfer-Cohen 2001. The symbolic realms of utilitarian material culture: The role of lithics. In *Beyond Tools*, eds. I. Caneva, C. Lemorini, D. Ampetti & P. Biagi. Berlin: Ex Oriente, 257–71.

Goring-Morris, N., & A. Belfer-Cohen 2002. Symbolic behaviour from the Epipalaeolithic and early Neolithic of the Near East: Preliminary observations on continuity and change. In *Magic Practices and Ritual in the Near Eastern Neolithic*, eds. H.-G. K. Gebel, B. D. Hermansen & C. Hoffmann Jensen. Berlin: Ex Oriente, 67–79.

Goring-Morris, N., & L. K. Horwitz. 2007. Funerals and feasts during the Pre-Pottery Neolithic B of the Near East. *Antiquity*, 81(314), 902–19.

Grosman, L., N. D. Munro & A. Belfer-Cohen. 2008. A 12,000-year-old Shaman burial from the southern Levant (Israel). *Proceedings of the National Academy of Sciences*, 105, 17665–9.

Guenther, M. 1999. From totemism to shamanism: Hunter-gatherer contributions to world mythology and spirituality. In *The Cambridge Encyclopedia of Hunters and Gatherers*, eds. R. B. Lee & R. Daly. Cambridge: Cambridge University Press, 426–33.

Hamilton, N. 1996. Figurines, clay balls, small finds and burials. In *On the Surface: Çatalhöyük, 1993–1995*, ed. I. Hodder. Cambridge: McDonald Institute for Archaeological Research, 215–63.

Hansen, S. 2007. *Bilder vom Menschen der Steinzeit*. Mainz: Verlag Philipp von Zabern.

Hauptmann, H. 2007. Nevali Çori. In *Die ältesten Monumente der Menschheit-Karlsruhe*. Karlsruhe: Badisches Landesmuseum, 86–93.

Hauptmann, H., & K. Schmidt. 2007. Anatolien vor 12 000 Jahren: Die Skulpturen des Frühneolithikums. In *Die ältesten Monumente der Menschheit*. Karlsruhe: Badisches Landesmuseum, 67–82.

Henry, D. 1989. *From Foraging to Agriculture: The Levant at the End of the Iceage*. Philadelphia: University of Pennsylvania Press.

Hodder, I. 1990. *The Domestication of Europe*. Oxford: Blackwell.

Hodder, I. 2006. *The Leopard's Tale: Revealing the Mysteries of Çatalhöyük*. London: Thames and Hudson.

Hodder, I. 2007. Çatalhöyük in the context of the Middle East Neolithic. *Annual Review of Anthropology*, 36, 105–20.

Hodder, I., & L. M. Meskell. In press. A 'curious and sometimes a trifle macabre artistry': Some aspects of symbolism in Neolithic Turkey. *Current Anthropology*.

Hutton, R. 1997. The Neolithic Great Goddess: A study in modern tradition. *Antiquity*, 71(271), 91–9.

Ingold, T. 1999. On the social relations of the hunter-gatherer band. In *The Cambridge Encyclopedia of Hunters and Gatherers*, eds. R. B. Lee & R. Daly. Cambridge: Cambridge Univerity Press, 399–410.

Kemp, B. J. 2000. The colossi from the early shrine at Coptos in Egypt. *Cambridge Archaeological Journal*, 20(2), 211–42.

Kenyon, K. M. 1981. *Excavations at Jericho. Vol. 3: The Architecture and Stratigraphy of the Tell*. London: British School of Archaeology Jerusalem.

Kozlowski, S. K. 1992. *Nemrik 9: PrePottery Neolithic Site in Iraq 2*. Warsaw: University of Warsaw Institute of Archaeology.

Kozlowski, S. K. 2002. *Nemrik 9: An Aceramic Village in Northern Iraq*. Warsaw: University of Warsaw Institute of Archaeology.

Kuijt, I. 2008. The regeneration of life: Neolithic structures of symbolic remembering and forgetting. *Current Anthropology*, 49(2), 171–97.

Kuijt, I., & M. Chesson 2005. Lumps of clay, pieces of stone: Ambiguity, bodies and identity as portrayed in Neolithic figurines. In *Archaeologies of the Middle East: Critical Perspectives*, eds. S. Pollock & R. Bernbeck. Oxford: Blackwells, 152–83.

Levi-Strauss, C. 1963. *Structural Anthropology*. New York: Basic Books.

Lewis-Williams, D. 2004. Constructing a cosmos: Architecture, power and domestication at Catalhoyuk. *Journal of Social Archaeology*, 4(1), 28–59.

Mellaart, J. 1967. *Çatal Hüyük: A Neolithic Town in Anatolia*. London: Thames and Hudson.

Meskell, L. M. 1995. Goddesses, Gimbutas and New Age archaeology. *Antiquity*, 69, 74–86.

Meskell, L. M. 2007. Refiguring the corpus at Çatalhöyük. In *Material Beginnings: A Global Prehistory of Figurative Representation*, eds. A. C. Renfrew & I. Morley. Cambridge: McDonald Institute Monographs, 137–49.

Meskell, L. M. 2008. The nature of the beast: Curating animals and ancestors at Çatalhöyük. *World Archaeology*, 40(3), 373–89.

Meskell, L. M., & C. Nakamura. 2005. Çatalhöyük Figurines. *Archive Report on the Çatalhöyük Season 2005* (www.catalhoyuk.com).

Meskell, L. M., C. Nakamura, R. King & S. Farid 2008. Figured lifeworlds and depositional practices at Çatalhöyük. *Cambridge Archaeological Journal*, 18(2), 139–61.

Mithen, S. 2004. *After the Ice*. Cambridge, Mass.: Harvard University Press.

Mithen, S., B. Finlayson & R. Shaffrey. 2005. Sexual symbolism in the Early Neolithic of the Southern Levant: Pestles and mortars from WF16. *Documenta Praehistorica*, 32, 103–10.

Molleson, T., P. Andrews & B. Boz. 2005. Reconstruction of the Neolithic people of Çatalhöyük. In *Inhabiting Çatalhöyük: Reports from the 1995–1999 Seasons*, ed. I. Hodder. Cambridge: McDonald Institute for Archaeological Research, 279–300.

Morsch, M. G. F. 2002. Magic figurines? Some remarks about the clay objects of Nevali Çori. In *Magic Practices and Ritual in the Near Eastern Neolithic*, eds. H.-G. K. Gebel, B. D. Hermansen & C. Hoffmann Jensen. Berlin: Ex Oriente, 145–62.

Nadel, D. 1990. Ohalo II: A preliminary report. *Mitekufat Haeven*, 23, 48–9.

Nadel, D. 2006. Residence ownership and continuity: From the early Epipalaeolithic unto the Neolithic. In *Domesticating Space*, eds. E. B. Banning & M. Chazan. Berlin: Ex Oriente, 25–34.

Nakamura, C., & L. M. Meskell. 2006. Çatalhöyük figurines. *Archive Report on the Catalhöyük Season 2006* (www.catalhoyuk.com).

Nanoglou, S. 2006. Regional perspectives on the Neolithic anthropomorphic imagery of Northern Greece. *Journal of Mediterranean Archaeology*, 19(2), 155–76.

Nanoglou, S. 2008. Building biographies and households: Aspects of community life in Neolithic northern Greece. *Journal of Social Archaeology*, 8(1), 139–60.

Nergis, S. 2008. *Yakin Dogu Neolitikinde Phallus Sembolü Sorunu* (The problems concerning the phallic symbols in the Neolithic of the Near East). Ph.D. dissertation. Istanbul: Prehistory Section, Faculty of Letters, Istanbul University.

Noy, T. 1991. Art and decoration of the Natufian at Nahal Oren. In *The Natufian Culture in the Levant*, eds. O. Bar-Yosef & F. R. Valla. Ann Arbor, Mich.: International Monographs in Prehistory, 557–68.

Özdoğan, M. 2001. The Neolithic deity: Male or female. In *Lux Orientis, Festschrift für Harald Hauptmann*, eds. R. M. Boehmer & J. Maran Rahden. Rahden: Verlag Marie Leidorf, 313–18.

Özdoğan, M. 2002. Defining the Neolithic of Central Anatolia. In *The Neolithic of Central Anatolia: Internal Developments and External Relations during the 9th–6th Millennia cal BC – Proceedings of the International CANeW Round Table, Istanbul, November 23–24, 2001*, eds. F. Gérard & L. Thissen Istanbul. Istanbul: Ege Yayınları, 253–61.

Özdoğan, M. 2003. A group of Neolithic stone figurines from Mezraa-Teleilat. In *From Village to Cities: Early Villages in the Near East*, eds. M. Özdogan, H. Hauptmann & N. Basgelen. Istanbul: Arkeoloji ve Sanat Yayinlari, 511–23.

Özdoğan, M., & N. Başgelen, eds. 1999. *Neolithic in Turkey: The Cradle of Civilization, New Discoveries*. Istanbul: Arkeoloji ve Sanat Yayınları.

Peters, J., D. Helmer, M. Saña Segui & A. Von Den Driesch. 1999. Early animal husbandry in the Northern Levant. *Paléorient*, 25(2), 27–48.

Politis, G. 2007. *Nukak: Ethnoarchaeology of an Amazonian People*. Walnut Creek, Calif.: Left Coast Press.

Rollefson, G. O. 2008. Charming lives: Human and animal figurines in the late Epipaleolithic and early Neolithic periods in the greater Levant and Eastern Anatolia. In *The Neolithic Demographic Transition and Its Consequences*, eds. J.-P. Bocquet-Appel & O. Bar-Yosef. New York: Springer, 387–416.

Rosenberg, M. 2007. Hallan Çemi. In *Die ältesten Monumente der Menschheit*. Karlsruhe: Badisches Landesmuseum.

Rosenberg, M., & R. W. Redding. 2000. Hallan Çemi and early village organization in eastern Anatolia. In *Life in Neolithic Farming Communities: Social Organization, Identity, and Differentiation*, ed. I. Kuijt. New York: Kluwer, 39–61.

Rudebeck, E. 2000. *Tilling Nature: Harvesting Culture*. Stockholm: Almquist and Wiksell.

Russell, N., & L. Martin 2005. The Çatalhöyük mammal remains. In *Inhabiting Çatalhöyük: Reports from the 1995–1999 Seasons*, ed. I. Hodder. Cambridge: McDonald Institute for Archaeological Research, 33–98.

Russell, N., L. Martin & H. Buitenhuis. 2005. Cattle domestication at Çatalhöyük revisited. *Current Anthropology*, 46(5), S101–S8.

Russell, N., & K. J. McGowan. 2003. Dance of the cranes: Crane symbolism at Catalhoyuk and beyond. *Antiquity*, 77(297), 445–55.

Russell, N., & S. Meece. 2006. Animal representations and animal remains at Çatalhöyük. In *Çatalhöyük Perspectives: Reports from the 1995–1999 Seasons*, ed. I. Hodder. Cambridge: McDonald Institute for Archaeological Research, 209–30.

Schmidt, K. 2006. *Sie bauten den ersten Tempel: Das rätselhafte Heiligtum der Steinzeitjäger*. Munich: C. H. Beck.

Schmidt, K. 2007. Göbekli Tepe. In *Die ältesten Monumente der Menschheit*. Karlsruhe: Badisches Landesmuseum, 74–5.

Simmons, T., & D. Nadel. 1998. The avifauna of the early Epipalaeolithic site of Ohalo II (19,400 years BP), Israel: Species diversity, habitat and seasonality. *International Journal of Osteoarchaeology*, 8(2), 79–96.

Solecki, R. L., & T. H. McGovern. 1980. Predatory birds and prehistoric man. In *Theory and Practice: Essays Presented to Gene Weltfish*, ed. S. Diamond. The Hague: Mouton, 79–95.

Stevanovic, M., & R. Tringham. 1998. The BACH 1 Area. Çatalhöyük Archive Report 1998 (http://catal.arch.cam.ac.uk/catal/Archive_rep98/stevanovic 98.html).

Stordeur, D. 2000. New discoveries in architecture and symbolism at Jerf el Ahmar (Syria), 1997–1999. *Neo-Lithics*, 1, 1–4.

Stordeur, D., M. Benet, G. der Aprahamian & J.-C. Roux. 2000. Les bâtiments communautaires de Jerf el Ahmar et Mureybet PPNA (Syrie). *Paléorient*, 26(1), 29–44.

Talalay, L. 2004. Heady business: Skulls, heads and decapitation in Neolithic Anatolia and Greece. *Journal of Mediterannean Archaeology*, 17(2), 139–63.

Twiss, K. C., A. Bogaard, D. Bogdan, T. Carter, M. P. Charles, S. Farid, N. Russell, M. Stevanović, E. N. Yalman & L. Yeomans. 2008. Arson or accident? The burning of a Neolithic house at Çatalhöyük. *Journal of Field Archaeology*, 33(1), 41–57.

Valla, F. R., F. Le Mort & H. Plisson 1991. Les fouilles en cours sur la Terrasse d'Hayonim. In *The Natufian Culture in the Levant*, eds. O. Bar-Yosef & F. R. Valla. Ann Arbor, Mich.: International Monographs in Prehistory, 93–110.

Verhoeven, M. 2002. Ritual and ideology in the Pre-Pottery Neolithic B of the Levant and Southeast Anatolia. *Cambridge Archaeological Journal*, 12(2), 233–58.

Watkins, T. 2004. Building houses, framing concepts, constructing worlds. *Paléorient*, 30, 5–24.

Watkins, T. 2006. Architecture and the symbolic construction of new worlds. In *Domesticating Space*, eds. E. B. Banning & M. Chazan. Berlin: Ex Oriente, 15–24.

Weinstein-Evron, M., & A. Belfer-Cohen. 1993. Natufian figurines from the new excavations of the el-Wad Cave, Mt. Carmel, Israel. *Rock Art Research*, 10, 102–6.

Yartah, T. 2005. Les bâtiments communautaires de Tell 'Abr 3 (PPNA, Syrie). *Neo-Lithics*, 1(5), 3–9.

3

Spiritual entanglement: Transforming religious symbols at Çatalhöyük

LeRon Shults

The overall aim of the three-year interdisciplinary project at Çatalhöyük was to explore the extent to which spiritual life and religious ritual may have been involved in the momentous shift toward sedentism and agriculture, which are typically connected to the emergence of "civilization." In *The Leopard's Tale* (2006) Ian Hodder offered his own initial analysis of the role of the religious sphere (among others) in the social transformations that are evident through time and space at Çatalhöyük, proposing a theory of "material entanglement." I find his interpretation plausible and compelling, and in this essay suggest a complementary perspective on the data that develops and makes use of the idea of "spiritual entanglement" as a conceptual framework for beginning to respond "theologically" to the four interrelated research questions that guided the project.

My strategy will be to take Robert Neville's pragmatic theory of religious symbolism, which deals primarily with axial age religions and has been applied to contemporary interreligious dialogue, and apply it imaginatively to the study of religious transformations during the early Neolithic. Besides its general illuminative power, Neville's model also commends itself to this task because its use of the semiotic metaphysics of C. S. Peirce provides a point of contact between the disciplines of theology and archaeology. Neville's emphasis is on what symbols *do*, on their transformative power and the way in which they are transformed by intentional agents in concrete communities. As we will see, he describes *religious* symbols as those that persons "take" in particular contexts in their pragmatic attempts to engage the ultimate boundary-making conditions of their lived world.

Many of the terms in the preceding two paragraphs are highly charged and controversial. The concept of "religion" itself is ambiguous and highly contested. The pairing of "spirituality" with "materiality" could easily raise suspicions about ancient and early modern dualisms, both metaphysical and epistemological. Moreover, many readers might have qualms about the very idea of an engagement between archaeology and theology as disciplines. In what follows I hope to provide enough clarification of my use of these terms, and of philosophical developments that have shaped the self-understanding of the academic field of theology (and religious studies), that at least some of these concerns will be alleviated and new possibilities for mutual interdisciplinary enhancement can emerge.

Matter, spirit and the bounds of religion

In one way or another all of the research questions addressed by the 2005–8 Çatalhöyük project have to do with religious boundaries: how to identify them and their causal efficacy (if any) in relation to human agents tending to the boundary conditions of social life. One of the reasons the project was so tempting to a theologian interested in interdisciplinary dialogue was the openness of the archaeological team to facing the difficult task of exploring the religious dimension of Neolithic sociality rather than ignoring it or trying to disentangle it from the web of causal forces in human life.

Nevertheless, all interdisciplinary boundary crossings bring challenges as well as opportunities. The idea that an engagement between archaeology and theology is even possible, much less potentially fruitful, may well be met with suspicion from participants in both fields. This is exacerbated by the lingering anxiety (on both sides) that the available options for interpreting the emergence of religion in human culture remain mired in an either–or dichotomy: either reduce everything to *material* explanations or introduce a separate interpretation that appeals to the *spiritual*. On this (stereotypical) model, archaeologists use objective tools to analyze material artifacts while theologians explore the subjective domain of spiritual intentions – and never the twain shall meet.

The good news is that scholars in both disciplines have increasingly challenged this forced choice between metaphysical monism and dualism, as well as the methodological ramifications that derived from impaling oneself on either horn of this dilemma. One of the most significant developments in this regard is the increased attention to theories of emergent complexity in the philosophy of science. Although some uses of the term "emergence" in the 20th century were (ironically) tied to both positivism and vitalism, the theories I have in mind here use the term in a way that is explicitly designed to avoid both of these outmoded approaches.

Instead of choosing between naturalistic reductionism and supernaturalistic interventionism, or between physicalism and dualism, emergence theorists can argue for a third way out of these forced dilemmas. As Philip Clayton explains, "Emergence is the view that new and unpredictable phenomena are naturally produced by interactions in nature; that these new structures, organisms, and ideas are not reducible to the sub-systems on which they depend; and that the newly evolved realities in turn exercise a causal influence on the parts out of which they arose" (2004: vi). This means, in the case of human agency or religious intentionality, that such phenomena are understood to be complex cases of autopoiesis, the naturally emergent self-organization of complex structures with new functionalities and capacities (cf. Gregersen 2003; Juarrero 2002; Murphy & Stoeger 2007).

For our purposes here it suffices to say that such approaches are philosophical elaborations of scientific insights into the nature of the relation between "matter" and "energy." Insofar as the term "spirit" was typically used in ancient and early modern philosophy to indicate that which *energized* or moved things in the world, any continued use of the term "spiritual" in dialogue with contemporary science ought to account for relevant shifts in our understanding of such concepts. Early modern (Newtonian) classical mechanics reduced causality to the interaction of material bodies in absolute space ($F = ma$). Late modern (Einsteinian) physics insists that what we call "matter" is inseparable from the energetic flux of space-time ($E = mc^2$). The following exposition, therefore, will presuppose that the sphere of human "spirituality" is not quarantined from the material sphere – as though we were dealing with two types of substance (material and immaterial) – but wholly entangled within (albeit emergent from) the sphere of materiality.

We can see a similar shift in the social scientific study of religion. As Arweck and Keenan observe in the introduction to *Materializing Religion*, all religions "dwell amongst us" in material means, embedded and embodied within physical forms. However, rejecting a Neoplatonic (or Cartesian) notion of spirituality as detached from "matter" does not require rejecting the "spiritual" tout court. "Discarding this

limiting dualism allows the pursuit of an integrated or holistic intellectual approach which might trace along those fuzzy, yet critical margins
where body-spirit and mind-matter fuse, mix and mingle . . . the boundaries between explication and appreciation, particularly in areas of the religious 'imaginary', are much thinner, and less dispensable, perhaps, than
those of a more positivistic disposition are inclined to view" (2006: 8–9).

In the dialogue with archaeology, however, one resource for over-
coming the dualism of matter and spirit, and its concomitant disciplinary
dichotomizing, stands out as particularly promising. The work of the
American pragmatist philosopher C. S. Peirce has been increasingly
retrieved among both archaeologists and theologians. The "Peircean
alternative" to structuralism, with its incipient dualism that dominated
archeology for decades, is outlined in Robert Preucel's book *Archaeological Semiotics* (2006). Peirce's triadic (rather than dyadic) and pragmatic (rather than idealistic) theory of signs has contributed to new
modes of archaeological interpretation. As Preucel observes, Peirce's
metaphysics resisted Cartesian dualism while acknowledging the real difference between types of symbol use. On this model, intentionality and
meaning-making are fully embedded within the dynamic semiotic network that constitutes nature. I will explore Neville's theological appropriation of Peirce in more detail later.

At this stage it is important simply to point out that Peirce's argument
for the complex ways in which signs may be "taken" or engaged by inter-
preters is embedded within his commitment to metaphysical synechism
and a triadic theory of knowledge. Avoiding a simple dualism between
sign and object (signum–res, etc.), Peirce stressed the *triadic* relation
between sign, object and interpretant. "A Sign, or Representamen, is a
First which stands in such a genuine triadic relation to a Second, called
its Object, as to be capable of determining a Third, called its Intepretant,
to assume the same triadic relation to its Object in which it stands itself
to the same Object" (Peirce 1998: 272). Peirce is careful to emphasize
that this cannot be reduced to dyadic semiotic relations or even to a
complex of such dyadic relations. The mediating (triadic) relationality of
signification is genuine and irreducible. Moreover, signs (including symbols) are not "merely" intelligible or ideational, but as "real" as all other
phenomena in their dynamic continuity.

Before outlining the theories of Hodder and Neville and attempting to
entangle them, I must return briefly to the notion of religious boundaries.

One of the difficulties of interdisciplinary endeavors is attending to the semantic shifts within and across fields of study. This is especially true when the subject is a phenomenon as contested and ambiguous as "religion," which in this day and age deserves scare quotes. The intrepidity, contestability and ambiguity of this phenomenon, however, should not lead us to avoid the task of trying to make sense of it. Interdisciplinary discussions about recognizing the "religious" and attributions of causality to religion are complicated by the fact that members of one discipline are often suspicious of the "other" discipline and sometimes force the other into conformity with the same categories with which their own discipline operates. Avoiding such hegemonic temptations requires humility and patience.

For the sake of this essay I will use a rough working definition of the "religious" dimension as that emergent sphere of human life in which social groups tend to their fascination with and fear of ultimate boundedness, which shape and are shaped by all of the other dynamic modes of social (and material) binding and being-bound. As even its etymological root (*re-ligere*) indicates, religion has to do with the way in which one is ultimately bound together with others. Various sciences focus on particular proximate modes of social binding, on binding practices and practical boundaries. "Theology" (in the sense used here) is also interested in sociality but tends to the ultimate conditions for sociality itself. How do humans deal with their experience of being-conditioned, with limitation per se, with questions about the ground for all social (and material) binding whatsoever? How do humans attempt to bind themselves to that which confronts them as unbounded and unbindable? This requires attending to "infinity" (in the sense described later) as well as "sociality."

The metaphors of "binding" and "entanglement" can reinforce one another. In a variety of disciplines, from quantum physics to marriage therapy, the concept of entangled fields of force has shown its illuminative value. As hinted in my subtitle, the question is about *transforming* religious symbols. How do symbols themselves change over time and in what sense do they change those who engage them? Religious symbols are transformed *and* transformative. Their entanglement within the bonds of human life makes them a force in transformation. In what follows, I will use Neville's pragmatic theory of religious symbols as a starting point for a way of thinking about "spiritual" entanglement that can be brought into dialogue with Hodder's interpretation of transformation at Çatalhöyük.

Ian Hodder's theory of material entanglement

In this short essay I cannot do full justice to Hodder's analysis in *The Leopard's Tale* (2006), but I do want to point to two specific themes: his emphasis on the way in which the people of Çatalhöyük were *bound* together and his understanding of the dynamics that shaped the *transformation* of these bindings. What I find fascinating is that Hodder's archaeological thesis that "more material entanglement and objectification lead to faster change" (2006: 258) could also be applied to historical developments during the past nine thousand years as well and, indeed, to our own technologically, electronically, informationally entangled age. From a theological point of view, it is interesting to explore what we can learn from studying this crucial period also for the sake of recognizing our own entanglement and capacity for transformation.

Part of the background for Hodder's analysis is the broader debate among archaeologists on the roles played by factors like sendentism, domestication, symbolism, tool use and art in the origins of "civilization." Like Cauvin (2000), Hodder believes that symbols played an important part in the emergence of culture, and like Renfrew (2001), Hodder argues that symbolism cannot be understood apart from human material engagement. However, Hodder's theory of "material entanglement" offers a unique proposal of how these features of human civilization came to be:

> Material entanglement produced a representation in the object world of the social structure such that it could be contested and changed. . . . As material entanglement increased, the human as agent becomes more apparent. . . . I would argue that this shift towards a centering of human agency came about as the inverse of the entanglement process. People became more invested in a web of material relations so that their social relations were 'objectified.' . . . the social world became more malleable and susceptible to *transformation* . . . humans came to see themselves more clearly as agents able to *transform* social lives by *transforming* material objects, artifacts, monuments and environments. (2006: 204–5; emphasis added)

In other words, "civilization" evolved slowly as a result of small changes in the way persons were increasingly bound to material objects and as their relation to one another became increasingly mediated through such objects.

Much of Hodder's analysis in the book is meant to provide warrant for his claim that phenomena like sedentism and domestication can be interpreted as the unintended by-product of a growing entanglement with material objects. As the quote indicates, he is particularly interested in understanding the changes or transformations within and around the "town" over time, especially the apparent increase in awareness of the power of human agency, which is displayed in the art and (arguably) the figurines.

To make sense of these transformations, Hodder introduces the idea of "spheres" of entanglement, spheres that "are comprised of groups of activities that involved sets of entanglements in social, material, productive, symbolic and other realms" (2006: 59). These spheres are not separate domains but reciprocal, dense networks that are intersecting and interdependent. This entanglement intertwines the spheres, networking webs of material, social and conceptual relations. Hodder illustrates this by demonstrating how practices such as the use of plaster for the walls and the burial of obsidian with ancestors require and reinforce such entanglement. This is consistent with his proposals (elsewhere) that archaeological analysis should recover its interest in the role of meaning, agency and intention that was lost in some processual approaches (e.g., Hodder 1990, 1999).

However, in this context he goes out of his way to emphasize the irreducible role of *materiality* in his analysis of the dynamics and patterns evident in the way in which people are tied together and bound in their social relations at Çatalhöyük. "By engaging in material things more fully, humans were able to extend social ties in the giving of gifts. . . . So the social world produces the material explosion, but we have also seen that materiality involves sociality. . . . So there was a dual process of social and material entrapment pushing entanglement forward in a positive feedback loop" (2006: 240). The more people became entangled with the materiality of their interactions with clay, obsidian, bones and symbolic markers of animals, as well as hiding and revealing, the more the "house" became increasingly important as a bonding force for life together. However, the growing significance of the house and its productive potential throughout the Çatalhöyük time sequence cannot be explained in merely material terms; it emerged through different sets of entanglements that "involved practical, symbolic, economic and aesthetic dimensions in a seamless web" (63).

Hodder observes that material objects "tie people together in the practicalities of their use. The objects are pursued because they allow greater sociality. But they also mean greater dependencies (material and social), and thus further shifts in practices, concepts, beliefs and orientations" (242). It was this "daily spiraling" of material-social engagements that led through a slow "march of the mass" to the conditions that allowed for an elaboration of the "prowess–animal spirit–hunting–feasting" network. Boundaries of all kinds are constantly teased and explored, hidden and revealed. The fascination with tensions such as fleshiness and permanence, living and dead, domestic and wild, presence and absence is brought within the houses in a variety of ways, including the use of plaster on walls and skulls, the use of horns and claws and burials (and the unearthing of skeletons), all within the house itself.

For Hodder the key question is not "Why was a new symbolic world created?" but "Why were symbolic worlds materialized at this time?" He argues that community was crafted slowly as people's agency became more materially entangled in their social lives and as their material lives became more socially entangled. This entanglement was an important factor not only for driving the process toward sedentism and domestication, but also for the development of a stronger sense of human agency. Materializing social relations made them easier to change and organize, on the one hand, and enhanced their ability to endure, on the other. The increased sense of awareness of human agency is suggested by the prevalence of human forms in the art of the early Neolithic, contrasting significantly with Palaeolithic, which typically represents animals and other figures.

On the one hand, the individual "self" at Çatalhöyük was thoroughly embedded within the social, within the practices and relations of the house and its symbolism. But on the other hand, these practices and increased materiality "also produce a partitioning and a greater sense of difference as the practices are carried out. The individualized self does emerge as identified in its difference from others, and from the very emphasis on boundaries themselves – the ridges, edges, pedestals and the distinctions in symbolism, burial and activity. This is a social process that creates individual difference . . . [material and social] practices draw attention to the boundaries of an individual self" (228).

For Hodder, the material and spiritual spheres are not mutually exclusive. "People crafted their own worlds by crafting the gods. They began to use things to effect change – economically and socially, but also *spiritually*. They became invested in materiality as part of trying to make sense of and control the world" (205, emphasis added). The material and social entanglement of the self as agent also shaped the "hunting–feasting–prowess–ancestry" network and contributed to culturally binding forms of interaction that would commonly be identified as religious or spiritual in some sense, including the "control of knowledge about and the objects of the spirit world" (250). One of the other few times that Hodder uses the term "spiritual" is in the context of the houses as connected to ancestors and possibly to interceding with animal gods or spirits: he observes the possibility "that elders within houses protected people with their knowledge of spiritual and material effects" (189).

Although Hodder does not deal in this context with the philosophical issues of Peircean metaphysics or emergent complexity theory, his theory of entanglement meshes nicely with such antidualistic and nonreductionistic models. He has engaged Derrida and Ricoeur more heavily than Peirce, but Hodder's approach seems consonant with many of the intuitions of pragmatic semiotics. Before beginning to weave a theory of spiritual entanglement in relation to the patterns of human life exhibited at Çatalhöyük, I need to introduce one more type of conceptual webbing – an explicitly theological interpretation of human engagement that attends to the material, the social and the spiritual without collapsing back into a deleterious dualism.

Robert Neville's theory of religious symbols

As indicated, I have selected Neville as a resource for the interdisciplinary dialogue because, more than any other theologian engaged in comparative religion, he has demonstrated the value of Peirce for interpreting religious symbols in late modernity (cf. Shults, in press). In *The Highroad Around Modernism* (1992), Neville argues that Peirce avoids the problems of both Enlightenment (especially Cartesian) modernism and pernicious and relativist forms of postmodernism. In *Religion in Late Modernity* (2002), he commends Peirce's pragmatic theory of symbols in the context of a broader argument about the public role of theology in contemporary culture. Neville summarizes much of his prior work and outlines his approach to theology as "symbolic engagement" in his more recent *The Scope and Truth of Theology* (2006).

My suggestion will be that his approach to interpreting religious symbols can be applied not only to contemporary comparative religions, but *mutatis mutandis* to ancient forms of human life as well. For our purposes here we can limit ourselves for the most part to Neville's *The Truth of Broken Symbols* (1996). In that volume the relevant features of his proposal are sufficiently clear: an emphasis on interpretation as *engagement*, on the way in which symbols "break" when engaging the *infinite*, on the significance of intentional interpretants in particular *contexts* for understanding the meaning of symbols and on the pragmatic effectiveness of religious symbolic engagement for the *transformation* of persons.

Building on the insights of Peircean *pragmatic* semiotics and metaphysics, Neville's analysis focuses on what symbols *do* (chap. 1). The human mode of being in the world, argues Neville, is best expressed not as a "mirroring" of reality in the mind (which assumes dualism), but as an "engagement" within the world. All organisms engage their particular environment in order to sustain themselves. Humans engage through the synthetic activity of imagination, which is a real interaction with realities, including people's responses, habits, orientations and so on. Like Peirce, Neville rejects a dyadic separation between sign (or symbol, idea) and thing signified (object, reality). Reality is understood to be a dynamically interconnected web and human interpretation to be an irreducibly triadic (sign, object, interpretant) semiosis pragmatically embedded within that web.

What about *religious* symbols? For Neville, symbols are not "essentially" religious (or nonreligious). Like all other symbols, they are "taken" in a particular context with a (more or less intentional) pragmatic purpose. What makes religious symbols unique is that they are taken to engage the boundary conditions of the world, or the world-constructing boundaries of a person's imaginative cultural engagement. For Neville, the human way of imaginatively engaging the world is (in a general sense) always and already *religious* insofar as its basic function is world-making or world-constructing. This is because "imagination cannot frame its experiential elements in a human way without the orienting importance of certain pervasively or seasonally appearing images that function as boundary conditions for worldliness."

Religious symbols intend to refer, according to Neville, to borderline or world-making things, "to things having to do with the very worldliness of the world, thus referring always jointly to the finite border and to the infinite within which the border is constituted" (1996: 11). A religious symbol may fail to engage this border, or engage it poorly, but what marks it off as religious is the intention to so engage these real boundary conditions. Here Neville proposes to use the technical phrase "finite/infinite contrast" for the intended (direct or indirect) referent of religious symbols:

> The logic of the borderline contingency conditions, registered in at least many of the symbols of them, is that they mark the boundary between the finite and the infinite. That is, by focusing on some finite thing as a boundary condition orienting the experiential world. . . . They suppose a contrast with what would be the case without the boundary condition. . . . Precisely in being symbolized as contingent, as the focal points of contingency, as those things on which all other worldly orientation hangs, the boundary conditions are imaged as finite/infinite contrasts. (1996: 58)

Neville describes religion as the "enterprise that shepherds the symbols of the boundary conditions" of cultures (55), a description that plausibly fits Çatalhöyük as well, as we will see.

The problem (or solution, depending on how you look at it) is that – as Neville puts it in chap. 2, "Symbols Break on the Infinite." *Religious* symbols are meant to point (indexically) to the infinite or unconditioned. When taken for this purpose, symbols "break" because the infinite (the unconditioned or ultimately conditioning condition) cannot be indicated under the same conditions as finite realities; otherwise, it would not truly be infinite. Insofar as they refer at all, religious symbols always refer indirectly, not only because they have networked polysemous layers and diverse practical uses, but most important because any such reference is – and can only be – through finite elements of the world.

Religious symbols or objects are finite things, but what makes them "religious" is that they also have "some world-constructing importance, either in a cosmological sense or a sense having to do with the ground, meaning and goal of human life" (1996: 70). This importance means that the object of reference is not simply the finite thing (bull's horn, bird image, plastered skull) as such but "the finite thing in contrast with the infinite, with its supra-finite context, with the situation that would obtain if the finite thing did not exist or have its world-constructing importance. In short the contrast has to do with the importance of the finite thing for the contingent existence of the world, in some respect, or the world of human meaningfulness." The first main point appropriated from Neville's theory, then, is that religious symbols have to do with the attempt to engage the infinite in some sense.

The second insight from Neville is his emphasis on taking symbols in context (chap. 4). Following Peirce, Neville insists on the pragmatic effect and engagement of the interpreter's intentional taking of a symbol as constitutive for the meaning and reference of the symbol. He stresses that the way in which (or extent to which) broken symbols engage a finite/infinite contrast truly must be understood in light of the *intentional* context of the interpreter. The possible interpretations within an extended semiotic code are *extensional* interpretations. However, the extension within the semiotic system is not itself interpretation. For Neville the primary meaning of an interpretant is "an *intentional* act of actually interpreting something for which the semiotic code contains possible forms" (115).

Interpreting a symbol always takes place in a context, an existential location, and there is always purpose (intention) behind such interpretation; this must be taken into account in understanding any symbol's effectiveness. Neville argues that the interpretation of religious symbols "consists in the impact of the symbol's referent, usually some one or several finite/infinite contrasts, on the experience of the interpreter for interpreting community, as mediated by the symbol; this impact is the symbol's content meaning integrated into practice" (119). However, the way in which (or purposes for which) an interpreter "takes" a religious symbol to refer in a certain respect to a religious object impacts the difference that putative referent makes in the experience of the interpreter.

Neville's treatment of the kinds of contexts in which religious symbols can be taken is shaped by his own context in a Western university, and so he begins with the context of academic theology itself. For Neville, academic theology (in distinction to religious studies) aims to express the truth about divine matters by presenting a coherent set of symbols, which are always in need of correction (given human finitude). In such a context, one should acknowledge that all symbolic engagement that is intended to refer to "divine matters" must be taken as hypothetical and provisional. It would take us too far afield to discuss the nuances of his theological method, his theory of truth and his interest in interreligious dialogue, but this is not necessary for our purpose in this essay. The people of Çatalhöyük (so far as we can tell) did not engage in academic theology any more than they did in academic archaeology (although they clearly engaged "divine matters" in a general sense and were interested in digging up the past).

We can limit ourselves here to Neville's observations about four other kinds of (overlapping) contexts in which religious symbols are taken, and explore the extent to which these observations might also shed light on our analysis of the transformations of Çatalhöyük. The first is what he calls *cultic* life. Among the things that religious symbols do is organize the life of a community, shaping the norms and actions of the community in response to the sacred, divine matters or most generally "finite/infinite" contrasts. In such contexts, argues Neville, religious symbols typically have double interpretants. An interpretant is "the meaning of a sign that is assigned to a referent in an act of interpretation" (113). In cultic contexts, a religious symbol is "taken" both representationally and practically. That is, the meaning of the symbol is related both to the finite/infinite contrast (the religious object) and to the practical life of the community. This is perhaps most obvious in the case of rituals, which are both linked to the divine (or world-constructing boundary) and shape social and moral codes.

The second context is what Neville calls *ordinary* life. He notes that he is using this term in the way developed by Charles Taylor, which demonstrates that Neville's own context is shaped by social concerns after the rise of secularism. Ordinary life means "the realms of production (work) and reproduction (domestic life generally) as the locus of principal religious and moral significance in modern culture" (148). In most premodern societies (including Çatalhöyük), a strong distinction between cultic and ordinary life would not hold in the same way. Nevertheless, as a sphere of human life, the concept might still be applied if appropriately qualified. The religious symbols at Çatalhöyük were clearly brought into (entangle with) work and domestic life, which were not so separated (or gender biased) as in Western cultures. For the sake of analysis, however, we might speak of "ordinary" life at Çatalhöyük as that sphere in which the religious symbols were shaping concrete behaviors that supported the livelihood of the community.

Neville also refers to *extraordinary* life as a phenomenon in modern societies. Here he points to persons who push the envelope of ordinary life, who seek to test the boundaries and accomplish something new or rare. He gives examples of great artists and poets, musicians and explorers or outstanding religious leaders. This third context in the late modern world may not be explicitly shaped by religious symbols, but Neville suggests that for some at least their pursuit has a performative religious reference (in the sense that he defines "religious"). In other words, such persons "offer their lives as ways to be rightly related to the ultimate boundaries of things" (149). Like the spheres of cultic and ordinary life, so with the context of extraordinary life the way of engaging "religious" symbols involves double interpretants; the symbols are "taken" (more or less explicitly) both representationally and practically – linked both to the boundary-constituting (world-making) object and to the practical shaping of the person in social relations.

The final context that is relevant for our purposes is what Neville calls *devotional* life. In this context, religious symbolic engagement involves not two interpretants (modes of taking), but two referents. In other words, argues Neville, the taking of religious symbols in the context of a person's attention to his or her own transformation in relation to ultimate boundary conditions has "dual reference, primarily to finite/infinite contrasts and secondarily to the state and stage of the specific devotee" (152). The devotee's taking of symbols intentionally in order to transform (or appropriately shape) his or her relation to ultimate reality involves a reference both directly to "the divine" and indirectly to the person him- or herself as symbolically engaged with the divine. Understanding what religious symbols do in this kind of intentional context requires awareness of the developmental stage and psychological condition of the individual who attempts to engage ultimate reality.

All symbols break on the infinite, but "broken symbols are a dime a dozen if they are dead," that is, if they are not live options to persons seeking to engage "the divine." The taking of broken symbols in devotional contexts may be more intense than in other contexts. The devotional use of symbols "stretches symbols beyond safe theological representationalism and responsible practical application to have a power of transforming the soul. The transformations at stake are radical, such as dissolving the soul completely, filling it with the infinite, transporting it across the finite/infinite boundary" (153). Often religious symbols must be bizarre or even terrifying to "work" in such contexts. Neville insists that the criteria for judging whether the symbols "work" devotionally will be case specific and quite different from how they work in other contexts. Such criteria must be pragmatic; either a religious symbol existentially engages a finite/infinite contrast in a way that transforms the person or it does not.

This approach to religious symbols obviously cannot be transferred directly to the data at Çatalhöyük, not only because it is a premodern society for which categories like "cultic," "ordinary" and "extraordinary" would be anachronistic, but also because we cannot know much if anything about the psychological stages of particular devotees or even which symbols they "took" religiously. Nevertheless, Neville's pragmatic theory of the contextual taking of religious symbols for engaging finite/infinite contrasts may provide a starting point for a theological response to the research questions about the role of spiritual life in the transformations of this ancient "town."

Toward an interdisciplinary theory of spiritual entanglement

What I now want to attempt is what Peirce himself would call an "abductive" move: reconceptualizing Hodder's analysis of the phenomenon of social transformation as material entanglement in light of Neville's insights on the engagement of religious symbols in order to develop a complementary model of spiritual entanglement. The dynamics of "spiritual entanglement" have to do with the way in which persons take religious symbols (more or less) intentionally as they engage world-constructing boundaries (or finite/infinite contrasts) in various contexts, such as the overlapping spheres of public, cultic, ordinary, extraordinary and devotional life. This conceptual framework will need to be tested in other concrete cases to prove (or disprove) its illuminative power, but my goal here is simply to offer some initial indications of its potential application for Çatalhöyük.

As we have seen, the appropriation of Peircean categories in both theology and archaeology has helped to overcome the deleterious effects of dualisms such as matter versus spirit. For Neville, the human engagement with the sense of being-confronted by ultimate limitations that are world-constructing is symbolically meditated, and symbols are not "in the mind" (as opposed to the real, material world) but pragmatically and semiotically functioning throughout reality. For Hodder, all sociality is entangled within – and I would say emergent from while mutually causally implicated in – materiality. Elsewhere (Shults & Sandage, 2006) I have outlined a way of speaking about spirituality that incorporates a holistic anthropology and the insights of emergent complexity science. This approach is consistent with many of the theoretical models of materiality and symbolism in contemporary archaeology (cf. Gamble 2004; Malafouris 2004; Shults 2007).

Human engagements with questions of ultimate limitation are embedded within and emerge out of the dynamics that characterize the spheres of material and social entanglement. "Spiritual" entanglement describes a particular emergent feature of human relationality that supervenes upon material entanglement and is causally efficacious in relation to this and other spheres. It has to do with the desire and fear that characterize attention to the ultimate boundary conditions of the lived material world as it appears to shape the binding and being-bound of human sociality. This tending to one's experience of being-conditioned and (more or less) intense longing for transformed and transforming intentionality in relation to ultimate reality are entangled within but not reducible to the tensions that characterize the material, social and other spheres of human life.

It is crucial to keep in mind that the use of the idea of *spiritual* entanglement as developed in what follows is not meant to be in competition with the theory of *material* entanglement, but to be a different perspective on a different dimension or sphere of human life. This "spiritual" sphere, in my view, is as (metaphysically) entangled in the "material" as any other sphere. We are not talking about a separate substance or compartment of human life that is untouched by or released from the material. Human "spirituality" is entangled within "materiality" but not reducible to it, any more than sociality is "nothing more" than the aggregation of material things. However, each distinctive sphere must be explicated in a way that respects the integrity and emergent complexity of relations integral to that sphere, and not be reduced to the explanatory scope of another sphere.

One of the most significant tensions that shape the existential field of *sociality* is the dialectic of fear and love. Like all living organisms, humans tend to avoid that which seems to threaten destruction and pursue that which seems to promise pleasure. Social interaction is structured by both our longing for and dread of being bound to one another. Our social experience of being-limited is ambiguous. We fear being suffocated or absorbed by needy others, but we also fear being isolated or abandoned by significant others whom we hope will fulfill our needs. We desire independence from the painfully overwhelming demands of others, but our overwhelming desire for pleasurable intimacy demands our dependence on others. And so sociality is characterized by pushing away and pulling close, an interactive play of repulsive and seductive forces in which we are entangled.

In addition to the finite tensive dynamics of sociality, scholars of religion (and especially theologians) are also interested in the role of an agent's understanding and engagement of ultimate reality (or ultimate value, meaning) in his or her social and material entanglement. A *theological* interpretation of limitation (per se) requires us to attend also to the experience of being-limited itself, and especially to the longing among human persons for the transformation of and within their contexts vis-à-vis questions of ultimate concern. Such longing is fully entangled within the materiality of human life in all its sociality, but in the symbolic engagement with *infinity* we are dealing not with how persons engage in the finite space-time of sociality but with the question of the conditions for agency "at the limits" of human engagement.

Discourse on infinity does not escape the conditions of sociality (or materiality). It is embedded within a complex semiotic coding process, always and already signaling and being signaled in acts of signification. However, the discipline of theology (as the term is being used here) focuses on the significance of limitation itself, that is, on the existential negotiation of the ultimately significant limit of human existence. Religious phenomena emerge within the complex, dynamic field of human sociality, which itself is constituted by tensive personal relations always and already materially entangled. However, the phenomenon of religious engagement with(in) the world is distinguished by the way in which persons are (more or less) explicitly attentive to their openness to and longing for a right relation to that which ultimately conditions any and all valuation whatsoever.

As humans attend to their material entanglement, they attempt to control (so far as possible) the various finite forces that might threaten them and finite resources that might nourish them. As humans respond to their spiritual entanglement, they also try to control forces and resources, those that feel utterly out of their control. Rituals and other "religious" practices are often oriented toward controlling or appropriately binding the self or community to ultimate powers or the forces that constitute and control ultimate boundary conditions. Materiality, sociality and infinity all have to do with limits, with our struggle within and against our being-limited by and for others, a struggle saturated by both fear and love. Theological reflection on these overlapping spheres focuses on the way in which human interpretations of a sense of the infinite, the sacred or the ultimate world-constructing reality shape their understanding and practice of spirituality.

If we think of "religion" as having to do with the way in which humans bind themselves to that which they imagine ultimately conditions and orients their finite desires and fears then, *ex hypothesi*, all humans are "religious" in this sense. On this definition, the inhabitants of Çatalhöyük nine millennia ago were also religious, reflecting and acting and feeling within the bounds and bonds of life together while (implicitly or explicitly) thematizing, imagining ultimate boundaries. Insofar as the attempt to illuminate and explicate the dynamics and value of particular contextual engagements with ultimate boundary conditions is one of the goals of academic theology, the following reflections on Çatalhöyük are meant to be initial "theological" responses to the research questions that guided our three-year interdisciplinary project.

QUESTION 1: HOW CAN ARCHAEOLOGISTS RECOGNIZE THE SPIRITUAL, RELIGIOUS AND TRANSCENDENT IN EARLY TIME PERIODS?

While it is notoriously difficult to define religion or even to list universal characteristics for identifying it, most people agree that they "know it when they see it." This was true as well for the working archaeologists with whom I interacted at Çatalhöyük. How might the concept of spiritual entanglement help archaeologists feel more confident about recognizing the religious sphere in early time periods? If spirituality has to do with engaging the limits of highest *significance* to human life, then material artifacts that signal high engagements with world-constructing boundaries may plausibly be identified as examples of spiritual entanglement. In other words, accentuated practices that appear to manifest the inhabitants' attempts to mediate, control or otherwise engage what they took to be the ultimate boundaries that conditioned their social and material life can plausibly be taken as potential indicators of a "religious" dimension within early cultures.

3.1. Painting of vultures and headless corpses from Çatalhöyük. *Source*: J. Mellaart and Çatalhöyük Research Project.

Combining the insights of Hodder and Neville, we can say that the religious sphere (or dimension) of human life has to do with the way in which persons (in community) attempt to make sense of their experience of the ultimate boundedness, of the world-making limits that constitute the conditions for social (and material) entanglement. Using this definition, we can suggest that archaeologists (or theologians) can warrant their claims that a particular artifact or pattern at Çatalhöyük (or other early sites) signifies the impact of human "religious" engagement with and in the world by showing how it indicates an imaginative way of dealing with ultimate world-making conditions that shape the boundaries and the bonds of everyday life.

For example, the dialectic of defleshing and refleshing that is found at Çatalhöyük (see Hodder and Meskell, Chapter 2) may be indicative of an attempt to deal with (and to some extent control) what they perceived to be an ultimate world-making boundary condition, namely, between the fleshiness of the living and the forces that deflesh (vultures, wild animals). The artistic representations of vultures taking heads and flesh (Figure 3.1) can be plausibly related to the wider narrative of hunting, baiting, feasting and prowess, and to the practice of the (postmortem) dis-articulation and burying of skulls. The refleshing of these skulls suggests some attempt to engage this boundary, perhaps to protect or energize or placate the ancestors or the forces that defleshed them. The almost continual replastering of the walls may also have had to do with attending to such boundaries. The burial and retrieval of plastered (and other) objects may plausibly be taken as evidence of the imaginative attempt to engage this world-constructing experience of the threat of defleshing and the hope for refleshing, and therefore of "religion" or "spiritual" entanglement in the senses developed earlier.

QUESTION 2: ARE CHANGES IN SPIRITUAL LIFE AND RELIGIOUS RITUAL A NECESSARY PRELUDE TO THE SOCIAL AND ECONOMIC CHANGES THAT LEAD TO "CIVILIZATION"?

This question gets at the issue of causality. Did "religion" contribute to the emergence of changes such as domestication and sedentism? Despite disagreements about how to define "religion," there was virtual unanimity among the team that this question should be given a positive answer. However, causality is a tricky concept for all disciplines. Some archaeologists, like Cauvin and Renfrew, have emphasized the causal force of the symbolic, including the "religious," on these transformations. Hodder's theory of material entanglement does not deny this but warns against a unilateral understanding of the causal direction of the shift toward civilization. As we have seen, he prefers to imagine a mutual relation between the material and the symbolic that has a spiraling effect; more material binding leads to more social binding and vice versa.

We can also think of *spiritual* entanglement as an integral part of this spiraling, an intensification of the human fear of and fascination with boundaries and the experience of being-bound. Insofar as the increased attention to that which conditions or shapes the limits of human life is entangled within the emergence of material, social and economic structures, perhaps we could say that changes like sedentism and domestication emerged alongside changes in human ways of tending to finite/infinite contrasts. In Çatalhöyük these "civilizing" transformations emerged through the intensification and complexification of the entanglements of the material and the spiritual spheres. It is not that one is a "prelude" to the other, but that they worked together (symphonically) as "interludes" of social change.

As these spheres became increasingly entangled, their "hold" or binding force was intensified as new modes of dealing with boundaries (of all kinds) became more complex. One of the benefits of this pragmatic approach is that it helps us explain what religion *does* – what practical effects spiritual entanglement has on the rest of life. If we accept Neville's idea that religion is the "cultural enterprise of shepherding the symbols of the boundary conditions for experiential worldliness," then we can ask how this shepherding may have worked at Çatalhöyük over time as its inhabitants struggled to gather and guide their materially entangled symbolic engagements with(in) the conditions of ever intensifying economic and social structures.

This spiraling mutuality can be illustrated, on the one hand, by the way in which the material engagement with bulls early in the Çatalhöyük sequence shaped the "spirituality" of that period, whereas bull imagery declined in the art and architecture as bulls disappeared from the landscape. Earlier sites like Göbekli utilized a rather different animal imagery. On the other hand, the capacity for increasing temporal representation and the creation of time-depth, which was connected to the memory of buried (and occasionally unearthed) ancestors, altered the way in which materials were procured, valued and stored. This is perhaps most evident in the roles that obsidian played in material production and spiritual mediation, roles that should be understood to be robustly pragmatic in both cases.

QUESTION 3: DO HUMAN FORMS TAKE ON A CENTRAL ROLE IN THE SPIRIT WORLD IN THE EARLY HOLOCENE, AND, IF SO, DOES THIS CENTRALITY LEAD TO NEW CONCEPTIONS OF HUMAN AGENCY THAT THEMSELVES PROVIDE THE POSSIBILITY FOR THE DOMESTICATION OF PLANTS AND ANIMALS?

The first part of this question requires archaeological analysis, and the answer appears to be a relatively confident yes. The second part lends itself more readily to theological reflection. As in response to Question 2, I would prefer using the terminology of spiraling intensification rather than saying that the centrality of human forms "leads to" new concepts of human agency. As humans became increasingly entangled materially and socially, awareness of intentionality became more intense. Most likely the increase in human forms in art and the growing capacity for intentionally controlling flocks and crops intensified together. As contemporary social science has shown, human agency is dialectical. That is, becoming aware of one's self as agent is mediated through one's entangled relations with those who are not-self. Attention to identity and attention to otherness emerge together, as does the complexity of the agent's capacity to tend to the other and the self.

The art at Çatalhöyük offers itself as a case study for thinking about the contexts that Neville identifies as cultic, ordinary, extraordinary and devotional life. Of course, we cannot apply them directly to early human cultures, but they may serve a heuristic purpose. It seems plausible to suggest that aesthetic engagement at Çatalhöyük was entangled within all these contexts. Although specialists may have produced the art on the walls (extraordinary life), the figurines appear to have been constructed and handled by almost everyone, being molded within and in a sense molding ordinary life. If the inhabitants were biologically (and psychologically) modern humans, then we can imagine some of them "taking" symbols (figurines, paintings, obsidian) in devotional contexts, engaging ultimate limitations in fear and trembling, as well as with desire and fascination. Most likely such symbols were also intimately linked to (perhaps modeled after) rituals that were "taken" in cultic contexts as well. Understanding what religious symbols *did* at Çatalhöyük will require imaginatively indwelling the different "contexts" within which they might have been "taken" by its inhabitants to engage their world-constructing boundaries.

The relation between agency, spirituality and domestication can be illuminated by focusing on the element of control, which I suggested earlier is a natural element of the human engagement with boundaries and the experience of boundedness. We can imagine a spiraling effect between anxiety about the encounter with forces apparently outside human control and increased success in controlling some of those forces. Domesticating plants and animals would have empowered and strengthened the human sense of agency, but it also would have intensified the awareness of other, more powerful forces and the desire to mediate such boundaries. We can also see the issue of control in the structure of the houses. On the one hand, they are all huddled together and yet, on the other hand, each has its own walls. Attempts to balance and control collectivity and individuality are expressed in the architecture itself. Moreover, it is reasonable to interpret activities such as burying skulls or obsidian under posts as evidence of agency – the intention to control, both materially (holding up collapsing walls) and spiritually (creating or reinforcing history houses).

QUESTION 4: DO VIOLENCE AND DEATH ACT AS THE FOCI OF TRANSCENDENT RELIGIOUS EXPERIENCE DURING THE TRANSITIONS OF THE EARLY HOLOCENE IN THE NEAR EAST, AND ARE SUCH THEMES CENTRAL TO THE CREATION OF SOCIAL LIFE IN THE FIRST LARGE AGGLOMERATIONS OF PEOPLE?

Nothing forces us to face our ultimate limits (finitude) more than death, and nothing draws our attention to the threat of death more than violence. I agree with the team's general consensus that the house society structure, with its differentiations and the dominance of history houses, can best be explained by appealing to the performance of rituals dealing with violence and death rather than to ordinary material production, and that this suggests a positive answer to the first part of the question. I believe that the definition of religion developed earlier in this essay and the concept of spiritual entanglement can be of service in reflecting on the second part of the question. If increased "spiritual" attention to ultimate boundaries, world-constructing limits and the human relation to them is entangled within (albeit emergent from) "material" and social life, then it makes sense that the one sphere would shape the other, as seems to have been the case in the Çatalhöyük practice of burying (hiding and sometimes revealing) the dead.

Death is the most existentially significant limit of human life, and an intensification of tending to this ultimate boundary would understandably contribute to the creation of new modes of social binding and being bound. Here too we might spell this out in terms of the engagement with finite/infinite contrasts in various contexts. The first large agglomerations of people appear to have been characterized by an intensification of the desire to control or engage the ultimate boundary that limits (or transcends) ordinary life.

If this "spiritual" sphere is entangled (or causally enmeshed) within the other spheres (including and especially materiality) that shape human sociality, then it follows that changes in "religious experiences" would creatively shape the emergence of social life in all of its material, economic and aesthetic dimensions. Death represents the most intense encounter with limitation, and we can plausibly conjecture that the inhabitants of Çatalhöyük "took" symbols that attempted to engage this existential

boundary in ways that were intended to organize the cultus, guide ordinary life, encourage extraordinary expressions and transform devotees at
various stages of development.

Conclusion

My argument has been that we can use shared resources from the pragmatic turn in theology and archaeology to develop ways of conceptualizing spiritual entanglement that are complementary to Hodder's theory
of material entanglement. This opens up a way of discussing the same
differentiated phenomena (embodied human experiences of boundaries
that shape sociality) from a new perspective: the human encounter with
infinity (the boundary conditions for being-limited). I have suggested
that we can refer to the latter dynamics as "spiritual" but insisted that
this is not another substance or separate compartment of human life, but
rather (like the social sphere) an emergently complex phenomenon that
intensifies over time. It is not "immaterial" but an energetic spatiotemporal tending to our confrontation with ultimate boundaries of meaning,
value and reality.

As I hinted at the beginning of the essay, engaging Çatalhöyük is not
only a scientific exercise; it may also help us tend to our own existential
anxiety about and longing to control our limitations. In her book *Object
Worlds in Ancient Egypt*, Lynn Meskell explores a similar entanglement
between things, subjects, objects and symbols in Egyptian artifacts. She
points not only to the object worlds evident in the materiality of Egypt,
but also to the way in which contemporary consumers are fascinated with
and desire connection to such objects. Why are we so interested in these
past objects? "It is the spiritual resonance, esoteric and secret knowledge,
notions of permanence and timelessness, aesthetics and bodily beauty,
scientific achievement, and finally the possibility of life eternal, that are
all tacitly embraced in both real and reproduced materials, and in the act
of possessing them" (2004: 219).

The material object worlds of Çatalhöyük have not (yet) become (as)
consumerized, but our fascination with this part of our human past is
certainly increasing. The art and other artifacts from this ancient town
display an increasing capacity among the inhabitants over time to mold
and form their social and material lives. Their way of engaging religious
symbols was transformative and transforming. Just as they were probably

not always aware of this slow movement of the mass (Hodder), in the same way most of them probably did not explicitly thematize the slow shifts in their spiritual lives as they dealt with death, violence and other constant reminders of their finite limits. However, we can imagine that some mystics, shamans, prophets or artists among them became intensely aware of the sense of ultimate boundaries and the importance of tending to them.

Today we are faced with the same kinds of questions, concerns and practical challenges, even if they are in some ways more complex. How can we intentionally shape our social (and material) lives in ways that respect and care for that dimension of our lives that makes us *Homo sapiens* – the longing for wisdom (*sapientia*) – as we tend to one another in relation to questions of ultimate value?

REFERENCES

Arweck, E., and W. Keenan, eds. 2006. *Materializing Religion: Expression, Performance and Ritual*. Aldershot: Ashgate.

Cauvin, Jacques. 2000. *The Birth of the Gods and the Origins of Agriculture*. Cambridge: Cambridge University Press.

Clayton, Philip. 2004. *Mind and Emergence*. Oxford: Oxford University Press.

Gamble, Clive. 2004. Materiality and symbolic force: A Paleolithic view of sedentism. In *Rethinking Materiality: The Engagement of Mind with the Material World*, eds. E. DeMarrais, C. Gosden and C. Renfrew. Cambridge: McDonald Institute for Archaeological Research Monographs, 85–93.

Gregersen, N. H., ed. 2003. *From Complexity to Life: On the Emergence of Life and Meaning*. Oxford: Oxford University Press.

Hodder, Ian. 1990. *The Domestication of Europe*. Oxford: Blackwell.

Hodder, Ian. 1999. *The Archaeological Process: An Introduction*. Oxford: Blackwell.

Hodder, Ian. 2006. *Çatalhöyük: The Leopard's Tale*. London: Thames & Hudson.

Juarrero, A. 2002. *Dynamics in Action: Intentional Behavior as a Complex System*. Cambridge, Mass.: Massachusetts Institute of Technology.

Malafouris, Lambros. 2004. The cognitive basis of material engagement: Where brain, body and culture conflate. In *Rethinking Materiality: The Engagement of Mind with the Material World*, eds. E. DeMarrais, C. Gosden and C. Renfrew. Cambridge: McDonald Institute for Archaeological Research Monographs, 53–61.

Meskell, Lynn. 2004. *Object Worlds in Ancient Egypt*. Oxford: Berg.

Murphy, N., and W. Stoeger, eds. 2007. *Evolution and Emergence: Systems, Organisms, Persons*. Oxford: Oxford University Press.

Neville, Robert C. 1992. *The Highroad Around Modernism*. Albany, N.Y.: SUNY Press.

Neville, Robert C. 1996. *The Truth of Broken Symbols*. Albany, N.Y.: SUNY Press.

Neville, Robert C. 2002. *Religion in Late Modernity*. Albany, N.Y.: SUNY Press.

Neville, Robert C. 2006. *The Scope and Truth of Theology*. New York: Continuum.

Peirce, C. S. 1998. *The Essential Peirce*, vol. 2 (Peirce Edition Project). Indianapolis: Indiana University Press.

Preucel, Robert W. 2006. *Archeological Semiotics*. Oxford: Blackwell.

Renfrew, Colin. 2001. Symbol before concept: Material engagement and the early development of society. In *Archaeological Theory Today*, ed. I. Hodder. Cambridge: Polity Press, 122–86.

Renfrew, Colin. 2004. Toward a theory of material engagement. In *Rethinking Materiality: The Engagement of Mind with the Material World*, eds. E. DeMarrais, C. Gosden and C. Renfrew. Cambridge: McDonald Institute for Archaeological Research Monographs, 23–31.

Shults, F. LeRon. 2007. Spirituality and figuration. In *Image and Imagination: A Global Prehistory of Figurative Representation*, eds. C. Renfrew and I. Morley. Cambridge: McDonald Institute for Archaeological Research Monographs, 337–40.

Shults, F. LeRon. In press. Religious symbols at the limits of human engagement. *Theology and Science*.

Shults, F. LeRon, and Steven J. Sandage. 2006. *Transforming Spirituality*. Grand Rapids, Mich.: Eerdmans.

4

Coding the nonvisible: Epistemic limitations and understanding symbolic behavior at Çatalhöyük

J. Wentzel van Huyssteen

I

For scientists deeply embedded in archaeological and anthropological work, it might seem unusual, if not rather strange, that someone with a theological or religious perspective might be interested in the Middle Eastern Neolithic. However, in my recent work on possible interdisciplinary connections between theology and palaeoanthopology/archaeology, I argued that an integrative praxis for 'theology and the sciences' can be found in a dialogue that proceeds from the highly contextual to the transversal as we pick up threads from different disciplinary discourses and weave them into an emerging pattern that transcends strict disciplinary boundaries (van Huyssteen 2006). I have also argued that the standard 'theology and science' dialogue has woefully neglected the importance of palaeoanthropology and archaeology for understanding human origins and human nature in general. And although I will not repeat my argument here, I will presuppose that philosophically there are in fact remarkable methodological links between a postfoundationalist approach to theology and some of the important voices in contemporary palaeoanthropology/archaeology today (van Huyssteen 2006). For this reason these sciences, specifically palaeoanthropology and archaeology, by focusing on human origins and modern human behavior, may turn out to intersect in exciting ways with theological concerns and thus help to redirect theological understandings of what it means to return to the prehistoric past and try to come to grips with the very fact of our humanness.

Against this background I believe that in any attempt to understand the Middle Eastern Neolithic, the Upper Palaeolithic in western Europe will provide at least an initial, valuable background for understanding symbolic behavior in the Middle Eastern Neolithic and, quite specifically, the culture of Çatalhöyük. Here too, as in the dark caves of western France, we have to wonder if it makes any sense to ask about the 'meaning' of prehistoric imagery or, even more challenging, what might have made the artifacts, wall paintings, sculpture, bucrania and house burials meaningful for the people of Çatalhöyük. In Catalhöyük's array of paintings, sculptures and burials within which bulls, predatory birds and leopards are so prominent, the evidence suggests that the economic changes that led from hunting and gathering to farming were intimately related to religious ideologies. Steven Mithen has correctly concluded that it may be nearly impossible to reconstruct these prehistoric religious ideologies in any meaningful sense (Mithen 2004). Mithen has also argued, however, that an adequate theory of prehistoric religion or modes of religiosity (cf. Whitehouse 2004) can in fact enrich our interpretations of specific aspects of the archaeological record, make some interpretations more plausible than others and help us identity previously unrecognized causal links between religious practices and political structures. Therefore, although it is unlikely that archaeological evidence can provide a formal test for anthropological theories of religion, it can provide longer-term perspectives on how religiosity develops in relation to economy and society (Mithen 2004: 19). It is in this sense that I too want to argue that the embeddedness of religious themes present at Çatalhöyük must be located within the broader context of prehistoric religion.

An interesting part of our self-perception and the way we tend to look at the evolution of modern humans, of course, is that it is often the less material aspects of the history of our species that fascinate us most. We seem to grasp at an intuitive level that language, imagination, self-awareness, consciousness and mythology are probably the elements that really make us human (Lewin 1993: 4). Yet exactly these elements that most suggest humanness are often the least visible in the prehistoric record. For this reason palaeoanthropologists have correctly focused on more indirect, but equally plausible material pointers to the presence of the symbolic human mind in early human history (van Huyssteen 2006: 167).

Today a growing dissatisfaction with past approaches to prehistoric imagery could indeed be seen as a direct result of an insufficient attention to concrete times and places when the images were actually produced and used. Olga Soffer and Margaret Conkey's views embody a strong reaction against unwarranted uniformitarian assumptions and broad ahistoric, abstract and often decontexualized frames of reference (1997). Any abstract assumption, then, that a transhistoric level of the meaning of this prehistoric 'art' may exist and that this may be 'true for all humans at all times and at all places' does seem to be troublesome and highly acontextual in its own right. Epistemically we have to recognize and accept that the ground on which we stand when trying to represent the viewpoints of others in the distant, prehistoric past is not firm, but is rather tectonic and shifting (Soffer and Conkey 1997: 3). The archeological record, therefore, indicates that the prehistoric past reveals a complex mosaic rather than a linear trajectory. Moreover, there are important temporal and even spatial discontinuities in the production of images in different regions in early human history – for example, the virtual disappearance of image making in western Europe with the advent of the Holocene versus its proliferation in the Levant at the same time. Therefore, a 'catholic', or comprehensive, view that takes location and context absolutely seriously is indeed crucial in reorienting the entire field of inquiry (Soffer and Conkey 1997: 3). For the theologian entering into an interdisciplinary dialogue with archaeology/palaeoanthropology, this will be crucial. Our view of the fascinating but enigmatic Neolithic period at Çatalhöyük is going to be necessarily fragmentary and pluralist, and may leave us with a mosaic of interpretative possibilities.

Even though the material works of 'art', as we will see, strongly suggest a spiritual mind-set, they will always be difficult to interpret. Given the rich material so typical of Çatalhöyük, however, they do suggest questions, such as what were the beliefs of these Neolithic peoples, what were their customs, what were their legends and how were their social structures organized? It is difficult to escape the implication that the Neolithic wall paintings, artifacts and burial practices suggest some or other definite narrative frame of mind that might have led directly to their construction. Although we may never know fully the meaning of these fascinating expressions of the human mind, and although we have to be careful not to project our own categories and interpretations onto these artifacts, there might be good reasons for arguing that these paintings and artifacts could have functioned as links between the mythological natural and the supernatural worlds. But how would we know? Which scientists are arguing this position, and how plausible is their argument for seeing the artwork as symbolic, possibly even as religious artifacts? I will argue that, if indeed there are plausible arguments for the symbolic, or even just tentative religious meaning of some of these cultural products, this symbolic heritage of the Neolithic population of Çatalhöyük may reveal something about the emergence of the earliest forms of religiosity, and thus support the naturalness and rationality of religious faith. Moreover, precisely because every human society, at one stage or another, possessed religion in some form, complete with origin myths that purportedly explain the relationship of humans to the world around them, religion cannot be discounted from any discussion of typically human behaviors (Tattersall 1998: 201; 2003).

In a very specific sense, then, religious belief is one of the earliest special propensities or dispositions that we are able to detect in the archaeological record of modern humans. There is indeed a naturalness to religious imagination that challenges any view that religion or religious imagination is esoteric or an isolated faculty of the human mind that developed later. Even if we are not certain what exactly the artistic productions of the people of Çatalhöyük represented to the people who made them, it is nonetheless clear that this early 'art' reflected a view held by these people of their place in the world and a body of mythology that explained that place. One of the major functions of religious belief has indeed always been to provide explanations for the deep desire to deny the finality of death and the curious reluctance of our species to accept the inevitable limitations of human experience. This is exactly why it might be possible for us to recognize that the artistic artifacts and burials of Çatalhöyük culture go beyond mere representation and as such could embody a broadly religious symbolism. In this sense Ian Hodder has argued that an elaborate symbolic world might indeed be reconstructed for Çatalhöyük (2006: 13).

In fact, what Hodder has argued about the famous representations of the leopard at Çatalhöyük may very well be extended to all art forms at this famous site: while we may never be able to detail precisely what beliefs and myths surrounded the leopard at Çatalhöyük, we can go some way down the road in making sense of a set of values, taboos or restrictions (Hodder 2006: 12). In spite of the epistemic limitations imposed on us by the mysterious, ambiguous material, then, it should be possible in some tentative way to reveal and reconstruct the elaborate symbolic world from so long ago. Çatalhöyük certainly reveals a series of slow but important changes that began in the Upper Palaeolithic and continued through later periods, including the Neolithic.

Particularly interesting is Hodder's reference to David Lewis-Williams's valuable, if controversial work on the San and on early shaman-istic practices. The latter facilitates an interpretation of the Neolithic world and the art at Çatalhöyük in terms of a three-tiered cosmos whereby installations on the walls of houses can be understood in the context of the movement of animal spirits from the spiritual world through the house walls into the house (Hodder 2006). In this prehistoric spiritual realm, movements between the spiritual world and daily life could be facilitated by, and, for example, assist in, the flow of power from bulls in the form of bucrania to people in their daily lives (Hodder 2006: 29). Hodder does carefully nuance this by saying that Çatalhöyük appears dimly through these comparisons, and although parallels can be drawn, there will always be differences (2006: 29).

In the symbolic world of Çatalhöyük, the status of individuals and families may have been linked to their ability to reveal what was hidden behind the walls as represented in the art (Hodder 2006: 170). Whether we want to call them 'shamans' or not, there must have been those who could intercede with the spirit world, the animal world, the world of the dead and the ancestors through altered states of consciousness. These were the individuals who would have revealed what was hidden by directing the performances and rituals of painting and uncovering, of digging up skulls and reusing them through this process of postmortem manipulation. Skulls and sculptures were therefore dug up and recircu-lated, and skulls were thus kept over time. It was this material circulation that created the fabric of the house-centered group and incorporated the revelatory component in the process (Hodder 2006: 170).

The connection with the spiritual dimension was thus hidden as well as revealed in places where the ancestors of animal spirits were – that is, beneath the floors and behind the walls. For this reason Hodder can state that the power of revelation occurred largely on a local, domestic scale – that is, in each house (2006: 170). The great challenge, of course, is to ask what exactly was hidden and revealed at Çatalhöyük. But what we do know is that the major symbolic window onto this was ritual symbols like bucrania, human and animal skulls and even obsidian. Hodder has dis-cussed the evidence for a focus on the hiding and revealing of significant symbols, and has added to that the important role of obsidian hoards that were placed beneath floors and periodically retrieved (2006: 171). In his own extensive work on the role of obsidian at Çatalhöyük, Tristan Carter has provided an analysis of the temporal and spatial contexts within which one can locate the Çatalhöyük hoards and has also focused on the conceptual underpinnings of the very act of the burial and retrieval of obsidian. Within this context Carter has distinguished between obsidian hoards and obsidian grave goods, exploring the idea that there is a conceptual or ritual/symbolic link between the burial and retrieval of obsidian and the burial and exhumation of people (Carter 2007). In Chapter 5, Whitehouse and Hodder offer the interesting perspective that the burial and retrieval, hiding and revealing of obsidian were most typical of the lower levels of the Çatalhöyük site. In the upper levels these hoards cease and obsidian becomes more bound by new specialist technologies, an observation that contributes to the authors' eventual argument for a gradual shift from imagistic to more doctrinal forms of religiosity.

II

In my recent book, *Alone in the World? Human Uniqueness in Science and Theology* (2006), I argued that, from a palaeoanthropological point of view, human uniqueness or species specificity emerges as a highly contextualized and embodied notion and is directly tied to the embodied, symbolizing minds of our prehistoric ancestors, as materially manifested in the spectacularly painted cave walls of the Upper Palaeolithic. This opened up not only the possibility of converging arguments, from both evolutionary epistemology and palaeoanthropology, for the presence of religious awareness in our earliest Cro-Magon ancestors, but also the plausibility of the larger argument: since the very beginning of the emergence of *Homo sapiens*, the evolution of those characteristics that made humans uniquely different from even their closest sister species – characteristics like consciousness, language, symbolic minds and symbolic behavior – always included religious awareness and religious behavior.

In this chapter I want to extend this argument and ask, from a theological perspective, what we could plausibly argue about the symbolizing minds of the people of Çatalhöyük. First, I will presuppose the role of culture and language in the evolution of symbolic and imaginative human behavior. A discussion of palaeoculture revealed that adaptability and versatility are remarkable human capacities in which symbolic language is a crucial factor (van Huyssteen 2006). It also revealed that the prehistoric material 'art' from the Upper Palaeolithic exemplifies a profound dimension of imagination and symbolic meaning, in which the presence of spoken language has to be presupposed. In fact, the painting of images on cave walls could have emerged only in communities with shared systems of meaning, mediated through language. Second, I will focus briefly on some of the current discussions in neuroscience and neuropsychology, and explore the possibility of transversal links to the symbolic propensities of the human mind, specifically in the Neolithic and as exemplified by Catalhöyuk. This may reveal that wall paintings, bucrania, burials, sculptures and other important artifacts are reliable windows through which we can glimpse the symbolic minds of these ancient people. Moreover, a neuroscientific perspective on the embodied human mind and human consciousness not only yields the possibility of a neurological bridge to the Neolithic, but also raises the possibility that our universal human capacity for altered states of consciousness both provides a link to the remarkable scope of prehistoric human imagination and challenges us to consider a very early form of shamanism as a plausible, if minimalist interpretation of at least some of these earliest forms of religious imagination. Third, religious imagination will emerge as central to any palaeoanthropological or theological definition of humanness. Although I cannot deal with this issue within the limited scope of this chapter, this idea will challenge the ability of neuroscience and/or cognitive psychology to effectively explain religious experience: although biological origins have directly shaped human origins and human understanding, the genesis of religions, so unique to humans, is not something that we can unproblematically extrapolate from earlier explanations in biology or neuroscience.

We know today that already within Upper Palaeolithic contexts the origin of language, and of cultural capacities so distinctive to humans, greatly enhanced the chances of adapting to environmental instability, and this enhancement decoupled early modern humans from any single ancestral milieu (Potts 1996: 265). Trying to understand humanness from a palaeoanthropological and archaeological point of view inevitably reveals the overarching influence of symbolic ability, and thus the means by which humans create meaning. Clearly, then, human cultural behavior involves not only the transmission of nongenetic behavior, but also the coding of thoughts, sensations, things, times and places that are not empirically available or visible. What we have here is an argument from science that not only the material culture of prehistoric imagery as depicted in the spectacular cave 'art' of France and Spain, or in the very different, complex Neolithic cultural world of Çatalhöyük, but also the heights of all human imagination, the depths of depravity, moral awareness and a sense of the divine, must depend on this human capacity for the symbolic coding of the 'nonvisible'. This coding of the nonvisible through abstract, symbolic thought also enabled our early human ancestors to argue and hold beliefs in abstract terms. In fact, the concept of God itself would eventually follow from the ability to abstract and conceive of 'person' (Potts 1996: 265). This strongly suggests that human mental life includes biologically unprecedented ways of experiencing and understanding the world, from aesthetic experiences to spiritual contemplation.

Like many scholars in contemporary evolutionary epistemology and palaeoanthropology (cf. van Huyssteen 2006), it is significant that a neuroscientist such as Terrence Deacon could conclude that the symbolic nature of *Homo sapiens* explains why mystical or religious inclinations can indeed be regarded as essentially universal attributes of human culture (Deacon 1997: 436). As we saw earlier, there is in fact no culture that lacks a rich mythical, mystical and religious tradition. The coevolution of language and the brain not only implies, however, that human brains have been reorganized in response to language, but also alerts us to the fact that the consequences of this unprecedented evolutionary transition for human religious and spiritual development must be understood on many levels. More recently Deacon (2003) argued that there are reasons to believe that the way that language can symbolically refer to things provides the crucial catalyst for the transition from species with no inkling of the meaning of life to a species in which questions of ultimate meaning have become core organizers of culture and consciousness. It is these symbolic capacities that are ubiquitous among humans and are largely taken for granted when it comes to spiritual and ethical realms. For Deacon (2003) this is precisely where crucial differences in ability mark the boundary between humans and other species. It is in this sense that one could say that the capacity for spiritual experience itself can be understood to be an emergent consequence of the symbolic transfiguration of cognition and emotions.

III

Deacon's argument that the spectacular cave 'art' from the Upper Palae-olithic as well as the burial of the dead that accompanied it strongly sug-gest early shamanistic or religious-like activities (2003) resonates remark-ably well with Jean Clottes and David Lewis-Williams's intriguing pro-posal for a shamanistic interpretation of at least some of the imagery from this important prehistoric period. In one of his recent works, *The Mind in the Cave* (2002), Lewis-Williams has returned to this theme and developed a much stronger argument for seeing neuroscience, as well as neuropsychological research on altered states of consciousness, as provid-ing the principal access to what we might know today about the mental and religious life of the humans who lived and painted in western Europe during the Upper Palaeolithic.

As has become clear by now, in spite of the remarkable progress in palaeoanthropology and archaeology it often seems that we are no closer to knowing why the people of the Upper Palaeolithic penetrated the deep limestone caves of France and Spain to make spectacular images in total darkness. We still do not really know what the images meant to those who made and to those who viewed them, and the great mystery of how we became human, and in the process began to make art, continues to tantalize us. In spite if this, however, Lewis-Williams believes that a century of research has indeed given us sufficient data, the 'material conditions', to attempt a persuasive, general explanation for much of Upper Palaeolithic art. Moreover, we are now in a position to explain some hitherto inexplicable features of the imagery and its often bizarre contents. It is in this sense that Lewis-Williams has argued that what is needed is not more data, but rather a radical rethinking of what we already know (2002). In his most recent work, *Inside the Neolithic Mind* (with David Pearce; 2005), Lewis-Williams has made a similar argument for the Neolithic, and especially for Çatalhöyük.

In developing his own methodology for approaching this interdisci-plinary problem, Lewis-Williams, echoing Margaret Conkey's rejection of metatheories for interpretating prehistoric imagery, shies away from overly generic explanations, while at the same time avoiding the overcon-textualization of some relativist forms of interpretation. Lewis-Williams's sensitivity to contextuality emerges as a focus on the social and historical context of the Neolithic society at Çatalhöyük. A keen sense of embodied materiality also drives him to seriously consider the role of intelligence and consciousness in prehistory. He argues that most researchers have consistently ignored the full complexity of human consciousness and have presented us with a one-sided view of what it is to be an anatomically and cognitively fluid modern human being (Lewis-Williams 2002: 9). It is against this rich background that he proceeds to examine the interaction of mental activity and social context. Lewis-Williams has argued that for scientific work to present us with 'better' explanations it has to be focused on verifiable, empirical facts, and any hypothesis must relate explicitly to the observable features of specific data. It also has to be internally consistent in that no part of a hypothesis should contradict any another. Most important, though, *any hypothesis that covers diverse fields of evidence* is always more persuasive than one that pertains to only one, narrow type of evidence. In this sense complementary types of evidence that converge to address the complex problems posed by Upper Palaeolithic or Neolithic 'art' can in fact produce persuasive hypotheses. This points directly, I believe, to the superiority of an interdisciplinary approach to issues in palaeoanthropology/archaeology and, by implication, in theology. It is in this sense too that useful hypotheses have strong heuristic potential, and as such lead to further creative questions and research. Lewis-Williams also argues that for us to understand the historical trajectory of Upper Palaeolithic or Neolithic research, we have to be especially alert to the social embeddedness of our own scientific work and research and its interactive potential with the material at hand (2002: 49). I believe this lends strong support to the fact that in our own interactive relationship with Palaeolithic or Neolithic imagery and artifacts, even if the 'original meaning' of these is lost forever, a sense of patternedness will emerge that reveals enigmatic narrative structures, even if the full meaning of these original narratives is lost forever.

For Lewis-Williams, allowing for the effects of social contexts, while at the same time emphasizing a real historical past and the possibility of constructing hypotheses that may approximate this past, now surfaces as a key epistemological principle, and we can proceed to address the enigma of what happened to the human mind in the Neolithic. To try to unlock the enigma of these images, we must therefore look more closely at the human brain, the mind, intelligence and what Lewis-Williams has called the shifting, mercurial consciousness of human beings (2002: 68).

Lewis-Williams is rightly critical of any overemphasis on intelligence and the evolution of intelligence, which has often tended to marginalize the importance of the full range of human consciousness in human behavior and has marginalized the fuller spectrum of human consciousness by suppressing certain altered states of consciousness as irrational, marginal, aberrant or even pathological. This is especially true of altered states of consciousness, which in science and even within mainstream religion normally have been eliminated from investigations of the deep past. In a move highly reminiscent of Antonio Damasio's work, Lewis-Williams suggests that we think of consciousness not as a state, but as a continuum, or *spectrum*, of mental states (2002: 121). Following the work of Colin Martindale (1981), Lewis-Williams first describes the spectrum of states of consciousness that encompasses a trajectory from being fully awake to a state of sleeping.

In addition to this spectrum of consciousness from shifting wakefulness to sleep, Lewis-Williams suggests another trajectory that passes through the same spectrum but with different effects. He calls this an *intensified trajectory* of consciousness, and it is more profoundly concerned with inward direction and fantasy. Lewis-Williams argues that dreamlike autistic states may be induced by a wide variety of means other than normal drifting into sleep; for instance, fatigue, pain, fasting and the ingestion of psychotropic substances are all means of shifting consciousness along the intensified trajectory toward the release of inwardly generated imagery. At the end of this trajectory pathological states such as schizophrenia and temporal lobe epilepsy emerge and take consciousness to the far end of the intensified trajectory. Hallucinations may thus be deliberately sought or may emerge unsought (Lewis-Williams 2002: 124). For Lewis-Williams this second trajectory has much in common with the one that takes us into sleep and dreaming, but there are also important differences. Dreaming gives us an idea of what hallucinations are like, but the states toward the far end of the intensified trajectory – visions and hallucinations that may occur in any of the five senses – are generally called altered states of consciousness (2002: 125). Lewis-Williams argues that this phrase can equally be applied to dreaming and to 'inward' states on the normal trajectory, even if some prefer to restrict its use to extreme hallucinations and trance states. More important, however, this kind of description reveals an essentially Western concept of the 'consciousness of rationality', and thus implies that there is an 'ordinary consciousness' that is considered genuine and good, and then there are perverted, or 'altered', states. For Lewis-Williams less focus on rationality should reveal that all parts of the spectrum of consciousness are equally important and equally genuine (2002: 125). All the mental states described here are generated by the neurology of the human nervous system, and they are thus part and parcel of what it is to be fully human. In this sense they are literally 'wired into the brain', although we have to remember that the mental imagery humans experience in altered states is overwhelmingly, although not entirely, derived from memory and thus is culture specific. This is why Inuits see polar bears in their visions, the San see eland and Hildegard from Bingen experienced the Christian God (Lewis-Williams 2002: 126). The spectrum of consciousness, therefore, is indeed wired, but its content is mostly cultural.

For Lewis-Williams the concept of a spectrum of consciousness will ultimately help us to explain many specific features of Upper Palaeolithic as well as Neolithic imagery by linking it directly to experiences of altered states of consciousness, which is remarkably consonant with experiences along the intensified spectrum of consciousness. In fact, it provides us with a neurological bridge that leads back directly to the prehistoric past, especially if we take a careful look at the visual imagery of the intensified spectrum and see what kinds of percepts (the representation of what is perceived) are experienced as one passes along it.

All anatomically modern people, not only from the Upper Palaeolithic and Neolithic, but also from our own time, had, or still have, the same nervous system and therefore cannot avoid experiencing the full spectrum of human consciousness, dreaming, the potential for ecstatic experiences or the potential to hallucinate (Lewis-Williams 2002: 130). And exactly because our Palaeolithic and Neolithic ancestors were fully human, we can confidently expect that their consciousness was as shifting and fragmented as ours, though the ways in which they regarded and valued various states would have been largely culturally determined; Lewis-Williams strikingly refers to this as the 'domestication of trance' (2002: 131). Thus, these people were as capable as we are of moving along both trajectories of consciousness as described by Lewis-Williams, although the content of their dream and autistic imagery would have been different. And it is in exactly this sense that Upper Palaeolithic and Neolithic imagery becomes accessible to us through this neurological bridge to the prehistoric past.

Various scholars have therefore concluded that the capacity to experience altered states of consciousness is a universal psychobiological capacity of our species. The patterning of these altered states of consciousness, however, is always culturally determined, but ecstatic experience is certainly a part of all religions (Lewis-Williams 2002: 1). Among hunter-gatherer communities, this sort of experience is called 'shamanism'. However, Lewis-Williams uses this controversial term carefully and argues that shamanism usefully points to a universal in the makeup of the human mind – the need to make sense of shifting consciousness. 'Shamanism' need not be a generic label, however, and the term certainly need not obscure the diversity of worldwide shamanism anymore than 'Christianity' obscures theological, ritual and social differences among the Russian Orthodox, Greek Orthodox, Roman Catholic and Protestant churches.

Since the people of the Upper Palaeolithic were all hunter-gatherers, Lewis-Williams is very specific about what he means by 'shamanism' and identifies some of its most important characteristics. In all states of 'deep trance', shamans are believed to have direct contact with the spiritual realm. But we must beware of stipulating some naively simple altered state of consciousness as *the* shamanistic state of mind. Lewis-Williams puts it well: the shamanistic mind is a complex interweaving of mental states, visions and emotions (2002: 135). At the heart of this argument lies the deeper conviction, however, that altered states of consciousness are directly related to the genesis of religion. The practice of shamanism, although we could never prove it today, indeed seems to be related to the very origins of human religious practices and beliefs. James McClenon has also persuasively argued (1997: 349) that shamanism, the result of cultural adaptations to a biologically based capacity for altered states of consciousness, is the origin of all later religious forms. And in this specific sense some have even called it the de facto source of all forms of religious revelation, and thus of all religions (Lewis-Williams 2002: 135).

IV

Against the background of his work on the Upper Palaeolithic, Lewis-Williams (now with David Pearce) has argued that the early Neolithic period is arguably the most significant turning point in all of human history (Lewis-Williams and Pearce 2005: 6). The full sweep of this period occurred approximately 10,000 to 5,000 years ago; it was the time during which agriculture became a way of life and people began to domesticate plants and animals, as well as to develop complex belief systems that, seemingly, focused on the dead (Lewis-Williams and Pearce 2005: 17). What interests me about this period is the mysterious and often unresolved connection to the Upper Palaeolithic in western Europe. Crucial questions arise with the advent of the Neolithic: What factors could have generated these enormous changes in societies? Why did people start to domesticate plants and animals? Why did they make plastered skulls and other ritual objects? Today we know that there is no simple way to answer questions of such complexity. We do know that the religion and symbolic repertoire of the people of Çatalhöyük was certainly adapted to suit the new means of making a living (Lewis-Williams and Pearce 2005: 21).

Although there may be no direct connection between artifacts and paintings created during these two periods, clearly the same symbolic human minds were at work. At Göbekli Tepe and other sites in southeastern Turkey, even before the adoption of farming, people were carving large stone pillars, embellishing them with fine carvings of animals, birds and reptiles and erecting them in sunken chambers (Lewis-Williams and Pearce 2005: 6). This kind of generality can indeed be ascribed to the universality of the neurological functioning of the human brain (Barrett 2004) and its perpetual striving to make metaphysical and religious sense of its world. This universal human trait, however, is always balanced by the specific contents of individual human minds, and their thoughts, images and memories, and is deeply embedded in specific cultural contexts.

The Middle East was indeed where agriculture and large settlements started, and it was in this process that Çatalhöyük played a central role. This famous site has preserved evidence for the ways in which its inhabitants lived and, more important, for the way they thought, what they might have believed and some of the rituals they performed. The strange and often inaccessible imagery at Çatalhöyük provides extremely valuable entry points into what held meaning for these ancient people. But as Lewis-Williams and Pearce remind us, meaning is a difficult concept. We have to ask questions like: For whom is the meaning (Lewis-Williams and Pearce 2005: 7)? To what extent did Neolithic people try to consciously express their beliefs? How might this meaning have been articulated with action, and did 'action' as portrayed in the famous paintings or the placement of artifacts and burials in houses 'concretize' any specific form of meaning? These questions must be asked in light of the fact that the uniqueness of individual cultures can be understood only if balanced with the universal aspects of our mental abilities for language, memory and symbolic behavior. This interaction between neurologically generated universals and cultural specifics will be of supreme importance in trying to understand the mysteries of Çatalhöyük; we will not be able to approach this material with the assumption that all human behavior can be explained in terms only of rational, ecological and adaptive grounds. In fact, as will become clear, all symbolic behavior and certainly all religious behavior, as was argued earlier, have ecstatic components and all religious behavior involves altering human consciousness to some extent by prayer, meditation, chanting, dancing and many other techniques. Thus, one can indeed say that shifting consciousness is a factor with which every society, past and present, has to deal (Lewis-Williams and Pearce 2005: 10).

In Çatalhöyük it is highly plausible that the people of the time, much like their counterparts in the Upper Palaeolithic, constructed clear cosmologies and worldviews for their own time. In this sense, related to the painted caves of the Upper Palaeolithic, houses built for daily shelter and living could become models of the cosmos, including the burial of the dead in a realm believed to lie beneath living floors. Thus, even if we never know the specific myths of the people of Çatalhöyük, it will make a difference to consider what role these elusive mythologies might have played in giving daily life a sense of transcendent reality.

Arguing from a cognitive science of religion perspective, Harvey Whitehouse has made an important distinction between imagistic and doctrinal modes of religiosity and so, I believe, has created room for including precisely ecstatic, high-arousal forms of altered-states-of-consciousness religious experiences in an imagistic mode of religiosity. Imagistic modes of religiosity are highly arousing and exemplified by ecstatic practices, extreme rituals, altered states of consciousness and highly emotive, revelatory experiences that draw primarily on episodic memory (Whitehouse 2004). Doctrinal modes of religiosity, on the other hand, rely on depersonalized, abstracted experiences, depend on semantic memory for the nature of religious knowledge and are characterized by the repetition of specific rituals and the acceptance of shared sets of belief. Whitehouse's further argument is that archaeological and historical evidence supports the fact that these imagistic modes of religiosity are also the most ancient forms of religious activity, an argument that seems to dovetail with Lewis-Williams and Pearce's argument for the earliest, prehistoric forms of religious experiences as ecstatic, visionary or shamanistic. Whitehouse has argued explicitly that imagistic modes of religiosity appear in the archaeological record as far back as the Upper Palaeolithic period (2004: 77; see also Whitehouse and Hodder, Chapter 5, this volume). Lewis-Williams and Pearce go further and suggest that religious experience, belief and practice are possible stimuli for the revolutionary changes in the Neolithic period. What seems to be clear is that at the beginning of the Neolithic and in the Mesolithic (the period between the Upper Palaeolithic and the Neolithic), access to spiritual realms was no longer gained through caves (as it was for the Upper Palaeolithic people of France and Spain), but through structures and cities built above ground (Lewis-Williams and Pearce 2005: 59).

In addition, in an attempt to answer the question of why Middle Eastern Neolithic people performed such elaborate burial practices, Lewis-Williams and Pearce oppose a functionalist explanation according to which the rituals created social cohesion and thus contributed to the society's adaptation to its environment. Instead, they suggest that Neolithic people practiced serial burials for mythological, especially cosmological, reasons, and not simply because those religious practices were adaptive to environmental conditions. Thus Lewis-Williams and Pearce suggest that their view of the cosmos entailed multiple stages of postmortem existence that were lived out in multiple cosmological levels: the living 'helping' the dead from one stage to the next with a series of widely spaced mortuary rites (2005: 78). But this is still only half of the answer: it is clear that only some corpses were selected for exhumation, disarticulation, special treatment and reburial. And those who kept these customs alive and explained them were undoubtedly powerful, influential people with special insight into spiritual matters. The selected dead were probably believed to have the same powers even after death.

This problem goes to the heart of the attempt by the current team at Çatalhöyük to discern whether there might indeed be a gradual transition in the Neolithic history of Çatalhöyük from an imagistic to a more doctrinal form of religiosity. One the one hand, what Steven Mithen argued for the Pre-Pottery Neolithic seems to be plausible for early Çatalhöyük too: we should avoid thinking of the people of Çatalhöyük as engaging in some form of formal worship of their ancestors. Instead, we should envisage a constant dialogue with the dead, with ancestors whose state of being is left undiscussed and whose presence in the world is more tolerated (Mithen 2004: 35). This kind of imagistic inter-pretation of the archaeological evidence would indeed imply the absence of a formal priesthood, and we should then be thinking of the burial rites at Çatalhöyük as rituals conducted and interpreted within family/house and individual bases. However, if the mortuary rites that involved skull caching and the placement of primary and secondary burials in contexts associated with domestic activities might have involved priestlike, special individuals, whose skulls then underwent the special treatment of plas-tering and decoration, then we may have a gradual transition to a more doctrinal mode of religiosity. In Chapter 5 Whitehouse and Hodder address exactly this problem in an attempt to answer Mithen's question as to the possibility of the nature of religiosity evolving over time in a major site such as Çatalhöyük (Mithen 2004: 33).

In this way the Neolithic can be seen against the background of the Upper Palaeolithic, even if we know very little about the Upper Palae-olithic and Epipalaeolithic in the Middle East. In the European Upper Palaeolithic people clearly believed in a suite of subterranean spirit ani-mals and beings *before* they started to make images of them in caves (Lewis-Williams and Pearce 2005: 83). Clearly, at the end of the Upper Palaeolithic there was a marked shift away from this kind of cosmol-ogy and religion. But what are the major changes that we can observe in the archaeological evidence? Most important, in the Neolithic peo-ple constructed exemplars of the cosmos above ground. Thus, Neolithic people eliminated the complexity of the subterranean passages of caves and replaced it with the greater predictability and simplicity of structures of their own design. For Lewis-Williams and Pearce this means gaining greater control over the cosmos and the ability to adjust beliefs about it to suit social and personal needs (2005: 85).

Lewis-Williams and Pearce in this way want to see their approach to the Neolithic as broadly in line with the kind of cognitive archaeology that both Mellaart and Ian Hodder pursue: here views of the Neolithic are shifting away from austere artifact analysis to a holistic understanding of belief and rituals (Lewis-Williams and Pearce 2005). And in this sense the richly decorated rooms and plastered bulls' heads – the so-called bucra-nia – can indeed be seen as evidence for a mythical world. Lewis-Williams and Pearce go one step further, however, and ask whether, in the light of the neurological heritage of all humans and what we know today about prehistoric religion, the effect of this on the cosmology and belief systems of the people of Çatalhöyük makes sense of and may coordinate the diverse finds at Çatalhöyük. Specifically they argue for clear cosmological implications embedded in the Çatalhöyük architecture. Also, and post-Mellaart, no imposed distinctions are made between sacred and secular concepts, or between sacred and secular spaces and relationships (Lewis-Williams and Pearce 2005). On this view domestic and ritual activities were not rigidly separated but holistically integrated. This view, however, would also probably imply a distinct move away from Whitehouse's imagistic mode of religion where no formal religious ideology would be associated with the figurines, cult buildings or burial practices; these religious artifacts would then have been no more than highly personal interpretations and experiences of ritual performances, which would have been loosely allied to a set of shared beliefs that remained largely undiscussed (Mithen 2004: 21). Importantly, however, Hodder and Whitehouse also argue that, although imagistic and doctrinal modes of religiosity in many respects seem to contrast starkly, they also often occur together within one single tradition as relatively discrete phases of domains or operations (Chapter 5).

I do believe, against the background of this broader discussion, that Lewis-Williams and Pearce's basic premise, that the physical structure of the human mind creates specific kinds of images and ways of viewing the world under altered states of consciousness, is plausible and has an impact, especially on what we see in the earlier levels of Çatalhöyük. It is also plausible that geometric and other nonfigurative patterns could be directly linked to what people see in altered states of ecstatic consciousness (Hayden 2006: 278). More speculative, and therefore less convincing, is their attempt to relate the conception of the world as a tiered cosmos to the neural structure of the brain, even if a three-tiered cosmos was definitely part of the Upper Palaeolithic and Neolithic worldviews. Altered states of consciousness were probably a central characteristic of Neolithic religion, and the early 'shamanistic' overtones of this were clearly objectified in the way that bucrania, vulture and other skulls were embedded in walls so as to appear to be emerging from these liminal structures. Animal heads that are not only part of the walls, but also *look out* from the walls indeed seem to be powerful arguments for an early form of shamanism (Lewis-Williams and Pearce 2005: 111; Hodder 2006: 70). This is also true of the fact that humans and animals were treated in the same way in death, as is seen in the plastered skulls of humans from other Neolithic sites and the molded, plastered bucrania. While Lewis-Williams and Pearce's detailed descriptions and comparison between the Upper Palaeolithic experience of moving through dark limestone caves and crawling through small openings between rooms at Çatalhöyük seems far too speculative (2005: 105), Whitehouse's imagistic mode of religion captures much more accurately the highly emotive events, the type of revelatory experiences that became embedded in episodic memory and that must have surrounded the crafting of bucrania, the embedding of vulture and other skulls in walls and the plastering of human skulls. Furthermore, what Steven Mithen states in relation to early Natufian burials must have been equally true at Çatalhöyük: the reburial of bones and the creation of skull caches would have been highly emotive experiences in this ongoing dialogue with the dead (2004: 27–35).

Conclusion

In our thinking about religion or spirituality in the Neolithic, we should not expect to discover some clearly demarcated, separate domain that we could identify as 'religion' as such. What this means is that we should avoid making easy and uncomplicated distinctions between natural and supernatural, between material and spiritual. The complex material culture of Çatalhöyük clearly demands a more holistic approach in which not just special artistic objects and artifacts but daily material life itself (houses and other structures) must have been deeply infused with spirituality for the people of Çatalhöyük. This implies that archeologists can indeed recognize the spiritual or religious in early time periods only through the material legacy of the people of that time. Imagery, sculptures and other artifacts may not always be exclusively symbolic but may point to normal living spaces as symbolic realms.

A holistic approach to the world of Çatalhöyük thus enables us to link the art discovered at this Neolithic city to the archaeological legacy from daily life – that is, the houses, their structures, burials and apparent rituals (skull removal and replacement) – and also see the houses as ritualized living spaces where bucrania, vulture and weasel skulls are enigmatically embedded in the walls. On this view it should not be far-fetched to link this symbolic material world, so typical of imagistic modes of religion, to the neurasthetic ability of the uniquely symbolizing human mind.

This sense of a deep material–spiritual entanglement not at all implies a generic 'shamanistic' reading of the Neolithic material at Çatalhöyük. However, it would be safe to assume that the neurological functioning of the human brain, like the structure and functioning of other parts of our bodies, is a human universal and that at least some of the material from Çatalhöyük clearly suggests an early imagistic, deeply religious culture, of which important experiential and ritual elements would have been carried through to later, more doctrinal modes of religiosity.

Even if we epistemically acknowledge a neurological bridge to this Neolithic culture, it is still extremely difficult to cross the vast interpretive bridge and try to probe the beliefs and meaning systems of this ancient culture. From a cognitive science of religion point of view, a holistic approach to the material culture of Çatalhöyük would presuppose that whatever the symbolic context and enigmatic ritual practices meant for the people of the time, it seems to be unmistakenly true that religious practices of all kinds have always presupposed worldviews, deep convictions and beliefs of what the empirical practices were about. This has direct implications for palaeoanthropology and archaeology: we may never know what the religious beliefs of the Neolithic were about, but observing paintings on the walls of houses as artifacts of vanished cultures does not take away from the fact that these ancient art forms clearly presuppose symbolic and other narratives, dreams, hopes and anxieties that we may never be able to decipher but that for these people represented a way of coping with the world. In this sense beliefs and their accompanying rituals sacramentally integrate the natural and the supernatural, and thus ultimately define religion, even if we may never know what those beliefs really represented.

Due to the neurological substratum of prehistoric and other religions, however we may want to define religion, minimally it always seems to have a 'universal patterning' that is exemplified by (1) belief systems that are (2) experienced and (3) ritualized. I would argue that this is true for both Harvey Whitehouse's imagistic and doctrinal modes of religion, even as abstract belief systems are much more abstractly doctrinalized in doctrinal modes of religion. These three basic characteristics of religion probably are the most important reason that Whitehouse and Hodder could argue that doctrinal and imagistic modes of religiosity, even when in many respects they contrast starkly, can occur together within a single tradition as relatively discrete phases of this operation (Chapter 5).

These three elements of religion are always highly contextualized and, as in the case of Çatalhöyük, can be known only in their cultural specificity. Without any doubt the Çatalhöyük society had its own culture, its own sets of beliefs, intense ways of experiencing them and norms and rituals that exemplified them, and that individuals learned from birth to creatively interact with. And if we can accept David Lewis-Williams's argument that it is human consciousness that enables the interaction between neurologically generated patterns and cultural specifics, then one could indeed say that all religions have an ecstatic or mystical component and all involve altering human consciousness through prayer, meditation, chanting, dancing and so on. The material entanglement of Neolithic religion with Çatalhöyük culture would indeed, through these ancient, unknown myths, have clothed daily life with a sense of spiritual reality and a living of daily life in a three-tiered cosmology.

In Chapter 5, Whitehouse and Hodder have argued plausibly that there is at least some independent archaeological evidence that low-frequency rituals associated with hunting, feasting, dancing and the burial of human remains were occasions that also involved high levels of peak emotional arousal. Evidence for this is found partly in pictorial remains of crowds of people teasing and baiting wild animals, as well as hunting scenes that show animals with erect penises. Hodder and his team also show that bull horns (bucrania) installed on the walls of houses were the main markers of significant feasting events and rituals and that these events, along with foundation rituals and burials, were fairly rare occurrences, involving highly charged cultural myths and practices (Chapter 5). Later the evidence from stamp seals, and especially pictorial depictions with a clear narrative component that seems to have become part of a discourse about ritual acts, suggest a homogenizing move across the settlement, consistent with the emergence of a more doctrinal mode of religiosity. This is convergent with a decline in the occurrence of actual bull horns and other installations of wild animal parts in the upper levels of the Çatalhöyük site. One of Whitehouse and Hodder's final, intriguing suggestions is that elders, ritual leaders and 'shamans' associated with the history houses increasingly developed doctrinal strategies by building discursive forms of knowledge out of earlier, preexisting imagistic forms.

Also important, however, is the extent of architectural conformity among buildings regarding the locations of domestic fittings and wall art. Hodder's program has indeed verified claims for annual replastering of walls within the main rooms, and in some cases at much more frequent intervals, along with the regular replastering of bull head sculptures. This kind of conformity and routinization in the lives of the people of Çatalhöyük does indeed seem more compatible with Whitehouse's notion of doctrinal religiosity (Mithen 2004: 37).

Religion cannot be discounted from any discussion of typical human behavior, and in my recent work I have tried to show that, in a very specific sense, religious belief is one of the earliest dispositions detected in the archaeological record of modern humans. Even if it is not clear what exactly the art of the Upper Palaeolithic or Neolithic represented to the people who created it, it is abundantly clear that this early art reflected a view held by these early humans of their place in the world and a body of mythology that explained that place. A minimalist shamanistic interpretation of some of the art and ritual might help us to understand more comprehensively the imagistic mode of religion, so prevalent in the early history of Çatalhöyük. The argument for a limited religious (shamanistic) interpretation for some of the art does suggest the high plausibility of the naturalness of religious belief, also in the lives and behavior of our prehistoric ancestors. This may sound like a circular argument, but the circle is not vicious: if our Cro-Magnon and Neolithic ancestors were 'us' in every possible way, then we should rightly argue not only for their self-consciousness, moral awareness and aesthetic imagination, but also for a shared universal religious disposition to make sense of the world – and for meaning beyond this world.

Of course, at the heart of even a minimalist shamanistic hypothesis lies the deeper conviction that altered states of consciousness are directly related to the genesis of religion. I argued in my recent book that shamanism can be seen as the result of cultural adaptations to a biologically based capacity for altered states of consciousness and can even be called the source of all forms of religious revelation, and thus of all religions (van Huyssteeen 2006). This goes to the heart of the broader issue of the nature of the symbolic human mind and is crucial also for the evolutionary origins of our moral and spiritual capacities. This is also why I believe that mystical and religious inclinations can be regarded as a universal attribute of human culture. In my book I argued that it is precisely this symbolic capacity that distinguishes humans from other species, and in this sense one could then argue that the capacity for embodied spiritual experience can be understood as an emergent consequence of the symbolic transformation of cognition and emotion.

REFERENCES

Barrett, J. L. 2004. *Why Would Anyone Believe in God?* Lanham, Md.: AltaMira Press.

Carter, T. 2007. Of blanks and burials: Hoarding obsidian at Neolithic Çatalhöyük. In *Technical Systems and Near Eastern PPN Communities.* Antibes: Editions APDCA, 343–55.

Deacon, T. 1997. *The Symbolic Species: The Co-Evolution of Language and the Brain.* New York: W. W. Norton.

Deacon, T. 2003. Language. In *Encyclopedia for Science and Religion*, vol. 2, ed. J. W. van Huyssteen. New York: Macmillan, 504–8.

Hayden, B. D. 2006. Prehistoric imaginings. *American Scientist*, 94, 278–80.

Hodder, I. 2006. *The Leopard's Tale: Revealing the Mysteries of Çatalhöyük.* London: Thames & Hudson.

Lewin, R. 1993. *The Origin of Modern Humans.* New York: Scientific American Library.

Lewis-Williams, D. 2002. *The Mind in the Cave: Consciousness and the Origins of Art.* New York: Thames & Hudson.

Lewis-Williams, D., and Pearce, D. 2005. *Inside the Neolithic Mind.* New York: Thames & Hudson.

Martindale, C. 1981. *Cognition and Consciousness.* Homewood, Ill.: Dorsey Press.

McClenon, J. 1997. Shamanic healing, human evolution, and the origin of religion. *Journal for the Scientific Study of Religion*, 36(3), 349–50.

Mithen, S. 2004. From Ohalo to Çatalhöyük: The development of religiosity during the early prehistory of western Asia, 20,000–7000 BCE. In *Theorizing Religions Past: Archeology, History, and Cognition*, eds. H. Whitehouse and L. H. Martin. Walnut Creek, Calif.: AltaMira Press, 17–43.

Potts, R. 1996. *Humanity's Descent.* New York: William Morrow.

Soffer, O., and Conkey, M. 1997. Studying ancient visual cultures. In *Beyond Art: Pleistocene Image and Symbol*, eds. M. Conkey, O. Soffer, D. Stratmann and N. G. Jablonski. San Francisco: Allen Press, 1–15.

Tattersall, I. 1998. *Becoming Human: Evolution and Human Uniqueness.* New York: Harcourt Brace.

Tattersall, I. 2003. Response to Robert Proctor's 'Three roots of human recency: Molecular anthropology, the refigured Acheulean, and the UNESCO response to Auschwitz.' *Current Anthropology*, 44(2), 232–4.

Van Huyssteen, J. Wentzel. 2006. *Alone in the World? Human Uniqueness in Science and Theology.* Grand Rapids, Mich.: Eerdmans.

Whitehouse, H. 2004. *Modes of Religiosity: A Cognitive Theory of Religious Transmission.* Lanham, Md.: AltaMira Press.

5

Modes of religiosity at Çatalhöyük

Harvey Whitehouse and Ian Hodder

Introduction

Social and cultural phenomena are organized and transmitted in highly patterned ways. Understanding the nature and causes of these patterns can help us to reconstruct some features of prehistoric societies that might otherwise remain undiscovered. The patterns we consider in this chapter concern the relationship between certain features of *ritual performance* (especially emotionality, frequency and exegetical thinking), on the one hand, and certain features of *social morphology* (especially the scale, structure and cohesiveness of ancient cults), on the other. We will show that from comparatively fragmentary information concerning the nature of prehistoric rituals at Çatalhöyük we can infer a surprisingly rich picture of how religious knowledge may have been constituted, transmitted and transformed over the lifetime of the settlement and how ritually based coalitions formed, interacted and changed. Our aim is to use a broad understanding of modes of religiosity to throw light on the evidence from Çatalhöyük and to open up discussion of some of the causal links between ritual performance and social and political structure at the site. By combining broad anthropological understanding with the specific data from Çatalhöyük, we believe that some interpretations can be shown to be more plausible than others.

The theory of modes of religiosity

The patterns we seek to investigate at Çatalhöyük stem from two rather different ways of conducting and experiencing rituals. A striking observation from the cross-cultural study of contemporary and historical rituals is that the intensity of *emotional arousal* experienced by participants in a ritual is inversely proportional to the *frequency* of performance. Rituals that are only very rarely performed are usually quite exciting and dramatic occasions, punctuated by a great deal of sensory pageantry. By contrast, rituals that are performed on a regular basis are on the whole comparatively tame affairs. Thus, rituals tend to occur in two main varieties: (1) low-frequency, high-arousal (typical examples would be rites of passage, royal and state rituals, millenarian cults) and (2) high-frequency, low-arousal rituals (e.g., liturgical rituals, blessings, propitiatory rites).

Investigations into this bifurcation of ritual forms led to a more general theory of 'modes of religiosity', based on a distinction between doctrinal and imagistic dynamics (Whitehouse 1995, 2000, 2004). The doctrinal mode is based on frequently repeated teachings and rituals. Much of the religious knowledge is codified in language and transmitted primarily via recognized leaders and authoritative texts. High-frequency ritual performances allow complex networks of ideas to be transmitted and stored in memory as relatively schematized encyclopedic knowledge, leading to the standardization of teachings in collective memory. Unauthorized deviations from the standard canon thus become easy to identify. At the same time, routinization tends to suppress certain kinds of creative thinking about the meanings of the rituals, reducing the risks of innovation. For both reasons, frequent repetition of rituals and creeds contributes to (and correlates highly with) the establishment of religious orthodoxies. The emphasis on verbally codified doctrines and narratives facilitates highly efficient and rapid spread, through processes of evangelism and missionization. The emphasis on oratory and learning also facilitates the emergence of venerable leaders and teachers: gurus, prophets and priests. This fact, and the emphasis on standardization and orthodoxy, facilitate the emergence of centralized ecclesiastic hierarchies, exerting influence over the content and organization of authoritative religious knowledge.

By contrast, the imagistic mode of religiosity is based on rare, climactic rituals – for instance, the traumas of initiation, collective possession and mystery cults – typically involving extreme forms of deprivation, the infliction of physical pain or participation in psychologically disturbing acts. Such practices trigger enduring and vivid episodic memories for ritual ordeals, encouraging long-term rumination on the mystical significance of the acts and artifacts involved. Imagistic practices are much harder to spread than doctrinal traditions. A major reason for this is that the religious knowledge emerges out of collective participation in rituals

Table 5.1. Modes of religiosity contrasted

Variable	Doctrinal	Imagistic
Psychological features		
1. Transmissive frequency	High	Low
2. Level of arousal	Low	High
3. Principal memory system	Semantic schemas and implicit scripts	Episodic/flashbulb memory
4. Ritual meaning	Learned/acquired	Internally generated
5. Techniques of revelation	Rhetoric, logical integration, narrative	Iconicity, multivocality and multivalence
Sociopolitical features		
6. Social cohesion	Diffuse	Intense
7. Leadership	Dynamic	Passive/absent
8. Inclusivity/exclusivity	Inclusive	Exclusive
9. Spread	Rapid, efficient	Slow, inefficient
10. Scale	Large scale	Small scale
11. Degree of uniformity	High	Low
12. Structure	Centralized	Noncentralized

Source: Whitehouse (2004).

rather than being summed up in speech or text. Traumatic rituals also create strong bonds among those who experience them together, establishing in people's memories who was present when a particular cycle of rituals took place. The tendency is toward localized cults, based on patterns of following by example, and so we never find the same kind of scale, uniformity, centralization or hierarchical structure that typifies the doctrinal mode.

All religious traditions dominated by the doctrinal mode by definition incorporate highly repetitive forms of ritual and oratory. Under certain conditions, however, this kind of routinization can give rise to boredom and lowered motivation. What we find is that, in conditions of demoralization, techniques of policing the orthodoxy typically become less effective, resulting in the emergence and spread of more idiosyncratic (nonstandard) versions. This in turn commonly triggers a backlash in the form of movements of doctrinal reform. Often these reformations entail high levels of religious excitement, triggering imagistic-type revelations and a rejuvenation of doctrinal authority. Once the religious police are back in power, we typically witness a return to routinization. Thus, although doctrinal and imagistic modes of religiosity in many respects contrast starkly (see Table 5.1), they also often occur together within a single tradition, as relatively discrete phases or domains of operation. Indeed, the vulnerability of the doctrinal mode to over- and underpolicing makes periodic imagistic outbursts more or less inevitable.

The modes theory is intended to capture and explain certain recurrent trends with respect to religious organization and transformation globally and historically. Much effort has been invested in testing the modes theory using detailed case studies from religions around the world and stretching back into the recorded past (Whitehouse and Laidlaw 2004; Whitehouse and Martin 2004, 2005). Currently a new project is under way that seeks to test the core predictions of the modes theory[1] against 645 religious rituals selected from a sample of 75 cultures around the globe.[2] The advantage of this method is that it will enable us to quantify more precisely correlations between variables that are predicted to covary within doctrinal and imagistic clusters and to assess statistically the impact of historically contingent factors influencing those correlations. In relation to our efforts to apply the modes theory to Çatalhöyük, the claims put forward in this chapter are evaluated in relation to the specific data from the site, but they also stimulate further data acquisition so that the claims can be made more or less plausible.

In a series of publications Whitehouse has argued that the imagistic mode of religiosity is much more ancient than the doctrinal mode. In his original formulation, imagistic practices dated at least as far back as the Upper Palaeolithic, whereas doctrinal dynamics emerged only in concert with the establishment of early state formations. Whitehouse

---

[1] These core predictions may be enumerated as follows: (1) The frequency of a ritual will be inversely proportional to the level of arousal it induces in participants (arousal inducers include sensory pageantry, singing, dancing, music, altered states of consciousness and painful or traumatic procedures). (2) Lower-frequency rituals will entail higher peak arousal than will higher-frequency rituals. (3) Lower-frequency rituals will generate greater volume and elaborateness of Spontaneous Exegetical Reflection. (4) Conversely, higher-frequency rituals will occur in traditions that transmit greater volume and elaborateness of verbally (or textually) transmitted doctrine and narrative. (5) The frequency of a ritual will be inversely proportional to the level of cohesion it induces in ritual participants. (6) Religions with high-frequency rituals will spread faster than traditions that lack high-frequency rituals. (7) Religions with high-frequency rituals will be larger than traditions that lack high-frequency rituals. (8) Religions with high-frequency rituals will be more hierarchical than traditions that lack high-frequency rituals.

[2] This research forms part of an international collaborative project funded by the European Commission, details of which may be found at http://www.cam.ox.ac.uk/research/explaining-religion.

argued that one of the key sites of spontaneous emergence of the doctrinal mode was Lower Mesopotamia some six thousand years ago. A prominent bone of contention with regard to this argument has been, not whether doctrinal practices are in evidence during that early flowering of civilizations, but whether the doctrinal mode *was triggered by the advent of writing systems* (as proposed by Goody 2004; Boyer 2005) or whether the appearance of doctrinal dynamics *helped to foster the development and spread of inscribing practices* and ultimately fully developed literate traditions (as argued by Whitehouse 2000, 2004; Johnson 2004; Mithen 2004).[3] The evidence presented in this chapter would support the latter view. But it would also place the emergence of the doctrinal mode in western Asia at a rather earlier point in the region's prehistory than originally proposed. We argue in this chapter that the seeds of the doctrinal mode were already germinating by the end of the period of settlement at Çatalhöyük.

We are not the first to consider this possibility. Steven Mithen recently noted the evidence for modes of religiosity at Çatalhöyük as part of a more ambitious effort to discern the operation of imagistic dynamics and the gradual appearance of the doctrinal mode in western Asia between 20,000 and 7000 BC.[4] He argued, as we do, that the modes theory could 'enrich our interpretations for specific aspects of the archaeological record, make some interpretations more plausible than others, and help us identify previously unrecognised causal links between religious practices and political structure' (Mithen 2004: 18). Nevertheless, Mithen's

---

[3] As Mithen observes, 'The sheer size of the settlement, the suggestion of a deity and rulers, and the architectural conformity of the structures would suggest that we are dealing with a type of religiosity that tends toward the doctrinal rather than imagistic mode in Whitehouse's terms, even though there is no evidence of literacy' (2004: 36).

[4] According to Mithen, 'In these regards, therefore, the interpretations of Çatalhöyük emerging from the 1990s research appear more compatible with an imagistic mode of religiosity. But one key aspect of Mellaart's interpretation remains valid – the extent of architectural conformity among buildings regarding the locations of domestic fittings and wall art. Hodder's program of work has verified claims for annual replastering of walls within the main rooms, and in some cases at much more frequent intervals, along with regular replastering of the bull-head sculptures (W. Matthews, personal communication). From this, one gains an impression of immense conformity and routinization in people's lives that seems more compatible with Whitehouse's notion of doctrinal religiosity. Whether this impression will be verified by full publication of the new research remains to be seen' (2004: 36).

assessment of the evidence was inconclusive with regard to the emergence of doctrinal dynamics at Çatalhöyük. We think we can offer a bolder and also more detailed account.

Low-frequency, high-arousal rituals at Çatalhöyük

The most reliable diagnostic feature of the imagistic mode is the presence of collective rituals that are performed no more frequently than once a year (in many cases much less frequently than that). Setting aside for the moment what we mean by the term 'ritual' (this issue becomes more pressing later), we describe such rituals as 'low frequency'. Low-frequency rituals typically evince higher peaks of emotional arousal among participants than can be discerned in frequently performed rites. Widely recurrent triggers of arousal in such rituals include the infliction of pain by means of beating, whipping, burning, piercing, scarification, tattooing, removal of body parts, laceration of the tongue or insertion of bones or other sharp objects through sensitive tissue. Commonly, however, such rituals also entail psychological torments, such as threatening, abandoning, kidnapping, humiliating, incarcerating, insulting and browbeating. Along with these ordeals it is common for participants to undergo trials of endurance: fasting, dehydration, athletic feats, solitary confinement or sleep deprivation. Given the emphasis on negatively valenced arousal, these practices have been dubbed 'rites of terror' (Whitehouse 1996), but some low-frequency rituals also entail an ecstatic component either due to masochistic aspects (e.g., the autoeroticism of penis-bleeding procedures reported in Papua New Guinea; Lewis 1980) or a sense of intense relief at having surmounted the ordeals. While it is hardly surprising that few cultural traditions require the performance of rites of terror on a daily or weekly basis (or confine such routine torture to a select minority of adherents), a more astonishing observation is the scarcity of low-frequency rituals that do not also entail exceptionally high levels of peak arousal, occasioned by the kinds of ordeals just outlined. Insofar as low-frequency, low-arousal rituals occur at all, they generally turn out to be variants of high-frequency rituals, cobbled together and spiced up so as to mark special occasions of various kinds. But genuinely low-frequency rituals (comprising clusters of procedures only rarely encountered by most participants) are typically very emotive.

This claim has been demonstrated using a large sample of contemporary religions,[5] and at Çatalhöyük there is at least some independent archaeological evidence that low-frequency rituals associated with hunting, feasting, dancing and burial of human remains were occasions that also involved high levels of peak emotional arousal. Having considered this evidence, we will turn to the general causal mechanisms responsible for ensuring that low-frequency ritual performances carry such a powerful 'kick'.

Evidence for low-frequency, high-arousal rituals at Çatalhöyük comes in part from pictorial remains. Two houses in Levels V and III have wall paintings that show the teasing and baiting of wild animals (bulls, deer, boars, a bear) by crowds of people, in one case clearly bearded (Mellaart 1966, 1967). The hunting and baiting scenes show animals with erect penises. In the deposits on the site it is clear that the meat-bearing parts of wild bulls are often associated with feasting events. The meat-bearing parts of deer and boars are rarely found on-site, and researchers have so far found the claws of only one bear. Other rare finds are a leopard claw and the talons of large raptors. So it seems possible to argue that on rare occasions wild animals and birds were killed, perhaps at times in association with male feats of bravery and strength. Consumption of many of these animals took place off-site, but the wild bull meat was eaten and distributed to feasts on-site. The hard and dangerous parts of these animals (claws, horns, antlers, tusks, talons) were then inserted as trophies or memories into the walls of the houses, where they were repeatedly plastered over as part of the general plastering of the house walls. The scale and emotional tonus of teasing and baiting at Çatalhöyük can be determined partly by the large number of human figures in scenes depicted in surviving artwork at the site. The haunches of the wild bulls at Çatalhöyük stood 2 m in height. Bringing down or teasing and baiting such an animal would have presented grave danger (perhaps even resulting in fatalities). The teasing and baiting scenes seem to be accompanied by dancing and music (as seen in the apparent rattles and drums depicted).

---

[5] Comparison of more than 500 rituals recorded in the Human Relations Area Files database, carried out by Quentin Atkinson, and Harvey Whitehouse, shows a striking inverse correlation between performance frequency and peak emotional arousal (full results yet to be written and published).

Feasts resulting from such kills at Çatalhöyük would have been moments of high social drama, not only because of the fear and danger occasioned by the quarry but also because of the sheer scale of such social events. It has been estimated that the meat from a wild bull could have fed a thousand people (based on figures from contemporary feasts using domestic cattle in central Anatolia). And the faunal remains at Çatalhöyük provide additional clues to the scale and frequency of feasting events on-site. As to scale, it seems possible that parts of animals were distributed to houses or house groups, as there is often some sidedness involved in the distributions of parts. For example, Building 52 had 11 left bull horns stacked above a bucranium. It seems that certain houses received certain parts of animals in feasts. Even so, a considerable number could have been involved, and the feasting deposits often contain the remains of bones of more than one animal. As to frequency, if we identify the installations of bull horns on walls as the main markers of significant feasting events and rituals, the maximum is 6 in one house, and a stack of 11 uninstalled horns has just been mentioned. Similarly, few deposits have been found that seem to result from major feasts – in the region of 1–3 per house. If we estimate the houses as enduring for about 80 years, then we have events involving feasting and wild animals occurring every 7–80 years.

Foundation rituals associated with the houses would have occurred every 70–100 years, and in some cases they appear to be associated with feasts. There is frequent evidence that house foundation was associated with highly charged events such as the burial of neonates and young children, and the placing of human skulls at the base of house posts. In the case of Building 42, the foundation of the house was accompanied by the burial of a man holding the plastered skull of a woman. The burial of neonates and young children in the foundations of houses perhaps implies involvement with a larger group than the inhabitants of these houses (suggested to be five to eight people per house on average, too small a group to produce a cluster of neonate burials at the time of house foundation). There may, in fact, have been some association between the closure and foundation of a house and the death of significant individuals in the house. The care taken in preparing houses for closure and rebuilding suggests elaborate ceremony and intense focus.

Determining the frequency of burial is complicated by a number of factors at Çatalhöyük, including the fact that some houses (the 'history houses') can have up to 62 burials in them, while others can have none or very few. Clearly the dead were preferentially buried in certain houses. It is also likely that not all people were buried in houses on the site (as is seen from the human remains in the off-site KOPAL Area). Infant burials are common, but it is difficult to know whether all infants were buried in houses. But if the average number of noninfant burials per house at Çatalhöyük is 5–10, and if buildings last for 70–100 years, then burial for each house (though not necessarily in that house) would have occurred every 10 years or so. The burial ritual itself involved little in the way of elaborate artifacts or bodily treatment – the bodies were often tied in a tight crouched position before being deposited with few artifacts. In some cases, heads were later removed, and a significant factor in burial would have been the disturbance and handling of bones that had earlier been placed in the grave. As for other performative ritual, throughout the Middle Eastern Neolithic there is evidence of an association between treatment of the dead and birds of prey, including vultures. At Çatalhöyük there are depictions of vultures with apparent human legs, and a crane dance has been suggested by Russell and McGowan (2003) on the basis of the treatment of some crane wing bones at the site. It is possible that the dressing up of people as birds is indicative of the 'trickster' figure seen in many myths and rituals (Hodder and Meskell, Chapter 2). Other, highly charged aspects of the burial ritual included the careful removal of skulls and other body parts from already buried and partially decayed bodies. The care shown in the removal of the heads and body parts belies an elaborate anatomical knowledge and a delicate attention to detail. There are cut marks on some bones resulting from head removal, and it is probable that obsidian blades were used for the task. A skull was in one case replastered, and there are other instances of red paint being applied to skulls. All this suggests that burial was a relatively rare occurrence, involving collective decision making (as in the decision regarding the location of the burial) and highly charged cultural myths and practices.

Mystery cult at Çatalhöyük

Wherever we find low-frequency, high-arousal rituals, we generally find traditions of esoteric revelation and ritual exegesis, typically stewarded by elders and ritual experts. This pattern has been repeatedly observed across a broad range of traditional societies in the contemporary world, from

West African male cults (e.g., Højbjerg 2004) to Amazonian shamanism (e.g., Verswijver 1992) and from New Guinea initiations (e.g., Barth 1987) to firewalkers in northern Greece (Xygalatas 2008). It has also been discerned time and again in the documented past: from studies of early Christians (Leopold 2004) to medieval nuns (e.g., Clark 2004) and from the religions of ancient Greece (Martin 2004) to the Dionysian cults of the Roman Empire (Beck 2004). Unpacking the causes of this pattern will furnish us with an explanation of the strong correlation observed between low-frequency ritual performances and elevated emotional intensity.

Rituals that are seldom performed but carry a powerful emotional punch are remembered as distinctive episodes in people's lives. These 'episodic' memories (Tulving 1972) specify all kinds of details about the acts and artifacts involved in the ritual performance, as well as many other unique features of the experience. These memories tend to last, perhaps even enduring for a lifetime. And often they incorporate a certain vividness or realism that has led some researchers to use the label 'flashbulb memory' to designate episodic recall with a particular canonical structure, specifying details not only of what happened, but of who was present, how one felt, what happened immediately afterward and so on (Winograd and Killinger 1983). Extensive psychological research into the workings of flashbulb memory has helped to explain how the distinctiveness (rarity) of an event, combined with its emotional impact, results in such durable and vivid recall (Conway 1995). But we are only now beginning to understand the implications of activating this kind of memory system in recall for *ritual* events. This is where we need briefly to clarify what we mean by 'ritual'.

There may be a number of ways of distinguishing behaviors that are ritualized from those that are not. But the salient feature for our purposes is that ritualized actions are never entirely reducible to a set of technical motivations. They incorporate features that do not contribute in any practical fashion to the goal of the action and are not intended to do so. In some cases rituals are composed entirely of acts for which no technical motivation is patently evident. One cannot infer from the actions or the intentions of the actor why such procedures should be performed at all. A matter of conventional stipulation, the origins of ritual scripts lie with those who came before, the details often lost in the mists of time. This state of affairs offers great scope for exegetical interpretation. Sometimes we are told the meanings of ritual procedures by acknowledged authorities. Sometimes we have no idea what the details of a ritual might mean. Only in rather unusual circumstances do we dwell at length on questions of exegesis. Low-frequency, high-arousal rituals are occasions of that kind. Since the memories of these unusual experiences endure, so does the puzzle of what it all meant. Consider the following concrete example.

In northern Greece, a community of orthodox Christians calling themselves "Anastenaria" dance on red hot coals as part of a cycle of rituals to honor various local and national saints. This moderately low frequency ritual involves predictably high levels of emotional arousal, assisted by loud music, frenetic dancing and bloody animal sacrifice. But by far the most dramatic and emotionally intense feature of the rituals is the act of walking on red hot coals. Anthropologist Dimitris Xygalatas (2007) gathered extensive statements about the meanings of various rituals in the Anastenaria. The rituals were not accorded any official or authorized meanings – indeed, the Greek Orthodox Church, which normally assumed an authoritative position in matters of doctrine and ritual exegesis, officially took a rather dim view of the tradition. As a result people felt at liberty to interpret the rituals as they pleased. Xygalatas found that the number of people capable of proffering interpretations of the rituals of the Anastenaria increased in direct ratio with the degree of emotional arousal that the rituals evoked. In relation to rituals that (although they had emotive qualities) were not associated with especially intense affective states (e.g., the use of candles or incense, commensality, the handling of icons of the saints), only relatively few people were able to explain their significance and meaning. By contrast, many more people offered interpretations of the most arousing aspects of the annual rituals – like the slaying of animals or the frenetic music and dancing. But the most striking finding concerned the terrifying ordeal of walking on coals. This part of the ritual produced by far the highest arousal levels. And on that topic, the proportion of informants offering exegetical commentaries rose dramatically. This was not because the firewalking had a widely known meaning; in fact, participants had highly varied notions of what it meant to walk on red hot coals. They seemed to be arriving at their own interpretations quite independently, via a process of 'spontaneous exegetical reflection'.

In order to understand better the psychological mechanisms that make low-frequency, high-arousal rituals more likely to trigger deep reflection on issues of ritual meaning, Whitehouse and colleagues have been conducting psychological experiments, using artificial rituals (Richert, Whitehouse and Stewart 2005). In these studies, participants are divided into low-arousal and high-arousal groups. Although the ritual procedures are never varied, participants' emotional states are manipulated by a variety of techniques, including 'high-tech' special effects. Afterward, participants are asked by trained interviewers to describe the entire ritual process and proffer any thoughts as to the possible meanings of each element of the ritual. The resulting exegetical commentaries are then coded for both volume and analogical specificity. Such experiments have repeatedly shown that in the high-arousal condition participants score significantly better on both measures.

Taking together the evidence from ethnography, historiography and psychological experiments, it would seem that the clustering of features already noted is an outcome of cultural selection. Low-frequency rituals that lack a significant emotional kick would be incapable of generating the mnemonic and exegetical effects needed to give salience to the acts involved. Low-frequency rituals that survive will be ones that evince powerful emotions and lasting and vivid memories, and thus encourage long-term rumination on esoteric puzzles of exegetical meaning. This is the essence of mystery cult. What these investigations suggest is that where low-frequency but highly arousing rituals flourish, we will also inevitably find that people reflect deeply on religious mysteries and problems of ritual exegesis, on the notion that hidden or nonobvious features of the world can be revealed, brought out into the light through slow and painstaking processes of reflection on questions of ritual meaning and purpose.

Such a picture of religious life at Çatalhöyük sits well with the archaeological evidence. Hodder has discussed elsewhere the evidence for a focus on hiding and revealing of significant symbols at Çatalhöyük (Hodder 2006). Obsidian hoards were placed beneath floors in the early part of the sequence and periodically retrieved. Paintings were made and then covered over, often then being remade and recovered. The spots on a pair of leopards were repainted in new designs 40 times in Building VIB.44 and more than 7 times in VII.44 (Mellaart 1967: 119; Todd 1976: 57). The claws of bears, the teeth of foxes and weasels, the tusks of wild boars and the beaks of vultures were placed in walls, covered over and then repeatedly covered over while being present as protuberances. Burials were reexcavated to retrieve skulls and body parts. There was a continual process of hiding and revelation.

Bucrania (plastered bull heads installed in walls of houses and on the upright posts) as well as bull horns set along benches may have provided a daily focal point for rumination on male cult rituals. The horns, claws and tusks placed in and hidden in the walls, sometimes visible only because of the swelling of plaster over them, 'presenced' the bull killing and feasting. At least in the first half of the occupation of Çatalhöyük (when the bucrania and installations are more common), the symbols of feasting and ritual power were ever present in the house, continual reminders of significant dramatic events.

Religious coalitions at Çatalhöyük

A further feature of the imagistic mode concerns social morphology, specifically the relationship between patterns of ritual frequency, emotionality and revelation, on the one hand, and the scale, structure and interaction of ritual groupings, on the other. Rare, climactic, revelatory rituals bind participants tightly together into highly cohesive groups. In part this is because the emotionality of the shared experience binds people together, a well-established principle in social psychology that requires little additional evidential support. But it is also partly a consequence of episodic recall – the fact that most people can remember exactly who else was present when the major ritual took place (Whitehouse 1992, 2004). Cohesive ritual communities forged in this way are therefore somewhat exclusive, in that one cannot easily fabricate a memory that somebody was present who was not or excise from memory the recollection of another's participation. This exclusivity and cohesiveness also promotes a somewhat egalitarian ethos among members of the in-group and, above all, a sense of loyalty in the face of danger. As such, groups formed by such means lend themselves admirably to perilous exploits where temptations to defect would otherwise be hard to resist. In many societies where the imagistic mode flourishes, this means that ritual groupings constitute military cells or raiding parties. But at Çatalhöyük, as has also been found in many other places, cohesive ritual groups were probably essential for the cooperative hunting of exceptionally dangerous wild animals. The pursuit of wild bulls and other large aggressive animals in the vicinity of Çatalhöyük would undoubtedly have been a hazardous undertaking requiring high levels of social cohesion and cooperation. Pictorial depictions of hunting suggest that upwards of 30 individuals would have been needed to capture a bull.

There are strong reasons also to connect hunting activities with mortuary practices. The finding in 2008 of a platform within Building 77 containing burials but entirely surrounded by, embraced by, protected by wild bull horns expresses the connection well (Figure 12.1). Again, this connection occurs from early on in the Neolithic. Schmidt (2006) argues that the 'temples' at Göbekli Tepe, replete with their carvings of bulls and other wild animals on monumental stone stelae, functioned as temples for the dead.

Closer examination of mortuary practices at Çatalhöyük fits well with our hypothesis that the imagistic mode fragmented the community into a multiplicity of small cohesive coalitions, each pursuing its own distinctive variants of a wider revelatory tradition. Most houses excavated to date contain no or few (up to five or six) burials beneath the floors. However, some houses seem to have acted as repositories of burials for small groups of houses. Approximately three to five houses, sometimes connected by crawl holes and the sharing of ovens and hearths, buried their dead (62 individuals in Building 1, but more commonly 20–30 individuals) preferentially in one ancestral building ('history houses', i.e., houses rebuilt on the same place four or more times that became the preferential repositories of burials and material symbols; see Chapter 7). Houses were often 'pushed and shoved' to be near these ancestral houses, and at times the houses were so packed together that the houses were very small. Sometimes they seem so small that they may have acted as symbolic 'place savers', claiming a presence close to the ancestral home. Abandonment and foundation feasts and rituals may also have taken place at this scale. There are examples of construction 'rafts' connecting pairs of houses and implying contemporary construction, and there are, especially in the lower levels of the site (up to Level VI), feasting deposits associated with founding and abandonment events. The cult of the dead also involved vultures, as seen in the wall art, and the removal of human heads from burials. These heads were themselves involved in founding houses (placed at the base of upright posts) and in abandoning them (placed in abandonment deposits). There is evidence also in the wall paintings that humans dressed up in vulture costumes, and we also have evidence of crane dance costumes (Russell and McGowan 2003). So the cult of the dead involved small corporate groups, linked by descent in houses, and a series of ritual themes and practices involving birds, dancing and the manipulation of skeletal remains.

Current evidence suggests that most burial involved the interment of wholly fleshed and tightly bound bodies. These were placed in shallow graves beneath the burial platforms in northern parts of the rooms, though neonates and very young children were often buried in the southern, oven and entrance part of the house. Later burials were added into the burial platforms, leading to the disturbance and rearranging of earlier skeletons. Skulls from earlier burials were removed from the bodies of important individuals by digging down into the graves and cutting off the partially fleshed heads using obsidian knives that left cut marks on the upper vertebrae. These skulls were often kept and, in one known case, were 'refleshed' by molding facial features in plaster and painting the plaster red. In another case, the head was left on the body but the legs and arms, including scapulae and clavicles, were carefully and neatly cut off, showing a detailed knowledge of the human corpse (Building 49). There are examples also of the skeletal form of an individual being re-created from the bones of several individuals, as well as the removal of teeth from an earlier jaw and their placement in a later grave in the same building sequence (see Chapter 7). There are also examples of secondary reburial of bodies or body parts – for example, into the 'history house' Building 1.

In many ways, the burial practices at Çatalhöyük replicate those found throughout the early Neolithic in the Middle East and in central Anatolia. And there are many practices that are common across the site, such as crouched burial within houses and with few grave goods. But at a more detailed level, there are many differences in the ways that the dead were treated in the small corporate house groups at Çatalhöyük. For example, in Space 129 in Level VII we found an utterly unusual burial. Animal bones never occur in graves at the site. But in this one grave a whole sheep with its front and back legs extended was laid out close to the body of a male. In two other cases the body was stacked with the scat from a small carnivore such as a weasel (Jenkins 2005). In another case the body was laid on its back with legs apart, and a mat and plank were placed over the body (Hodder 2006). While Mellaart claimed regularities in the platforms under which the different sexes were buried (females under the central eastern platform and males under the northeastern platform), the more recent excavations have found marked variability in the relations between age and sex and burial location. Where there are continuities these seem vertical within house clusters. Thus in the sequence of four houses, 65–56–44–10, in the same place, repeating the same foundations, there is a recurring use of the central eastern platform for burial and the burial of infants in the southwest corner of the main room (Regan 2007).

There is much evidence that there were clear memories within house clusters of the exact location and significance of the burials beneath the platform floors. Later digging down led to the precise location of earlier graves and skulls. These memories must have extended over considerable intervals. The average number of burials per house is about eight. And yet the average duration of houses is 70–100 years. Thus burial in houses may have occurred every 10 or so years. Cessford (2005) has estimated that about one-third of the population was buried off- site, and it is here that we would expect to find practices related to the scenes shown in the paintings of excarnation of headless bodies and the removal of flesh by vultures. There is no evidence of excarnation on the bodies found on the site. But in the KOPAL trench off-site we found human body parts treated in the same way as animal bones and mixed in with them and other 'refuse'. We know little about the treatment of human remains off-site, but they occurred still more rarely than those on the site.

The emergence of the doctrinal mode at Çatalhöyük

The Templeton project has focused attention on the gradual shift at Çatalhöyük toward more discursive styles of transmission in the upper levels of the site, based on evidence from stamp seals and pictorial depictions that suggest narrative interpretation. This transition also suggests that increasingly widely distributed narrative traditions may have been homogenizing across the settlement, consistent with the emergence of a doctrinal mode of religiosity. Such developments would have required relatively high frequency transmission. Imagistic practices are too low in frequency to sustain bodies of discursive religious knowledge. In order for a relatively stable corpus of cosmology, narrative and ritual exegesis to form and spread, much higher transmissive frequencies would be required.

There is a decline in the occurrence of actual bull horns and other wild animal part installations in the upper levels of the site. While some bucrania continue, these often have plaster rather than real horns. Indeed, there is much evidence that hunting declined in the upper levels of the site; there may have been fewer wild bulls present in the landscape. Rather than real bull horns and heads, small symbolic bull heads are found from Level V as handles on pottery. As already noted, the paintings of teasing and baiting scenes also occur from Level V onward, and these have a clear narrative component. They have become part of a discourse about ritual acts.

The greater discursive component of religious life in the upper levels of the site is also seen in the emergence after Level V of stamp seals. These may have been used to stamp human or animal skin, and they employ a distinct array of codified signs (Türkcan 2005). These signs are abstract but some refer to hands and perhaps to navels, while there are a few examples that indicate a leopard and a bear.

In the lower levels of the site, as already noted, obsidian is 'presenced' in hoards or caches below the floors. In the upper levels these hoards cease and obsidian becomes more bound by new specialist technologies. Pottery too becomes more complex and more specialized after Level V. It gradually becomes more decorated until, by the time of Çatalhöyük West (Chalcolithic, from 6000 BC), it is heavily decorated with complex designs. By the time of the West Mound as well, burial in houses of adults largely ends. It is presumed that burial occurs off-site and perhaps in cemeteries. Certainly the earlier fragmentation of burial practices is replaced by something larger scale and perhaps more centralized. The rituals involved in the abandoning of houses also change. Now frequently houses are burned (from Level VI onward on the Neolithic East Mound). This suggests uniform, sitewide practices.

Thus in the upper levels at the site there is less evidence of dramatic and rare imagistic events and more evidence of higher-frequency, low-intensity and discursively elaborated rituals. How can we account for the emergence of increasingly routinized religious life at the site – its dispersal into daily codes and practices, in contrast to the presencing of powerful indices of dramatic events seen in the earlier levels?

One hypothesis is that the doctrinal mode emerges from within the interstices of the imagistic mode. We have seen that the presencing of trophies of dramatic and dangerous events was a key component of the imagistic mode at Çatalhöyük. Brought into and installed in the house, the hard and dangerous parts of wild animals and birds were continually present, able to be ruminated upon, the power of the event continually felt and referred to and lived with. These active symbols were continually reawakened by replasterings and sometimes repaintings (such as the continual repainting of designs on the bucrania in Mellaart's Shrine EVI.8; Mellaart 1963). The walls of the houses at Çatalhöyük were replastered every season and perhaps every month in a new white marl slurry, carefully prepared and applied. There was, then, something highly repetitive and routinized even within this imagistic religious mode.

Indeed, the repetition and routinization were themselves central components in the building of histories within long-term buildings – those we have dubbed 'history houses'. The latter houses become dominant in the lower levels of the site in the sense that they have more burials and are to some degree more elaborate in terms of architectural fittings (Düring 2001). The history houses are distinguished by the amassing and passing down of trophies and ritual symbols. But they are also distinguished by the careful repetition of house practices, the internal arrangements of the house and the multiple layers of plasters on the floors and walls. They do indeed distinguish themselves in terms of amassing and creating histories.

It seems possible that the elders, ritual leaders, 'shamans' associated with the history houses increasingly developed doctrinal strategies by building discursive forms of knowledge out of the preexisting forms. Rather than the largely embodied practices in the lower part of the site, discursive modes could be built in the upper levels. It is possible that the increasingly discursive religious practices of the doctrinal mode exploited and extended ideas originating in the imagistic cult complexes, the latter periodically invigorating and underscoring them.

A simple contributing impulse would have been the 'hunting out' of wild cattle that we seem to see in the upper part of the site. By the time of the West Mound, domesticated cattle are in use. It is likely that other wild animals (leopards, boars, etc.) were less present in the landscape than before and were thus less available for celebrating and presencing the imagistic mode. At the same time, in the upper part of the site, centralizing tendencies are increasingly present in pottery and obsidian production, and in the emergence of large houses based on integrated and more intensive production of domesticated plants and animals. This social transformation seems to have been associated with the transformation of history houses into large complex centers of production, greater specialization and the development of more doctrinal modes.

Conclusions

This chapter has sought to reconstruct certain features of religious life at
Çatalhöyük based on a combination of generalizable theory and the interpretations that we and others have made of the archaeological evidence.
Others have taken on comparable tasks (e.g., Lewis-Williams and Pearce
2005), and always the danger is that the interpretations will become
'infected' with the cross-cultural model such that Çatalhöyük gets forced
into an interpretive scheme when other interpretations remain possible.
Archaeological data are often underdetermined, and despite the richness
of our evidence from the site, the interpretation of religion at Çatalhöyük
remains open to revision and reinterpretation. Have we, in this chapter,
avoided the temptation to force a complex cross-cultural scheme on the
data?

We concur with Mithen (2004) that the clearest evidence from
Çatalhöyük concerns low-frequency rituals that would have had high-
arousal components. There seems little doubt that socialized and ritualized interactions with large and dangerous animals, and concomitant
feasting, would have occurred relatively infrequently and would have
been high-arousal events. Other aspects of the Çatalhöyük data can be
interpreted as conforming to the expectations of the imagistic mode
summarized in Table 5.1. For example, as the hard, pointed parts of
the animals killed in hunting or teasing and baiting were brought into
individual houses, there must have been much variation in the specific
interpretations that were made. Thus there must have been multivocality
and multivalence, as is indicated by the great diversity of specific interactions with the bucrania and other animal body parts in individual houses.
For example, usually the benches with bull horns occur on the east side
of main rooms in houses, but in Building 52 a bench with bull horns
occurs on the west side.

It also seems likely that, according to the imagistic mode expectations,
Çatalhöyük society was relatively decentralized, although in Chapter 7,
Hodder and Pels argue for some social differentiation between history
houses and other houses, and the possible role of a 'trickster' figure is discussed by Hodder and Meskell in Chapter 2. But it is perhaps the burial
practices that offer the greatest interpretive challenge. These have imagistic components in that death and burial, at least of adults, were relatively
infrequent, and they presumably involved emotions of bereavement and

interactions with dead and decaying bodies that can be interpreted as high arousal. But we also need to proceed cautiously in drawing inferences of this kind. It is possible that the inhabitants at Çatalhöyük rejoiced in their proximity to the dead, content to dwell in their remains and odors and to touch and handle the skin and bones. Given that, for example, the skulls of the dead were present in daily life, funerary and body disarticulation ceremonies need not have been highly arousing events. So although we may be able to show that low-frequency features of ritualized behavior invariably entail moments of comparatively high peak arousal (against a baseline of more frequent rituals), at least on the evidence of contemporary and historically documented cases worldwide, we may never be able to specify in detail how those moments were constructed and experienced by the people living at Çatalhöyük.

Another set of challenges surrounds the diversity of cult practices and exegetical traditions at Çatalhöyük and beyond. The imagistic mode anticipates localized cults, based on patterns of following by example, in contrast to the large scale and uniformity of traditions typical of the doctrinal mode. It is certainly the case that symbolic and ritual differences between houses can be discerned at Çatalhöyük. It is also the case that on a regional scale there are many specific differences between sites and regions, also supporting our view of a religious landscape richly fragmented into myriad local traditions. But much as Whitehouse discovered in his surveys of imagistic initiation cults and millenarian movements in Papua New Guinea (1995, 2000), we also find remarkable continuities over huge areas from what is now central Turkey into northern Syria and even into the southern Levant, for instance with regard to the importance of human head removal, the plastering of human heads, the role of vultures in death rituals and the centrality of dangerous wild animals (as Hodder and Meskell note in Chapter 2). In other words, certain broadly similar patterns of behavior can replicate widely and endure for very long periods of time even while they sustain a great profusion of localized variants in the details of ritual practice and exegetical interpretation. In the absence of a fuller understanding of these variable features, it may prove difficult to discriminate between evidence of wide diffusion of ancient patterns associated with imagistic dynamics versus evidence of truly standardized doctrinal creeds. What we think justifies our proposals regarding the emergence of the doctrinal mode at Çatalhöyük, however, is evidence not merely of *recurring themes* in the construction of acts and artifacts at the site but, more tellingly, we venture, of the increasingly *discursive* deployment of those themes in standardized ways and the emergence of *authoritative* versions.

The emergence of doctrinal mode dynamics constitutes a major milestone in the evolution of social formations, paving the way for more centralized, large-scale and hierarchical patterns of political association. In the most general terms, the shifts toward the doctrinal mode of religiosity in the upper parts of the Çatalhöyük East sequence occur through the 7th millennium BC and the formation of the West Mound at Çatalhöyük with its more fully doctrinal mode occurs at 6000 BC. These developments thus occur at about the same time as the shift to the Pottery Neolithic in the Levant and the emergence of the elaborate decorated pottery of Hassuna in Mesopotamia. The latter is followed by the Samarran and Halafian styles in Mesopotamia that lead into Ubaid and Uruk and the emergence of Sumer in the 3rd millennium BC. It is difficult to argue for simple continuities across these huge areas and times, and indeed many would argue for radical breaks – for example, after the Pre-Pottery Neolithic in the Levant. But there is much to be said for arguing that some elements of the doctrinal mode that has emerged by around 6000 BC do indeed presage the more complex centralized political systems of Mesopotamia.

The shift to the doctrinal mode, among other changes in social and economic realms, seems to have been an important factor in setting the stage for the complex centralized societies of the Middle East. Much social theory assumes that the great transition is rooted in changing technology and modes of production. For instance, deterministic theories of literacy have been repeatedly used to account for the emergence of the doctrinal mode (e.g., Goody 2004; Boyer 2005). Theories inspired by Marxist traditions and cultural materialism have meanwhile in various guises emphasized the role of forces and relations of production in shaping early state formation. The account presented here suggests a rather different view: that it is the relationship between divergent modalities and frequencies of ritual transmission that provides the impetus for increasingly complex social morphology.

REFERENCES

Barth, F. 1987. *Cosmologies in the Making: A Generative Approach to Cultural Variation in Inner New Guinea*. Cambridge: Cambridge University Press.

Beck, R. 2004. Four men, two sticks, and a whip: Image and doctrine in a Mithraic ritual. In *Theorizing Religions Past: Historical and Archaeological Perspectives*, eds. H. Whitehouse and L. H. Martin. Walnut Creek, Calif.: AltaMira Press, 87–103.

Boyer, P. 2005. A reductionistic model of distinct modes of religious transmission. In *Mind and Religion: Psychological and Cognitive Foundations of Religiosity*, eds. H. Whitehouse and R. N. McCauley. Walnut Creek, Calif.: AltaMira Press, 3–29.

Cessford, C. 2005. Estimating the Neolithic population of Çatalhöyük. In *Inhabiting Çatalhöyük: Reports from the 1995–1999 Seasons*, ed. I Hodder. Cambridge: McDonald Institute for Archaeological Research / British Institute of Archaeology at Ankara Monograph.

Clark, A. L. 2004. Testing the two modes theory: Christian practice in the later Middle Ages. In *Theorizing Religions Past: Historical and Archaeological Perspectives*, eds. H. Whitehouse and L. H. Martin. Walnut Creek, Calif.: AltaMira Press, 125–42.

Conway, M. A. 1995. *Flashbulb Memories*. Hillsdale, N.J.: Erlbaum Associates.

Düring, B. 2001. Social dimensions in the architecture of Neolithic Çatalhöyük. *Anatolian Studies*, 51, 1–18.

Goody, J. 2004. Is image to doctrine as speech to writing? Modes of communication and the origins of religion. In *Ritual and Memory: Towards a New Comparative Anthropology of Religion*, eds. H. Whitehouse and J. Laidlaw. Walnut Creek, Calif.: AltaMira Press, 49–64.

Hodder, I. 2006. *Çatalhöyük: The Leopard's Tale*. London: Thames & Hudson.

Højbjerg, C. 2004. Universalistic orientations of an imagistic mode of religiosity: The case of the West African Poro Cult. In *Ritual and Memory: Towards a New Comparative Anthropology of Religion*, eds. H. Whitehouse and J. Laidlaw. Walnut Creek, Calif.: AltaMira Press, 173–85.

Jenkins, E. 2005. The Çatalhöyük microfauna: Preliminary results and interpretations. In *Inhabiting Çatalhöyük: Reports from the 1995–1999 Seasons*, ed. I. Hodder. Cambridge: McDonald Institute for Archaeological Research / British Institute of Archaeology at Ankara Monograph.

Johnson, K. 2004. Primary emergence of the doctrinal mode of religiosity in prehistoric southwestern Iran. In *Theorizing Religions Past: Historical and Archaeological Perspectives*, eds. H. Whitehouse and L. H. Martin. Walnut Creek, Calif.: AltaMira Press, 45–66.

Leopold, M. A. 2004. Syncretism and the interaction of modes of religiosity: A formative perspective on Gnostic-Christian movements in late Antiquity. In *Theorizing Religions Past: Historical and Archaeological Perspectives*, eds. H. Whitehouse and L. H. Martin. Walnut Creek, Calif.: AltaMira Press, 105–21.

Lewis, G. 1980. *Day of Shining Red: An Essay on Understanding Ritual*. Cambridge: Cambridge University Press.

Lewis-Williams, D., and Pearce, D. 2005. *Inside the Neolithic Mind: Consciousness, Cosmos, and the Realm of the Gods*. London: Thames and Hudson.

Martin, Luther H. 2004. Toward a scientific history of religions. In *Theorizing Religions Past: Historical and Archaeological Perspectives*, eds. H. Whitehouse and L. H. Martin. Walnut Creek, Calif.: AltaMira Press, 7–14.

Mellaart, J. 1963. Excavations at Çatal Hüyük 1962: Second preliminary report. *Anatolian Studies*, 13, 43–103.

Mellaart, J. 1966. Excavations at Çatal Hüyük, 1965: Fourth preliminary report. *Anatolian Studies*, 16, 165–91.

Mellaart, J. 1967. *Çatal Hüyük: A Neolithic Town in Anatolia*. London: Thames and Hudson.

Mithen, S. 2004. From Ohalo to Çatalhöyük: The development of religiosity during the early prehistory of Western Asia, 20,000–7000 BC. In *Theorizing Religions Past: Historical and Archaeological Perspectives*, eds. H. Whitehouse and L. H. Martin. Walnut Creek, Calif.: AltaMira Press, 17–43.

Regan, R. 2007. Building 65 sequence. *Çatalhöyük Research Project Archive Report 2007*, 100–12 (http://www.catalhoyuk.com/downloads/Archive_Report_2007.pdf).

Richert, R. A., Whitehouse, H., and Stewart, E. 2005. Memory and analogical thinking in high-arousal rituals. In *Mind and Religion: Psychological and Cognitive Foundations of Religiosity*, eds. H. Whitehouse and R. N. McCauley. Walnut Creek, Calif.: AltaMira Press, 127–45.

Russell, N., and McGowan, K. J. 2003. Dance of the cranes: Crane symbolism at Çatalhöyük and beyond. *Antiquity*, 77, 445–55.

Schmidt, K. 2006. *Sie bauten die ersten Tempel: Das rätselhafte Heiligtum der Steinzeitjäger: Die archäologische Entdeckung am Göbekli Tepe*. Munich: C. H. Beck.

Todd, I. 1976. *Çatal Hüyük in Perspective*. Menlo Park, Calif.: Cummins.

Tulving, E. 1972. Episodic and semantic memory. In *Organization of Memory*, eds. E. Tulving and W. Donaldson. New York: Academic Press, 381–403.

Türkcan, A. 2005. Some remarks on Çatalhöyük stamp seals. In *Changing Materialities at Çatalhöyük: Reports from the 1995–1999 Seasons*, ed. I. Hodder. Cambridge: McDonald Institute for Archaeological Research / British Institute of Archaeology at Ankara Monograph.

Verswijver, G. 1992. *The Club-Fighters of the Amazon: Warfare among the Kaiapo Indians of Central Brazil*. Gent: Rijksuniversiteit te Gent.

Whitehouse, H. 1992. Memorable religions: Transmission, codification, and change in divergent Melanesian contexts. *Man* (N.S.), 27, 777–97.

Whitehouse, H. 1995. *Inside the Cult: Religious Innovation and Transmission in Papua New Guinea*. Oxford: Oxford University Press.

Whitehouse, H. 1996. Rites of terror: Emotion, metaphor, and memory in Melanesian initiation cults. *Journal of the Royal Anthropological Institute* (N.S.), 2(4), 703–15.

Whitehouse, H. 2000. *Arguments and Icons: Divergent Modes of Religiosity.* Oxford: Oxford University Press.

Whitehouse, H. 2004. *Modes of Religiosity: A Cognitive Theory of Religious Transmission.* Walnut Creek, Calif.: AltaMira Press.

Whitehouse, H., and Laidlaw, J., eds. 2004. *Ritual and Memory: Toward a Comparative Anthropology of Religion.* Walnut Creek, Calif.: AltaMira Press.

Whitehouse, H., and Martin, L. H., eds. 2004. *Theorizing Religions Past: Historical and Archaeological Perspectives on Modes of Religiosity.* Walnut Creek, Calif.: AltaMira Press.

Whitehouse, H., and Martin, L. H. eds. 2005. History, Memory, and Cognition. *Special issue of Historical Reflections / Reflexions Historiques,* 31(2).

Winograd, E., and Killinger, W. A. 1983. Relating age at encoding in early childhood to adult recall: Development of flashbulb memories. *Journal of Experimental Psychology: General,* 112, 413–22.

Xygalatas, D. 2007. Forthcoming. *The Burning Saints: Emotion and Motivation in the Fire-walking Rituals of the Anastenaria,* London: Equinox.

Xygalatas, D. 2008. Firewalking and the brain: The physiology of high-arousal rituals. In *Evolution of Religion: Studies, Theories, and Critiques,* eds. J. Bulbulia, R. Sosis, E. Harris, R. Genet, C. Genet and K. Wyman. Santa Margarita, Calif.: Collins Foundation Press, 189–95.

6

Is there religion at Çatalhöyük...
or are there just houses?

Maurice Bloch

A cautious introduction

On what expertise can a social anthropologist draw that might be useful for the interpretation of an archaeological site such as Çatalhöyük? When facing that question, the anthropologist must accept the uncomfortable fact that he or she has probably much less relevant expertise than the professionals already working, either directly or indirectly, at the site. Not only do they use wonderful techniques in order to obtain data from the remains they uncover, they have also been trained in interpreting their findings with a good deal of theoretical sophistication, which is the fruit of the history of their discipline. Furthermore, they dispose of much more expert general knowledge about the geographical and historical context. They therefore know best how to squeeze interpretation from their material. The social anthropologist coming into such a project will, simply because he or she is innocent of the history of archaeology, run the risk of appearing a blundering, ignorant amateur who, as amateurs often do, simply repeats the mistakes of the past that the discipline has subsequently and painfully learned to avoid. Thus, is not a social anthropologist, let loose on a 21st-century archaeological site, likely to simply prove to be a 19th-century archaeologist in matters of interpretation? The risk is great. The amateur's temptation to attribute fanciful meaning to this or that aspect of the findings on the basis of undisciplined analogies is evident. Characteristic of such mistakes is the assumption that features, or objects, that look vaguely the same as those used by contemporaries must have had similar associations in the past.

In order to avoid the worst pitfalls of this sort of jaunt in another discipline, a severe self-examination on the part of the anthropologist seems therefore necessary. He or she must ask: What might I bring to the process of interpretation that others cannot do better? In what way can I avoid incompetent or misleading attributions of meaning? The answers must come from what the anthropologist can pretend to know better than the archaeologists. In my case I have tentatively two things to offer. First, a theoretical approach that I consider might be helpful even though it is not widely shared and, second, detailed knowledge of a couple of contemporary societies and cultures in Madagascar.

The relevance of this ethnographic knowledge is, however, far from obvious. After all, these locations in Madagascar are obviously very remote in time and place from early Neolithic Çatalhöyük. What is the relevance of my studies of the Zafimaniry, for example, the small forest Malagasy group I have studied for almost 40 years, to the central Anatolia of 10,000 years ago?

There was a time in the history of the social sciences when the answer to such a question would have been easy. It would have run something like this: The people of Madagascar have a simple type of technology that can be equated with that of the inhabitants of prehistoric Çatalhöyük, and so it is a fair guess that many ideas, values and practices would be shared by both places. This would mean that I could then project what I know of the Zafimaniry onto Çatalhöyük. The fallacy of such reasoning is by now familiar. Necessary, or even probable, linkages between technology and such things as religious and kinship systems have proved illusory because of the complexity of human history, itself the product of the cognitive character of our species. Moreover, while the people of Çatalhöyük are quite probably my genetic and cultural ancestors, as they are ancestors of the majority of humankind, the forest people of Madagascar are not in any way the remote ancestors of anybody. Their history and the changes it has brought are just as long as that of any other contemporary. Much more likely, indeed most probably, the people of Madagascar are, like us, partly the cultural and genetic *descendants* of the people who lived in central Anatolia in the early Neolithic. Thus, any direct analogies between the Zafimaniry and Çatalhöyük on the basis of mere unanalyzed resemblances of this or that trait should be treated as merely a superficial anecdote.

There is, however, a little ray of hope for thinking that a person such as myself might be of more help than any random body on the Clapham omnibus. If I propose that what I know in Madagascar suggests what may have also been true in Çatalhöyük, this must be not only because elements of what we find in Çatalhöyük are reminiscent of elements I find in Madagascar, but also because in Madagascar these elements are part of a pattern for which it can be argued that the different parts of the pattern imply each other for general reasons. Furthermore, it is necessary to explain why this pattern will recur in unrelated places and times. These explanations must inevitably depend on the proposition of chains of causation that ultimately go back to general characteristics of our species. This is a tall order, but only if such causation can be proposed can my suggestions that not directly documented aspects of Çatalhöyük have certain significance have any legitimacy. The recognition of similarities *must* be accompanied by theoretical arguments that explain why one thing is reasonably likely to imply another for reasons that go beyond and do not depend on any specific cultural formulation. This is what this chapter will attempt to do.

An implication of this approach is that I shall take into account only those findings from Çatalhöyük that are part of recurring patterns and that therefore suggest necessary connections among elements. A rather lamentable effect of this method is that I shall have to ignore nearly all of the exciting finds that have made the site famous, and this in spite of the feverish stimulation they produce in me, as in everybody else. I shall have nothing to say of the lady (if she is a lady) surrounded by the figures of the two leopards, or about the plastered skull, or the more bizarre headless burials, the leopard's claw and so on. I shall have hardly anything to say, in print at least, about the too easily thought provoking murals. The reason is that all these things are one-off instances that can, therefore, not be associated systematically with other elements, while it is the *pattern* of association that makes ethnographic analogies potentially relevant. Instead, I shall concentrate on those aspects of Çatalhöyük houses that occur again and again, since it is only the pattern of recurrences that can with any degree of assurance be linked to general reasons that might explain how and why such a pattern might be caused.

Çatalhöyük houses

One thing about Çatalhöyük is clear. For most of the period of occupation, this was a place where houses mattered. Houses mattered in ways that went well beyond their practical functions. The careful orientation of the different parts and the elaborate wall decorations show that these were no casual edifices.

Furthermore, a specific aspect of these houses is emphasized. There seems good evidence that the continuity of the house was a major value. The period of occupation of houses in Çatalhöyük varies, but many were lived in for periods of up to a hundred years. Such long occupation implies continual maintenance, and this is very evident in many of the houses excavated at the site. What is striking is the emphasis on a type of maintenance that must have been intended to keep the house the same through time. The continual replastering that in the end forms such a thick covering illustrates this and shows, at the same time, the irony of the situation. This apparent stability was achieved, as is the case for life in general, through incessant movement. I assume the replastering was intended to maintain, and indeed achieved the maintenance of, the original whiteness that would be rapidly threatened by the soot from the fires. This "restorative" aspect went much further when decorations such as painting and molding that would be obscured by the new layers were carefully reproduced onto the new surfaces. The investment in this activity would be heavy, and the aesthetic value of such an activity would have been inseparable from the ethical.

As equally significant as the maintenance of the state of decoration, the internal organization and layout of Çatalhöyük houses is unchanging and is restored when damaged. This means that the various activities that occurred in the space, probably the most important time-consuming activities of life, were made to appear as repetitions of the same activity since they occurred in the same, identically constructed, place a stability that must have so framed activities that these had to have been performed in largely the same way as is suggested by the skeletal modifications of the inhabitants. This immobile–mobile repetition implies not only a static aspect to the perception of the passage of time but, in the case of long-lived houses, a concept of replacement of persons. The woman crouching by the fire would not always be the same individual, but these different persons would be in the same place doing the same things with the same movements. This stability of roles would not be merely framed by the house but would actually be imposed on the inhabitants by its recurrent maintained structure. Thus, it is in the house rather than in the body of the living that the longer-term continuity of the society would reside.

What suggests most strongly the emphasis on continuity is the way house replacement occurred on similar sites. It is clear that houses were occasionally destroyed so that a new house could be built on the same site, but making the new house a replacement for the old created an aspect of immobility. Repetition was obviously of great significance, as is shown by the fact that posts would be placed in the same location, as would all the practical and decorative features, which would either be transferred or reproduced. The destruction of houses through intentional collapsing or fire would thus be a matter of continuity rather than ending.

Finally, what emphasizes the significance of houses and their continuity is not only the elaboration and longevity of houses but the absence of any other competing focus. It is as though the meaning given to social life was all there in the houses. There are no symbolical meeting places for large communities, no great houses that could be palaces, courtrooms or meetinghouses. There are houses and that's it. Thus, the prominence of houses, their continuity and their contiguity suggest a pattern that implies, on the basis of our present knowledge, what the whole of Çatalhöyük would be like.

Zafimaniry houses

The kind of emphasis on houses and their continuity, which the findings in Çatalhöyük suggest, is, for the social anthropologist, reminiscent of many of the aspects that have recently led to the proposal that there objectively exists a class of societies that have been labeled "house based." Indeed, the existence of such societies and what we know about them has inevitably influenced even the cautious guesses I have outlined in the preceding section. Asking whether this is a risky procedure and how it might be justified is the main purpose of this chapter. However, before considering the matter more theoretically and in order to explain to the reader the temptation of seeing Çatalhöyük as a "house-based" society, I shall outline those points that are most suggestive by describing very briefly the situation among the Zafimaniry (for more detail see Bloch 1995).

Among the Zafimaniry it is also evident that houses matter, if only because they are strikingly solid, elaborate and decorated in a part of the world where houses of most other groups are flimsy, temporary and plain. The sturdiness of Zafimaniry houses and their decorative motifs have led the carving skills of the group, originally intended for the decoration of posts, walls and windows, to be recently recognized by UNESCO as of World Heritage significance. These carvings are a celebration of the lasting hardness of the wood of which the houses are made. The emphasis on continuity is everywhere. Zafimaniry houses and their contents are oriented and therefore repeat the pattern of activities that take place within them. This is standard in rural Madagascar, but the emphasis on fixed spatial organization is far more elaborated and celebrated there than anywhere else on the island. The maintenance and beautifying of the house are the most important kinship duties of the relatives of the householders. No greater offense to morality exists than to harm an important house (Bloch 1996).

Finally the symbolical dominance of the house over any other possible symbolical foci is clear. There are meeting places in some Zafimaniry villages but these are hardly noticeable, in sharp contrast to what is the case for neighboring groups. Most remarkable in the Malagasy context of related groups such as the Betsileo and the Merina, the Zafimaniry are little concerned with tombs that are famously the symbolical and aesthetic focus of the social of the other people.

In these general linked aspects the Çatalhöyük and Zafimaniry situations are similar, but inevitably there are further aspects that we can know in the Malagasy case and only guess at in the Anatolian one. The permanency of houses is foremost in both cases and therefore contrasts with the transformability and replaceability of people. In the Zafimaniry case it is thus not surprising that the house, instead of the tomb, is the place where one communicates with ancestors, ancestors who are thought of not simply as progenitors but, in an equally important way, as previous householders. Perhaps the relation of the inhabitants of Çatalhöyük to the dead buried under parts of the floor in their houses implied the same sort of connection we find in Madagascar. We shall never know, but such a situation is found, for example, in another house-based society: Tikopia, thoroughly studied by Firth. Here an area of the house was used to bury the dead under the floor, and succession was more a matter of a link between present inhabitants of the house with that of previous householders buried under the floor than simply a matter of kinship filiation (Firth 1936: 76).

Another aspect of Zafimaniry houses is thought provoking for Çatalhöyük. Zafimaniry houses are, above all, places where couples exist.

They are places where masculinity and femininity come together fruit-fully. This is true of gendered activities and of the material side of these activities. Thus, the Zafimaniry stress how a house brings together the hearth and the tools of the hearth associated with the creative, procreative and transformative contribution of women and the house post associated with the creative, procreative and nurturing contribution of men. This coming together in a joint enterprise is often rhetorically illustrated by the combination of the supports of the roof from either side of the main beam that require each other to hold up the single structure that covers the house.[1] These are elaborate ideas that are most unlikely to have existed in the same form in Anatolia, but it seems clear that the Çatalhöyük house was also a locus of the coming together of a variety of creative and transformative activities that were probably gendered.

Toward theory: House-based societies

These two very brief sketches, which can easily be complemented with the existing publications on both places, may have convinced the reader of the possibility of a recurrence of a simple basic pattern. In any case it is the recurrence of this pattern in a number of places that has led to the development of the middle-level theory of "house-based societies."

The idea of house-based societies, *sociétés à maisons*, gained its modern form in the work of Claude Lévi-Strauss (1979). Lévi-Strauss's idea can be understood only within his vast and somewhat personal theory of social evolution. For Lévi-Strauss the way ancient peoples represented to themselves the process of human life and its differentiation from that of nonhumans was focused on the need for exchange that the people of these early societies imposed on themselves. Above all it was the exchange of spouses, made necessary by the existence of the incest taboo; that was the key to early human society. In these systems symbolical social reproduction thus occurred in the space *between* exchanging groups. Then, in an unspecified period, which it can reasonably be claimed to have been intended in the work of the French anthropologist to be the early Neolithic, a shift occurred. Instead of the locus of symbolic reproduction being created by the maintenance of lasting distance of

---

[1] These supports on one side must be even numbered, as even numbers are associated with males and odd numbers on the other side are associated with females.

nonetheless exchanging groups, it migrated to the achieved union where the exchange created something new. The focus became the completed unit reproducing as a result of successful conjunction. This new creation, inevitably of a woman and a man, became in many cases instantiated in a material form: the house. This material form then took over the continuity of society from the abstract concept of repetitive exchange that had characterized what he had called "elementary structures." In this new form, reproduction is caused by conjunction *within* a totalizing building. As is typical of the work of Lévi-Strauss, we are not quite sure what we are dealing with. Is he talking of history or of the logical possibilities of systems? How does the theory relate to specific cases? This is a particularly thorny question, since the ethnography he cites in support has struck the specialists as very oddly interpreted. Yet, as is again so often the case in the work of Lévi-Strauss, in spite of these obscurities the theory has turned out to be fruitful and illuminating in a number of unexpected ways. First, the theory simply made anthropologists focus on the importance of the house itself. Second, it encouraged scholars to concentrate on the nature of the connection between material culture and social organization. Third, it encouraged high-level theoretical reflection about what had previously been considered mundane activities such as cooking, cleaning, sleeping and house building, as well as in a number of other ways.

The Lévi-Strauss scenario is a "just so story" for which there is very little evidence, but it has struck many chords among anthropologists who have studied societies where houses seem to be the foci of the symbolic reproduction of life and where the very materiality of the building becomes an aspect of social reproduction. Before Lévi-Strauss's work on house-based societies, there had been many studies of places where the architecture of houses seemed to express the core value of people (e.g., Cunningham 1964). However, it was as a result of the inspiration of his writing that in 1990 a group of anthropologists got together to pool their specific knowledge of a number of highly varied places in order to explore what reality might be given to Lévi-Strauss's speculations. The meeting led to the book *About the House* (Carsten and Hugh-Jones 1995). This book brings together a variety of cases, including that of the Zafimaniry, occurring in very different parts of the world. These cases loosely link up one with another through certain themes, many of which had been predicted by Lévi-Strauss. It thus became possible to argue for the existence of a phenomenon that transcends the specificity of locality and time: "house-based societies."

The common themes that recur in the various examples examined in the Carsten and Hugh-Jones book have already been touched on in the discussion of the Zafimaniry houses. These seem also to be applicable to Çatalhöyük because they are entailed by the simple fact of houses being the main, or the only, focus of the representation of social continuity.

Houses are places where a range of activities take place. They are adapted so that these activities occur in certain dedicated parts, which is inevitably the case for activities such as cooking. This being so, a temporal dialectic is established between the actions and the place for them. This is because, although cooking occurs only some of the time, although who cooks and what is cooked will vary, the hearth remains in time the material abstracted and stabilized location of cooking irrespective of circumstances. The material hearth can thus be said to be similar to an abstract "concept" in the way that the concept indicated by the word "cat" is an abstract concept with a complex relation to the multitude of specific animals existing at an infinity of specific times, to which it can legitimately refer. The hearth can thus be said to be a kind of concept for indicating the actual activities and the social relations that make these activities possible.

It is this simple connection between the reality of cooking events and the "hearth" concept that explains its meaning. Such a relation is much more powerfully determinant than would be conveyed by the idea of "symbolic meaning," which always implies an arbitrary signifier–signified relation, as in the old, and very misleading, semiotic model. Further elaborations may be built up on the "concept" base of the hearth, but these will always depend on the fact that the concept depends on the reality that cooking is done there, although concept and activity are phenomena of a radically different order. The hearth is a concept but it is a motivated concept and this applies in a similar way to the concept "house" itself. In the case of the hearth any further accretion of meaning will always be partially determined by the human-wide activity of cooking, by the physical characteristics of fire, by the chemical transformation of matter exposed to heat and so on. This is why it makes sense to talk of "house-based societies" as a natural category; it is why there are such recurrences in the significance given to houses, although every case of the concept will have unique aspects, and why, therefore, it is not unreasonably rash to make a guess at what was going on in Çatalhöyük. It is also why the association of the word "symbol" as commonly used in the social sciences is so misleading because it suggests a lack of motivation.

The situation with cooking applies to other aspects of houses in house-based societies. Houses in most house-based societies not only are places where cooking and eating take place but are usually, though not universally, places where couples are established and reproduce, and this becomes again and again an essential part of what they are about. Again and again parts of the house are seen as female and others as male. However, in these types of societies it is the *conjunction* that matters and thus the house becomes the core of social reproduction. This is what Lévi-Strauss meant when he contrasted "house-based societies" with those societies where it is the exchange between descent groups that has this function. However, as with cooking, the fertile conjunction of male and female that the house "houses" has a motivated relation to the actual processes of reproduction. By its very materiality the house stabilizes, and to a certain extent transcends, its very temporality. Concepts are now understood to have at their core related theories about the world. This is true of houses in house-based societies, and a key theory of the concept "house" in house-based societies, also motivated, is the "theory" of social continuity (see Medin and Wattenmaker 1987). The motivation of the "concept" makes possible a situation, such as that among the Zafimaniry, where the houses of forebears and their continuing beauty indicate the promise of the continuing fertility of the offspring and the offspring of offspring, and so on, long after the originators' death.

One can go even further. Houses in "house-based societies" are usually situated inside groups of houses. These groupings of houses must, if the "concept" of houses is charged in this way, create derived "concepts" that can indicate a wider social system based on locality and contiguity but whose conceptual core, nonetheless, remains houses.

The work of Lévi-Strauss and the Carsten Hugh-Jones collection therefore suggest a recurrent pattern, which, given the indications that have been unearthed, might well have occurred in Çatalhöyük. This, however, is so only because the notion of house-based societies can be grounded in things about the world and about our species that motivate the meanings houses can be given. This motivation is what makes it probable that the historical path that has led to the specific formulations we find in different places and different times will have been taken, again and again, in the history of humankind without necessarily any kind of contact between the cases.

Such a conclusion therefore gives me a little hope that my contribution, as a social anthropologist, to the understanding of what might have gone on in Çatalhöyük is a little bit more informed than that of someone who believes that what has been found there is the result of the influence of little green men from Mars. There is, however, another element that underpins the all-important motivation of the form "house-based societies" that applies to the great majority of human societies and that, although much more general, explains why human societies might be tempted to take paths *of the sort* of which house-based societies are one, and only one, example.

Why humans might be tempted to create, again and again, house-based societies

In order to go to this much more general level it is necessary to focus on a characteristic of human societies – that they are built on representations of their continuity in time that transcend the moment. Such a representation is to a certain extent counterintuitive in that the empirical appearance of human beings and their interaction is continual movement, incessant change and modification. The representation of the social as permanent therefore requires a cognitive feat of imagination. It is the need for a foundation of some sort for this feat of imagination that leads to the appropriateness of houses as concepts on which a particular take on the social – the transcendental – can be built.

In what follows I summarize what was already merely a programmatic article written in 2008 (Bloch 2008). Many aspects of the social organization of animals closely related to our species such as the chimpanzees or bonobos are reminiscent of humans. In all three species there is continual politicking and competition for power, rank and alliance. This side of things I call the transactional. However, there is also, at least, one fundamental difference between nonhumans and us. Humans phenomenologically create what have been called roles and corporate groups. These, in some way, have an existence that transcends the people who are endowed with these roles or who belong to these groups. What I mean by "transcend" here is that these roles and groups seem to exist independently of people and on a very different timescale (Gluckman 1962). A role such as that of a king, for example, is famously separate from the holder, and this is made evident by the fact that one can become a king by being given certain material paraphernalia that are said to "embody" the kingship – that is, such things as specters, stools and crowns. Corporate groups, such as clans or nations, similarly seem to have a life of their own, of which temples or origin sites are an indication. Thus, although they may involve many people, they are often said to be one body. They survive irrespective of the birth, death or other transformations of the members. These aspects of the social can be said to be transcendental in that they seem to negate the empirical flux of life.

Because the transcendental social implies a "life" beyond that of people, it involves a complex game with time. People are in a continual sate of flux, as are the relations that exist between them; this is the transactional phenomenology of the everyday. The transcendental social, however, appears to possess great stability. This is true of roles that in extreme cases can ideally be passed on unchanged from person to person. Groups can appear to have extraordinary continuity, so that it is possible for members of a clan to say such things as "We came to this country three hundred years ago" even though it is obvious that this is in no way true of the speaker or those being addressed or the other living referees of the word "we." Furthermore, roles and corporate groups link up to form apparent patterns, which some earlier anthropologists called, somewhat misleadingly, "social structure." This largely invisible transcendental social, separate from people and the strategies of their lives, is something quite absent from the social of animals other than humans.

An obvious question about this transcendental imagination is how it is that it can be given phenomenological reality. Probably the most important mechanism for doing this is ritual. It is, of course, one of the most widely recognized facts about rituals, such as initiation rituals, that they "create" roles or memberships of corporate group. The theory of rites of passage has always stressed this. One "becomes" a member of Christendom through baptism, or one "becomes" a knight through the ritual placing of the sword.

Another familiar point about such rituals is that they require, in their initial stages at least, a removal of the individual from the ordinary world of continual modification and transaction toward the transcendental world of roles and corporate group membership with its apparent fixity and stability. Thus, initiation rituals first separate people from the mundane world, as Van Gennep and Turner stressed.

It is worth noting why ritual in general removes from the everyday. Human interaction of a normal sort, as in the case of language, depends on the mutual reading and adjustment of intentionalities (Grice 1982; Sperber 1986). It is our continually modified and adjusted understanding of others that governs our interpretation of their actions or of their words. This continuous, ever-changing flux is what is denied in the transcendental world of roles and corporate groups, and it is not surprising, therefore, that one of the principal aspects of the usual meaning of the word "ritual" is that it makes intentionality impossible to locate (Humphrey and Laidlaw 1994; Bloch 2004). This is because ritual defers intentionality in the sense that the imagined originators of the actions, or of the sounds of ritual, be they words or otherwise, are not the actors or speakers. These latter defer to others, in the sense that they *follow* those who showed them how to act in ritual circumstances. If they were the intentional originators of the form of the words and actions used, then these words and actions would not be ritual. Ritual thus leeches out intentionality and the tumult of a life continually created by actions to make it the static world where roles and corporate groups can exist. This is the transcendental social.

But there is also another way in which the invisible imaginary world of the transcendental social can be given some phenomenological reality. That is through material culture associated with it. This can serve as the visible material trace of the invisible transcendental. To return to examples used earlier: crowns and thrones remain the invisible trace of the rituals when the transcendental that was ritually instantiated has now disappeared. These objects may well have been created for the ritual and the transcendental – this is the case for crowns and specters – but this function can also be achieved by material things, which have a quite other raison d'être but which may be incorporated into ritual because they lend themselves to such use. A common example is landscape, which plays such a central role in Australian Aboriginal rituals. In such a case the landscape is obviously not just ritual become ritualized and an anchor for the permanent social. This, however, requires that it be transcendentalized into a "concept" that exists beyond its empirical manifestation.

This is what happens with houses in house-based societies or with parts of them, such as the hearth. Obviously these houses have a practical side in these societies, but they are also made to vanquish time and thus become "concepts." They then can be seen as a visible residue of the transcendental social and the rituals that bring it to life. However, the relationship between the transactional and the transcendental side is closer and more complex than that between the Aboriginal landscape and the initiation of boys. This is because, as discussed earlier, houses are sites of continual activities at the same time as they become stable points in the system of the transcendental social. This both denies the fluidity of the house process and draws its meaning from it. The transcendental cannot be separated from very common human-wide practical activities.

So the reason the anthropological record can be used with a certain degree of confidence for suggesting what happened in Çatalhöyük is that house-based societies are doubly motivated. The reasoning goes like this. We can assume that like all human societies (there are a few doubtful exceptions) Çatalhöyük society involved a transcendental, time-denying social element and that this required support. Such a support very often involves a material manifestation of this invisible transcendental social. A readily available way of using the material to express this social is to build houses. This is because houses, by their very nature, lend themselves to the representation of a continuity that transcends the moment. They and the activities that go on in them readily become concepts and as such are suited to the purposes of the transcendental social. But the concepts so created are not arbitrary but linked to the practical. The concept "house" in these societies is determined both by the universal needs of the transcendental and by the transactional and practical that go on in them.

The repetition of pattern that we find in house-based society is thus the product of a not necessary universal, but frequent causal chain that ultimately derives from a particular combination of a number of human-wide characteristics. The category "house-based societies" is therefore a recurrent phenomenon repeatedly engendered by a combination of recurring factors. So we can suggest that what went on in Çatalhöyük can be illuminated by what goes on in Madagascar and in other places with house-based societies.

Dangerous further steps

However, can we go further? So far, only very little information from the Çatalhöyük finds has been used in the argument. This is for the reasons outlined at the beginning of this chapter. In this final part I shall take more risks by considering another recurrent characteristic of Çatalhöyük houses: the aesthetic uses of strong wild animals, particularly cattle, which are evident in the use of bucrania on walls and in the occasional pictorial representation of scenes such as the famous "bullfight."

In Çatalhöyük there does seem to be an emphasis on wild animals for decoration and a significant lack of use of domesticated animals, especially sheep. This is surprising for the period when they were domesticated and when they must have represented an important economic asset. On the basis of this fact and the choice of the other animals that appear to have been focused on, I propose that two aspects were probably prominent in explaining these choices. One is the strength of the animals and perhaps their virility, perhaps exemplified by their horns, which are prominent in Çatalhöyük, since these often have this role. The second is the fact that these strong beasts have been mastered and killed, perhaps in corrida-style slaughter.

These somewhat tendentious proposals are, of course, again influenced by my knowledge of the ethnography of other parts of the world and must, therefore, also be justified in terms of motivated meanings, in the way that I have already done.

In order to make my argument I refer briefly to the theory I outlined in *Prey into Hunter* (Bloch 1992). In that book I argued that the phenomenological creation of what I have called the transcendental social always creates a metaphysical problem. The transcendental social requires a ritual removal from the transactional in order to construct an invisible world of roles and groups within which people act some of the time. This removal inevitably implies a movement out of life and vitality, since the world of the transcendental is not one of transformative beings. This leads to the dramatic acting out in rituals of what I have called "rebounding violence," the dramatic reconquest of vitality in a conquered form, which then "reanimates" the transcendental. For example, many of the rituals that have been called sacrifices display this element but so do many others.

Reanimation ideally involves the absorption of vitality, and contact with large, strong animals is often used for this. These animals may be domesticated, but when this is the case they are often re-represented as wild. This is the case in Hispanic corridas. The general reason for this is that wildness is associated with untamed nondomestic strength. Often, however, the animals are wild in the first place – for example, the lions used in Roman sacrifices.

Using this theory, I would *very tentatively* suggest that the prominence of wild cattle in Çatalhöyük houses is to be explained in this way. Houses, as we have seen, are probably anchors for the disembodied transcendental, but the ritual creation of this image requires a negation of the fluid, changing aspects of transactional life. To create the houses of house-based societies, the continually changing phenomenon of living things needs to be ritually removed. This is evident in the first stages of initiation rituals mentioned earlier. Thus, the phenomenologically stable, time-defying "concept" of house replaces the fluid ephemeral life of people and their activities. The ethereal transcendental house so created then requires ritual reanimation. The reanimating element must be subordinated to the house; otherwise the houses' very existence would be threatened. Thus, the strength must be returned, even emphasized, but *only* in a conquered, controlled form. The dramatic introduction of conquered and killed wild cattle, and probably the consumption of their flesh, would then be the reintroduction of vigor and life-in-time to the house. The bucrania would thus either achieve this revivifying of the transcendental or celebrate moments when it occurred in sacrificial-like rituals.

What about religion?

The Templeton initiative that led to the publication of this book was about religion at Çatalhöyük, yet this chapter has not mentioned the word once. This is no accident. The reason is that I am confident that there was no religion in Çatalhöyük, any more than there was among the Zafimaniry before Christianity arrived there. Looking for religion is therefore a misleading wild goose chase. The English word "religion" inevitably refers to what English speakers have known, and no amount of redefinition or manipulation of the term can escape the associations that a particular history has created. It is clear that calling the phenomena usually indicated by the words Hinduism and Buddhism "religions" has similarly simply led to misunderstandings (Fuller 1992). The kind of phenomena that the English word "religion," and the associated word "belief," can be made to evoke have, at most, a history of five thousand years. This is thousands of years after the establishment of Çatalhöyük. I have tried in an earlier publication to suggest the processes that might have led to the creation of religion, and these inevitably made use of preexisting cultural and cognitive phenomena (Bloch 2008). These elements that were so used were and could have been used for a host of other developments. These preexisting elements have to do with the nature of the human social. Some of them are found in a specific form in house-based societies, and this is why I have talked of houses, roles, corporate groups and the transcendental rather than about religion.

REFERENCES

Bloch, M. 1992. *Prey into Hunter: The Politics of Religious Experience*. Cambridge: Cambridge University Press.

Bloch, M. 1995. The resurrection of the house. In *About the House*, eds. J. Carsten and S. Hugh-Jones. Cambridge: Cambridge University Press, 69–83.

Bloch, M. 1996. La consonation des jeunes homes chez les Zafimaniry de Madagascar. In *De la Violence*, ed. F. Heritier. Paris: Odile Jacob, 201–22.

Bloch, M. 2004. Ritual and deference. In *Ritual and Memory: Toward a Comparative Anthropology of Religion*, eds. H. Whitehouse and J. Laidlaw. Walnut Creek, Calif.: AltaMira Press, 123–37.

Bloch, M. 2008. Why religion is nothing special but is central. In *The Sapient Mind: Archaeology Meets Neuroscience. Philosophical Transactions of the Royal Society*, June 2008, 2055–62.

Carsten, J., and Hugh-Jones, S., eds. 1995. *About the House*. Cambridge: Cambridge University Press.

Cunningham, C. 1964. Order in the Atoni house. *Bijdragen tot de taal – Land – en Volkekunde*, 120, 34–68.

Firth, R. 1936. *We the Tikopia*. London: George Allen and Unwin.

Fuller, C. J. 1992. *The Camphor Flame: Popular Hinduism and Society in India*. Princeton, N.J.: Princeton University Press.

Gluckman, M., ed. 1962. *Essays on the Ritual of Social Relations*. Manchester: Manchester University Press.

Grice, H. 1982. Meaning revisited. In *Mutual Knowledge*, ed. N. Smith. London: Academic Press, 223–43.

Humphrey, C., and Laidlaw, J. 1994. *The Archetypal Actions of Ritual*. Oxford: Oxford University Press.

Lévi-Strauss, C. 1979. *La voie des masques*. Paris: Plon.

Medin, D., and Wattenmaker, W. 1987. Category cohesiveness, theories and cognitive archaeology. In *Concepts and Conceptual Development*, ed. U. Neisser. Cambridge: Cambridge University Press, 25–62.

Sperber, D. 1986. *Relevance*, Oxford: Blackwell.

7

History houses: A new interpretation of architectural elaboration at Çatalhöyük

Ian Hodder and Peter Pels

This chapter deals with building variation at Çatalhöyük. Such a theme is relevant to the discussion of religious ritual at the site because Mellaart initially interpreted architectural variation among buildings in terms of whether they were 'shrines'. The work of the current project has demonstrated conclusively that all buildings at Çatalhöyük, however much burial, symbolism and ritual they contained, served as domestic houses. But Mellaart was right that some buildings seem more elaborate than others, even though the site as a whole is relatively egalitarian. How, then, are we to understand the more elaborate buildings, and how did they come into being? What social and religious roles did they play? This chapter explores, first, quantitative variation in the architecture at Çatalhöyük in the light of the results of recent work. It subsequently sets these findings about building variation in the context of a reinterpretation of more elaborated buildings as 'history houses'. It focuses on Çatalhöyük itself and does not include comparisons and parallels with other sites. We acknowledge a debt to studies of the politics of tell house sequences through time in southeast Europe (see Tringham 2000; for a general review see McAnany and Hodder 2009).

The history of work on variation among buildings at Çatalhöyük includes Mellaart's (1967) identification of 'shrines' concentrated in a 'priestly quarter' in the southwest part of the East Mound. Others have focused on social differentiation (e.g., Wason 1994). Tim Ritchey (1996) showed that in terms of architectural elaboration (numbers of platforms, pillars, paintings, etc.) the buildings in any one occupation level showed a smooth and regular falloff when ranked from the most to the least elaborate. The very thorough and systematic work by Düring (2006) on the architectural elaboration of buildings excavated by Mellaart showed that elaborate buildings sometimes have a large number of burials, and they sometimes endure through several rebuilds. There has been little previous work on house size (although see in particular Cutting 2005) – perhaps because house size seems superficially to vary little.

Study of the material collected and published by Mellaart provided some indication that certain types of obsidian cores and figurines were concentrated in more elaborate buildings (Conolly 1996; Hamilton 1996), but the evidence for both these claims is weak. Buildings are known to vary in that they have different types of fill and abandonment, different dates, different functions (e.g., some buildings concentrating on bead manufacture) and so on. We also have defined 'sectors' on the site – that is, large groups of houses (10–30 or more) bounded by refuse areas or alleyways (see also Aşıklı Höyük; Esin and Harmankaya 1999). Nested within these sectors, smaller groupings of houses have been assumed based on evidence for the shared use of burial houses (Building 1) and micro-traditions in architecture among nearby houses (dominant use of western benches, sticking-out ovens attached to walls, etc.).

In this study we build on Düring's (2006) suggestion that houses were not equal and may have developed specific symbolic and political or economic dependencies on each other. This requires an examination of architectural variation of houses at Çatalhöyük in relation to building size and burial frequency. We then argue for the identification of 'history houses' – buildings in which Çatalhoyuk people accumulated more transcendent knowledge and symbolic capital than in others – and for a situating of such houses within a specific interpretation of the wider category of 'house societies'. Examples of the latter have come to be recognized widely in archaeology in recent decades (e.g., Boric 2007; Chesson 2003; Joyce and Gillespie 2000; Kuijt 2000), and a wider framework for the identification of such societies at Çatalhöyük is discussed in this volume by Bloch (Chapter 6).

Quantitative analysis

The identification of some Çatalhöyük houses as 'history houses' is based on (1) interpreting Çatalhöyük by an analogy to the ethnographic record of 'house societies', (2) acknowledging the differentiation between individual houses within the settlement and (3) hypothesizing that such

7.1. Building 5 has the typical arrangement of rooms at Çatalhöyük, with a central main room containing hearth, oven and platforms, as well as side rooms usually associated with storage and production. North is to the top in this building, and the hearth, oven and ladder entry are usually toward the south of the main room. *Source:* J. Swogger and Çatalhöyük Research Project.

differentiation might indicate a relative measure of both hierarchy and specialization and exchange between houses.

For this study, buildings have been used for which there is a full plan as a result of recent excavation at least down to the latest floors and often the retrieval pit bottoms. All data from the recent excavations have been lumped together from the lower levels up to Levels IV/V. The TP area has not been included, and Building 3 does not occur on the graphs (as this building is being published separately; Stevanovic and Tringham 1998, in press). Data from Mellaart's excavations have been included where we have continued excavating his buildings and can verify his plans and drawings to some degree (as in the sequences that lead up to 'Shrines' 1, 8 and 10; see Hodder 2007a). The spaces in buildings have been defined as main rooms (where the ladder enters and where burial normally occurs) and side rooms (entered off the main room and where storage often occurs). The areas of rooms are measured as the internal areas (Figure 7.1). In what follows it has not been possible to illustrate and show plans of all the buildings referred to in the text. Plans of all buildings are available in the public online database at www.catalhoyuk.com.

In order to quantify architectural variation among buildings, a measure of architectural elaboration needed to be devised (see also Ritchey 1996). The measure used here simply sums, for any one phase of a building, the numbers of floor segments, basins, benches, installations (protuberances on walls, including bucrania and other animal fixtures), pillars and paintings in the main room of the building. There are numerous problems with such a measure. Sometimes, for example, it is difficult to define the main room. In Building 5 in Figure 7.1, for example, the eastern room has characteristics that might be argued to imply that it was part of the main room, but here it has been defined as a side room because a wall separates it from the larger central room. In other cases, there are partition walls that may or may not have been full height, and so it is not clear whether a side room should be defined. In this study, rooms have been defined when bordered by complete or partial brick walls (rather than slim partitions).

Another problem is that it is often difficult, especially when not all the floors in a building have been excavated, to be sure that all the 'elaborate' features are present at any one time in the phase of a house. On the whole, most such features tend to be fairly stable in a phase of a building, but this is certainly not true of paintings that are very short lived. In counting the numbers of paintings for the elaboration index, any clear traces of painting (including red washes) seen in the wall plasters have been included, regardless of whether they are all exactly contemporary. Different paintings on the same phase of one wall have been counted as one painting.

These problems are exacerbated in the case of Mellaart's buildings. The recent excavations have shown that buildings go through many phases within one level in the site's occupation, but Mellaart tended to conflate these (into his Levels I, II, III, etc.). It is thus especially difficult to know which elaborate feature goes with which; his plans and drawings probably have more features on them than were present at any one phase. Also he tended to be imaginative in his account of elaborate features – for example, interpreting wall plaster slump as bull horns. Thus, as we will see, the Mellaart building data have averages for the elaboration index that are rather higher than the averages for the building data from the current excavation. In the charts described later, the Mellaart data are often shown separately.

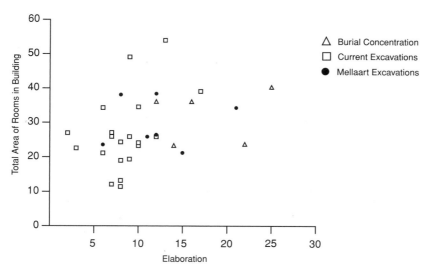

BUILDING TOTAL SIZE AND ELABORATION

7.2. The relationship between the elaboration index (described in the text) and the total internal area of buildings. The buildings are divided into those from the Mellaart and those from the current excavations. Buildings with more than 12 burials beneath the floors are also indicated. *Source:* Laura Baker and Çatalhöyük Research Project.

The numbers of posts in the main room have not been included in the elaboration index. This is because through time the use of posts declines, to be replaced by the use of brick columns, which can be very residual (as in Building 44). Numbers of hearths and ovens have also not been included. These get replaced so much that it has proved very difficult to know what to count – every relining of an oven or every relocation of an oven? The numbers of hearths are very compromised by this problem. In addition it seems that in earlier levels there are either more ovens and hearths or they were relocated a lot more.

The scatter plot in Figure 7.2 shows the total internal area of buildings against the elaboration measure. There is visually a weak association between the two variables for the current data (excavated by the current team since 1993), though covariation is less apparent when the Mellaart data are included. On the graph the buildings with large numbers of burials have also been indicated (for the difficulties with these data see Hamilton 1996). Where the current excavations stopped before floors were excavated, the presence of burials is unknown. Within these limitations we see that buildings with more than 12 burials tend to be more

MAIN ROOM SIZE AND ELABORATION

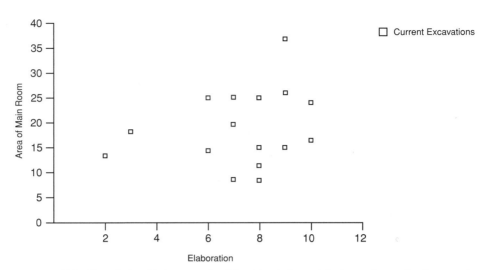

7.3. The relationship between the elaboration index and the internal area of main rooms in buildings excavated by the current project. *Source:* Laura Baker and Çatalhöyük Research Project.

elaborate. This observation confirms results obtained by Düring. The multiple burial buildings are not, however, especially large.

The weak correlation between size and elaboration in the current data could simply be the product of increasing house size. As more space is available in a building, so there might be more space for platforms, benches, installations and so on. This argument does not work for paintings. It could also be the case that large numbers of burials need a large amount of space, but as noted already, the larger burial numbers do not occur preferentially in the largest buildings.

The scatter plot in Figure 7.3 suggests that the size (area) of the main room too may correlate weakly with elaboration. This plot shows only the data from the current excavations. When the Mellaart data are added (Figure 7.4), a weak relationship between the two variables remains. In addition we can again see the tendency for the Mellaart buildings to be defined as more elaborate. As already noted, this is probably the result of the collapsing of features from different phases into one plan. Nevertheless, the buildings with multiple burials (in both the Mellaart and recent data) tend to be more elaborate.

It is possible to explore variation in building elaboration through time in particular building sequences. The continuity in the use of space

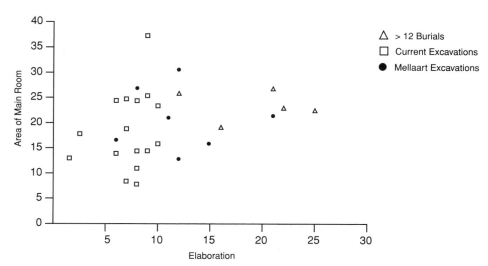

MAIN ROOM SIZE AND ELABORATION

7.4. The relationship between the elaboration index and the internal area of main rooms in buildings. The buildings are divided into those from the Mellaart and those from the current excavations. Buildings with more than 12 burials beneath the floors are also indicated. *Source:* Laura Baker and Çatalhöyük Research Project.

in buildings as they are rebuilt over generations has been discussed by Hodder and Cessford (2004; see Figure 7.5; see also Düring 2007). Figure 7.6 takes the same data as in Figure 7.2 but adds information about sequences of rebuilds. Included here are two sequences from the current excavations: Building 5 to Building B1.2B to B1.2C, and Building 65 to 56 to 44 to 10. Also included are three sequences that have been partly excavated by Mellaart and partly by the current team. These are the 'Shrine 10' sequence (17, 6, 24, 'Shrine 10'), the 'Shrine 8' sequence (18, 16, 7, 20, 'Shrine 8') and the 'Shrine 1' sequence (23, 22, 21, 8, 'Shrine 1'). All of these sequences except the Building 65 to 10 sequence end in a major fire, after which smaller or less elaborate buildings are sometimes constructed on a rather different plan. One example is B1.4, which is built in the burned remains of B1.2C. Another example of the effect of a fire is the small Building 51, which was built in the burned remains of the much larger Building 52 (which was not itself part of a long sequence). In both of the latter cases we see a major fire (whether accidental or intentional is unclear) leading to a very different and smaller building. There are other examples on-site (e.g., Building 45 and the Level VI Buildings 79 and 80) where a major fire leads to a lack of

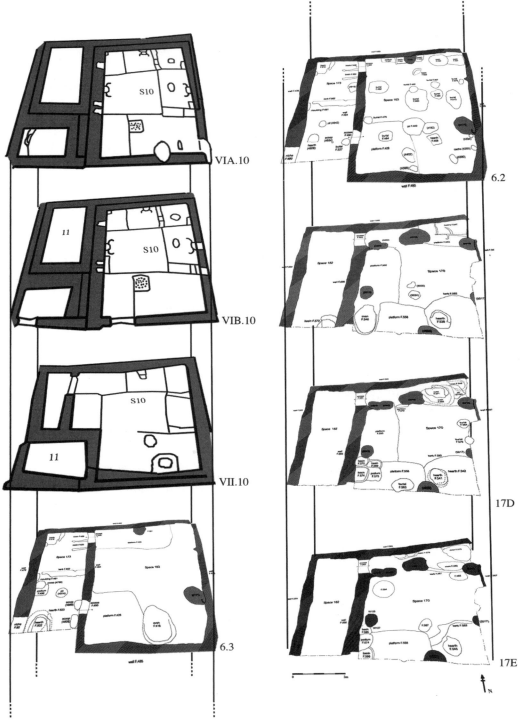

7.5. Example illustrating the continuity of buildings in one location over time. The building was rebuilt from Building 17, Phase E (in the bottom right-hand corner), through the phases of Building 6 and into Mellaart's 'Shrines 10' in his Levels VII, VIB and VIA. *Source:* Tim King and Çatalhöyük Research Project.

MAIN ROOM SIZE AND ELABORATION

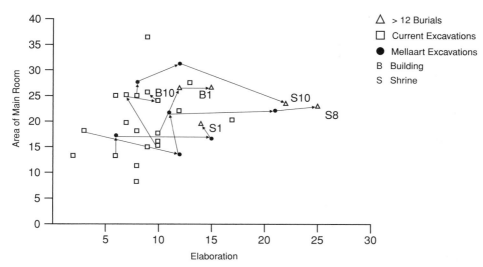

7.6. The relationship between the elaboration index and the internal area of main rooms in buildings as shown in Figure 7.4, but in this case with sequences of rebuilds of individual buildings. The buildings at the end point of sequences are shown, such as Buildings 1 and 10 (excavated by the current project) and Mellaart's 'Shrines' 1, 8 and 10. *Source:* Laura Baker and Çatalhöyük Research Project.

growth or a reorganization of space, although the building placed above burned Building 77 followed the walls of Building 77 with only a slight deviation. Returning to the sequences used in this study, VIA 'Shrines' 10 and 8 are replaced by Mellaart's S3 and S6 respectively in Level V, but there is little information available from Mellaart about these buildings and their stratigraphical relationships to the 'Shrine 10' and 'Shrine 8' sequences.

Figure 7.6 explores these five sequences up until the point at which there is a major burning and a decrease in building size. We see that in four of the five cases, the sequence of increasing elaboration or size culminates in a building with a large number of burials. In the fifth case, toward the end of the sequence that culminates in Building 10, the penultimate building (Building 44) has 10 burials. It could be argued that these increases in size and elaboration are simply overall trends in time. Mellaart's 'Shrine' 1, 8, 10 sequences all start in Level IX or X (or earlier in the case of 'Shrine 1') and peak in Level VI, and so perhaps the whole site sees increasing size and elaboration through these levels. Hamilton (1996) demonstrates the concentration of burials in Level VI.

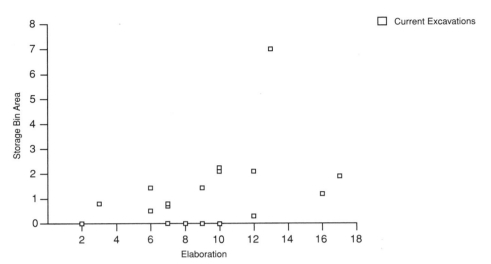

7.7. The relationship between the elaboration index and the total bin storage area in buildings excavated by the current project. *Source:* Laura Baker and Çatalhöyük Research Project.

However, the 65, 56, 44 sequence probably covers Levels VI–IV, and Düring (2007: 146) shows concentrations of burials in Level VII in the building sequences of 'Shrines' 9 and 31, so there is not one single sitewide process of increasing burials from Levels X to VI.

In order to understand the processes involved in the long-term increase in elaboration of certain buildings, it is helpful to understand the role of storage and production in these buildings. In Figure 7.7 there is a weak relationship between bin storage area and elaboration. There are difficulties in measuring bin storage area. Data from Mellaart's buildings have not been included, as many bins are slight and difficult to discern. In the current excavations bins, like ovens, often seem to change location and to go in and out of use, and we cannot always be sure of the phasing in relation to other features in the building. There is often uncertainty about whether a feature is a bin or a basin; if the walls have been heavily truncated the feature could be either a bin or a basin. In some cases (e.g., as in the southwest room in Building 5 shown in Figure 7.1) we can clearly see the height of the bins as plaster traces on the walls, and in such cases we could work out volumes, but in most cases this is not possible. Rather than assume the heights of the bins and guess at volumes, we have used bin area for Figure 7.7.

MAIN ROOM AND SIDE ROOM AREAS

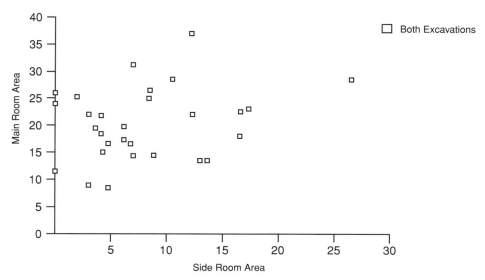

7.8. The relationship between the areas of main rooms and side rooms in buildings excavated by the current project and those included in this study from the Mellaart excavations. *Source:* Laura Baker and Çatalhöyük Research Project.

A very slight relationship is shown in Figure 7.8 between main room area and side room area. Side rooms are used for a variety of functions. They often contain bins, ovens and work areas, and they usually have little plaster on the walls. There is often a higher density of micro-artifacts in these rooms; they can have dirty or clean, white plaster floors. The size of side room space is an approximate measure of storage and productive space, although bins and ovens also occur in main rooms. The weak relationships noted in Figures 7.7 and 7.8 could simply be a function of size – of the building and of the occupying unit. As the building increases in size, there may be more space for side rooms and storage. As the number of people using the building increases, more productive and storage space is needed.

In summary, the sizes of buildings at Çatalhöyük do vary. The variation of the size of buildings and main rooms correlates weakly with architectural elaboration and storage and productive space. None of this, so far, suggests a clear differentiation between dominant and subordinate buildings. The variation could all be due to variation in the size of the buildings and the occupying units. This latter point is clarified in Figure 7.9. Here we see that there is no trend if we plot elaboration against

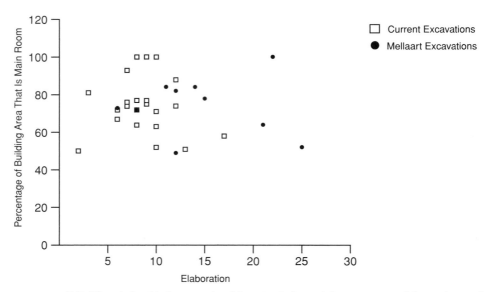

7.9. The relationship between the elaboration index and the percentage of the total area of a building that is taken up by the main room. The buildings excavated by the current excavations and by Mellaart are distinguished. *Source:* Laura Baker and Çatalhöyük Research Project.

the percentage of the total interior space of buildings that is used for the main room. On the whole the percentage remains much the same regardless of elaboration (and the same is true of overall size). Thus, there is no category of buildings so far discernible that has more than the usual proportion of side, storage and productive space. This does not suggest some buildings controlling production and storage or depending on the production and storage of others.

So it is not the case that the more elaborate buildings have relatively more side room production and storage. But what might we expect in individual building sequences? So far we have seen that more elaborate buildings are associated with more burials, and that as buildings are rebuilt in the same place over many generations they sometimes become places where burial and elaboration concentrate – until there is a burning associated with a sudden decrease in size and a break in the exact replication of house by house. But what happens to the relative amount of space given over to side rooms and storage in these sequences?

Figure 7.10 shows what we might expect as buildings become more elaborate through time and as they come to focus on burial. The measure

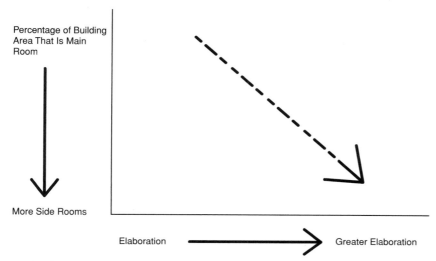

7.10. The relationship between the elaboration index and the percentage of the total area of a building that is taken up by the main room that would be expected if buildings that became more elaborate also had more storage and productive space. *Source:* Laura Baker and Çatalhöyük Research Project.

of elaboration includes installations – defined in terms of protuberances on walls largely made up of bucrania and other animal heads and body parts placed in walls. Access to the wild animals from which these parts were taken may have been obtained by scavenging and hunting, but the paintings also suggest a wider context. Social groups were active in the teasing and baiting of wild animals. We also know that feasting remains on-site include a disproportionate number of wild bulls. The provision of installations in houses thus suggests an ability to provide significant economic and social resources in the form of feasts. We might expect that, as buildings become more elaborate and have more installations, they need or can support relatively more storage and productive space. This might occur as they become dominant in the social-ritual spheres and also become dominant in terms of production and storage. So we might expect that, as buildings become more elaborate, they have more side room productive and storage space.

But if we look at the information from the current excavations, the opposite happens (Figure 7.11). For Figures 7.11 and 7.12 the same building sequences as described in Figure 7.6 have been used. In the

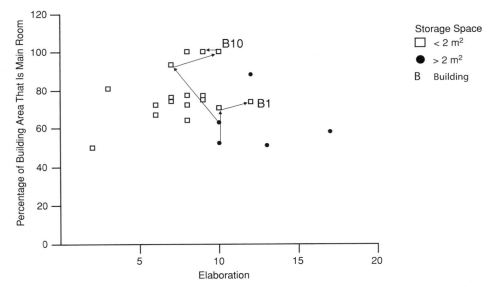

7.11. The actual relationship between the elaboration index and the percentage of the total area of a building that is taken up by the main room in building sequences excavated by the current project. Buildings with more than 2 m² of storage area are also shown. *Source:* Laura Baker and Çatalhöyük Research Project.

current excavations, the 65, 56, 44, 10 sequence as well as the 5, B1.2B, B1.2C sequence shows a decrease in side room space through time. Their total internal space becomes dominated by the central main room. Also shown in this figure are the buildings with more storage space (>2 m²). If the Mellaart sequences are considered (Figure 7.12), we see that all the sequences move to the right; the relative amount of side room space stays much the same through the sequences. We can also see specifically in Figure 7.13 that those buildings with multiple burials have less bin storage space than other buildings with similar amounts of elaboration.

To summarize the building sequences, as buildings become more elaborate (and sometimes larger), and as they become places for multiple burials, they keep the same relative amount of side and storage space or they decrease it. The main room gradually takes over more of the overall space, or there is a gradual reduction in side room space or a gradual diminution of productive activities (ovens, hearths, bins, etc.) in the main room.

BUILDING ELABORATION, SIDE ROOM SPACE

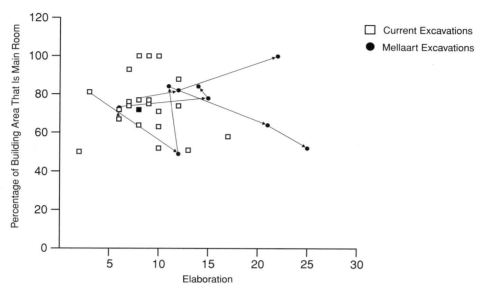

7.12. The actual relationship between the elaboration index and the percentage of the total area of a building that is taken up by the main room in building sequences partly excavated by Mellaart. *Source:* Laura Baker and Çatalhöyük Research Project.

BIN AREA AND ELABORATION OF BUILDING

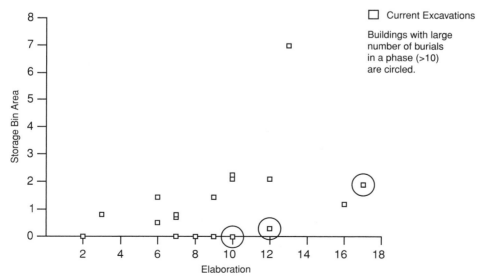

7.13. The relationship between the elaboration index and the total bin storage area in buildings excavated by the current project (see Figure 7.7). Buildings with more than 10 burials are indicated. *Source:* Laura Baker and Çatalhöyük Research Project.

One interpretation of this evidence is that, within an overall relatively undifferentiated society, through time some houses manage to transfer productive success into symbolic elaboration and burial. We know from the 5, B1.2B, B1.2C sequence (for a detailed description see Hodder 2007a; Hodder and Cessford 2004) that more people come to be buried in the building than could have lived in it. The building came to be used for burial by other houses, presumably related in some way. Buildings also gradually accumulated objects such as bucrania and skulls; these are part of their increasing elaboration through time. The clearest pattern in our data is that large numbers of burials occur in more elaborate buildings (Figures 7.2 and 7.4). We have also seen that more elaborate buildings with many burials often emerged over time (Figure 7.6). It seems not unreasonable to term such long-lived houses that amassed objects of memory 'history houses'. It is possible that these history houses came to provide or control ancestors and rituals for a larger kin or other group or 'house' (some larger collection of buildings in a 'house society'). The central history houses may have had less productive and storage space because others in the kin, ancestral or 'house' group provided resources and food for them.

Stevanovic and Tringham (in press) have noted that the Bach building (Building 3) also sees a shift from a focus on production and storage to burial. They interpret this shift in terms of the varying size of the occupying unit – as a result of changes in the size of the family in the family life cycle. This interpretation seems possible for the short-lived Building 3. This building was constructed on midden and it was never rebuilt. It contained few burials. Its shifts through time occur over the different phases of use of one building. True history houses seem to have endured over considerable periods of time. The VIA and VIB 'Shrines 1, 8, 10' are substantial buildings with much buildup of floors (such that the bucrania in 'Shrine 10' gradually sank beneath the frequently renewed floors). The sequences from Level X to VIB and VIA may have lasted 500 years (Cessford 2005). It is difficult to interpret the gradual shift to elaboration and burial in such sequences in terms of the waxing and waning of family size.

It is clear that not all large and elaborate houses became history houses. This is seen in Figures 7.2 and 7.4 where there are large and/or elaborate houses that do not have many burials. Some of these do not seem to have been occupied for long periods (they have few plaster layers on the floors and walls). So what are the differences between large elaborate buildings without many burials and those with burials? Is it just a function of time? That is, given enough time and enough opportunity to 'build history', do all large and elaborate buildings become history buildings (see Keane, Chapter 8)? Or is there some difference in the productive strategies of elaborate buildings that do or do not become elaborate burial buildings? Larger samples of different types of building need to be examined before we can answer such questions.

Discussion

It seems possible that in a relatively egalitarian society certain houses managed through time to amass a 'history' (although one should ask what 'history' here means; see later in this section). This may have been maintained over many centuries in that some of the continuous building sequences have distinctive characteristics that are maintained over four to six rebuilds, and on average each rebuild has been shown to last around 70–100 years. The 'history' that was accumulated seems to have included human remains. Building 1 had 62 humans buried beneath the platforms, including parts of bodies interred as secondary burials, perhaps initially buried in other or earlier buildings. In recent work Başak Boz has identified teeth taken from a skeleton in a house in the 65, 56, 44, 10 sequence and placed in the jaw of an individual in a later building in the same sequence. There is clear evidence that pits were dug down from later houses to retrieve installations on walls in earlier houses (Hodder 2006). It is likely that the bull horns and other enduring parts of wild animals were kept and passed down and incorporated into houses.

In a number of instances we have discovered human skulls removed from bodies and inserted at the base of house posts, or placed in burials, or in abandonment deposits. In one case, the skull had been plastered to represent the flesh of the face (see Chapter 2). These individual skulls have been found in a number of types of houses. But the clearest evidence for the bodies from which they have been removed comes from history houses. The sample size is not large. One headless burial occurred in Building 1, two in Building 44 and another in Building 6 in the 'Shrine 10' sequence. Other headless burials have been found in Building 49, which is a very elaborate building with a large number of plaster layers on the walls and a large number of burials (20 overall), and in Building

60, which continues on from the very large Building 59 and a yet lower unexcavated building (information regarding headless burials from Lori Hager and Başak Boz). All these seem long-lived houses, with multiple rebuilds where we can see the evidence, and they tend to be larger or more elaborate. It seems possible, although the small size of the sample needs to be emphasized, that heads (and perhaps other body parts) were removed from individuals in history houses and placed in other houses. In these ways alliances with history houses could be built up through the circulation of the dead.

The construction of 'histories' in place, in the repetition of houses, emerged early and was a long-term component of Neolithic societies in the Middle East (Hodder 2007b). Others have made similar arguments in relation to the circulation and deposition of human skulls (e.g., Kuijt 2008; see also Chapter 2, this volume).

The identification of possible 'history houses' in this chapter is a starting point from which to formulate new interpretations and hypotheses. So far we have defined history houses empirically, as those with numerous burials, more elaboration and evidence of multiple rebuilds in the same location. What is now needed is an examination of the notion of a 'history house' and a discussion of where such a notion leads further research. Düring (2001, 2006) has argued on the basis of a reanalysis of Mellaart's findings that ritually elaborate houses may form the center of a cluster of houses, but that in the higher levels of the settlement (post–Level VI) this clustering seems to decrease. A further examination of the full range of evidence from 'history' and nonhistory houses, therefore, both in space and in time, is needed to see if any differences can be discerned in terms of production and consumption and daily and ritual practices within the houses. The degree of sharing (of food, burial, obsidian, etc.) between groups of houses clustered around 'history houses' needs to be discerned, and the possibility of various forms of dependence between houses explored. It seems particularly important to develop hypotheses about how some houses managed to become 'history houses' while others started and failed. What are the conditions that allowed some buildings to amass histories while others did not? What are 'houses' in the first place, how do they come to contain 'histories' and what makes them different from other houses?

At this point some reflections on the notion of a 'house' and a 'house society' may be useful (see also Chapter 6). From Claude Lévi-Strauss's first formulation onward (1975), 'house societies' have been seen as societies where the 'house' is a major symbol and organizing principle of social organization. If Lévi-Strauss thought of them predominantly in terms of a type of kinship organization, later approaches inspired by Bourdieu (1977) and Bachelard (1964) emphasize the processual aspect of a house, and take both kinship relations and the material environment – both houses as embodied things and houses as built things – as elements of an analysis that saw them as evolving in time (Carsten and Hugh-Jones 1995; Joyce and Gillespie 2000). Two aspects of Lévi-Strauss's analysis remain salient, however: the constitution of the house as a 'moral person' (see Gillespie 2000: 24) and the fact that a 'house' is a kind of 'naturalization' of kinship relationships (Carsten and Hugh-Jones 1995:12). House societies often naturalize houses as individuals with a life span and a continuity that go beyond those of the human generations that occupy them (see Bloch, Chapter 6). This continuity already implies an identity of the house that is both dependent on and distinct from the identity of the building (as a physical structure with its own history of construction and use) and from the identity of the household (which may or may not be congruent with the people living in the physical building). The house, while distinct from any individual member of it, therefore also has an individual development distinct from both the physical building and the household sharing food and work, for while the permanence of the building is the sine qua non of the house, the building itself changes shape and signification on the basis of use, as does the composition of the group of people who eat its food and contribute to its economic reproduction.

This view of 'house' and 'house societies' implies that we can associate with Çatalhöyük three aspects of sociality that are not commonly associated with traditional, small-scale societies: (1) processes of individualization that produce idiosyncracies and a measure of social atomization (but here, of house collectives rather than human beings), (2) processes of the division of labor that distinguish the role of one house from another and (3) a central role of history in differentiating individuals (but here as members of houses rather than of nation-states). These three dimensions of differentiation can be interpreted to work together to produce the house as a 'moral person' (analogous to the way in which modern people talk, e.g., of 'legal persons' who are not congruent with any human being as such) – but as a process, an identity constituted over time, rather than a fixed category.

'History houses', therefore, get their name from a process of differentiation of houses that is universal throughout the settlement but
that identifies certain houses as specializing in modes of incorporating
'history'. The Çatalhöyük evidence as a whole gives many indications
that, indeed, people began to link themselves to specific pasts, by burying pots, tools, humans and hunting trophies in ways that indicate particular memories rather than a generic reference to a group (Hodder
2006: 149). Burials, for example, seem particularly 'historical', since we
may presume that people remembered these human beings as distinct
persons; bucrania and other hunting trophies seem too idiosyncratically
located in specific buildings – or, put differently, associated with too
particular 'individual' houses – to be only 'mythical'. The continuity
over time of particular buildings, or their erasure and/or abandonment,
implies decisions, taken by different generations of inhabitants, to either
continue or discontinue a house – decisions that therefore do not possess
the generic character of myth either. The continuities found from one
building level to the next by the particular moldings of leopards, paintings
of hands and paintings of vultures give a clear indication that houses were
marked by 'individual' characteristics. While no direct correlation can be
found between figurine deposits and the elaboration of houses (Meskell
et al. 2008: 150) – let alone between figurines and what Mellaart called
'shrines' – it is striking that some figurine deposits show that buildings
have individual 'biographies', one containing almost more figurines than
all others taken together, another containing the only find in recent
research of stone human figures and yet another containing almost only
figurines of quadrupeds (Meskell et al. 2008: 145–8). (Paintings may
only *seem* 'historical': if we do not interpret them as depicting events,
but as showing a desirable state to be reached in the future, such as
the abundant presence of wild game, they do not celebrate a particular
memory.)

Differentiation between houses raises the crucial question of the political economy on which its signs of distinction were based. Since the
evidence about household economy throughout the life span of the settlement indicates that it was highly integrated, without sharp discrep-
ancies between genders, the question might become what a differentiation of houses across generations was for. Again, the term 'history
house' points to the accumulation of historical memory (as opposed to

habituated and/or mythical memory) as a resource. The available evidence might indicate that it was precisely the capacity to remember events (of feasts and hunts, burials, caching and hiding things) and their places that grounded this differentiation, and thus indicate the 'foundation' of history houses in more powerful households counting members – most likely but not necessarily exclusively elders – whose capacity for remembrance was most highly developed (and, of course, entangled with the materiality of the history house as a mnemonic device). These houses may also have been, at certain phases in the development of the settlement, the central foci of neighborhood and/or community attention, if we can interpret memory (not only of events, but also of the accumulation of certain specialized skills) as a resource to be exchanged with other houses, possibly on unequal terms.

Thus, one might hypothesize that the household that animated a building and turned it into an individual 'house' consisted of several generations of nuclear families, with or without adoptive kin, where authority was divided among different elders of both genders – articulating a certain division of labor between agriculture, herding and hunting. Elders supervised and safeguarded the transmission of relevant socioeconomic skills (animal husbandry, social communication, manufacture, sexuality), and some of them were more skilled at or renowned for this than others and were sought out by a much larger number of people from other households – and acquired more authority and power as a result. This resulted in an increasing concentration of reproductive power in a limited number of houses, articulated by memory storage (expressed by interring both humans and animal bones in the house and marking them by platforms, plastering and/or sculpture or moldings) and, most likely, an accumulation of skills and knowledge based on specific events and experiences. As certain elders gained power and authority and lost physical stamina, they may have become increasingly confined to the house both in a practical sense and in the sense of becoming guardians of the goods, skills, capacities and identities stored there. A successful house transferred such guardianship capacities to another guardian in the next generation, either born into the family, adopted or recruited (or both, depending on the extent and nature of the kinship network and its classifications), thus increasing the need for a house to be rebuilt in the same way after structural defects appear or an important transfer of skills and capacities is required (in an isolated instance, the skull of a previous, renowned guardian was even buried together with one who took over these capacities in a later generation). These houses did, indeed, 'bring everything into' them (Hodder 2006:58), but in articulations that, for example, privileged the memory of wild cattle in reliefs and installations or deposits in many houses, and depictions of other wild animals (such as leopards) in more isolated instances. The more domestic (feminine?) parts of household production were not articulated, or perhaps even downplayed. Each house thus had its own history, as articulated vis-à-vis other, more elaborate houses, or marked in the different events and actions that memorialize a house's individuality.

If this is a plausible interpretation, a number of possibilities remain to be further discussed and researched: Is there any evidence of the routes of dispersal of houses? Households will probably have seen some measure of fission, with younger couples splitting off to form their own house, suggesting that specific patterns – such as ultimogeniture – may have been preferred if older children move out first. Also, fission might explain a certain amount of clustering of houses, as it is more likely that close family members like to stay close. This would imply that, in a way, history moves not only into the house, but also out of it.

Finally, the gradual changes taking place in the settlement as a whole might indicate particular moments in which the pattern of central 'history houses' begins to lose some of its coherence because the individualization of the house (measured by the growing independence of the building and the household) became less tied to specialized memorializations. Following Düring, Pels (Chapter 9) argues that the settlement becomes less concentrated around specific houses in the higher building levels. While history houses do not disappear after Level VI and many houses are equally if not more marked by numbers of burials, they nevertheless seem to change under the influence of, for example, the sharply decreasing life span of the house, the decrease of memory-by-installations and the installation of hunting trophies, the lesser works needed for the making and transportation of bricks and the greater elaboration of pottery. Thus, it may be suggested that households have become increasingly independent, prior to and simultaneous with a slow dispersal over the East Mound, toward the West Mound and away from the settlement, leading to a decrease in the period during which a 'history house' could exert a certain influence over its direct neighbors.

REFERENCES

Bachelard, G. 1964. *The Poetics of Space.* New York: Orion Press.

Boric, D. 2007. First households and 'house societies' in European prehistory. In *The Durable House: House Society Models in Archaeology*, ed. R. A. Beck, Jr. Center for Archaeological Investigations, Occasional Paper No. 35. Carbondale: Southern Illinois University.

Bourdieu, P. 1977. *Outline of a Theory of Practice.* Cambridge: Cambridge University Press.

Carsten, J., and S. Hugh-Jones, eds. 1995. *About the House: Lévi-Strauss and Beyond.* Cambridge: Cambridge University Press.

Cessford C. 2005. Absolute dating at Çatalhöyük. In *Changing Materialities at Çatalhöyük: Reports from the 1995–1999 Seasons*, ed. I. Hodder. Cambridge: McDonald Institute for Archaeological Research / British Institute of Archaeology at Ankara Monograph, 65–99.

Chesson, M. S. 2003. Households, houses, neighborhoods and corporate villages: Modeling the Early Bronze Age as a house society. *Journal of Mediterranean Archaeology*, 16(1), 79–102.

Conolly, J. 1996. The knapped stone. In *On the Surface: Çatalhöyük, 1993–95*, ed. I. Hodder. Cambridge: McDonald Institute for Archaeological Research / British Institute of Archaeology at Ankara Monograph, 173–98.

Cutting, M. V. 2005. *The Neolithic and Early Chalcolithic Farmers of Central and Southwest Anatolia: Household, Community and the Changing Use of Space.* British Archaeological Report S1435. Oxford: Archaeopress.

Düring, B. S. 2001. Social dimensions in the architecture of Neolithic Çatalhöyük, *Anatolian Studies* 51, 1–18.

Düring, B. S. 2006. *Constructing Communities: Clustered Neighbourhood Settlements of the Central Anatolian Neolithic, ca. 8500–5500 Cal. BC.* Leiden: Nederlands Instituut voor het Nabije Oosten.

Düring, B. 2007 The articulation of houses at Neolithic Çatalhöyük, Turkey. In *The Durable House: House Society Models in Archaeology*, ed. R. A. Beck, Jr. Center for Archaeological Investigations, Occasional Paper No. 35. Carbondale: Southern Illinois University, 130–53.

Esin, U., and S. Harmanakaya. 1999. Aşıklı in the frame of Central Anatolian Neolithic. In *Neolithic in Turkey: The Cradle of Civilization – New Discoveries*, eds. M. Özdoğan and N Başgelen. Istanbul: Arkeoloji ve Sanat Yayınları, 115–32.

Gillespie, S. D. 2000. Beyond kinship: An introduction. In *Beyond Kinship: Social and Material Reproduction in House Societies*, eds. R. A. Joyce and S. D. Gillespie. Philadelphia: University of Pennsylvania Press, 1–21.

Hamilton, N. 1996. Figurines, clay balls, small finds and burials. In *On the Surface: Çatalhöyük, 1993–95*, ed. I. Hodder. Cambridge: McDonald Institute for Archaeological Research / British Institute of Archaeology at Ankara Monograph, 215–64.

Hodder I. 2006. *Çatalhöyük: The Leopard's Tale*. London: Thames and Hudson.

Hodder I., ed. 2007a. *Excavating Çatalhöyük: South, North and KOPAL Area Reports from the 1995–99 Seasons*. Cambridge: McDonald Institute for Archaeological Research / British Institute of Archaeology at Ankara Monograph.

Hodder, I. 2007b. Çatalhöyük in the context of the Middle Eastern Neolithic. *Annual Review of Anthropology*, 36, 105–20.

Hodder, I., and Cessford, C. 2004. Daily practice and social memory at Çatalhöyük. *American Antiquity*, 69, 17–40.

Joyce, R. A., and S. D. Gillespie, eds. 2000. *Beyond Kinship: Social and Material Reproduction in House Societies*. Philadelphia: University of Pennsylvania Press.

Kuijt, I. 2000. Near Eastern Neolithic research: Directions and trends. In *Life in Neolithic Farming Communities: Social Organization, Identity, and Differentiation*, ed. I. Kuijt. New York: Kluwer Academic / Plenum Publishers, 311–22.

Kuijt, I. 2008. The regeneration of life: Neolithic structures of symbolic remembering and forgetting. *Current Anthropology*, 49, 171–97.

Lévi-Strauss, C. 1979. *La voie des masques*. Paris: Plon.

McAnany, P., and I. Hodder. 2009. Thinking about stratigraphic sequence in social terms. *Archaeological Dialogues*, 16(1), 1–22.

Mellaart, J. 1967. *Çatal Hüyük: A Neolithic Town in Anatolia*. London: Thames and Hudson.

Meskell, L. M., C. Nakamura, R. King and S. Farid 2008. Figured lifeworlds and depositional practices at Çatalhöyük. *Cambridge Archaeological Journal*, 18(2), 139–61.

Ritchey, T. 1996. Note: Building complexity. In *On the Surface: Çatalhöyük, 1993–95*, ed. I. Hodder. Cambridge: McDonald Institute for Archaeological Research / British Institute of Archaeology at Ankara Monograph, 7–17.

Stevanovic, M., and R. Tringham. 1998. The BACH 1 Area. *Çatalhöyük Archive Report 1998* (http://catal.arch.cam.ac.uk/catal/Archive_rep98/stevanovic98.html).

Stevanovic, M., and R. Tringham. In press. *The BACH Area at Çatalhöyük*. Los Angeles: Cotsen Institute.

Tringham, R. 2000. The continuous house: A view from the deep past. In *Beyond Kinship: Social and Material Reproduction in House Societies*, eds. R. Joyce and S. D. Gillespie. Philadelpha: University of Pennsylvania Press, 115–34.

Wason, P. 1994. *The Archaeology of Rank*. Cambridge: Cambridge University Press.

8

Marked, absent, habitual: Approaches to Neolithic religion at Çatalhöyük

Webb Keane

One motive behind the quest for prehistoric religion has been a search for those elements of human existence most characterized by independence from sheer necessity. In this view, religion is an especially strong version of a general cultural capacity to transcend what is merely given. It embodies people's ability to create and to respond to new realities, to project as yet unrealized futures, to exercise their agency in and upon the world. At the same time, religions characteristically displace or deny human agency. Indeed, the displacement and the exercise of agency may be dialectically inseparable from one another. Unknown ancient humans learned to make fire, but if their descendants are to recognize themselves in the deed – *to recognize that it is a deed at all* – Prometheus must steal fire from the gods. Objectified agency makes possible the reflexivity that transforms habit into inventive, or morally responsible, or simply audacious actions. If one accepts these claims, it follows that religion would seem well suited to play a crucial role in the development of new forms of human agency in the Neolithic.

In this chapter I both develop and challenge these assertions. I begin by criticizing certain assumptions found in theories of Neolithic religion and propose some heuristics for thinking about prehistoric religion. I then turn to Çatalhöyük's artworks, animals and houses, drawing on my own ethnographic materials as a stimulus to reflection. The category of

The project was directed by Ian Hodder with funds from the Templeton Foundation. The other participants at the field site at the same time as me in 2006 were Maurice Bloch, Peter Pels, LeRon Shults and Harvey Whitehouse. Lynn Meskell and Shahina Farid were also very active in the work of the group. I am grateful for the invitation to join this project, and for the insights offered and challenges posed by all the participants. For comments on the manuscript, I thank George Hoffman, Adela Pinch, Andrew Shryock, Mary Weismantel, Norm Yoffee and especially Ian Hodder.

"religion" groups together a wide range of practices, ideas and experiences from diverse sources. I argue that what looks to us like religion may emerge from the convergence of practices that produce effects I call "markedness" and "absence." These effects stand out from, and take their place amid, the habitual and repetitive activities that surround them. In Çatalhöyük, for instance, the cattle horns that remain after dramatic events of killing and feasting end up marking certain houses whose ongoing reproduction, like that of all houses, is shaped by largely unmarked cycles of birth, nurturance and death. In addition, some houses conceal things (human burials, animal remains inside walls, paintings that have been plastered over) that may point toward potent absences in the midst of those same unmarked activities.

The dialectic between markedness and absence, on the one hand, and the habitual, everyday world, on the other, may lead people to recognize, reformulate and reappropriate their own and others' agency. People who reflect on agency become capable of imputing responsibility for, and judging the value of, the actions of humans and nonhumans. These evaluations feed back into the production of new forms of agency. This is one way in which those practices we retrospectively call "religion" can have historical consequences. In conclusion, I suggest that attending to the materiality of social phenomena, and the semiotic ideologies that mediate people's responses to that materiality, may help archaeologists avoid some of the temptations of teleological thinking.

Art, religion and utility

Much of the speculation about religion at Çatalhöyük is based on its visual displays. The site has yielded some of the earliest known paintings on human-made surfaces. Paintings and reliefs are found in many excavated houses. Along with patterns and handprints are some striking figural images of animals and humans. Interior walls also contain painted plaster reliefs of leopards and bears. It is immediately apparent that both paintings and reliefs feature wild animals whose remains are rare in the settlement, in contrast to those of sheep and goats, which are by far the most common faunal remains (Russell and Twiss 2008). Embedded in walls, pillars and benches are bucrania, the plastered-over skulls and horns of wild cattle, and skulls of foxes and weasels. Some walls also bear protuberances, within which were hidden the lower jaws of wild boars.

In contrast to work built into the physical structure of the house, large quantities of tiny figurines are found, mostly in domestic rubbish heaps between houses (Hodder 2006: 194; Nakamura and Meskell 2008). The figurines were quickly made and in most cases are smaller than the palm of a hand. Among these figurines is perhaps the most famous object from Çatalhöyük, resembling a heavy-set human, apparently a female, her arms resting on two felines. This image helped give rise to the early speculations that Çatalhöyük was home to a mother goddess cult (Gimbutas 1982; Mellaart 1967; cf. Meskell 1998). Most, however, are more roughly shaped to form vaguely human or animal-like forms.

This art has been taken to exemplify the increased symbolic activity that marks the Neolithic. It has also been a chief focus of speculation about its inhabitants' religion. In fact, the relationship between art and religion is virtually predetermined by the way in which the writers have defined them. The main diagnostic for identifying material remains as art or evidence of religion is their supposed lack of utility. If the absence of utility is diagnostic of the symbolic, then the explanation of the symbolic is usually taken to lie in its meaningfulness. This definition of symbol thus isolates a domain of meaning from the practical. Not only does this separation threaten to render the practical meaningless, it also defines art and religion in terms of meaning, which, as I will suggest later, is equally misleading.

According to Jacques Cauvin, for example, the symbolic revolution was manifested early through the appearance in Pre-Pottery Neolithic B of flint knapping on bipolar nuclei to produce fine regular blades and the use of a flat lamellar retouch on blades, which, he says, takes them beyond the requirements of utility (2000: 243). Of the display of bull skulls, he writes, "These devices are obviously symbolic, for very little hunting of the wild bull itself took place" (2000: 238). Similarly, Bleda Düring's (2001) analysis of the data on houses at Çatalhöyük shows a regular contrast between clean and dirty areas, the latter associated with food preparation (Hodder 1999:186), an observation confirmed by micro-analysis (see Matthews, Wiles and Almond 2006). From this, Düring draws the conclusion that these are respectively the "symbolically charged" and the domestic areas of the house. This pattern of diagnosis is widespread in treatments of the material record: in the absence of apparent utility, the assumption runs, we must be in the presence of the symbolic.

According to a venerable tradition in British social anthropology, lack of utility virtually defines something as religious. This way of thinking persists in some more recent definitions of religion. For instance, in Harvey Whitehouse's opinion, "What both ritual and art have in common is their incorporation of elements that are superfluous to any practical aim and, thus, are irreducible to technical motivations" (2004: 3). Similarly, Steven Mithen writes, "Artefacts which relate directly to religious ideas lack any utilitarian explanation" (1998: 98). If the symbolic is defined as the meaningful, then religion is the quintessential expression of the symbolic. And if religion is defined by meaning, then the central question one should ask is, what does it mean?

There are a number of problems with the assumptions these approaches display. First, of course, is the sheer difficulty of accurately identifying a lack of utility. Just as the absence of proof cannot be taken as a proof of absence, so too the investigator's inability to imagine a use for something may demonstrate nothing more than the limits of his or her imagination – or breadth of ethnographic knowledge. What, for example, could be more useless in modern times than the study of a "dead" language like Latin? But it is useless only if one does not, say, think it is the actual language of God or has magical powers, or if one ignores the social utility of status display through conspicuous educational consumption. When Constantine placed the Christian *labarum* sign on his soldiers' shields, it was not as a useless symbol: he was activating divine power to a very practical end, victory in warfare. Conversely, efficient European state bureaucracies emerged out of ecclesiastical structures designed to serve religious purposes (Gorski 2003). Anyone familiar with American car culture will recognize the inseparability of transportational function from status, sex and power. And surely we ought not to be forced into deciding that American baseball and European football are either religious or practical.

Efforts to isolate "the symbolic" as a distinct set of empirical observations reproduce an invidious dichotomy, in which the symbolic stands apart from the truly useful. To separate the archaeological evidence into things that are useful and those that are symbolic implies that the practical side of human activity is *not* symbolic. Yet an enduring insight of cultural anthropology is that even hunting reflects cultural choices made on the basis of certain values (Sahlins 1972). So we might turn back to Cauvin's bull skulls. Suppose they were displayed by people who regularly ate

the animals; would that make their display any less symbolic? Not necessarily – look at rice in East Asia (Ohnuki-Tierney 1993). Nor can we
know that apparently more humble aspects of life in Çatalhöyük were not
symbolic. Furthermore, even if we were to demonstrate a lack of utility
in any given instance, this would be neither necessary nor sufficient to
count as an instance of religion. Religion may be, for some people, the
ultimate utility. What could be more functional than protection against
misfortune, access to divine powers or guidance to the good life?

It is no doubt significant that the inhabitants of Çatalhöyük portrayed
and displayed the skulls only of animals they hunted and that were not
their primary sources of food.[1] And this pattern does suggest that such
animals were foci of particular kinds of attentiveness and interest. It does
not follow from this that the display of bucrania is peculiarly symbolic in
ways that the making of pottery, the harvesting of lentils or the marrying
of cousins are not; the ethnographic and archaeological record is full of
examples of the "meaningfulness" of precisely "practical" things (Bradley
2005; Fogelin 2007; Walker 1998). Nor is this evidence that wild animals
are somehow more symbolic than domesticated ones. People on Sumba,
the Indonesian island where I have done fieldwork, keep water buffalo.
They talk endlessly about their qualities, represent them on tombs and
display their horns on houses. They are an expensive sacrifice and offering
to ancestral spirits. But this makes them neither more nor less useful –
nor more or less meaningful – than deer, horses, wild boars, dogs or
chickens. Rather, it marks them out against an unmarked surround, a
process I return to later.

Religious ideas?

If one identifies necessity with the material world of cause and effect, and
religion with its opposite, it typically follows that the latter will be identified with immaterial ideas. To the extent that the symbolic is a distinct
domain and identifiable with a certain class of noninstrumental objects,
those objects themselves have a distinctive relationship to the world of
thought and activity. That relationship is usually one of representation:

---

[1] In 2008 a single sheep's skull was found embedded in a wall and plastered over
(Çatalhöyük Research Project 2008), but it is not clear if the animal was wild or
domestic (Nerissa Russell, pers. comm.).

the material object expresses, and is logically secondary to, the idea that gave rise to it. But as Carolyn Nakamura and Lynn Meskell remark:

> The notion of representation entails a remove from the real, it depicts a likeness, rendition or perception rather than the immediacy of the object in question. . . . By employing the notion of representation we infer that figurines stand in for something real and are a reflection of that reality, of someone or something. And yet these objects are not necessarily referent for something else tangible, but could be experienced as real and tangible things in themselves. (2006: 229)

The point does not just hold for the distant world of the Neolithic. Early Christian icons functioned to make divinity present, not to depict it (Belting 1994); in India, the figure of a god furnishes that eye before which the worshipper makes himself or herself visible (Davis 1997; Pinney 2004; cf. Morgan 2005). Some visual images, such as Navaho sand paintings (Newcombe 1937) and designs in various media by Australian Walbiri (Munn 1973), are above all outcomes of the processes by which they were created, and eventually destroyed; they are not images meant primarily for the gaze (nor, for that matter, are the visual patterns created by most modern-day crossword puzzles). Something similar is very likely in the case of Çatalhöyük's paintings, which were plastered over and seem to have had a short life span as "rare, transient events" (Matthews et al. 2006: 285).[2] Even an image that is meant to be viewed by a spectator presupposes significant material conditions. As Holl observes of Saharan rock art, "The conversion of these media into cogent ideas is subject to sensory and motor capabilities as well as skill and understanding" (2004: 5). To treat artifacts, or even pictures, as representations is to look *beyond* their fundamental materiality and all that makes it possible and that follows from it.

Discussions of prehistoric religion at Çatalhöyük have tended to treat material objects as representing ideas.[3] Cauvin, for instance, pays special

---

[2] Interior walls, which presumably grew sooty fast, were plastered on a regular, repeated basis; e.g., one wall was washed and replastered 700 times in 70 years (Matthews 2005). Paintings would have required special efforts to preserve, and indeed, the reliefs did receive such efforts, being renewed through periodic replastering.

[3] Not all major theories of religion in Çatalhöyük are subject to this criticism. David Lewis-Williams (2004), e.g., tries to reconstruct a phenomenology of life within the houses. Unfortunately, his conclusion, that Çatalhöyük was home to shamanism, is

attention to the bull horns embedded in the walls and what he takes to be females carved in stone and molded in clay. From these he concludes, "These two figures, the woman and the bull, were destined to represent the divine couple, the mother-goddess and bull-god, which were to persist in the Near East and the eastern Mediterranean from the Neolithic until the classic period; the bulls, for instance, foreshadow the Phoenician and Hittite god Ghada, also represented as riding a bull" (2000: 238). There are good reasons to be wary of this reading and its bold leap across millennia.[4] What I want to stress here is how the representational approach can incline one in this direction. First, the very category of representation leads Cauvin to see horns and figurines as part of a single complex: male bulls, female figurines. But why should such different kinds of things be any more connected than any other set of objects in Çatalhöyük? Apparently it is the concept of representation, rather than anything about their form, means of production, location or evidence of treatment, that induces Cauvin to see them as related. They form a complex because they are both representations. Much of his interpretation depends on this initial step of grouping them together by virtue of their membership in this dubious class.

The representational approach to material evidence plays an especially important role in the major cognitivist interpretations of Çatalhöyük religion. This is perhaps not surprising, given the two foundational premises of the latter approach. One, already mentioned, is that religion, like art, is defined in opposition to practicality. The second is that religion consists primarily of beliefs. It follows that material objects, like practices, are secondary to the beliefs they serve to express. The task, then, is how to get from the object to the belief. For Mithen, this means taking the paintings of Çatalhöyük as literal depictions of the content of people's ideas. A similar representational interpretation to Çatalhöyük is given by Trevor

---

largely unsubstantiated by the actual evidence. He claims shamanism derives from universal neurophysiological experiences, but like all such claims, this one fails to account for why those experiences are elaborated only in some social worlds and not others. Moreover, if neurophysiology is already sufficient to produce those experiences, it would seem unnecessary to reproduce those phenomena in wall paintings and other manipulations of the external environment.

[4] Nakamura and Meskell (2008) argue that the figurines indicate no particular interest in sexuality or reproduction, the usual explanation of "mother goddesses." In many cases even the identification of the figures as female is uncertain (Voigt 2000: 283).

Watkins. He describes the transition from Palaeolithic to Neolithic as a shift in balance between nature and culture, in which people "devised means of embodying abstract concepts, beliefs and ideas about themselves and their world in externalized, permanent forms" (2004: 97). In both cases, Mithen and Watkins treat material things as evidence for immaterial concepts. There is certainly nothing wrong with this as speculative strategy. But it becomes problematic when it also leads us to ignore the implications of their materiality, and to assume that things function *in order to* express concepts, rather than as indexical entailments like those left by *any* mode of activity, no matter how mundane and utilitarian. As I will suggest in the conclusion, to see them as indexical is to situate them in the causal nexuses through which they circulate socially and endure historically.

Ideas leave material traces only to the extent that they take the form of activities. But this is not merely a methodological scruple. It may be a more realistic way to think about mental life, as it is lived within society (Keane 2008). Once we try to look *past* the things, in our effort to get at ideas, their materiality ceases to be informative. But that materiality is crucial to their place within social life, and not just as a determinant. It is as material things that pictures and figurines, houses and burials have causes, effects and histories. It is as material things that they enter into people's perceptions, stir memories, provoke thoughts, conjure up actions. As material they are conditions for possibilities that may, or may not, be realized. Being material, things are part of the shared experiences and actions that mediate sociality. They are not just sensory inputs for individual cognitions.

Elements of religion

The ethnographic variety of historically known societies suggests these general axioms for the investigation of prehistoric religion:

Function: Religion does not serve some particular psychological or sociological function. In any empirical setting it may serve many functions or none, and those functions may shift from context to context.

Genealogies: Trying to link prehistoric remains to much later religions not only is questionable on grounds of evidence, but also encourages a teleological bias toward what persists in later periods at the expense of important elements of the prehistoric context that failed to do so.

Beliefs: Religion is not necessarily defined by any *particular* beliefs, much less the contemplation of deep meanings.[5] It may, for instance, consist of practices and disciplines around which, historically, ideas develop and change. And even granting that religious practices are unlikely to endure without involving ideas of some sort, similar beliefs can sustain different practices, and different beliefs can underlie the same practices, which may thrive despite conflicting interpretations.

Deities: Religion is not necessarily defined by the presence of supernatural agents. This follows in part from the injunction against placing beliefs at the definitional heart of religion. But it also follows from ethnographic observation, that sometimes it makes no sense to draw a line between religion and magic, which requires no agents (Du Bois 1993; Keane 2007; Pels 2003), or between spirits, ancestors and elders, who are not supernatural (Kopytoff 1971).

Religion: We should not assume there is always and everywhere some clearly demarked domain we can call "religion" as such (see Asad 1993; Masuzawa 2005; Saler 1993).

These axioms are not meant to dissolve an important dimension of human societies. Rather, I will suggest that much of what seems to fit received categories of religion lies at one end of a continuum of forms of attention and hierarchies of value that range from relatively unmarked to marked. That marked end of the spectrum brings together a heterogeneous variety of practices, ideas and institutions. There may well be no single source for those phenomena that have come to look like "religion" to observers today. More likely, a wide range of experiences, cognitive potentials and sociological phenomena provided material that could come together in different formations that would eventually be called religion. The list should be kept open-ended, and surely it involves experiences and ideas that range along a spectrum from those that are clearly not "religious" to those that are excellent candidates for "religious" (see Smith 1982).

---

[5] Ethnographers have long known that practitioners of ritual, magic, divination, trance, etc. may lack any theory of how or why these work, and even find the question uninteresting. The centrality of beliefs may also be challenged in philosophically self-conscious contexts as well (e.g., Kellner 2006; Lopez 1998; Sharf 1998).

The marked and the absent

The materials from Çatalhöyük suggest two aspects of experience that would count as candidates for "religious," those that are *marked* for attention and those that seem to point toward some significant or potent *absence*. Neither is confined to phenomena that we might call "religious." They are neither necessary nor sufficient to define religion. But markedness and absence seem characteristic of experiences that have been classified under rubrics like "spirituality" and "transcendence." Unlike those terms, however, "markedness" and "absence" lend themselves to the task of sorting out material evidence.

By "marked," I refer to any features of an activity or experience that convey a sense of being unusual and demanding special attention, in contrast to unmarked alternatives (Keane 2008). What is crucial here is that the sense of being marked arises from the evidence, and not from our own a priori assumptions about what is or is not ordinary. We cannot know in advance what will strike other people as normal or strange, taken for granted or hard to believe. To one who is socialized to expect that there are witches or spirits all around, they may seem quite ordinary. But this does not mean that life presents itself to people as an unvarying plane of sameness. There are elements in any social or cultural world that seem strange *to the people themselves.* In any instance, however, outside observers cannot rely on their own intuitions to decide what those elements will be. They must attend to the ways in which things *are made* the focus of special attention, are marked in some way.

For example, everyone has noticed that large cattle are accorded special treatment in Çatalhöyük that marks them as unusual relative to small or domesticated animals. But that special treatment itself is likely to be a dialectical response to an emergent sense of the distinctiveness of cattle in a world within which some animals have become domesticated. As wild cattle came to stand apart in ordinary experience, special treatment began to mark them as apart in ways that demand yet further attention and may have produced further markedness. That attention might not derive entirely from unmediated experience. Ian Hodder (pers. comm.) points out that wild animals might already have been in close relation with humans at Çatalhöyük, so there may have been no sharp distinction between the wild and the domesticated. Yet the distinction in the treatment of their remains seems fairly clear. The practices of killing and display may have helped sharpen a distinction that was less evident in ordinary experience. Then, as cattle became increasingly domesticated, this marking may have become less interesting, relevant or plausible. Perhaps, given the widening scope of people's powers of domestication, mastery of cattle seemed a less potent image of human powers than other manifestations of agency. This may be one reason that bucrania installations and the proportion of cattle remains relative to that of sheep decrease in the higher levels at Çatalhöyük.

My hypothesis is that, on the one hand, marking for attention will not be drawn to just *any* aspect of experience but, on the other, *not all* things that stand apart in experience will come to be so marked.[6] Once some things (such as wild cattle) *are* marked out for attention by certain practices, however, the distinction between them and the background of ordinary things (such as sheep) will become accentuated and thus more perceptible, making them more interesting and subject to still further attention. This further attention may have contributed not just to religion but to domestication too.

Actions that are marked tend to seem, to the practitioners, linked to some sort of risk, difficulty or hard work. Rituals are not always rigid, rule-bound or repetitious, but they do seem to require some degree of attentiveness *in response to* some special pragmatic challenge they face, such as communicating with invisible agents or counteracting an otherwise given state of affairs.[7] Activities called religious commonly invoke or produce the felt *absence* of a potent entity or force. For example, offerings are often designed to deal with the problem of conveying a material gift to an immaterial recipient; similarly, ritual speech is marked by the special efforts needed to communicate with an invisible and inaudible listener (Keane 1997a,b).

But to put the matter in these terms places beliefs prior to material activity. What if we start with material practices (as is often the case for

---

[6] Colin Renfrew (1994; cf. Renfrew and Bahn 1991) included "focusing of attention" in his list of indicators of ritual. Where my approach differs, I think, is in proposing that the marking process is not just something produced by a religious system, but a moment in an emergent set of dialectical responses to experience, *out of which* "the religious" may emerge. The mark may precede, ontogenically, the attention it draws.

[7] Ritual should not be conflated with religion (see Humphrey and Laidlaw 2007). However, definitional questions aside, the material evidence for prehistoric religion is most likely to have been produced by ritual (Kyriakidis 2007), which will perforce be my focus here.

participants, especially novices)? Through the special efforts they involve and their formal features, religious practices *construct the very difficulties they seem designed to overcome.* In the process, these activities constitute transcendence by means of transitions or transformations across semiotic modalities. By these means, they render available to experience the *very absence* they invoke (say, that of the dead or of protective spirits or demonic forces), and not other absences (e.g, travelers, other people's dead, lost property), and mark that relevant absence as a focus of attention.

This possibility is already built into the basic structure of human semiosis. The feint that might otherwise seem to be an aggressive punch points to and builds on the significance of a contrast between what is present and what is absent (Bateson 1972). Thus, a wall painting of cattle in Çatalhöyük, whatever else it does, takes its significance not only from making present the animal it portrays, but also from pointing to the *difference* between that painting and the animal which is *not present*.[8] This capacity to thematize presence and absence – and the potential reflexivity it may help develop – may be a more useful way of defining "the symbolic" than the more traditional focus on "meaning."

Marking certain aspects of experience for special attention does not necessarily produce religion: warfare or difficult craft skills might also call for such attention. And the production of absence likewise need not mean religion: any kinship group that extends beyond individuals who are physically present at the moment already deals in absences. But when markedness and absence converge and become thematized, those various things anthropologists have called religious may begin to emerge. In particular, by producing a sense of otherness, they help make agency into a more clearly delineated object of experience, reflection and reappropriation.

Killing and displaying wild animals

In Çatalhöyük, food plants, sheep and goats had been domesticated, but cattle and equids remained wild. The period was at a tipping point in

---

[8] Notice that this is consistent with the criticism of approaches to representation expressed by Nakamura and Meskell (2006), which I quoted earlier. Where they emphasize the consequences of focusing on the absent referent, at the expense of the present object, I stress the ways in which the present object can make the *distinction* between the two parts of its significance.

8.1. Bull horns stacked above a bull skull installed in the wall in Building 52, Çatalhöyük. *Source*: Jason Quinlan and Çatalhöyük Research Project.

the processes of domestication. I do not mean by this the teleological fallacy that assumes people in Çatalhöyük knew where they were heading in history, or in some sense *needed* to head in a certain direction (see Pels, Chapter 9). Rather, the sense of a tipping point may have taken the form of people's *sharpened awareness of contrasts that they found interesting*. Certain elements of experience came to be marked as possible foci for attention and, perhaps, innovative efforts.

In Çatalhöyük, foraging was giving way to agriculture, and hunting was coming to coexist with herding. The vast majority of faunal remains come from domesticated animals like sheep and goats, isotope analysis indicating they were the primary sources of dietary protein (Richards and Pearson 2005; Russell and Martin 2005). Yet the buildings display bucrania from wild bulls and depictions of bulls, deer, bears, leopards and equines (Figure 8.1). Moreover, there is more evidence of feasting on cattle than on sheep and goats. Taken together, this suggests that wild animals had some grip over people's imagination. No doubt such animals held power over the imagination for Palaeolithic hunters as well. What is important at Çatalhöyük is that hunting now offered a possible contrast to animals that were killed but not hunted. In this semiotic economy, not only were deer and bulls things that humans killed and ate, they were also animals that were not domesticated. The contrast between wild and domesticated seems to be not just an opposition that we, the observers, impose on the people of Çatalhöyük, but an approximation of a focus of attention and interest of their own that seems to be emerging from the material remains.

Some observers take the remains of bulls and the depictions of leopards as evidence that violence played a central role in Çatalhöyük religion. But the category of violence is excessively capacious, encompassing everything from the excited sadism of bear baiter or lynch mob to the indifference of the butcher or the professional hit man. Those who obtain meat themselves rather than from the market, and those who have never formed relations with pets, may not see the killing of animals to be violence at all.

Consider, as a provocation to the imagination, the slaughter of buffalo in contemporary Sumba. Sumbanese society in the 1990s was based on an economy of pastoralism and small-scale subsistence farming (Keane 1997a). Water buffalo and horses were used primarily as work animals, buffalo trampling rice fields to ready them for planting, horses affording transportation. They were also among the most valuable and prestigious items used in the ceremonial exchanges necessary for marriages and burials, among other major events. Most buffalo, and some horses, were eventually slaughtered and butchered, and their meat was distributed in public sacrifices. Virtually no meat was ever eaten outside the context of ceremonial feasting, and traditionally not even a chicken was killed without first being offered to the ancestral spirits.

As I mentioned, there are some clear contrasts between Sumba and Çatalhöyük. First, unlike aurochs but like the sheep and goats of Çatalhöyük, Sumbanese water buffalo are domesticated. Second, Sumbanese buffalo killing takes place within a hierarchy of sacrificial value that also includes offerings of betel nut and the killing of chickens, pigs and horses.[9] The hierarchy reflects the kind of labor, the extent of kinship ties and the powers of exchange relations that are concretized in the very existence of the animal. Third, the components that ritualists consider most important leave no material traces: prayers and divinatory reading of the entrails of the victim.

---

[9] Bucrania, mandibles and similar remains placed in houses offer the strongest evidence for the ritual use of animals in Çatalhöyük, but for speculation about the significance of cranes, see Russell and McGowan (2003).

8.2. Slaughtering buffalo for mortuary feast, West Sumba. *Source*: Webb Keane.

Sacrifice of chickens was far more common than that of larger animals, but the killing itself elicited little interest. The killing of small and weak animals lacks drama and offers little opportunity for spectatorship. Buffalo slaughter, on the other hand, is a hugely popular spectacle (Figure 8.2). It takes place in the village plaza, and everyone who is able to watch does so with great enthusiasm. But what is that enthusiasm about? First, there is a certain thrill in the sheer display of wealth and its expenditure. The killing produces huge quantities of meat, which people anticipate with enormous relish. Many spectators focus on the risk-taking bravado of the young men who undertake the killing. And people seem to find the fatal blow of the machete and the struggles of the buffalo to be fascinating, and sometimes to carry divinatory significance.

What did Sumbanese see in the spectacle? Power, domination, fear, the killers' display of athleticism, youth and masculinity, identification with or a vast sense of distance from the victim, sadism or empathy, excitement at the dramatic movements of the animals, amusement at the occasional slapstick may all be involved, even the joy of humiliating a great beast (Hoskins 1993) – a sentiment echoed, perhaps, in the painting at Çatalhöyük that might portray men teasing an auroch. The slaughter also results in meat. Sumbanese love to eat meat, but do so

8.3. Front veranda of a house in West Sumba in the mid-1980s publicly displays tokens from past feasts. Water buffalo horns are stacked along the exterior wall; rows of pig mandibles hang from cords running from wall to outer pillar. *Source*: Webb Keane.

only at ceremonial feasts. These bodily pleasures are inseparable from the giving and receiving they presuppose, the commensality and reciprocity. Confronted with evidence of killing, we cannot be sure that violence is the principal focus of attention. It may also be mere excitement, in which the killing is inseparable from the stimulation of being in a crowd and the anticipation of the feast.

So if Sumbanese objectify themselves in the form of the sacrificial animal, they also absorb that objectified beast into their own flesh. They are very aware of the pleasures of satiety and renewed vigor this produces. The dead body of the animal becomes part of the revitalized living body of the feasters; the animal rendered an object of human actions contributes to their constitution as subjects both through the agency by which they kill the beast and through the act of consumption by which they appropriate it to themselves. This is a kind of objectification, an externalization of an aspect of oneself, at the same time that it is a subjectification of the object world.

The objectification process leaves traces not just in the bodies of the eater, but in their houses. Across the ethnographic record, we find people discovering certain latent possibilities in the remains of feasts. For example, not only are cattle horns dramatic in their own right (being large, hard, pointed), but also since they are durable, they can be accumulated over time and, at any given moment, enumerated (Figures 8.3 and 8.4).

8.4. Buffalo horns depicted on contemporary stone tomb, West Sumba. *Source*: Webb Keane.

The houses of feast givers in Sumba display rows of mandibles and stacks of horns from past feasts (Keane 1997a; see also Adams 2005; Hodder 2005). These displays make immediately obvious the relative strength of each household as feast givers. They manifest both the inherent interest of certain animals and the social differentiation that feasting entails. Since horns accumulate over long periods of time (and some houses never develop the wherewithal to stage feasts), at any given moment they represent the *historical fact* of the house's situation within a multigenerational career. What is relevant to Çatalhöyük is that the difference between displays in houses is not necessarily categorical (some houses are by definition places where horns are displayed) but contingent (excavators are catching houses at different stages of development).

In Çatalhöyük, animals that are represented and those that are major sources of food exist in complementary distribution. Sheep and goats may be good to eat but they are not good to display. Viewed retrospectively as milestones on the road to domestication, they objectify human agency, yet they do not *stand for it* in the marked contexts. Why are cattle more interesting? Perhaps it is not just their danger, but the way they live at the very edges of human control: we can kill them but nothing is guaranteed. The fully domesticated animal, on the other hand, is too thoroughly subjugated; again, this may be one reason for the apparent dropoff in interest in cattle in the later houses.[10]

The point of killing need not be violence, or even life's end, as such. As Valerio Valeri observed, killing dramatizes the ubiquitous experience of transformation or transition from presence to absence: "Sacrificial death and destruction . . . represent the passage from the visible to the invisible and thereby make it possible to conceive the transformations the sacrifice is supposed to produce" (Valeri 1985: 69; cf. Bloch 1992). Sumbanese make clear that killing forms a bridge to the invisible world. Sacrificial animals must die in order to convey messages between the manifest world of the living and the invisible world of the dead.

Perhaps we do not have to decide which aspect of killing or feasting is the key one. These aspects are all bundled together (see Keane 2003). All components of this bundle of features (wealth, social power, domination over the wild, youthful folly, masculine bravado, plentitude and the feelings of meaty satiation, aggression, fear, transition from visible to invisible, from living animal to dead meat, incorporation of edible object into vital subject) are in principle available for attention, elaboration and development. Different components of this bundle may come into play in different circumstances; some that were only latent in one context may

---

[10] Interestingly, some Sumbanese myths suggest that cattle are held in contempt for having surrendered their powers of speech along with their autonomy in return for the ease of life in the corral (Hoskins 1993). It is almost as if Sumbanese wish there were still really dangerous wild beasts to contend with, yet also recognize they could sacrifice only mute ones.

become prominent in another, only to recede again in yet another. At any given historical moment and social configuration, the range of experiences and practices opens into multiple possible pathways. Nor need only one of those pathways prevail: herding may coexist with farming and trade, ancestors with animal spirits and deities.

In Çatalhöyük, the markedness of wild aurochs and deer, in contrast to the unmarked character of sheep and goats, suggests that the distinction between control and lack of control was quite salient for inhabitants. We might think of control over aurochs as a question of contested agency: aurochs have power of their own, against which human power is measured. This is perhaps one way of understanding Cauvin's speculation that Neolithic developments derived from "a certain existential dissatisfaction" (2000: 242) that drove the emergent human perception that nature is something that should be transformed.

Burials and habitual life in the house

I suggested that religion may emerge out of the convergence of different kinds of process. In Çatalhöyük, this convergence seems to have a physical dimension: the marked, the absent and the habitual are brought together in the daily life within the house. Wild, dangerous animals that had been mastered through punctate events of killing and, in some cases, eating were incorporated into the house, which was also, of course, a locus of the ongoing flow of daily routine. People in Çatalhöyük lived with the traces of wild animals. Some of these traces seem to have been designed to induce the experience of a potent absence. For example, the hidden mandibles were manifested as protrusions from the walls – pointing to something that cannot be seen. These were only some ways in which the houses seem to have pointed toward an absence. For example, paintings that were plastered over were no longer visible, but probably still remembered.

The most ubiquitous form absence takes in Çatalhöyük is perhaps that of the dead, who, buried in the platforms, coexist invisibly with the living in the house.[11] In contrast to the prominence of bucrania displays, given the small size of these houses, burials are understated. This

[11] Although not all houses hold burials, almost all known burials are inside houses (a few are in middens; Hodder and Cessford 2004: 29). A preliminary analysis (Düring 2001: 10–11; see also Düring 2003) showed that 20% of buildings have burials and moldings. Although houses are fairly similar in size and layout, burials are not evenly distributed

makes sense if we think of death as having a place within ongoing cycles of reproduction, along with birth, child rearing, cooking and feeding, unmarked habitual activities centered in the house. But intramural burials also seem to form a transition between the more marked and unmarked ends of the spectrum. We can assume human deaths were powerful events, and like cattle feasts, they would have a punctate, event-like character (if not, perhaps, the same display of agency that killing cattle might have shown), in contrast to the flow of everyday life. The treatment of some corpses, like that of wild animals, suggests special attention to the head. Certain corpses had had the heads removed, and it seems that some skulls were later dug up and reused in different contexts. The headless burials recall the paintings of headless humans and the many figurines whose heads were purposely broken off or designed to be detachable (Nakamura and Meskell 2006; Voigt 2000). Detached human skulls appear in some foundation and abandonment deposits (Hodder and Cessford 2004: 35). Like the bucrania, some human skulls were "refleshed" with plaster (Hodder 2006: 148). We cannot specify what this attention to heads means, or even that there is a single meaning, but these treatments seem good evidence for markedness.[12]

Human corpses, cattle horns, boar mandibles, paintings and reliefs all find their place in the house – in close proximity to cooking, eating and sleeping. As I suggested earlier, however, the display of horns and paintings might be traces of an individual house's place in an ongoing career or history rather than a purely categorical distinction. Horns and paintings form a gradient of accumulated markings that stand out against the unmarked background of ordinary habits that shape every house and render houses so uniform in other respects; this might even be true of the large number of burials that accrued to certain houses. Main rooms are always divided by platforms; ovens and hearths are usually on the south side, the entrance ladder nearby, art and burials to the north, large reliefs on the west walls (Hodder and Cessford 2004). This uniformity, along with the sheer density of habitation, is a striking feature of Çatalhöyük.

among them, but seem to cluster, with as many as 62 in a single house (Hodder and Cessford 2004: 35–6).

[12] In the past, Sumbanese took trophy heads in raids and displayed them on altars in the plaza in the center of the village; and to this day, it is widely believed that heads or entire corpses from human sacrifice are used in foundation rituals for unusually large, modern edifices (on headhunting see Keane 1997a: 41–3, 256–7). But headhunting is subject to a wide range of interpretations even by the actors themselves.

Not only are most houses alike, they often go through as many as 500–1,000 years of rebuilding on the same location with little variation in basic layout (Hodder and Cessford 2004: 20).[13] This seems to be the trace of habitus, the structuring repetitions that reflect the conditions that unconsciously produce regular ways of doing things, the somatic or aesthetic feel for the appropriate, the right procedure, the pleasing fit (Bourdieu 1977).[14] Evidence from Sumbanese houses suggests that this uniformity is an effect produced by habit, much as a trail is worn, not from a rule or a decision, but as one footstep absently follows another, along a line already laid out by predecessors. In Sumba, houses materialize aspects of cosmology. Their builders draw on their experiences of helping to erect previous houses, and they seem most comfortable raising the central pillars on the same spots as their predecessors, reusing what materials they can salvage. It is the materiality of former houses more than purposeful intentions and formal regulations that reproduces their form in new houses.

In Sumbanese daily routines, some habits fall near the self-consciously "religious" end of a spectrum: the modest shelf on which betel nut is left for the spirits, the display of pig mandibles from past sacrifices, the knowledge that the most recent ancestors are in the attic. Others are harder to mark off this way: the intuitive distinctions between spaces more suited for male or female activities, aligned with relatively outward and inward oriented spaces, the prohibition on moving a certain hearthstone. In a Sumbanese house, it simply feels right to locate sleep and sex in the innermost room where the ancestors' inalienable valuables are stored. This is how bodily habits realize cosmological models.

Human intentions are materialized in the house, which is the environment within which children are formed (Watkins 2004). Spaces are separated by solid walls (quite different from those of huts or tents) and rendered out of sight from one another: there are people on all sides,

---

[13] Some evidence suggests that old bucrania were dug out of older layers of the house to be retrieved for reuse when later houses were built (Hodder 1999: 189; Hodder and Cessford 2004).

[14] Hodder and Cessford use the word "rule" to describe the routine behaviors that produced this uniformity, but I think the word "rule" is misleading, since it suggests conscious representations, models that are external to the activity itself (Taylor 1993). The power of Bourdieu's concept of "habitus" lies in its *causal logic*, that bodies somatically reproduce the conditions that produced them without the necessary intervention of directives or prohibitions.

above and below, known, possibly heard, but not seen. The structure renders some things out of sight within itself as well: walls harbor mandibles and paintings that have been plastered over; platforms contain corpses. In such spaces, the play between the perceptible and imperceptible (but known), simple experiences of footsteps above and voices in other rooms may have provoked the imagination.

Çatalhöyük houses suggest that their inhabitants' daily experience involved a play of visible and invisible, presence and absence. Even descending by ladder from the roof into the house, and from bright day into the darkness below (Last 1998), or moving from one room to another, although utterly ordinary, may have prompted the imagination (and, given the open landscape of the Konya Plain, perhaps nowhere but in houses were such experiences likely). This everyday experience, along with the more marked signs of absence (burials, mandibles, bucrania, paintings), may have played into a more general aspect of the house, which could be experienced as a stage for appearing and disappearing, visibility and hiding. Its interior spaces are separated by walls and rendered out of sight from one another: there are people on all sides, above and below, known but not perceived (except, perhaps, by sound). The play between the perceptible and imperceptible, the present and absent (but known) is one ordinary experiential source from which a sense of transcendence might be produced. There is a very old theory that the concept of spirits might arise from witnessing the transition from life to death. Less familiar is the possibility that the concept might also be prompted by the sound of muffled voices from other rooms. The visual displays and hidden mandibles, the postmortem handling of human skulls and the digging up of old bucrania from earlier levels may all be evidence of the inhabitants' interest in controlling the transitions between presence and absence, between visible and invisible. The house, containing both the visibly present and the palpably absent, the marked and the habitual, could be a physical and, perhaps, conceptual point of convergence for those effects out of whose combination emerged something we might call "religion."

Subjects and their objects

The plastered or "refleshed" skull seems to reverse the process by which animals are reduced from fleshed, living things to bony objects of human actions. Less dramatically, the working of obsidian takes away from stone to produce an object of human agency; as a form of self-objectification, the process of making pottery is like the refleshing of a skull, producing a thing with a membrane-like surface from a nonthing. If killing effects a transformation from a living subject to a dead object, the crafting of artifacts undertakes the reverse, from objects to extensions of the subjects who made them. In both cases, the result is an expression of human agency and its abilities to transform the world.

The Neolithic in Anatolia was marked by a massive increase in the sheer quantity of things made by people, including buildings, pottery and textiles (Hodder 2006: 241, 2007). For the first time, people were spending their daily lives in environments that were largely of human construction or subject to ongoing human manipulation, in towns, agricultural fields and pastures (Watkins 2004).[15] Lynn Meskell remarks that the materiality of human artifacts "represents a presence of power in realizing the world, crafting thing from nonthing, subject from nonsubject" (2004: 249). The numerous figurines of Çatalhöyük, for instance, seem to be small presences. This is what a child's doll, a hex figure and a worshipper's amulet have in common: they are companions, social others who are smaller than me, over whom I can exercise some dominion. They can be carried about, manipulated, hidden, kept to oneself, passed around, lost accidently or on purpose. They are quintessential objects before my subjecthood as an agent in a physical world. At the same time, yet insofar as they invoke the agency of living beings, they may also represent my power over the agency, not just the physical being, of others. In this respect, we may see some parallel to the relationship between humans and animals.

Nakamura and Meskell (2006: 238) write of the clay figurines, "The figured world of Çatalhöyük directs our attention to heads and necks, stomachs and buttocks, with scant attention to arms, legs, feet, facial features. The torso is the main area of interest." Writing of the rounded form of these torsos, Voigt concludes that although we cannot tell if the figurines are fat or pregnant, their apparent heft means they "have a relatively high amount of leisure time and are exempt from the kind of heavy labor performed by village women today" (2000: 288). Although we

---

[15] As Pels (Chapter 9, this volume) points out, the increase in *artifacts* must not be confused with an increase in "materiality" per se; hunting and gathering take place within, and make use of, quite as material a set of circumstances as anything else.

should be careful not to assume that such images are representations of something other than what they are, the observation is suggestive. Ethnographic experience suggests that some images are powerful because they are *counterfactual*. This is more than just a matter of being memorable, as the cognitive approaches suggest. More specifically, they present alternatives to certain nagging anxieties or frustrations associated with core social values. In a society in which exchange is of central importance, such as Sumba, some myths enact fantasies of a world without the relentless pressure of one's exchange partners (Keane 1997a). In a world in which new forms of labor such as agriculture and herding are beginning to impinge on people, a life without labor may be especially interesting. Some images may offer, in effect, meditations on certain salient, morally loaded conditions of life.

Objects are under the agency, and can serve as extensions, of subjects. But they are also entities that stand apart from them. Whatever the original purpose of the decorations in houses, they became part of the environment within which human subjects come to know themselves. The house itself exemplifies this. Living within walls, people are contained within a microcosm that they know themselves to have produced and that requires maintenance and reproduction in the future. The walls produce a clear distinction between inside and outside, and the contents of the house might be seen as interiorizations of people's engagements with that outside world. As Tristan Carter put it in the 2006 workshop at Çatalhöyük, the house with all its contents could be seen as "your world in a box."

If the house is a container for a world, this may help explain the high degree of attention that is paid to their closure. Houses seem to have had continuous identities across episodes of rebuilding, sometimes for centuries. The end of a sequence is sometimes marked by purposeful actions. Storage bins and floors were cleaned, ovens and rooms filled in, timbers dismantled (Hodder and Cessford 2004: 32). Abandonment deposits include burned animal bone, horn and red deer antler, clusters of grindstone, polished stone ax heads, tools and worked bone, evidence of baskets or mats (e.g., House and Yeomans 2008: 39), scattered cattle scapulae and possibly digging tools (Russell and Twiss 2008: 119), and in some cases, houses may have been subjected to controlled burns (Hodder 2008: 2; but see Farid 2008: 27). In contrast to the habitual round of daily life, such attentive control over the end of a house, or a lineage of houses, may (like burials) manifest a self-conscious effort at control over the transition from visibility to invisibility, presence to absence.[16]

Watkins observes that the transition from Palaeolithic to Neolithic is one from an environment mostly untouched by human manipulation to daily life carried out in a constructed world of architecture. He proposes, "By means of architecture, they constituted . . . 'theatres of memory' in which the history of the community, its inhabitants and former inhabitants, and much else was recorded, retained, and transmitted" (2004: 97). As one would expect from the cognitivist approach, Watkins sees this theater as primarily a matter of ideas (rather than, say, the exercise of power or the inculcation of a bodily habitus), the elaboration of thinking about the structure of the world and the cosmos. This conceptual orientation treats religion as primarily contemplative and separate from practical and goal-oriented activities, a view I criticized earlier in the chapter. Nonetheless, Watkins's attention to architecture is valuable, especially as it does not rely only on "art" to carry the full weight of analysis. It invites us to see the house as a critical component of the materiality of religion in ways that studies of art tend not to.

But this should not lead us to conclude that people in Çatalhöyük lived in some simple mystical unity with the spirit world. In Çatalhöyük, the ways of marking cattle, raptors and leopards suggest that some aspects of experience were subject to greater attention, circumspection and discursive elaboration than others. Near the more marked end of this continuum, the conditions for the exercise of people's powers and social relations come to the foreground, objectified and thus made recognizable as the outcome of the processes by which they have been materialized. In objectified form, human and animal agency takes public form, available for people's perceptions and subject to their moral evaluations.

Marked and unmarked distinctions such as those between domesticated and wild, unelaborated house and elaborated, the manifest and the hidden indicate where we might find those hierarchies of value and attentiveness that start to give content to the category of religion. Dramatizing absence sharpens a contrast to the agency of people who are immediately present and draws attention to their power to bring about and control the transition between visible and invisible. People in the midst of their

---

[16] There is some evidence of foundation deposits as well (Hodder and Cessford 2004: 32).

ordinary routines are not likely to perceive agency or at least to reflect on it. Placed against the background of habits, the marked and the absent foreground actions, events and possibly their sources, and in this way may help objectify the very idea of agency, making it available for reflection, evaluation and transformation.

Toward a materialist semiotics

Steven Mithen asks, "Why are material symbols so fundamental to religious ideas and ritual?" (1998: 97). In response, we might ask, "Why do material things make us think of religious ideas?" I have already criticized the assumption that material objects that have no apparent use must be symbols, that they therefore represent ideas and that certain ideas define religion. Here I will conclude by proposing that a materialist semiotic will help us understand the social character of religion without merely returning us to functionalism (see Keane 2003; Preucel 2006).

Society may be impossible without ideas, but people cannot read minds. Their access to others' ideas, and thus the possibility that ideas become socially distributed and historically durable, depends on some materialization, some words, bodily gestures, artifacts, transformed environments and such. Materializations possess two important features. First, they are relatively independent of the intentions of those who produce them (e.g., words can be misconstrued; artifacts can be diverted to new purposes). Second, all materializations involve networks of causal relations. But this does not mean materializations are merely determinate effects of specific causes. Purposeful actions are characteristically future oriented, from which several things follow. First, in projecting into the future, people may *or may not* respond to hitherto unrealized possibilities in their material surround and will respond to *some* possibilities *but not others* (Keane 2003). Second, actions not only produce intended (and, of course, unintended) results, but may also bring about the preconditions demanded by those intentions (compare this with what Renfrew 2004 calls "engagement"). A materialist semiotic, combined with a fully social theory of objectification, can help us rethink the place of causality in the analysis of society and history, and in people's discovery and manipulation of their own agency.

Plastering the walls of a Çatalhöyük house required marl extraction plots, tools to dig the house, containers to carry the mud and some kind of division of labor and allocation of time (Hodder 2006: 60). Hodder surmises that these conditions would also have required ways of gathering and organizing people, killing animals and staging feasts, "a network of entanglement." One important aspect of this is that *material* entanglements produce and are produced by *social* ones; social ones in turn produce new material nexuses. There is no reason to privilege one or the other as a prime mover. The material artifacts this labor involves make possible a distribution of agency across a social field. The materialization of human activity makes it public and extends the activities of some people into those of others, in ways that are inseparable from – but not reducible to – material things (Latour 2005).

The material outcomes of people's activities make it possible for other people to treat them as indexical, drawing inferences about what made them possible (Keane 2003). When people do in fact draw such inferences (which depends on their semiotic ideologies), the meaningfulness of material things is part of a causal logic. For instance, the presence of plastered walls allows the inference that people had been organized to do the work, just as the presence of bucrania might index past feasts and that of fine obsidian access to distant resources. But such potential interpretations are not *necessarily* ever realized. Nor are they necessarily any guide for future actions. The conditions of possibility are only conditions, not goals. There is no reason to assume they are based on some particular set of utilitarian judgments or practical reasons that would be obvious to us. We must be wary of the temptations of teleological thought.

The hunt cannot be quite the same when there are also domesticated herds, at the level of either meaning (because now hunting stands in conceptual contrast to herding) or practice (time and energy spent hunting could have been used for the making of pots, flaking of obsidian, cultivation of fields, telling of myths, negotiating of marriages, etc.). The outcome of the hunt objectifies these possibilities. That does not necessarily mean that objectification is in itself meaningful, in the sense that it aims to give rise to specific concepts, or purposeful, in the sense that it derives from them. But once objectified, an activity or artifact is *available* for being rendered meaningful and subjected to evaluation. It can become an object for the acting, thinking, evaluating and choosing subject. The capacity to reflect on agency is shown both in assertions of agency we may reject (all kinds of magic) and in the denial of those we may accept (the human sources of rituals and scriptures).

An agent that can reflect on agency itself may also judge it, evaluating the merits of the action and the responsibilities of the agent. A subject that evaluates is potentially a moral subject. Reflection on agency makes it possible to link actors and consequences, to attribute responsibility (Keane, forthcoming). As I have suggested, a more useful distinction than that between symbolic and practical or material would be that among degrees of markedness of attention: objectification is one way to mark out certain parts of experience for special attention, vis-à-vis its relationship to human subjectivity, agency and values.

If during the Neolithic people found themselves within a context increasingly affected by human activity, whether they *recognized* and accorded any significance to the role of any distinctively *human* agency in their environment, is a distinct question (see Brown and Walker 2008). Human cultures vary widely in what entities (people, gods, spirits, etc.) they will recognize as agents in their surroundings, and even to what extent they recognize their own agency at work. In practice, how agency is recognized or not is mediated by *semiotic ideologies* (Keane 2007: 16–22), notions about what might count as an intentional sign or as evidence of a purposeful agent or not. Thus, if one believes in germ theory, disease is not normally evidence of an agent; if one is surrounded by witches, it is. Identical symptoms will have quite different semiotic statuses in each case, a point of caution for archaeological interpretation.

Self-recognition is not automatic: humans' ability to deny and displace their own agency is well attested. That very displacement may sharpen people's attention to agency as such. Artifacts are potentially indexical since they bear the traces of the actions of those who made them. Confronted with those artifacts, however, people may not necessarily recognize that agency, or find it interesting (Sumbanese traditionally thought that the archaic stone points they found were created by lightning spirits). Conversely, they may also impute agency to objects that we might consider natural in origin (Sumbanese also say that certain sacred valuables flee bad owners and cause fires). But to the extent that people do draw inferences about agency from the artifacts around them, those objects are indispensable media by which agency comes to be dispersed or distributed, and thus by which discrete actions in the past may become part of social worlds in the present. This may be the case for a house, a wall painting, even a herd of domesticated sheep, and holds true regardless of either explicit meanings or their apparent utility.

A materialist semiotics seeks out the logical-causal nexus behind and arising out of objectification. It takes seriously two aspects of the materiality of social life. First, all social action is mediated in some material form. It is therefore subject to causality, and thus to contingent precursors and unintended consequences, that is, to history. Second, all human experience is in part a response to the material forms that, at least since the Neolithic, were created by previous human actions, which form part of their context: however private the initial impulse behind an action, its materiality gives it an inevitably social character; its reach extends beyond any original intent or agent. Even the experience of transcendence, if it is to become socially viable, draws on the resources of multiple semiotic modalities and the relations among them. Those dimensions of experience and practice that we have come to group together as "religious" build on and develop the possibilities that begin with the marking of some parts of experience for special attention and the semiotic possibilities of pointing to absence. Marking and absence are aspects of material forms. It is no accident that material things are central to religion.

REFERENCES

Adams, R. L. 2005. Ethnoarchaeology in Indonesia: Illuminating the ancient past in Çatalhöyük. *American Antiquity*, 70(1), 181–8.

Asad, T. 1993. *Genealogies of Religion: Discipline and Reasons of Power in Christianity and Islam*. Baltimore: Johns Hopkins University Press.

Bateson, G. 1972 (1955). *Steps to an Ecology of the Mind*. New York: Ballantine Books.

Belting, H. 1994. *Likeness and Presence: A History of the Image before the Era of Art*, trans. Edmund Jephcott. Chicago: University of Chicago Press.

Bloch, M. 1992. *Prey into Hunter: The Politics of Religious Experience*. Cambridge: Cambridge University Press.

Bourdieu, P. 1977. *Outline of a Theory of Practice*, trans. Richard Nice. Cambridge: Cambridge University Press.

Bradley, R. 2005. *Ritual and Domestic Life in Prehistoric Europe*. London: Routledge.

Brown, L. A., and W. H. Walker, eds. 2008. Special Issue: Archaeology, animism, and non-human agents. *Journal of Archaeological Method and Theory*, 15(4).

Çatalhöyük Research Project. 2008. *Çatalhöyük 2008 Archive Report*. www.catalhoyuk.com/downloads/Archive_Report_2008.pdf (accessed October 13, 2009).

Cauvin, J. 2000. The symbolic foundations of the Neolithic Revolution in the Near East. In *Life in Neolithic Farming Communities: Social Organization,*

Identity, and Differentiation, ed. I. Kuijt. New York: Kluwer Academic / Plenum, 235–51.

Davis, R. H. 1997. *Lives of Indian Images*. Princeton, N.J.: Princeton University Press.

Du Bois, J. W. 1993. Meaning without intention: Lessons from divination. In *Responsibility and Evidence in Oral Discourse*, eds. J. H. Hill and J. T. Irvine. Cambridge: Cambridge University Press, 48–71.

Düring, B. S. 2001. Social dimensions in the architecture of Neolithic Çatalhöyük. *Anatolian Studies*, 51, 1–18.

Düring, B. S. 2003. Burials in context: The 1960s inhumations of Çatalhöyük East. *Anatolian Studies*, 53, 1–15.

Farid, S. 2008. A review of the Mellaart level system and the introduction of a new phasing system at Çatalhöyük 2008. *Çatalhöyük 2008 Archive Report*, 13–28. www.catalhoyuk.com/downloads/Archive_Report_2008.pdf (accessed October 13, 2009).

Fogelin, L. 2007. The archaeology of religious ritual. *Annual Review of Anthropology*, 36, 55–71.

Gimbutas, M. 1982. *The Goddesses and Gods of Old Europe, 6500–3500 BC: Myths and Cult Images*. Berkeley: University of California Press.

Gorski, P. S. 2003. *The Disciplinary Revolution: Calvinism and the Rise of the State in Early Modern Europe*. Chicago: University of Chicago Press.

Hodder, I. 1999. Symbolism at Çatalhöyük. In *World Prehistory: Studies in Memory of Grahame Clark*, ed. J. Coles. Proceedings of the British Academy 99. Oxford: Oxford University Press, 177–91.

Hodder, I. 2005. Socialization and feasting at Çatalhöyük: A response to Adams. *American Antiquity*, 70(1), 189–91.

Hodder, I. 2006. *The Leopard's Tale: Revealing the Mysteries of Çatalhöyük*. London: Thames and Hudson.

Hodder, I. 2007. Çatalhöyük in the context of the Middle Eastern Neolithic. *Annual Review of Anthropology*, 36, 105–20.

Hodder, I. 2008. Season review. *Çatalhöyük 2008 Archive Report*, 1–4. www.catalhoyuk.com/downloads/Archive_Report_2008.pdf (accessed October 13, 2009).

Hodder, I., and Cessford, C. 2004. Daily practice and social memory at Çatalhöyük. *American Antiquity*, 69(1), 17–40.

Holl, A. F. C. 2004. *Saharan Rock Art: Archaeology of Tassilian Pastoralist Iconography*. Walnut Creek, Calif.: AltaMira Press.

Hoskins, J. 1993. Violence, sacrifice and divination: Giving and taking life in Eastern Indonesia. *American Ethnologist*, 20(1), 159–78.

House, M., and Yeomans, L. 2008. Building 77. *Çatalhöyük 2008 Archive Report*, 38–52. www.catalhoyuk.com/downloads/Archive_Report_2008.pdf (accessed October 13, 2009).

Humphrey, C., and Laidlaw, J. 2007. Sacrifice and ritualization. In *The Archaeology of Ritual*, ed. E. Kyriakidis. Los Angeles: Cotsen Institute of Archaeology, 255–176.

Keane, W. 1997a. *Signs of Recognition: Powers and Hazards of Representation in an Indonesian Society*. Berkeley: University of California Press.

Keane, W. 1997b. Religious language. *Annual Review of Anthropology*, 26, 47–71.

Keane, W. 2003. Semiotics and the social analysis of material things. *Language and Communication*, 23(2–3), 409–25.

Keane, W. 2007. *Christian Moderns: Freedom and Fetish in the Mission Encounter*. Berkeley: University of California Press.

Keane, W. 2008. The evidence of the senses and the materiality of religion. *Journal of the Royal Anthropological Institute*, 14(1), 110–27.

Keane, W. Forthcoming. Minds, surfaces, and reasons in an anthropology of ethics. In *Ordinary Ethics*, ed. M. Lambek. New York: Fordham University Press.

Kellner, M. 2006. *Must a Jew Believe Anything?* Portland, Ore.: Littman Library of Jewish Civilization.

Kopytoff, I. 1971. Ancestors as elders in Africa. *Africa: Journal of the International African Institute*, 41(2), 129–42.

Kyriakidis, E. 2007. Finding ritual: Calibrating the evidence. In *The Archaeology of Ritual*, ed. E. Kyriakidis. Los Angeles: Cotsen Institute of Archaeology, 9–22.

Last, J. 1998. A design for life: Interpreting the art of Çatalhöyük. *Journal of Material Culture*, 3(3), 355–78.

Latour, B. 2005. *Reassembling the Social: An Introduction to Actor-Network-Theory*. Oxford: Oxford University Press.

Lewis-Williams, D. 2004. Constructing a cosmos: Architecture, power and domestication at Çatalhöyük. *Journal of Social Archaeology*, 4(1), 28–51.

Lopez, D. S. 1998. Belief. In *Critical Terms for Religious Studies*, ed. M. C. Taylor. Chicago: University of Chicago Press, 21–35.

Masuzawa, T. 2005. *The Invention of World Religions: Or, How European Universalism Was Preserved in the Language of Pluralism*. Chicago: University of Chicago Press.

Matthews, W. 2005. Micromorphological and microstratigraphic traces of uses and concepts of space. In *Inhabiting Çatalhöyük: Reports from the 1995–1999 Seasons*, ed. I. Hodder. Cambridge: McDonald Institute Monographs / British Institute of Archaeology Monograph 38, 355–98.

Matthews, W., Wiles, J., and Almond, M. 2006. Micromorphology and micro-analysis of archaeological surface materials and residues: An investigation of source material and the life-cycle of buildings. *Çatalhöyük 2006 Archive Report*, 285–94.

Mellaart, J. 1967. *Çatal Hüyük: A Neolithic Town in Anatolia*. London: Thames and Hudson.

Meskell, L. 1998. Twin peaks: The archaeologies of Çatalhöyük. In *Ancient Goddesses: The Myths and the Evidence*, eds. L. Goodison and C. Morris. London: British Museum Press, 46–62.

Meskell, L. 2004. Divine things. In *Rethinking Materiality: The Engagement of Mind with the Material World*, eds. E. DeMarrais, C. Gosden and C. Renfrew. Cambridge: McDonald Institute for Archaeological Research Monographs, 249–59.

Mithen, S. 1998. The supernatural beings of prehistory and the external storage of religious ideas. In *Cognition and Material Culture: The Archaeology of Symbolic Storage*, eds. C. Renfrew and C. Scarre. Cambridge: McDonald Institute for Archaeological Research Monographs, 97–106.

Morgan, D. 2005. *The Sacred Gaze: Religious Visual Culture in Theory and Practice*. Berkeley: University of California Press.

Munn, N. D. 1973. *Walbiri Iconography: Graphic Representation and Cultural Symbolism in a Central Australian Society*. Ithaca, N.Y.: Cornell University Press.

Nakamura, C., and Meskell, L. 2006. Figurine report 2006. *Çatalhöyük 2006 Archive Report*, 226–41.

Nakamura, C., and Meskell, L. 2008. Figurine report 2008. *Çatalhöyük 2008 Archive Report*, 110–19. www.catalhoyuk.com/downloads/Archive_Report_2008.pdf (accessed October 13, 2009).

Newcomb, F. J. 1937. *Sandpaintings of the Navajo Shooting Chant*. New York: J. J. Augustin.

Ohnuki-Tierney, E. 1993. *Rice as Self: Japanese Identities through Time*. Princeton, N.J.: Princeton University Press.

Pels, P. 2003. Spirits of modernity: Alfred Wallace, Edward Tylor, and the visual politics of fact. In *Magic and Modernity: Interfaces of Revelation and Concealment*, ed. B. Meyer and P. Pels. Stanford, Calif.: Stanford University Press, 241–71.

Pinney, C. 2004. *Photos of the Gods: The Printed Image and Political Struggle in India*. London: Reaktion Books.

Preucel, R. W. 2006. *Archaeological Semiotics*. Malden, Mass.: Blackwell.

Renfrew, C. 1994. The archaeology of religion. In *The Ancient Mind: Elements of Cognitive Archaeology*, ed. C. Renfrew and E. B. W. Zubrow. Cambridge: Cambridge University Press, 47–54.

Renfrew, C. 2004. Towards a theory of material engagement. In *Rethinking Materiality: The Engagement of Mind with the Material World*, eds. E. DeMarrais, C. Gosden and C. Renfrew. Cambridge: McDonald Institute for Archaeological Research Monographs, 23–31.

Renfrew, C., and Bahn, P. 1991. *Archaeology: Theories, Methods and Practice*. London: Thames and Hudson.

Richards, M. P., and Pearson, J. A. 2005. Stable isotope evidence of diet at Çatalhöyük. In *Inhabiting Çatalhöyük: Reports from the 1995–1999 Seasons*, ed. I. Hodder. Cambridge: McDonald Institute Monographs / British Institute of Archaeology at Ankara Monograph 38, 313–22.

Russell, N., and Martin, L. 2005. The Çatalhöyük mammal remains. In *Inhabiting Çatalhöyük: Reports from the 1995–1999 Seasons*, ed. I. Hodder. Cambridge: McDonald Institute Monographs / British Institute of Archaeology at Ankara Monograph 38, 33–98.

Russell, N., and McGowan, K. J. 2003. Dance of the cranes: Crane symbolism and beyond. *Antiquity*, 77, 445–56.

Russell, N., and Twiss, K. 2008. Animal bones 2008. *Çatalhöyük 2008 Archive Report*, 110–19. www.catalhoyuk.com/downloads/Archive_Report_2008.pdf (accessed October 13, 2009).

Sahlins, M. 1972 (1968). *Stone Age Economics*. Chicago: Aldine Publishing.

Saler, B. 1993. *Conceptualizing Religion: Immanent Anthropologists, Transcendent Natives, and Unbounded Categories*. Leiden: E. J. Brill.

Sharf, R. H. 1998. Experience. In *Critical Terms for Religious Studies*, ed. M. C. Taylor. Chicago: University of Chicago Press, 94–116.

Smith, J. Z. 1982. *Imagining Religion: From Babylon to Jonestown*. Chicago: University of Chicago Press.

Taylor, C. 1993. To follow a rule. In *Bourdieu: Critical Perspectives*, eds. C. Calhoun, E. LiPuma and M. Postone. Chicago: University of Chicago Press, 45–60.

Valeri, V. 1985. *Kingship and Sacrifice: Ritual and Society in Ancient Hawaii*, trans. Paula Wissing. Chicago: University of Chicago Press.

Voigt, M. M. 2000. Çatal Höyük in context: Ritual at early Neolithic sites in central and eastern Turkey. In *Life in Neolithic Farming Communities: Social Organization, Identity, and Differentiation*, ed. I. Kuijt. New York: Kluwer Academic / Plenum, 253–93.

Walker, W. H. 1998. Where are the witches of prehistory? *Journal of Archaeological Method and Theory*, 5, 245–308.

Watkins, T. 2004. Architecture and 'theatres of memory' in the Neolithic of Southwest Asia. In *Rethinking Materiality: The Engagement of Mind with the Material World*, eds. E. DeMarrais, C. Gosden and C. Renfrew. Cambridge: McDonald Institute for Archaeological Research Monographs, 97–106.

Whitehouse, H. 2004. *Modes of Religiosity: A Cognitive Theory of Religious Transmission*. Walnut Creek, Calif.: AltaMira Press.

9

Temporalities of "religion" at Çatalhöyük

Peter Pels

This essay starts from the assumption that the careful distinction of different temporalities indicated by the material evidence from the Çatalhöyük site may advance the study of whatever kind of specially marked "religious" or "transcendent" experiences occupied the life of its inhabitants. In writing it, however, I found that I needed a certain theoretical and methodological framing to make sense of my arguments about how "temporalities of religion" can become useful to analyze the material record of Çatalhöyük. As someone without archaeological experience, I was struck by the extent to which archaeological analysis is suspended between the twin anchors of the material record, on the one hand, and theoretical narratives of the *longue durée*, on the other. The effort of bringing these together in a process of abduction seems to be the essence of archaeological interpretation.[1] My effort to contribute to this process of abduction in

[1] Abduction is different from induction (reasoning from the material evidence) and deduction (reasoning from theoretically generated hypotheses), in that it infers or conjectures from mostly indexical signs how they should be valued within theoretical narrative. It therefore determines explanation and explanandum, theory and fact more or less simultaneously. Its mode of reasoning is common to clinical medicine, palaeontology, archaeology, historiography and ethnography, to name just a few disciplines (see Ginzburg 1983).

I am very grateful to Ian Hodder for the invitation to participate in the Templeton seminars at the Çatalhöyük site, his constant willingness to answer questions and discuss hypotheses and his incisive comments on an earlier draft. I also thank all others present at the 2006, 2007 and 2008 Templeton seminars for their contribution to what has so far been a very exciting research adventure into the, for me, uncharted territories of archaeology. Maurice Bloch, Başak Boz, Tristan Carter, Shahina Farid, Webb Keane, Serena Love, Wendy Matthews, Lynn Meskell, Carolyn Nakamura, Nerissa Russell, Nurcan Yalman and Katheryn Twiss have to be mentioned for their contribution to this essay in particular. Anke Kamerman did most of the library research on which it is based, and I thank her for bringing up a large number of important insights into the available material.

the case of Çatalhöyük, therefore, entails the following steps: First, I try to answer the question of what one may be looking at when looking for different timescales in the material record, and part of this answer is that one inevitably seems to look at facts that ultimately take their meaning from within a narrative of the *longue durée*. Second, I have to question the relevance of notions of "symbolism" and "religion" when applied to the Neolithic. Third, this effort has to be translated to my own version of the narrative of the *longue durée* as it appears to me on the basis of the material record of Çatalhöyük so far. It is, finally, only on this basis that a consideration of the temporalities of religion at Çatalhöyük becomes feasible.

In this process, several things will, I hope, come to stand out:

first, that generalizations about human material entanglements and their relationship to larger narratives of evolutionary change will have to explicate their temporal scales more explicitly if they are to make good their claims;

second, that making sense of the material evidence at Çatalhöyük may be more dependent on what one can call the "local" evolution of the settlement – its particularity – than on any universal evolutionary scheme;

third, that assessing the role of religion, the transcendent or the sacred at Çatalhöyük may be helped more by comparisons with – partly secularized – social arrangements in the modern world than with analogies with what seem to be more "traditional" predecessors; and

fourth, that it is in the overlap between timescales that we are most likely to find traces of the religious or transcendent characteristic of Çatalhöyük.

While working this out, however, I was struck by the numerous occasions on which I turned out to be mistaken or premature in my conclusions in the face of analytical insights already provided by the archaeologists working at the site. The following notes offer little more than suggestions about possible shifts in interpretive emphasis or preferences for one storyline over another, and often end up in a kind of interpretative limbo that should remain extremely modest in its claims to contribute anything to the interpretive and methodological rigor of the archaeological work done at the site since 1993.

Materiality and temporality

Archaeologists have, by theoretical tradition as well as the nature of the evidence available, rarely explicitly focused on short-term timescales (Fox-hall 2000), concentrating instead on "deep time" and the questions of human evolution that address, in the case of Çatalhöyük, the why and how of the "Neolithic Revolution" (see Keane, Chapter 8). While archaeologists at Çatalhöyük have, of course, zoomed in on smaller timescales as well (see Fairbairn et al. 2005; Hodder 2005b; Hodder & Cessford 2004; Matthews 2005b), it seems worthwhile to ask what the common archaeological preoccupation with an evolutionary timescale might mean in terms of assessing the material evidence.

Reflecting on how to integrate the data from Çatalhöyük, Ian Hodder adapts Colin Renfrew's suggestion that, with sedentism and farming, we can hypothesize a shift in materialization toward more "symbolic material culture":

> According to Renfrew, it was only with the Neolithic that materials took on a symbolic power so that the process of engagement led to social and economic change. But in the Upper Palaeolithic and earlier, objects certainly had symbolic power. So the problem becomes – what changes in material engagement occurred at the transition to farming, sedentism and bronze? ... How did materiality shift?" (Hodder 2005a: 9–10)

The conception of materiality employed here is important and distinctive: rather than focusing on the objects confronting and changing human beings as in the various forms of natural or technological determinism, the notion of a "shift in materiality" implies an overall change in the *relationship* between humans and objects, changing the nature of both. This reflects the recent renewal of interest in "material culture," caused, at least partly, by a theoretical move away from the fetishization of objects and technologies toward the realization that subjects construct objects just as much as objects construct subjects.[2]

---

[2] This renewal of interest can be traced to publications like those of Appadurai (1986), Gell (1992), Miller (1987), and Pietz (1985, 1987, 1988) and the publication of the *Journal of Material Culture* since 1996.

This, indeed, justifies starting to integrate the data on Çatalhöyük on the basis of Hodder's answer to the question posed earlier: "One thing that happened was that there just became a lot more of it – a lot more things made by people" (Hodder 2006: 241). I'd like to suggest that it may pay off, at this juncture, to be even more precise about the understanding of "materiality": while the importance of noting the "massive increase in the sheer quantity of things made by people" (Keane, Chapter 8) cannot be understated, it is not exactly the same as saying that there was a "massive increase in the amount of enduring materiality" (Hodder 2005b: 183) or that "there was a proliferation of material culture" (Matthews 2005b: 125) or that "human culture became more substantive, more material" (Renfrew 2001: 128) around the time of the "Neolithic Revolution." "Material culture" is, of course, a pleonasm, for how can we know or do culture unless by means of its material manifestations? While it is crucial to recognize that Çatalhöyük represents a moment in which "[h]umans get increasingly caught up in society through their involvement with objects" because of the productive entanglements that form these objects' conditions of possibility (Hodder 2005a: 10), that is not the same as saying that human culture becomes *more* material or substantive – unless one restricts the definition of "materiality" and "substance" to things *made by people*. This may reintroduce a subject–object distinction that the renewal of "material culture" studies since the 1980s meant to question in the first place. The "material record" consisting of human artifacts may, indeed, be the archive from which an archaeologist starts (cf. Hodder 2006: 185), but that does not imply that the life of a hunter-gatherer predominantly living with objects not made by human hands (animals, wild plants, the landscape) is any the less material.

I would argue that an understanding of materiality – that is, the relationship between human beings and objects – as being restricted to human-made "material culture" both draws on and conflicts with a set of assumptions about materiality that emerged in their present form in the 19th century, in the context of a cultural contest about the nature of truth and evidence. In this context, the meaning of "materiality" changed depending on the intellectual vectors along which it was plotted, so that "materialists" denied any statement not based on material evidence as "metaphysical," "spiritualists" denied that there was any evidential value in matter per se and Christian and agnostic scientists debated what evidence could count as cultural (and therefore variable and fallible) and what as natural (and therefore incontrovertible, "objective" and/or divinely manufactured; Pels 2008). I cannot go into this discussion here; suffice to say that one of the assumptions about matter that emerged as hegemonic in the 19th century was its essentially secular nature and its classification within a strong dichotomy of nature and culture. The statement that, during the Neolithic, human culture becomes "more material" seems to import some of these modern assumptions into the interpretation of the data. This is not necessarily a problem: these assumptions may be "etically" correct. However, it can be questioned whether they are always the most appropriate way to understand how the different generations of inhabitants of Çatalhöyük, their predecessors or their cattle-herding descendants related to their material environment. Again, "etically" we may say that humans become increasingly entangled in social relationships because social relationships are required to produce the house, pottery or domesticated plants and animals. But the semiotic ideologies that classified Neolithic houses, pots, sheep, corn, predators or game as natural or cultural, material or spiritual, agents or patients have to be conjectured, and one cannot therefore determine that Neolithic engagements were "more" material unless one assumes that natural things have to be regarded as less material than manufacture. This is at least hypothetically important for the interpretation of evidence from Çatalhöyük where it concerns the relative importance of the different material entanglements that go together with sedentism (houses and artifacts), with the herding of sheep and goats (demonstrably important for the life in the settlement) and with hunting and feasting (where wild animals were important), as each might have implied a different "materiality," at least as perceived by the inhabitants.

So far, I could be accused of relativist nitpicking and speculation hardly relevant to "deep time" archaeological interpretations. The uses of the rigorously relational understanding of materiality mentioned earlier, however, will turn out to be relevant to the assessment of which material relationship is most significant for which activity (e.g., when we contrast relationships with wild animals to those with manufactured goods or domesticized herds) and how that determines our understanding of both the temporalities and the transcendental features of Çatalhöyük data. More about that later; here, I'd like to further illustrate the use of differentiating temporalities by zooming in on some material and temporal aspects of the relationship between humans and houses.

At the evolutionary timescale, the shifts in materialization generate specific questions: Why did people start to build houses in the first place? Why at Çatalhöyük? What seems to be changing between Levels VI and V, ca. 6400–6300 BC? Why did people abandon the East Mound and move to the West Mound – or elsewhere? It seems reasonable to assume that at the timescales we are talking about here, few if any of these developments took root at the level of human consciousness (with the possible exception of the Level VI–V shift, but again, more about that later). The questions asked seem to refer to evolutionary beginnings and endings, possibly generalizable to other parts of the globe or at least to other human settlements in the Middle East – but in any case, to events within a narrative (Foxhall 2000: 485). The answers sought out, again, seem to be pitched at the level of universals, or at least invite comparison with other parts of the globe where people did similar things. Like the rise of mercantilism, the industrial revolution or the nation-state, such explanatory storylines call for a multivariate analysis, the complexities of which seem to go beyond an individual or even collective "emic" consciousness's capacity for understanding. The patterns we talk about are aggregate and probabilistic, and the outcome dependent on a *class* of human acts rather than these acts in the singular. "Materiality" in this narrative pattern is aggregate and therefore several abstractions removed from things dug up in specific places.[3]

Different questions and notions of materiality are generated when we move one level down, to the life span of a Çatalhöyük house – or building sequence (i.e., the maximum ca. 500 years in which different houses were built on each other in more or less the same building pattern). Here human agency plays a less abstract role because, rather than just adding one more datum to the aggregate, human beings would have to have purposely rebuilt houses in the same pattern – and therefore to have had some concretely explicable reason to do so. This, too, generates questions about beginnings and endings, but the questions are, to some extent, no longer exclusively "ours" as observers, for why was a house demolished and rebuilt in that way? Did it mark a beginning

---

[3] Mary Poovey (1998) has recorded how the shift from a concrete, Renaissance conception of factuality to a more abstract, statistical and aggregate 19th-century notion of "facts" took place.

for the builders, or had they, in a sense, "already" begun because they were conscious that a previous house pattern existed? What occasioned the end, or the destruction, of a house? At the same time, a life span of a house sequence of several hundreds of years also divorces the house from human agency, at least when the latter is defined by the life span of human beings. The pattern we discuss here is entangled with individual human events and acts, and therefore with human purposes and rationality, yet it is not fully determined by those acts because the intentions governing them do not apply to the full timescale concerned: the life span of the house. In a "weak" sense, one might say, the house or house sequence was an agent of continuity, and the human builders its "patients." (In order to know whether the house or house sequence was actually also an agent in the strong sense, we would have to have access to the semiotic ideologies by which the Çatalhöyük builders interpreted the house.)[4]

Yet other questions and materialities take prominence once we move to the level of the human life cycle. Although we are not sure whether anyone was actually ever born inside a house, we can presume that children grew up in it and developed their mature social dispositions in relation to it – the materiality that Bourdieu has famously discussed in the case of the Kabyle house in terms of habituation through the social pattern that the house itself objectifies. In Bourdieu's terms, this is the "form par excellence" of "the dialectic of objectification and embodiment" (1977: 87–9). Its distinctive characteristics are that, in order to work, it has to be locally materialized (rather than a product of an observer's translocal aggregation of data) and individually embodied (rather than the product of the objective material as agent). Moreover, it is more of a structure (generating a habitus) than an event, and therefore often implies a mediation of knowledge that remains below the level of discourse: it is not a product of an independent individual consciousness.[5] This is the kind of materiality that Foucault would include in what he called processes of "subjectivation" – of *making* a subject through the concrete pattern of objects.

---

[4] This may be a case of what Hodder, following Connerton, calls "commemorative" memory (2005b: 184).

[5] This is, of course, a case of "habituation memory" (Connerton, quoted by Hodder 2005b: 184); its importance for ethnographic interpretation was stressed by Comaroff (1985), De Boeck (1995), Bourdieu (1977) and Jackson (1983), among others.

These three patterns of materiality at different timescales are therefore quite different in their composition of objective and subjective factors and materials: while the last identifies materiality as the relationship that makes the local subject in a patterned interaction with the physical structure of the house, the second turns it into the event-like agency of a physical thing (a house) that defines the subjectivity of the builders by acts of commemoration and rebuilding. The first pattern, however, does not generate a local subject; its materiality is more geared to the production of the subject of the archaeologist. Yet despite these profound differences in the relation between materiality and temporality, we can also see that all of them would be required to understand what happened at Çatalhöyük in the relationship between humans and houses.

Çatalhöyük temporalities

Thus, it seems important to try to outline the different temporalities relevant to the interpretation of the Çatalhöyük data in more detail and think further about the relationships between the different timescales concerned. (I will turn to their relevance to thinking about "religion" later.) First of all, I was struck by the extent to which – perhaps contrary to Foxhall's suggestion (2000: 496) – the *longue durée* of archaeological periodization seems to remain the point of departure for any interpretation. Within that overarching timescale, however, it should be noted that the archaeological *longue durée* (often supported by artifact classifications) may be different from the *longue durée* originally posited by Fernand Braudel (which referred to the history of the Mediterranean as a communications infrastructure; 1972, 1973) or that posited by Giddens (which referred to the supra-human timescale of social institutions; 1979: 198). So far, the timescales identified are those of the history of the Çatalhöyük settlement as such, longer-term continuities and changes in the use of buildings (including successive buildings on the same pattern), the life course of a building, human lifetime cycles, annual cycles, seasonal and other intra-annual cycles and daily routines (see especially Matthews 2005b; also Foxhall 2000; Hodder 2005a,b; Hodder & Cessford 2004). It is important to note that an analysis of a specific timescale makes little sense without its contrasts with longer- or shorter-term cycles – not least because it is in many cases the perception of an *event* marking the beginning or end of a certain period or cycle that connects time frames, and this event is often itself located at a longer-term level. (This will become important once we consider the connection between temporalities and transcendence; see the conclusion.) Finally, the examples given suggest that the definition of "materiality" as a *relationship* between people and things (rather than as "things *an sich*") makes it vital to reflect on the possibilities of replacing definitions of timescales in terms of physical material (such as "the life course of *buildings*") with definitions of timescales in terms of social relationships (such as "the life course of *a house*") – which, in what I discuss later, usually translates into positing a necessarily tentative universal connection between material practices and forms of signification – or what I will call "marking" or "articulation." That said, I suggest that the following list covers most relevant possibilities:

- The life span of the settlement (7400–7100 cal BC to 6200–5900 cal BC). This reflects the common archaeological focus on a site and remains the master narrative of any interpretation of Çatalhöyük material, provided we understand it to include (1) the positioning of Çatalhöyük within longer-term developments in the Neolithic Middle East and (2) the major shifts within this life span, such as the transformations that take place between Levels VI and V (as discussed later). We cannot do without the analytic vocabulary of evolutionary shifts in agriculture, sedentism, aesthetic forms, the emergence of "house societies" and the like at this level or at any other.
- The life span of a house sequence (more houses built on each other in the same or similar pattern over a maximum of 500 years, especially in Levels X–VI). Its major patterns are given by continuity in floor plans and interments of bones and artifacts; its major events are erasure and demolition followed by either reproduction of the pattern or abandonment of the plan: the first level at which explicit memorialization (or forgetting) plays a role and, thus, where the relationship between etic classifications and emic understandings seems to appear first.
- The life cycles of "houses" (some reaching ca. 80 years of age, but not in all phases of the settlement's life span). The relation between "house" and house sequence raises the question of cross-generational continuity and rupture in terms of acts of commemoration (interment of bones and artifacts) as well as amnesia (erasure and demolition). Given an average individual life span of 35, a "house" would

have to be reproduced over at least three to four generations (of 20 years on average), at least in Levels VIII–VI.

- The life cycle of a household. A household can be defined by both normative (kinship and marriage) categories and practical (residential, commensal and economic) arrangements (Sanjek 1996: 286), indicating that here – as with the memorialization of "house" and house sequence – the interpretation straddles indigenous categories and material traces of practice. It is vital to realize (1) that "house" and "household" may be different units, especially when we consider commensal and economic arrangements (as in societies in which part of the household is absent for seasonal labor); (2) that the household is by definition composed of a multiplicity of gender- and age-differentiated persons (which may not apply to the definition of the "house"); and (3) that a household has, again almost by definition, to be reinvented and recomposed by every new generation: it is the primary temporal referent of the practices of initiating youngsters, and its change is necessary for a "house" to gain cross-generational continuity.

- The life cycle of a human being (average 35 years). This comprises all evidence of birth and childhood, maturation, gender differentiation, human fertility, the acquisition of technical competences, labor skills and specializations, travel, accumulation and hoarding, social stratification, seniority and aging and death.

- Annual, seasonal and other intra-annual cycles. It seems to make little sense to differentiate between annual and seasonal cycles since for the inhabitants of Çatalhöyük, in the absence of calendars and clocks, the experience of the annual cycle would have been completely dominated by the experience of winter, spring, summer and autumn. Moreover, to treat annual and seasonal cycles in conjunction highlights that, on this timescale, the material relationship between being "inside" and "outside" the settlement (of hunting and animal migration, transhumance and animal husbandry and agriculture) is most prominent. Last, longer-term cycles of heating or cooling, lightening and darkening, wetting and drying would have provided both practical and symbolic markers that are "good to think with" – for instance, about individual life cycles as well as the daily rounds of reproduction.

- Monthly cycles. Monthly experiences of time can be feminized when tied to menstruation and human fertility and sexuality or when tied to the moon and possibly night visibility and hunting. The connection with Çatalhöyük empirical data lies partly in the almost monthly plastering of walls and some interpretive possibilities to be suggested at the level of the human life cycle and menstruation. Both, however, can be subsumed under the discussion of other timescales, and I will not deal with this timescale further.

- Daily cycles. At the smallest timescale of human experience, one obviously concentrated on patterns of light and dark, warmth and cold, exertion and rest, waking and sleeping, hunger and satiation. By extension, this involves patterns of movement across thresholds, up and down ladders and between roof and interior of the house and out of and into the settlement (with the concomitant patterning of the landscape into degrees of being "inside" and "outside," or into the points of the compass as defined by where the sun rises, reaches its zenith and sets).

As argued earlier by means of the examples of humans and houses, these temporalities differ not only on a scale from the longer to the shorter term, but also in the materialities (defined as the relationships between humans and things, including animals, plants and landscapes) by which they are mediated and that define how a certain experience of time is objectified (and thus leaves a trace in the archaeological record). I would like to use this analytic of different temporalities to consider whether and how religious and/or ritual activity can be expected to leave such traces. Before I can do so, however, two further steps are required: first, a brief consideration of what kind of archaeological trace would count as "religious" or "ritual" or "magical"; and second, a specification of the "grand narrative" of Çatalhöyük, without which, as I argued in this section, no interpretation of anything, let alone anything "religious" or "ritual," at the site is possible.

Tracing the "religious"

One of the most salient features of James Mellaart's *Çatal Hüyük: A Neolithic Town in Anatolia* (1967) is the extent to which his argument relies on the equation of "art" – that is, traces of aesthetic elaboration – with religion or ritual. This interpretive strategy seems to be based on a particular line of reasoning, one that says that, first, anything that does not indicate any practical use must be artistic and, second, since prehistoric society does not possess the separate realm of art production of modern society, artistic production can take place only as devotion, in the service of (something akin to) the supernatural. This mode of reasoning is based on fallacious assumptions about materiality, signification and religion, and I have to discuss some of those fallacies in order to outline what could count as a material trace of something "religious." (This discussion owes much to Webb Keane's insightful Chapter 8 on similar themes.)

THE FALLACY OF "SYMBOLISM"

In a majority of cases in which we use the word "symbol," its meaning can be rendered as "a sign whose referent is absent or unknown." However, as a sign whose referent is absent, the symbol is only a very special case of sign (modeled on verbal signs) and, with the exception of certain written signs, not very salient to archaeology, where indexes (signs pointing to the activity that constituted them) are far more important and prominent items of analysis (Keane, Chapter 8). Even more important is the fact that, once we concentrate on indexical signs, we turn our attention from the absent and therefore immaterial and often unknown referent of the symbol to the materiality of the *present* sign or index. The next step would be to replace the theory of representation implicit in most notions of the symbolic with a theory of performance implicit in the notion of the index; for the index always points to some activity *for* some audience (a statement in which we once more recognize the theory of materiality-as-relationship I already used in the first section of this essay). This theory of the performative capacity of things is crucial for suggesting an alternative interpretation of something that does not appear immediately useful (i.e., that appears to be a "symbol"). Once we recognize that any material thing has a performative capacity – that is, that a wall or an ax is never just a material wall or ax, but also a sign of a wall or ax to human beings – we can see that one cannot divorce signification from its carriers, and therefore cannot make a dichotomy out of a thing and its uses, on the one hand, and its aesthetic elaboration, on the other. Once one recognizes the performative aspect of material things, utility and aesthetic elaboration are no longer opposed but reinforce each other: aesthetic elaboration indicates an extension, marking or articulation of use.

We are, of course, still faced with the difficulty of reconstructing how Çatalhöyük inhabitants would have perceived the use and performance of the material things by which they were surrounded. But the insight sketched earlier would in any case allow and require us to ask: What do wall paintings, bucrania, platforms, burials, stamp seals or ladders *do* to human beings (cf. Hodder 2006: 195)? How do they perform in everyday life and what agency does that give them? Again, one will notice the shift in theories of materiality that took place from the 1980s in this injunction. An excellent example of the consequences of such an approach is given by Ian Hodder when he suggests that "the art and symbolism at Çatalhöyük has little to do with representation and symbolism at all. It may be more like a tool, used to control or communicate with animals, spirits, and ancestors" (1999: 190). Note that such a perspective does not necessarily require the "religious," understood as a physically absent referent, since animals or ancestors may in fact be present through their indexes, interred in walls or floors.

THE FALLACY OF "RELIGION"

The equation of the not immediately useful with the religious (because prehistoric societies lack the modern institution of "art") is, of course, based on a secularist perception of religion, and therefore shows that this conception of religion dates from a period in which secularism had become hegemonic, at least in scholarly circles. Talal Asad has shown that the category of "religion" as such is based on this 19th-century comparativist and secularizing consciousness and that, therefore, our understanding of religion is paradoxically based in sociohistorical circumstances in which it first became possible to think of a public space or even a world without it (Asad 1993). Whatever definition of religion one wants to use or defend – and I would like to continue defending many of them for particular interpretive uses – they always arose and will still have to be understood in opposition to something called the "secular," so that the "religious" denotes a separate realm of social life. This applies to the two most important denotations of "religion" in modern scholarship: "church" (or "sect" or "cult"), which indicates an institution separated out from other parts of social life, and "belief," which emerged from the idea that there are propositions to which one can adhere on faith, that are separate from those that command adherence by their correspondence to a secular referent (marked as "knowledge").[6] Both denotations

[6] The emergence of a propositional understanding of religion is discussed by Baird (1998).

"exoticize" the religious in setting it apart from what is perceived as the prime marker of the modern world: knowledge of the secular. The fallacy of "religion," therefore, is that it makes us look for a distinct practice, with institutional and doctrinal unity or coherence, and based on propositions about entities that have no worldly or secular (and therefore usually material) presence. Mellaart's quest for "shrines" in a specific "priestly quarter" that were devoted to the worship of the male "bull-god" and the "mother goddess" is a perfect example of this fallacy (1967: 71, 100, 180, passim). But the assumptions criticized by Düring – that too many have taken the Çatalhöyük imagery as constituting a "unified, interconnected and coherent corpus" that can be interpreted as a "reflection of the symbolism and religion" of its people (2006: 191) – can also be identified as part of this fallacy's heritage.

An alternative practice of tracing the religious would be to "de-exoticize" the sacred by placing it within more familiar, less distanced modes of social action (cf. Rowlands 2004). One of the available models for this would be the common tendency of human beings to mark the salvation, nourishment or transformation that they desire material things to bring by "fetishizing" them – that is, attributing to them an agency to move people (cf. Gell 1998; Meskell 2004). Such attributions might not be doctrinally marked or part of a coherent conceptual model; when modern people "knock on wood," for example, they rarely use a specific doctrine or set of beliefs, but they *do* fetishize (unpainted) wood by their act of knocking. These acts may, moreover, not be transcendent in anything but the most mundane or secular meaning of the term – such as when some people claim to feel more comfortable, important or happy when they possess a Macintosh computer rather than a PC. Finally, they are usually based in the performative capacity of things discussed earlier – the capacities listed by the Macintosh user when he or she tries to convince us of its superior quality. This is not to propose that doctrines of salvation are not important in elaborating the sacredness of certain things – the famous 1984 advertisement that introduced the Macintosh computer as an individual liberation from "Big Brother" drew not only on intertextual references to Orwell's science fiction book, but on a decade of elaboration of an anarchistic hacking ideology – but to say that a less exotic understanding of religion could and should start with its rootedness in everyday practice (of, in this case, the spread of PCs into people's everyday lives). We could – as Marx,

Frazer and Malinowski intuited some time ago – compare "primitive" religion with our present society, rather than with the specialized religions conceived on the basis of medieval and early modern Christian models.

How can we trace "religion" in Çatalhöyük through such an alternative approach? Webb Keane (Chapter 8) suggests that we attend to the "degrees of markedness of attention" that we can connect to the traces we find, where we can define "marked" as an articulation of the performance of the material thing by human activity. A thing marked is a thing to which people have attributed agency, if only in the weakest sense of articulating (an aspect of) its performance. In the use of archaeological evidence, we will only rarely be able to spell out the precise understanding of this agency; the semiotic ideologies on which these are based remain largely out of reach unless we gain direct access to traces of discourse (that allow us, to use Keane's words, to distinguish goals from outcomes of human action; Chapter 8). But material traces index activities at several levels of analysis: a painting indexes at least mimetic action; a burial or interment of an animal skull indexes memorial action; rebuilding a house indexes an act of continuation; the house interior indexes the marking of a social pattern; the micro-traces of activities reinforce this pattern; and the sheer existence of an inside and an outside – house and roof, settlement and field, settlement and wilderness – indicates movement. In isolation, the material trace that is an index is not enough to even approach an assessment of the performance of the thing, let alone to reason from the outcome to the goal of the action indexed. However, I am particularly impressed by the strength of current archaeology, and of the Çatalhöyük Research Project in particular, to overcome such obstacles by the aggregation of traces into definable objects of study. One important and insightful example of this procedure is the assessment of a special marking in contrast with the absence of others: Hodder's attempt to outline "the leopard's puzzle" by means of the contrast between material things of almost everyday use (such as the remains of sheep and goats) that seem to remain completely unmarked and material things that seem very rare at the site but are marked by a considerable degree of elaboration (such as reliefs and paintings of leopards and wild bulls; see Hodder 2006: 9) is an important case in point; the conclusion that the former were regarded as mundane and the latter as in some degree sacred seems warranted in such cases.

I just used the term "sacred," and this may require a further elaboration of what it means to trace the "religious" in societies where its existence as a separate realm of belief and cultic behavior is not evident. What unites the fetishist, the Macintosh user and any other human being who expects something out of the ordinary from an object employed to better their lives is the emphasis on expectations, desires and wishes for an improved future, however mundane and conservative these desires may be. "Marking" or "articulating" this object is, at the very least, one step in a movement from the profane to the sacred, by the material expression of some enhancement of desire.[7] Thus, even if the whitewashing of the walls of a Çatalhöyük house can be reduced to sheer utility (to keep the house bright and clean), their being painted indicates an articulation of sacrality that goes beyond it. This sacrality, however, should not be mistaken for something necessarily "religious" in our strict sense of the word: it may only indicate a level of elaboration comparable to, say, that of a sitting or dining room in a modern house, in contrast to the more profane kitchen. More important, however, is that this allows us to speak of *degrees* of articulation in three different senses. First, markings or articulations of material items differ in their relationship to everyday life, some being more out of the ordinary (or less profane) than others. And this is precisely why it makes sense to turn the indexes of the leopard and the bull into an important and intriguing puzzle, for if the leopard, the bull and the vulture (for example) are not part of everyday experience in the settlement, their signs can be interpreted as indications of something transcending the profane – just as house burials indicate a transcendence of the temporality of the household living in the house at a specific moment. While it would be too hasty to translate these forms of transcendence into the existence of an otherworldly realm (of leopards, bulls or ancestor "spirits"; again, our access to such semiotic ideologies seems too limited to support such a conclusion), they certainly seem to indicate a different degree of sacredness than, say, a figurine thrown into a midden.

A second sense in which we can speak of degrees of articulation can be indicated by the aggregation of evidence of such markings, when,

---

[7] Note that Durkheim's opposition of sacred and profane is more appropriate here than the opposition of sacred (or religious) and secular, since it does not introduce the unwarranted assumption of an "otherworldly" realm opposed to the "this-worldly" meaning of "secular."

for instance, we try to distinguish "history houses" (Hodder and Pels, Chapter 7) on the basis of a *combination* of articulations – of, for example, repeated rebuilding in the same pattern, large numbers of burials and large numbers of paintings and/or interments of skulls or bones – thus again allowing for the interpretation that some houses became less profane and more transcendent or sacred over the course of their career. This is an approach to the transcendent that is certainly appropriate to the temporal analysis presented later. Finally, a third sense of differing degrees of articulation can be found in what Hodder identified as a practice of hiding and revealing things at Çatalhöyük (Hodder 2006: 183). Indeed, a dialectics of revelation and concealment is inherent in magical action (Pels 2003: 37; Taussig 2003) and, despite Mauss's distinction of "secret" magic from "public" religion (1972: 24), may also be part of many religious practices of articulating transcendent value (see Nakamura, Chapter 11). In this essay, however, I will not deal with this aspect of articulating materialities further; it will have to await more research and another occasion.

To tell a story

Whether one does qualitative or quantitative research, one always has to tell a story. With this, I do not mean to denigrate the value of non-verbal meanings or evidence, but to point out that the materiality of evidence consists of a "bundle" of possibilities that underdetermine how they can be interpreted (cf. Keane 2003) and that we need to use our interpretative imagination to conjecture from the material indexes the possible narratives that can be constructed on their basis (as I tried to do in the preceding section). In social scientific methodology, the phase of conjecture or abduction (see note 1) is usually subsumed (and often ignored) under the name of "validity" – the formulation of the best fit between the terms in which questions are asked and the situation the research aims to study. As discussed in the first section of this essay, I was struck by the extent to which, in archaeology even more than in other disciplines, the aggregate objects produced by periodization and defining temporal shifts in the *longue durée* are key to the interpretation of other, lower levels of temporality and aggregation. Thus, I feel I should spell out a possible story of Çatalhöyük – an imagined sequence constructed through my limited reading and experience at the site – before proceeding to the main aim of this essay: the detailing of temporalities of religion at Çatalhöyük. This is probably little more than a repetition of themes and insights already articulated by others and mostly brought together by Hodder in *The Leopard's Tale* (2006). Yet it is not so much meant to give statements about what Çatalhöyük was "really" like as to elaborate on what a methodology of detailing scales of temporality might produce when used to further refine the analysis. One salient feature of this methodology, in any case, is that – in keeping with the approach toward religion outlined in the preceding section and with Keane's advice (Chapter 8) – it focuses on the particular trace rather than the universal pattern, even when I will use plausible suggestions about human universals when trying to detail such particularities.

Broadly speaking, I assume that Çatalhöyük represents a unique phase in the settlement of the Konya Plain, wedged in between a phase in which the domestication of human beings proceeded from, on the one hand, ritual sites such as Göbekli Tepe toward house settlements with collective ritual centers such as Aşıklı Höyük and, on the other, a sequence in which, initially, the upper levels of settlement of the Çatalhöyük East Mound testify to the increasing independence of houses toward each other, possibly on the basis of a more "organic" form of mutual exchange or collaboration and a subsequent movement off the East Mound toward, among other sites, the West Mound, possibly associated with the domestication of cattle. In the course of that development, and especially between 7000 and 6400 BC (or Levels XII–VI), Çatalhöyük drew most of the inhabitants of the Konya Plain into a house settlement based on households that subsisted on plants, sheep and goats, suggesting an economy with a fairly stable pattern of interaction between the settlement as such (and the immediate environment of the resources needed to build and maintain it – water, clay, lime, etc.) and a wider environment of agricultural, herding and hunting grounds, with only occasional forays into farther regions for obsidian and timber.[8]

I zoom in on Levels VIII–VI of the excavation because of Düring's suggestion that one may discern a specific architectural pattern in those levels, one that seems to dissolve at least partly from Level V upward

---

[8] I am conscious of the problematic relationship between Mellaart's stratigraphy of levels and the drawing up of a coherent sequence of events (Cessford 2005a: 67; see also the discussion in Düring 2001b: 226–35) and have tried, as far as I am capable, to avoid its pitfalls here.

(Düring 2001a). This shift within the settlement's architecture is confirmed by shifts in artistic production, and especially a move from moldings of bucrania and other interments in the walls toward wall paintings, stamp seals and a "more narrative" art (Hodder 2005b: 189–90), accompanied by a shift in pottery production toward more variation in designs and sizes and more decoration by figural lugs and incisions (N. Yalman, pers. comm.), as discussed later (on specialization in obsidian production, see Conolly 1999: 798; Düring 2001b: 221, 235).[9] The architectural pattern that dominated building before this shift is characterized by an agglutinative settlement in which about one-fifth of the houses progressively developed into elaborated centers for commemoration (by burial, animal reliefs and interment of animal bones). While ritually elaborated houses marked mostly by burials persist after Level VI, these houses no longer seem to occupy the central position within the settlement that used to be marked by a high degree of connectedness to a number of less elaborate houses via roof access (Düring 2001a,b). Corresponding to this decrease in focus on houses, the post–Level VI and West Mound uses of art and stamp seals and the migration of wall design to pottery suggest "a gradual wresting of memory away from the house" (Hodder 2005b: 195). Also, the post–Level VI settlement seems to shrink in size or disperse on the mounds (Düring 2006: 246; Hodder 2006: 254).

What kind of story might this summary of material evidence produce? Bear with me while I flesh some of these bones with my imagination. Çatalhöyük appears to be a "house society" (Joyce & Gillespie 2000) that has settled down in a place where the raw materials for their material reproduction were available in abundance: near the clay and marl pits of the swamp where the Çarşamba River dispersed itself into the Konya Plain. The household that animated a building and turned it into a "house" consisted of several generations of nuclear families, with or without adoptive kin, where authority was divided among different elders of both genders – articulating the relative importance of a certain gendered division of labor between agriculture, herding and hunting.

---

[9] This pattern would be supported by the suggestion that a shift from male to female figurines can be found between Levels VI and V (Hamilton and Voigt, quoted by Hodder 2006: 254). Recent critical reexaminations of the figurine corpus, while throwing some of such conclusions into doubt (Meskell et al. 2008), seem to confirm that there is indeed a shift to female imagery in the upper levels.

Elders supervised and safeguarded the transmission of relevant skills (animal husbandry, social communication, manufacture, sexuality); some of them were more skilled or renowned for this than others and were sought out by a much larger number of people from other households – and acquired more authority and power as a result. This led to an increasing concentration of reproductive power in a limited number of houses, articulated by memory storage (expressed by interring both humans and animal bones in the house and marking them by platforms, plastering and/or sculpture or moldings) and, most likely, an accumulation of skills and knowledge. As certain elders gained power and authority and lost physical stamina, they became increasingly confined to the house, both in a practical sense and in the sense of becoming guardians of the goods, skills, capacities and identities stored there. A successful house transferred such guardianship capacities to another guardian in the next generation, either born into the family, or adopted or recruited (or both, depending on the extent and nature of the kinship network and its classifications), thus increasing the need for a house to be rebuilt in the same way after structural defects appear or an important transfer of skills and capacities is required (in a isolated instance, the skull of a previous, renowned guardian was even buried together with one who took over these capacities in a later generation). These houses did, indeed, "bring everything into" them (Hodder 2006: 58), but in articulations that, for example, privileged the memory of wild cattle in reliefs and installations or deposits in many houses, and depictions of other wild animals (such as leopards) in more isolated instances. The more domestic (feminine?) parts of household production were not articulated, or perhaps even downplayed. Each house thus had its own history, as articulated vis-à-vis other, more elaborate houses, or marked in the different events and actions that mark an individual house's memorialization.[10]

Houses were probably differentiated in their household composition: if an elaborated house was occupied by a guardian of memory and skills, its economy may have been more dependent on gifts in exchange for knowledge than in the case of a house occupied by a young nuclear family. The occupation of the house must have been different, in any case, depending on the seasons, more activity (herding, agriculture) taking

---

[10] While the manufacture and use of figurines seem more mobile and less tied to memory practices, they do support the emphasis on individual biographies of houses (Meskell et al. 2008: 148).

place outside the settlement or on the roofs during drier and warmer seasons, with people moving into the smoke-filled rooms from autumn to spring. Daily rhythms, too, necessitated movement in and out, if only to gather fuel and water. Given the Çatalhöyük people's diet, hunting feasts may have taken place only occasionally, and the daily rhythm in summer must have consisted mostly of herding sheep and goats and tilling the fields. Because of the heat, it is likely that summer life inside the settlement took place on the roof, turning the house over the summer into a container of goods more than people. Yet feasting off wild animals, especially cattle, took place, and wild animals were used to mark the integrity and/or transformation of a "house." Çatalhöyük seems to have been quite peaceful, suggesting that there was little pressure on people to compete among each other for resources – or perhaps too much pressure to survive to engage in internecine struggle. The only signs of struggle are with bulls, deer, bears, and boars, in paintings from the period after Level VI.

The controlled burning of houses took place from Level VII onward, and it may be too much to argue that the major fire in part of the site in Level VIA indicated a major disruption. Yet the changes between Level VI and Level V, accompanied by the start of the dispersal of the settlement, suggest a major but slow shift toward a different type of house society. As male figurines are being replaced by female ones, and bucrania and other moldings of wild animals give way to wall paintings of teasing and hunting animals, the settlement also seemed to concentrate less on specific elaborated houses than on mobile, locally produced art and stamp seals. Even more, pottery production from Level V onward suggests that this shift in material culture may not have been that different from the shift from houses as containers to pots as containers suggested for certain areas of the Levant (Gamble 2004: 92): while the pottery from Levels XII–VI shows gradual changes, such as increasingly thinner ware (in Levels VIII–VII) and the addition of lugs (in Level VII), there is a major shift from Level VI to Level V, from the common mineral-tempered black ware to a sudden variation of colors and materials used, a greater variation of design, including the addition of bowls and miniature cups, difference between pots for daily usage and more specialized containers and, significantly, decoration in the form of lugs in the shape of animal or human heads and carved incisions on the pots – the prize item being the beautiful cup carved with twin human and bulls' heads (Figure 2.8) also found at this level.[11] From Level V onward, it is more difficult to allocate ceramics to ware groups, and while innovations in technology and design continue to appear in Levels IV and III, a decisive break seems to be made only in Level V.[12]

This development seems also to relate to economic changes in the settlement. Faunal remains indicate that cattle become less common in the upper levels: trophy bones decrease and there seems to be less emphasis on hunting from Level VI, while the domestication of cattle takes place only several centuries after the dispersal of the settlement. A simultaneous increase of reliance on sheep and goat herding may not indicate transhumance but an increasingly integrated economy, with same-sex labor, that combines agriculture and pastoralism in the mosaic landscape close to the settlement; this suggests that households become both more integrated and more independent from each other than in a period in which the organization of hunting parties necessitated collective action.[13] If hunting was a male preserve, its decrease and the increasing integration of the economy with the settlement might explain why paintings of hunting scenes (rather than actual hunting trophies) appear at this stage, but also why symbols of the hunt (such as the leopard) now appear to be dominated by female figures (as in the famous "mistress of animals" statue discovered by Mellaart). The paintings suggest that masculinity was connected to material remains from hunting, that is, not made by human hands, and that this emphasis decreased from Level V onward. An increase in the independence of households also seems to appear from the evidence of bricklaying and building, although here the major shift (from wet-laid, in situ bricklaying to mold-made bricks probably dried in the sun outside the settlement) takes place between Levels VIII and VII (simultaneous with the shift from clay balls to pottery in cooking; Cessford & Near 2005: 180), and the fact that neighbors, even when using the same materials, used them differently

---

[11] The face on the cup shows a remarkable similarity to the way the nose was built up in the plastered skull that was held, forehead to forehead, by the buried corpse, also in Level V, at least as I saw in the the Konya museum (see also Hodder 2006: 23, plates 13 and 14). This would reinforce the interpretation that the cup displays transcendental indices – including the bull – similar to those found in the house.

[12] I thank Nurcan Yalman for this summary of her findings during a wonderful tour of the Çatalhöyük pottery lab on July 30, 2008.

[13] I thank Nerissa Russell and Katheryn Twiss for this information from the faunal remains lab, Çatalhöyük, July 29, 2008.

shows that some measure of independent house building was always going on.[14]

If this composite story is plausible, it suggests some highly intriguing questions about both shorter-term and long-term changes in the Neolithic Middle East: Is it possible that Çatalhöyük displays two relatively (for we should not exaggerate the speed with which the shift between Levels VI and V occurs) distinct periods of the settlement's economy? The first would be one in which a household is composed of the everyday, quotidian materialities of in situ house- and settlement-bound production *in combination with* longer-distance hunting and the feasting related to it. The other, later phase would then imply a more integrated economy of households that ceased to rely as much on hunting and its commemoration in the house, turned hunting into a painted representation and emphasized more domestic crafts instead. If those two phases were gendered differently (as the later hunting scenes seem to indicate), does the later phase of a more integrated economy indicate a kind of prehistorical feminizing wave (i.e, a decreasing emphasis on the economic necessity of extra-settlement-based male skills, like hunting)? We see here that the reinterpretation of "material engagement" from the exclusively artifactual to including the engagement with animals – and particularly, the wild animal as compared with the domestic – is interpretatively crucial.

Temporalities of "religion" at Çatalhöyük

This final section of the essay considers what we can say about "religion" – or, as argued earlier, how people articulate activities and relationships they find important by differing degrees of marking their sacrality or transcendence – once we consider the different timescales relevant to the analysis of Çatalhöyük material and the interrelations between them. This will necessarily be fragmentary and haphazard, in the sense that my aim is more to provide illustrations and examples of the viability of my approach (if any) than to give a comprehensive catalog of how different Çatalhöyük data fit the study of different timescales.

[14] I thank Serena Love for initiating me into some of the secrets of brickmaking at Çatalhöyük in several conversations during the 2007 and 2008 seasons.

THE LIFE SPAN OF THE SETTLEMENT

The question of "religion," I would argue, does not play a decisive role when we consider this longest of *longue durées*. If we discuss the positioning of Çatalhöyük within longer-term developments in the Neolithic Middle East, including questions about the rise of sedentism, agriculture and the domestication of animals, terms like "religion" and "symbolism" seem to confuse the issue to the extent that they introduce separations and significations into a situation foreign to them. The critical edge that the statement that "religion (or symbolism) (also) caused sedentism" may once have had totally disappears if one recognizes that no social pattern or its change occurs without the mediation by material signs, that is, of things acting on people. Such an insight does away with any simple technological or environmental determinism and therefore also with its opposite – that "culture" or "religion" is more important for human evolution.

However, this does not mean that "religious" issues are irrelevant to the assessment of what took place at the timescale of the settlement as such. To the contrary: a "wider picture" of the place of Çatalhöyük in the Middle Eastern context cannot fail to show that the excavation of an elaborate ceremonial center like Göbekli Tepe and the strong emphasis on ceremonial buildings in places like Çayönü and Aşıklı Höyük "have very much altered narratives of the development of village life" (Hodder 2006: 134), to such an extent that one may presume that human settlement was encouraged initially by the objectifications of the sacred made by corporate groups *before* humans developed the looser divisions of labor that characterized the Çatalhöyük house society (2006: 135).[15] In combination with the narrative I have outlined, this suggests that we might have to confront the evidence with the idea that Çatalhöyük indicates – in comparison with Cayönü and Aşıklı Höyük – a more atomized society based on relatively independent houses (up to ca. 6400 cal BC), which in its second phase loses even the possible settlement-wide organization of labor needed for large hunting parties (up to the abandonment of the

---

[15] Hodder's use of the Durkheimian distinction of mechanic and organic solidarity (2006: 134) here is, I feel, risky, especially since the notion of the mechanical solidarity of "the community" ignores the probably universal division of labor of all human groups into gender and age differences. The two phases of the Çatalhöyük settlement hypothesized in this essay suggest, if anything, a progression from a more organic division of labor (between hunters and domestic producers) to a more integrated (and hence more mechanical) solidarity – the opposite of the sequence proposed by Durkheim.

East Mound). Add to this that, in similar comparisons, burial customs at Çatalhöyük seem "conservative" (Hodder 2006: 124), and one gets the impression of a distinctly "local" cultural trajectory with a relatively "low" investment in collective, settlement-wide ceremonial activity.

The evidence for major shifts within the life span of Çatalhöyük gives rise to intriguing questions about the ways in which people marked things out for special degrees of attention. One of the ways in which the shift that seems to take place between Levels VI and V may be interpreted is that a society that concentrated memory in houses by interring both humans and animals in it became less interested in doing so as far as interring animal remains was concerned (while human burials continued to be important into Levels V–II on the East Mound). At the same time, houses seem to disperse, to no longer display the same continuity, and are less grouped around more central, elaborated buildings.[16] This would need to be coupled to other evidence of change occurring in the same period: more localized and specialized lithic production (Conolly 1999: 798), a radical reduction of the period of occupancy of a building (Cessford and Near 2005: 175), no "hunting" or "teasing" scenes in wall paintings before Level V and no figurative moldings later than Level VI (Düring 2006: 194, 199). Düring suggests that, after Level V, the link to the past "was no longer important in the way it had been before" (2001b: 222). Hodder suggests that the changes have more to do with an increase in domestic production (2006: 255), and as we have seen, it may indicate a more integrated household economy on the basis of the evidence of faunal remains.

Traces of memorialization, of course, are as close as we will get to the transcendental as experienced by Çatalhöyük people – with the qualification that I see no evidence of anything more transcendental than houses (as discussed later), ancestors and animals (whose spirits, if any, are of immanent descent).[17] Note that such interpretations of how Çatalhöyük

---

[16] I base this largely on Düring (2001a, 2006) and Mellaart's "table of shrines and houses" (1967: 82). I disregard the moldings that Mellaart called "mother goddesses" and Hodder designates as "some sort of bear–human hybrid" (2006: 142) – items for which I have yet to see a plausible interpretation.

[17] Here, I part company with Kopytoff's postulate of a continuity between ancestors and elders (1971) by the observation that while elders, once deceased, do not indeed change, most Bantu languages define a special "spiritual" realm (*kuzimu*; see Brain 1973), which the deceased enter after death. This does not, of course, prove that Çatalhöyük residents had a conception of a similar separate realm.

people memorialized ancestors and animals during a certain phase of the settlement's history completely rely on the observer's aggregation of data, yet provide hypotheses about the dialectic of objectification and embodiment that people actually experienced. This dialectic itself, however, properly takes place only in temporal sequences in which we can identify a "house."

THE LIFE SPAN OF A HOUSE SEQUENCE AND THE LIFE CYCLE OF A HOUSE

Once one tries to discuss some of the evidence for the special marking of the temporalities of houses, the life span of a house sequence and the life cycle of a house (or its physical substratum, the building) turn out to be inextricably entangled (see Matthews 2005b), and I will therefore deal with them together. The main categories of evidence here are continuities and discontinuities in floor plans; evidence of erasure and demolition of a building, with burning as a special instance; interment of bones and artifacts; and burials. The "house" is both more and less than the remains of a physical building, for its identity is tied to forms of memorialization and the repetition of floor plans that extend beyond it, and therefore to decisions about reproduction, memorialization and/or destruction that could take place only on a conscious level – just as much as the physical building contains elements forgotten by the builders and left out of the reproduction of the house. The "house" is, in this conception, a transgenerational entity that was definitely marked for special attention by acts of foundation and erasure. While this clearly indicates the house's transcendental status – and more aggregation of data may provide more clues as to its meaning for Çatalhöyük people – our understanding of these meanings remains limited by the difficulty of knowing precisely where to draw the line between its history and its myths (cf. Hodder 2006: ch. 6).

A study of continuities and discontinuities in Çatalhöyük floor plans shows that, again, Levels VII–VI show most continuity, especially in relation to a seeming break in continuity between Levels VI and V (see the diagram in Düring 2006: 219). This is reinforced by the evidence for ceremonial acts of foundation and erasure of a house brought together by Hodder, which all seems to refer to Levels XII–VII and which ties the special marking of the beginning and end of a house to the period in which long-term occupation of houses (up to 80 years) was common and house sequences could stretch up to 500 years (Hodder 2006: 117–18, 129–30). Interestingly, the possible break in continuity between Levels VI and V was accompanied by what Mellaart called a "conflagration" in the South Area – a large-scale fire that may have been deliberate and controlled (Cessford & Near 2005: 172). Even more, it seems that no burning was applied in the ceremonial erasure of buildings pre–Level VI, while it did occur more regularly in the upper levels of the mound, leading Cessford and Near to suggest that "the appearance of this phenomenon [the deliberate burning of buildings] coincides with a decrease in the typical length of time for which buildings were occupied" from an average of 110 years (ca. five generations) to an average of 25–35 years (i.e., the average age of a Çatalhöyük inhabitant or less) (2005: 175). Cessford and Near note the "transformative" character of fire and its "spectacular" nature (2005: 175, 182), which suggests that the reduction in the length of occupation of a house required a ceremonial "spectacle" of transformation by fire – perhaps as a way to neutralize the agency of the house in those cases where it was abandoned before it had had the chance to "grow old." Note, again, that such a line of reasoning requires a prior storyline, the aggregation of data into an "object" (in this case "house") and the subsequent focus on how this object was "specially" marked, before we come to the point of interpreting what these marks mean (in this case, the possible sacralization of the "house"). But given such a storyline, the evidence supports an interpretation of burning as a ceremonial act used by increasingly "individual" households to terminate their occupancy and clear the way for a new start.

Note, too, that paying attention to the relative timescales of the "house" at different levels of occupation suggests that, from Level V upward, the long house sequence of the previous levels becomes less prevalent. In the framework of the story presented in this essay, one could argue that this change represents the demise of a house society based on bringing into the house a fairly widespread combination of agriculture, building, herding and hunting, which required the "house" to specially mark its need for continuity through acts of foundation and repetition because this combination rested on social relationships extending beyond individual generations and, in the accumulation of indices of hunting, social relationships with the "wilderness" beyond the settlement and its immediately surrounding landscape. If, indeed, it is correct to assume that the restriction of the length of occupation of a building to a single generation led to the disappearance of the house sequence, one is led to the hypothesis that this is related to the socioeconomic changes that seem to indicate an increasingly integrated economy (as suggested by the faunal remains) and more emphasis on individual houses. The house still remained a main place of burial, at least until Çatalhöyük people moved away to the West Mound. Floor plans indicate houses became more diversified, or "multi-roomed" (Hodder 2006: 253). Brick sizes decreased, suggesting increasing self-sufficiency of people in building houses (2006: 252–3). Fewer and thicker layers of plaster suggest less "specially marked" walls, but while some decoration seems to shift to pottery, and pottery certainly becomes more varied and elaborate (Hodder 2006: 251; N. Yalman, pers. comm.), the more remarkable wall paintings of hunting or baiting or teasing animals occur only after Level V too (Düring 2006: 194). There is an increase in female burials and female figurines (including the famous "mistress of animals" found by Mellaart in a grain bin), and other evidence indicates an increasing emphasis on domestic production (Hodder 2006: 254–5). These traces, I would argue, all suggest that the house becomes less transcendental from Level V onward – without saying that it loses its transcendental status altogether. In any case, these traces index changes at the level of the household, showing that all such conjectures are necessarily based on an assessment of how different timescales relate to each other.

THE LIFE CYCLE OF A HOUSEHOLD

A household is something different from a house, tied initially to a network of relationships and activities that is relatively autonomous from the physical substratum of a building (cf. Matthews 2005b). A household was commonly treated by anthropologists in terms of kinship and marriage relations, but this cultural emphasis has had to give way to more social anthropological concerns, focusing on the residential, commensal and economic relationships that tie people together. I emphasize once more that the household ties in people who are, at times, physically absent from the building as such – on a daily basis for some of those who till the land or herd the sheep, on a seasonal basis when hunting, herding or trading becomes a longer-term endeavor – and that a household is by definition based in a division of labor along the lines of gender and age, if not other specializations, which requires it to reinvent itself for every new generation. This is, in fact, one of the most important functions of initiation ceremonies for youngsters as well as elders, where the intersection of gender and age is the usually explicit and central concern of the social (and usually sacred) transformation that has to be effected on the initiate. Initiation ceremonies, especially where they are meant to transform children into responsible and skilled adults, change constantly in order to keep up with the new conditions of the times – even beyond the point where state-introduced schools marginalized the household as a reproductive institution (cf. Pels 1999: chs. 3 & 4). Even while we do not seem to possess any unambiguous evidence about initiation ceremonies at Çatalhöyük, it is worthwhile to keep in mind the model of societies where households are being reproduced by the collective reproduction of adults through initiation, especially when this reminds us of the fact that the household is composed of relationships that engage the house (as in certain female initiation practices; Pels 1999: ch. 4) with the bush and the wider world (as in certain male initiation practices; Pels 1999: ch. 3).

I already discussed the *residential* focus of the household – the "house" – in the preceding section and need only recall the fact that, precisely because a household is materially entangled with the fields and the bush, it is not congruent with the house, yet turns the house into an entity transcending its material substratum, the building. The economic focus of the household – its incorporation of labor power and tools, accumulated knowledge about production and reproduction, the relative balance of food resources, the whole economy of building – is maybe something best left for discussion at a lower timescale, that of annual, seasonal and intra-annual cycles (but see later). The *commensal* focus of a household rests, of course, on the pyrotechnical installations of hearth and oven, and these also play a role at the level of daily rounds and rhythms. However, the existence of a number of ovens and hearths, shifting location during the life span of a building (Cessford & Near 2005: 177), clearly indicates the reinvention of the household over the course of this life span that I have referred to and results in the question to what extent such reinventions could be marked by degrees of attention to the sacred.

A final issue to be discussed at this timescale is the fact that, because the household can be seen as the major social unit of Çatalhöyük, it is also the level at which one can identify the social contradictions that, as Marx suggested, hold societies together. These are the tensions between individual and collective, between the specially marked "prowess–animal-hunting-and-feasting" complex and domestic production, and gender (Hodder 2006: 207) – and, not least, age (2006: 214–17). Such tensions are, in most societies, specially marked by an emphasis on one, usually dominant or hegemonic and therefore sacralized side of the contradiction. In the case of Çatalhöyük, one can discern several emphases from this perspective. First, it seems clear that the relation between the individual and the collective in the pre–Level V arrangements was articulated by some houses becoming more dominant than others, indicating that not all households were similar and that some households were tied into the work of reproducing houses in more complex ways than others. The changes that seem to occur from Level V upward may indicate more independence of the individual household toward the collective, in the sense that houses are less concentrated around elaborated houses, in the sense that female identity becomes more separately marked and in the sense that some material entanglements (such as bricklaying from Level VII upward) may have required less collective labor.

Second, this already indicates possible shifts in gender relationships and inequalities. If in the pre–Level V situation, gender remains singularly unmarked by burials, division of labor or diet (Hodder 2006: 210), and some of the transcendental signs that dominate the house are those of the "prowess–animal-hunting-and-feasting" complex, the very least we can argue is that both men and women were subject to this complex associated with the wild, and did not articulate the more "domestic" contributions to the household such as plants and herded animals. As already indicated, this glaring discrepancy (which made Hodder puzzle over the presence of the leopard) marks a degree of articulation of wild animals and hunting out of proportion to its profane role in everyday life. Coupled to the longer life span of a house and a building in the lower levels, this suggests that the social authority that was needed to ensure the perpetuation of a house over several generations required these indices of the wilderness and of hunting, and, mutatis mutandis, of the knowledge associated with it within the household. Conversely, the reduction of hunting to a painting (i.e., the *representation* of hunting rather than the presence of a bull or boar in the form of its bones) in the upper levels suggests, by means of a simple functionalist argument, that hunting lost its transcendental authority within the household, and this is in fact supported by the evidence from faunal remains. It is, therefore, tempting to associate the articulation of female identity in the upper levels with the increased importance of domestic production at the expense of a more masculine "prowess–animal-hunting-and-feasting" complex. The household may have become more exclusively dependent on an economy in which pastoralism and agriculture were integrated into a regime in which gender differences were no longer as predicated on the prolonged absence and the articulation of distance from the settlement, especially in terms of opposing the settlement against the "wild." The perpetuation of – and hence, the authority within – the household would then have become more dependent on different, more "in-house" skills, those required for the new variety in pottery production, new pyrotechnology (perhaps articulated by the new ceremonial prominence of fire), collective baking and the combination of pastoralism and agriculture in the immediate surroundings of the settlement more generally. This, however, does not explain why the upper levels seem to indicate a reduction of the life span of the house, unless we invoke several auxiliary and so far speculative hypotheses, such as the argument that hunting was an uncertain business that (following the thesis that uncertainty about outcomes requires a more magical articulation of an activity; Malinowski 1954) seemed to require more articulation of its results to safeguard future success and, conversely, that a more secure and abundant, integrated economy supporting the upper levels' society made such incantations and their enshrinement across generations superfluous.

Some of these reflections on gender and age divisions of labor and cultural articulations within the household at Çatalhöyük deserve, I feel, further empirical scrutiny at several levels of interpretation. It seems, for example, plausible to suggest that certain pyrotechnical abilities are initially exclusively associated with the house through the centers for domestic production, concentrated on hearth and oven, and articulated by the movements of both as house and household change shape. Fire is universally associated with transformation (cf. Cessford & Near 2005: 172) and in Çatalhöyük, because the location of hearth and oven is where neonates and infants are buried, also with birth. But fire also seems to proliferate through the settlement from Level VI upward – used to "give birth" to new houses, but also concentrated in the seemingly more complex firing of larger ovens. An assessment of the relationship of these activities to (the places and technologies of) pottery production would seem to be highly illuminating, if evidence were available. A revisiting of Craig Cessford's and Julie Near's exciting essay (2005) on the basis of newly aggregated evidence from different parts of the site and the findings in the laboratories would, when coupled to a specification of pyrotechnical skills with an eye to possible gendered relationships, be extremely helpful in constructing a more complex picture of relationships within the household than available so far.

Finally, the tensions within the household that one can associate with age deserve some consideration. Burial practices seem to indicate that birth (i.e., neonate burial) is associated with the foundation of a house, and very small children with the southern part, that is, the domestic production center of the interior. Adults and adolescents were buried mostly in the north and east platforms but, perhaps more important, must in some cases have been buried off-site (Cessford 2005b), which in itself suggests the possibility of an alternative, adult "marking" of household identity that was not directly congruent with the house as such. (We should, as I already suggested, use a conception of materiality that foregrounds that not "everything" was taken into the house at Çatalhöyük and that tries to specify what was not.) Secondary burial concerns only adults and adolescents, suggesting at the very least that both formed a single category after a certain age (Hodder 2006: 215). Finally, the fact that both old men and women were found with soot-filled lungs suggests that "elders" (whatever condition qualified a person for such status) became house bound by cultural choice or necessity or both (2006: 210). Hence, both the beginning and the end of a life within the household were more strongly associated with the house than was middle age (and how old would that be?), and "middle age" from adolescence onward strongly suggests an important locus of household activity outside the house – activity that remains unmarked (at least to us) but that must have been of daily significance. That age and gender were articulated on each other seems inevitable, even if we do not find traces of initiation ritual; this is supported by the simple fact that birth (which, next to the start of menstruation, would be a marker of female maturity) was specially marked in relation to (parts of) the house. Again, an increase in female burials in the upper levels (Hodder 2006: 254) may indicate that "elderhood" became more feminized in relation to the house as well.

THE LIFE CYCLE OF A HUMAN BEING

The average Çatalhöyük person did not live beyond 35 years of age, and at birth and in old age (up to 50 or 60 years old) persons seemed to be associated with the house. The fact that only adults and adolescents were secondarily buried suggests that maturation may have implied entering a separate category of personhood, a stage that may have been unmarked (as "natural") when girls began to menstruate (although I find that unlikely) but would have to have been culturally marked in the case of male adolescents. However, the link of evidence to initiation remains speculative (see Hodder 2006: 217). Likewise, we can say very little about the special marking or articulation of gender differences, although the connections of birth to hearth and oven referred to earlier suggest the possibility of demarcating a specifically female realm. This implies an almost total absence of any straightforward indices of fertility and sexuality – a blank precisely in the spot on which human beings universally tend to lavish a large amount of their available attention. Did Çatalhöyük youth experiment with their sexuality and, if so, where and at what age? Did Çatalhöyük people have sex in the house? How did partnerships form anyway? There seems to be little evidence available on these aspects of social life. We seem to have no indications of the cultural practices of fertility and sexuality; archaeologists generally do not seem to have access to such evidence.

Likewise, evidence for the acquisition of technical competences, labor skills and specializations, and the experience of and motives for travel and trade, is scant, in the Çatalhöyük case most likely because agriculture, herding, hunting and trading did, indeed, not take place in the settlement. Thus, the observation from the preceding section, that a household is different from a house and suggests a network of relationships that stretches beyond it, to some extent runs into the snag that the nature of the household, and ipso facto the human differences and specializations that give a person a specific place in it during his or her lifetime, cannot be adequately studied on the basis of the evidence from the house as such. But, conversely, this also warns against giving the evidence from the Çatalhöyük house too much weight in the attempt to reconstruct the settlement's history of social arrangements.

We do see evidence of accumulation and hoarding of artifacts, bodies as well as signs, and could treat this as evidence for progressive social stratification – that is, of special markers of status that might indicate modes in which forms of possession (of knowledge, memory or wealth) became sacralized and marked a person's progression through life. It does not seem too speculative to try to relate the evidence from especially elaborated houses to the existence of (a sequence of) especially distinguished "elders" in those houses. The evidence from the lower levels, when brought together and compared across houses, suggests that by Level VII–VI about one-fifth of the houses had emerged as more ritually elaborate than others. This perhaps went together with the accumulation of obsidian and figurines (Hodder 2006: 178), suggesting that some households, and some persons, accumulated more access to goods and knowledge than others. The great disparities in numbers of burials between houses indicates not only the status of a particular house, but also the need to memorialize specific persons associated with it. Finally, the disparity between houses with more or less moldings and other interments of wild animals indicates that those persons living within them had a need to articulate their difference vis-á-vis others living in other houses. Thus, the course of a Çatalhöyük person's career seemed to have been determined by his or her differential placement within a certain network of houses and households. This suggests that a social stratification of persons took place during their lifetimes that was based not just on the difference between houses, but also, importantly, on a collective – settlement-wide – conceptualization of authority that must have been sacralized by the marking of its transcendence (by, e.g., burial practices) that we find in the archaeological record of Çatalhöyük, even when direct evidence of "sacralized" moments of accumulation and social stratification in a person's lifetime seems, again, to be absent.

Finally, something similar goes for seniority and aging and for death: even if the degree of social differentiation seems to be slight (Hodder 2006: 179), we can presume that the burial of a woman holding a repeatedly plastered skull represents a special case of the elevation of certain persons to sacred status, because the skull itself is marked to an extraordinary degree (by plastering), but also because the man holding it is marked by the skull (and because the skull's visage looks similar to the more abstracted "face-cup" discovered in the same level).[18] It does not seem idle speculation to interpret this as an index of certain acts in the lives of the skull's owner and the man that separated them out from others in a way that necessitated articulation of both their heads – they touched foreheads in burial – to emphasize these *particular*, individual

---

[18] This is my personal interpretation of the visual appearance of skull and cup and may not be corroborated by further analysis.

human heads as linked containers of meaning. Even if we do not know what meaning they contained, we may presume that the burial articulated a specifically revered experience or knowledge accumulated by these individual persons in their own lifetimes. Whatever it means, the articulation of this burial was reinforced by the leopard claw interred at the same time.

A final piece of evidence about the special marking of the human life cycle is the fact that human heads are articulated in separation from the body (unlike animal figurines, which usually keep their heads; Düring 2006: 155),[19] suggesting that the head (or the representation of a head) was perceived as something that had a temporality, agency or life cycle different from the body (and may therefore have indexed as transcendence of the lifetime of the individual). This seems logical if the head of an elder was perceived as a transcending container in which knowledge about the house was stored.

ANNUAL, SEASONAL AND OTHER INTRA-ANNUAL CYCLES

A focus on the experience of winter, spring, summer and autumn by Çatalhöyük people immediately foregrounds the (possibility of) movement of people "inside" and "outside" the house, as well as the settlement and the possibilities for marking such movements, but also the extent to which annual cycles provided possibilities for "good thinking" or articulating other parts of social life. Conversely, we can ask what markings of these cycles are evident in the material record. It should be remarked, however, that it is a given that, at the level of seasonality, people all over the world engage in the most profane of transcendental imaginations, usually marked by the existence of numerous folkloric sayings that are as little religious as our everyday "knock on wood."

The seasonal schedule for activities in the settlement (Fairbairn et al. 2005: 97) shows both how Çatalhöyük people experienced the year and how they could have varied their presence in and use of the house. Seasonal temporalities point to questions about how accessible the country was from the house at different times of the year; in the cold winter, people may have congregated in the settlement, restricting outings to local wood collection, weeding, upturning the soil and sowing the winter

[19] This would suggest, contra Hodder 2006: 201, that the splayed figures Mellaart identified as goddesses were humanoid, since their heads were removed on abandoning a building.

crops – except for hunting, for which people would seem to be dependent on the movement of game (again, a warning against taking "materiality" as something dependent on human manufacture). In spring, increasing warmth and light would invite a move to the rooftops and fields, but this movement would be restricted by rain or floods. At the same time, sheep birthing, the germination of seeds and the gathering of birds' eggs would emphasize a particularly fertile and procreative part of the year. In summer, the occupation of the settlement would vary, because of hunting and herding, because the drought allowed for a wider wood collection and perhaps because travel conditions were easier. Hunters would be confronted with rutting game in late summer. Autumn would clearly be a period that emphasized moving into the house, if only for the storage of food and wood, as well as the penning of sheep and goats. There must have been differences in the temporalities of seasonal relationships to the landscape, with agriculture and herding more seasonally affected than hunting, which could take place throughout the year.

These annual/seasonal temporalities, therefore, once more highlight the problematic that Ian Hodder made into a central question of his *The Leopard's Tale*: the fact that the Çatalhöyük evidence so far indicates that activities relating to hunting and the consumption of wild animals in feasting (something he also associates with prowess and communication with animal spirits) are strongly marked in the Çatalhöyük house, while the common basis of subsistence – cultivated crops, gathered plants and domesticated sheep and goats – was not, or hardly, articulated at all (2006: 47). Hence, the Çatalhöyük house articulated its annual and/or intra-annual cycles in a very particular way: by emphasizing temporalities that seem to some extent both more permanent (in the sense that hunting cattle and pigs, and encountering rival, animal predators such as leopards, foxes and vultures, seem yearlong preoccupations) and more remote (in the sense of "wild"), and by *not* articulating what was in fact closest and most permanent about survival in the house itself. To put this differently: the Çatalhöyük house seems to have articulated and sacralized those entities and activities with which Çatalhöyük people were least materially entangled, and this in itself should warn us of a conception of materiality too closely based on its human-made components.

This discrepancy is not surprising, since in many societies powerful people employ a limited selection of the available representational possibilities to construct hegemony. In the peasant society where I did fieldwork, male initiation ceremonies in the early and middle 20th century took place in the "bush." They emphasized proper deference to elders, but subsequently mostly articulated the boys' possibilities in the remote outside world: hunting, trading, migrant labor and the cash economy. Tilling the field and building a house were not emphasized at all, partly because the boys knew this already, partly because house and field marked the core ideological position of women in the reproduction of the lineage home. In contrast, female initiation took place in the (parental) house itself, again teaching proper deference to the girl and articulating the power of the lineage, but subsequently mostly concentrated on sexuality as a resource and a liability. Neither of these ceremonies left any trace in the house itself, with the significant exception that boys coming back from the coast or the plantations would bring souvenirs that would be displayed (see Pels 1999). In this society as well as in Çatalhöyük, inequalities (between genders, between ages) were hardly marked in the house (or in the diet); the main subsistence activities were also left profane (with the exception of magic, which was articulated by charms and amulets in the fields or under the roof or threshold); and the only special marking that seems to have made a difference was that male activities were commemorated and female ones were not.

Did annual cycles provide Çatalhöyük people with possibilities for marking and/or sacralizing (parts of) everyday life? One possibility here is the extent to which the pattern of the house itself reflects seasonal differences, although this pattern is more properly discussed in the context of daily routines (as discussed later). The movement inside or outside and across the roof must have differed from season to season, suggesting, for example, that during winter, the roofs (at least of the closely huddled settlement of Levels VIII–VI) were more of a public space than in the summer, when occupancy of the roofs must have required a sharper articulation of which routes to take from roof to roof to reach a certain building without disturbing domestic activities or sleep.[20] Likewise, egress could be seasonally marked, since it seems unlikely that Çatalhöyük

---

[20] Düring's earliest reflection on the Çatalhöyük buildings, while highly interesting, makes too easy a connection between public spaces and streets, and the lack of public space with the absence of them (2001a: 1–2). It would be interesting to think of the Level VIII–VI roof spaces not in terms of private properties ("a front garden"; Düring 2001b: 232), but as spaces of limited public access (such as the implicit code that identifies crossing spaces of ships moored next to each other).

people failed to associate birth (at least of birds and sheep) and germination with spring and with wetness (of rain and floods). One does not need the presumption of a structuralist system to argue that such a pattern of articulation would have to coexist – harmoniously or in friction – with other associations with birth (such as the south part of the house, the sun at its zenith, the hearth, fire and domestic production). (The difference with structuralist and cognitive analyses here may be that the hypothesis is based on the observation of plausible material entanglements and mediations rather than cognitive regularities, which makes the signs discussed anything but arbitrary [cf. Keane, Chapter 8]).

A final example to discuss at this temporal scale is how to interpret the evidence of intra-annual cycles in the material record. That walls were plastered three to nine times a year, as discovered by Wendy Matthews (2005a), is both a highly distinctive articulation of the wall and an enigma: why do this? This frequency of applying plaster itself indexes a "performance" of the wall over and above its pragmatic functions of giving shelter and partitioning. Even if the wall had to be frequently whitewashed merely because sooting turned it too dark to reflect the limited amount of light that filtered down from the ladder opening or as protection against mosquitoes, this would have given the wall a particular meaning – one that, for example, would be difficult to square with an interpretation of the house as a separate "subterranean" realm of spirits to be contacted by a shaman (as proposed by Lewis-Williams, quoted by Hodder 2006: 196), for where would that "subterranean" light then come from? We could further explore such associations – for example, by systematizing the evidence for the uses of walls. Wall paintings, in any case, seem to have been equally ephemeral as the plasters themselves. Would it be too speculative to suggest that plastering and painting were associated activities (in contrast to the activity of bringing home animal bones or burying a family member) and that those who plastered walls were also those who painted them at special occasions? What, if that is plausible, can we infer from the fact that wall paintings before Level V seem to feature vultures, "kilims," hands and honeycombs (or geometric designs; see Hodder 2006: 166–7, 190), while we find only hunting and baiting scenes painted from Level V upward (Düring 2006: 194)? Does it signify a change in the relation of whoever painted the walls with a powerful "outside" world? More provocatively, could the monthly and ephemeral plastering and painting of walls at Çatalhöyük be an index of more profane domestic activity, while the interment of persons and animal remains indicates transcendence?

DAILY ROUTINES AND RHYTHMS

The smallest timescale of human experience is obviously generated by the alternation of light and dark, warm and cold, strenuous and restful, waking and sleeping, hungry and satiated periods. This involves patterns of movement that give meaning to "up" and "down," "inside" and "outside," and "front" and "back" that mesh with seasonal patterns and result in a patterning of the landscape on the basis of the points of the compass, at least as defined by where the sun rises, reaches its zenith and sets (see Wason, Chapter 10). By extension, such rhythms also highlight the everyday material relationships between bodies and things – of eating, sleeping, personal hygiene and, not least, producing waste. Almost by definition, the largest part of these activities remains unmarked and profane in any special sense, or marked only by that which we throw away; the latter becomes important in Çatalhöyük because of the distinction between clean and dirty areas in the house (Hodder 2006: 50), which is one of the main empirical markers of activities at this timescale. It seems reasonable to explore the special articulation of such a mundane pattern in at least two respects: (1) through the assumption that the profane pattern of daily activity will also to a large extent be used as a blueprint for anything extraordinary or transcendentally marked; and (2) by attending to the possibilities for the most universal and everyday form of religious activity: protection and wish fulfillment, often known as magic (see Nakamura, Chapter 12).

The larger part of the daily cycles we can identify can be summarized by the trajectory of the sun, which we can say is marked by the points of the compass. This suggests that the pattern of the use of the house itself is an important indication of the extent to which the basic pattern of daily activities could be employed in articulating degrees of the extraordinary or sacred. If we limit ourselves to the Level XII–VI houses, a "dirty" area in the south part around the fire installations can be identified, with most storage areas located in the southwest. Molded features and installations, benches and buttresses seem to concentrate in the east, with some in the north and west but a significantly lower number on the southern side of the house. Wall paintings are found in the north and east. Burials seem to be distributed all over the house, but if there is a pattern, it

seems to be associated with neonate and infant burial in the southern
part, and adult and adolescent second burials under the northern and
eastern platforms, and a general association of burial with platforms in
the northern part of the house (see Düring 2006: 185–8, 194, 200;
Hodder 2006: 215, passim). Thus, the pragmatic choice to work and
store in the southern part of the house, where there is more light, was
articulated by devoting the northern and eastern parts to a significantly
larger number of aesthetic and ritual elaborations. I already noted the
possible associations of the south with birth, light and warmth, whether
the latter derived from the sun or from fire installations. The north and
east, likewise, seemed at least statistically associated with death in the
form of human burial as well as animal bone installations, in addition to
vultures and more abstract painting. The west and north seem in most
cases the place where finished products of agriculture end up for storage.
There seems to be at least statistical evidence for a binary pattern of
articulation that opposed the northeast to the southwest of the house,
but the numerous exceptions to this pattern also suggest that it needed
to be reproduced by individual households along the lines of their own
creative trajectory. It would be an extremely interesting empirical exercise
to try to systematize these exceptions further by an analysis of the extent
to which they do or do not fit into such general patterns, and especially
how they are distributed over elaborate and less elaborate houses within
each level in general, and compared across the shift between the upper
and lower levels divided by Levels VI and V in particular.

Apart from the points of the compass, the daily cycle is also experienced by going up and down, and especially by the upward movement
through the house occasioned by the rising of the sun and the downward movement that accompanies its setting. "Up" and "down" in the
Çatalhöyük house have been interpreted as fitting into the three-tiered
cosmos that is said to characterize shamanistic societies, so as to link
a subterranean level to an intermediate level (in Çatalhöyük, the roof)
and to an upper level, the sky (Lewis-Williams, cited in Hodder 2006:
196).[21] I find this difficult to reconcile with a society that so manifestly
articulates up and down by means of its architecture and that invests so

---

[21] In the ethnographic record, the complex called "shamanism" is usually associated with
nomads of the arctic or of the primeval forest, and societies that experience regular
flooding do not seem to have a place for the subterranean in their landscape (for an
interesting account of the latter, see Harrison 2004). The "aboriginal" status of the

much energy in whitewashing and thus lightening its interiors, but the possible association between the inside, the dark, the downward and the foundation of the house, on the one hand, and the upward, the sun and the core work areas for domestic production cannot be lightly dismissed. In the absence of more information about what took place on roofs and in fields, it is hard to say more.

Finally, the daily cycle of consumption and waste is articulated in a number of ways: first, by traces of regular cleaning and, second, by what can be found in refuse areas as a result. Both raise questions about what one can call wish fulfillment – the first because such traces suggest that everyday routines included a desire for and articulation of a white-walled, hard-floor inside environment without vermin and dirt – and therefore raise questions about the (desired) contrast between the inside and the outside of the settlement in terms of what vermin and dirt were brought into the settlement by the constant movement of people. Personal hygiene is directly connected to this, not only in terms of sanitation, but also in terms of desires about personal health and beauty. With respect to health concerns, I would endorse an interpretation of many human figurines focused on the torso as "mundane" healing instruments, discarded into middens after they were used to affect bodies in a healing process (Meskell et al. 2008: 146). Stabbed quadruped figurines also found in middens would seem to suggest a similar act of wish fulfillment, but in those cases as accompaniments of a successful hunt (see Hodder 2006: 194), although recent analyses raise doubts about the figurines' connection to hunting (Meskell et al. 2008: 157). These "throwaways" may manifest a mundane type of magic, an articulation of sacrality close to modern "commodity fetishism" and not necessarily connected in any systematic fashion with larger cosmological schemes or semiotic ideologies – an interpretation supported by recent critiques of the association of figurines with fertility rituals (Meskell et al. 2008). Their articulation, however, is also determined by the context in which they are found: if middens are also full of human coprolites, then that suggests strongly that the figurines themselves were, indeed, waste – material that was valuable only during the process of its use and became valueless after it fulfilled its purposes (Meskell et al. 2008: 150).

San, on whom Lewis-Williams seems to base his interpretation, has been the subject of much controversy ("the Kalahari debate").

Conclusion

I hope to have shown that, in analytically distinguishing the temporalities that an analysis of the Çatalhöyük material has to reckon with, one gains a number of insights into the work of interpretation that might be useful in further research at the site. In retrospect, I am particularly struck by the fact that, in the Catalhöyük material studied in this essay, it is usually the *overlap* between temporal scales that gives the most interesting clues by which to abduct sacralized activities from material traces. Leaving aside, for the moment, the narratives of the grand scale of human evolution that are the sine qua non of archaeological interpretation (but I will get back to them), these overlaps show, to my mind, an empirical universal that we require as social scientists in order to make sense of any experience of the transcendental, however minute the timescale we target. At the most basic phenomenological level, "religion" implies perceptions of an order of existence that is not of the here and now (if we take the latter to be both profane and secular, both "ordinary" and "this-worldly"). This everyday phenomenology of "religion" remains to a large extent out of the grasp of prehistoric archaeology's knowledge production; in contrast, it is accessible to ethnographers because, once they encounter a puzzling act or artifact, they can ask people what they mean, want or desire by it. By this, I do not mean to propose an (exceedingly naïve) solution of the problem of interpretation in favor of ethnographers, but to bring out the obvious point that ethnographers can use interlocution to make people themselves relate their material environment to the immaterial and invisible orders of existence (which do not need to be supernatural; the past and the future have their transcendental side too), while prehistoric archaeologists have to reconstruct, if possible, such relationships. In the course of working on this essay, I have become more and more convinced that, in the study of religion, the systematic explication of temporalities and their overlap may substitute, at least to some extent, for the ethnographic possibility of asking people what a thing means, *because transcendence itself – literally – means that different timescales are being articulated on each other.*

This comes out most clearly in the case of the Çatalhöyük house, which figures as both the most complex social institution and the most material trace of its society. Where the house is articulated or marked as transcendent to become a "history house" (Hodder and Pels,

Chapter 7), we in fact see that a large part of the material evidence for this marks conjunctions of timescales: beginnings and endings such as foundations, births, erasures, purposeful demolition or burning, destruction of tools or pots, deaths and burials of animals and humans. Indeed, the attempt to reproduce a house that will outlive its inhabitants necessarily implies that the larger timescale of the house is articulated on the shorter timescale of the life cycle of the human being, to such an extent that the latter is incorporated into the former, and this is indeed what these markings of beginnings and endings seem to achieve. Likewise, one would expect that the daily round of activities is likewise "transcendentalized" by being articulated on the longer-term temporalities of house or building, and this is indeed what the differential use of the "clean" northern part and the "dirty" southern part of the house seems to suggest. In both cases, we see that the analysis of the overlap of temporal scales achieves the combination of observer and participant perspectives (or "etic" and "emic" views) that seems so "easily" accessible to the ethnographer. In both cases, too, it is reasonable to say that the overlap articulates transcendence. I have no doubt that more examples of such illuminating overlaps can be found, but this essay was meant to set out the possibilities of such an analytic, not to do a complete analysis.

Thus, we can add another observation to the answers I already gave to the question of how one can recognize traces of the "religious" in archaeological research. A first answer was that we should be wary of importing a distinction between the useful and the symbolic to situations in which this was not appropriate, because all material practice is inherently performative, and each thing is always its own sign or symbol, and that the marking of a thing also implies a minimal "fetishization" of its use. A second answer, following on this, was that it is possible to talk of different degrees of articulation, which include the contrast between a strong articulation and the presence or absence of articulations in everyday life (such as the leopard), the combination of articulations that gives them an aggregate degree of articulation and the articulation of things by means of their concealment and/or revelation. We can now add another mode of tracing the religious in dead matter: by attending to the temporalities that we can reasonably deduce from what we know about a specific society, as well as by looking for the places in the evidence where we can see that those temporalities overlap and where we might expect to find material traces of transcendence.

Finally, how does such an analytical approach relate to the narratives of the grand scale of human evolution that provide so much of archaeology's raison d'être? Bruce Trigger observes that, despite "major changes in interpretative fashion," many archaeological "classifications of artifacts" have endured (1989: 383), and something similar can be said for the narratives that these classifications have supported. Despite much outstanding critical work, the reputation of Çatalhöyük still rests on such classifications and narratives, especially so when we turn to the narrative of religion. The statement that such an evolutionary advance as sedentism was caused by religion still raises hackles, and during the preparation of this essay I found little support for my proposal to compare the house society of Çatalhöyük to our modern society. However, I do think that the evidence discussed here warrants the hypothesis that Çatalhöyük was not a particularly religious society – that in fact the life span of the settlement may indicate, in comparison with places like Göbekli Tepe and Aşıklı Höyük, a process of secularization in two phases: the first, where a "house society" emerged in which the articulation of forms of transcendence through the presence of wild animals and ancestors provided a fairly low key but still moderately public and collective practice, centered in the "history houses"; and the second, where the independence of households from public and collective action increased the individualization and privatization that are usually regarded as the key processes of secularization, to such an extent that the traces of public and collective transcendence in "history houses" become increasingly marginal and only individual "houses" marked by burial remain, until even they disperse off the mounds. It may, in fact, be appropriate to argue that Çatalhöyük displays a sequence in human history in which a massive increase in the human use of artifacts went together with a form of secularization, which is not unreasonable if we take account of the fact that people who manufacture things also perform (at least toward themselves) as creators, and therefore have less need of other forces creating the world for them. This does not, of course, mean that we can speak of this secularization process as a straightforward evolutionary advance; our knowledge of subsequent civilizing processes is sufficient to show the contrary. If processes of sedentism were alternated with processes of renewed nomadism in (pre)history (as Deleuze and Guattari argued some time ago; 1980: 434), we should be prepared to let the differential artifactual and animal, wild and domesticated materialities that the evidence confronts us with convince us of the possibility that our ancestors may have been less rather than more religious than "we" (whoever we are) have been, and interpret the residues of their activities accordingly. What this essay has shown is, I feel, that there are ways of dealing with the question of what is religious about Çatalhöyük without assuming its religious nature and turning it into a primitive mother goddess cult or an equally primeval shamanism. If that does not fit existing dominant narratives, it does at least fit an empirical attitude that treats Çatalhöyük as a material place *before* it is seen as a moment in the narrative space of evolution.

REFERENCES

Appadurai, A. ed. 1986. *The Social Life of Things: Commodities in Cultural Perspective*. Cambridge: Cambridge University Press.

Asad, T. 1993. *Genealogies of Religion*. Baltimore: Johns Hopkins University Press.

Baird, R. J. 1998. How religion became scientific. In *Religion in the Making: The Emergence of the Sciences of Religion*, eds. A. L. Molendijk and P. Pels. Leiden: Brill, 205–29.

Bourdieu, P. 1977. *Outline of a Theory of Practice*. Cambridge: Cambridge University Press.

Brain, J. L. 1973. Ancestors as elders in Africa: Further thoughts. *Africa*, 42, 122–33.

Braudel, F. 1972. *The Mediterranean and the Mediterranean World in the Age of Philip II*, vol. 1. New York: Harper & Row.

Braudel, F. 1973. *The Mediterranean and the Mediterranean World in the Age of Philip II*, vol. 2. New York: Harper & Row.

Cessford, C. 2005a. Absolute dating at Çatalhöyük. In *Changing Materialities at Çatalhöyük: Reports from the 1995–1999 Seasons*, ed. I. Hodder. Cambridge: McDonald Institute of Archaeological Research / British Institute of Archaeology at Ankara Monograph, 65–99.

Cessford, C. 2005b. Estimating the Neolithic population of Çatalhöyük. In *Inhabiting Çatalhöyük: Reports from the 1995–1999 Seasons*, ed. I. Hodder. Cambridge: McDonald Institute for Archaeological Research / British Institute for Archaeological Research/British Institute of Archaeology at Ankara Monograph, 325–28.

Cessford, C., and Near, J. 2005. Fire, burning and pyrotechnology at Çatalhöyük. In *Çatalhöyük Perspectives: Themes from the 1995–1999 Seasons*, ed. I. Hodder. Cambridge: McDonald Institute for Archaeological Research / British Institute for Archaeological Research/British Institute of Archaeology at Ankara Monograph, 171–82.

Comaroff, J. 1985. *Body of Power, Spirit of Resistance: The Culture and History of a South African People.* Chicago: Chicago University Press.

Conolly, J. 1999. Technical strategies and technical change at Neolithic Çatalhöyük, Turkey. *Antiquity*, 73, 791–800.

De Boeck, F. 1995. Bodies of remembrance: Knowledge, experience and the growing of memory in Luunda ritual performance. In *Rites et ritualisation*, eds. G. Thinès and L. de Heusch. Paris: Librairie Philosophique J. Vrin, 114–38.

Deleuze, G., and Guattari, F. 1980. *Mille plateaux: Capitalisme et schizophrénie.* Paris: Éditions de Minuit.

Düring, B. S. 2001a. Social dimensions in the architecture of Neolithic Çatalhöyük. *Anatolian Studies*, 51, 1–18.

Düring, B. S. 2001b. Cultural dynamics of the Central Anatolian Neolithic: The Early Ceramic Neolithic–Late Ceramic Neolithic transition. In *The Neolithic of Central Anatolia: Internal Developments and External Relations during the 9th–6th Millennia cal BC*, eds. F. Gérard and L. Thissen. Istanbul: International CANeW Table Ronde, 219–36.

Düring, B. S. 2006. *Constructing Communities: Clustered Neighbourhood Settlements of the Central Anatolian Neolithic, ca. 8500–5500 cal BC.* Ph.D. dissertation. Leiden: Nederlands Instituut voor het Nabije Oosten.

Fairbairn, A., Asouti, E., Russell, N., and Swogger, J. G. 2005. Seasonality. In *Çatalhöyük Perspectives: Themes from the 1995–1999 Seasons*, ed. I. Hodder. Cambridge: McDonald Institute for Archaeological Research / British Institute for Archaeological Research/British Institute of Archaeology at Ankara Monograph, 93–108.

Foxhall, L. 2000. The running sands of time: Archaeology and the short-term. *World Archaeology*, 31(3), 484–98.

Gamble, C. 2004. Materiality and symbolic force: A Palaeolithic view of sedentism. In *Rethinking Materiality: The Engagement of Mind with the Material World*, eds. E. DeMarrais, C. Gosden and C. Renfrew. Cambridge: McDonald Institute for Archaeological Research, 85–95.

Gell, A. 1992. The technology of enchantment and the enchantment of technology. In *Anthropology, Art and Aesthetics*, eds. J. Coote and A. Shelton. Oxford: Clarendon Press, 40–67.

Gell, A. 1998. *Art and Agency.* Oxford: Clarendon Press.

Giddens, A. 1979. *Central Problems in Social Theory: Action, Structure and Contradiction in Social Analysis.* Berkeley: University of California Press.

Ginzburg, C. 1983. Morelli, Freud and Sherlock Holmes: Clues and scientific method. In *The Sign of Three: Dupin, Holmes, Peirce*, eds. U. Eco and T. A. Sebeok. Bloomington: Indiana University Press, 81–118.

Harrison, S. 2004. Forgetful and memorious landscapes. *Social Anthropology / Anthropologie sociale*, 122, 135–51.

Hodder, I. 1999. Symbolism at Çatalhöyük. *Proceedings of the British Academy*, 99, 177–91.

Hodder, I. 2005a. Changing entanglements and temporalities. In *Changing Materialities at Çatalhöyük: Reports from the 1995–1999 Seasons*, ed. I. Hodder. Cambridge: McDonald Institute of Archaeological Research / British Institute of Archaeology at Ankara Monograph, 5–22.

Hodder, I. 2005b. Memory. In *Çatalhöyük Perspectives: Themes from the 1995–1999 Seasons*, ed. I. Hodder. Cambridge: McDonald Institute for Archaeological Research / British Institute of Archaeology at Ankara Monograph, 183–95.

Hodder, I. 2006. *The Leopard's Tale: Revealing the Mysteries of Çatalhöyük*. London: Thames and Hudson.

Hodder, I., and Cessford, C. 2004. Daily practice and social memory at Çatalhöyük. *American Antiquity*, 69(1), 17–40.

Jackson, M. 1983. Knowledge through the body. *Man*, 18, 327–45.

Joyce, R., and Gillespie, S. D., eds. 2000. *Beyond Kinship: Social and Material Reproduction in House Societies*. Philadelphia: University of Pennsylvania Press.

Keane, W. 2003. Semiotics and the social analysis of material things. *Language and Communication*, 232, 409–25.

Kopytoff, I. 1971. Ancestors as elders in Africa. *Africa*, 41, 129–42.

Malinowski, B. 1954 [1925]. *Magic, Science and Religion and Other Essays*. New York: Doubleday.

Mauss, M. 1972. *A General Theory of Magic*. London: Routledge and Kegan Paul.

Matthews, W. 2005a. Micromorphological and microstratigraphic traces of uses and concepts of space. In *Inhabiting Çatalhöyük: Reports from the 1995–1999 Seasons*, ed. I. Hodder. Cambridge: McDonald Institute for Archaeological Research / British Institute of Archaeology at Ankara Monograph, 355–98, 553–72.

Matthews, W. 2005b. Life-cycle and life-course of buildings. In *Çatalhöyük Perspectives: Themes from the 1995–1999 Seasons*, ed. I. Hodder. Cambridge: McDonald Institute for Archaeological Research / British Institute of Archaeology at Ankara Monograph, 125–49.

Mellaart, J. 1967. *Çatal Hüyük: A Neolithic Town in Anatolia*. London: Thames & Hudson.

Meskell, L. 2004. Divine things. In *Rethinking Materiality: The Eengagement of Mind with the Material World*, eds. E. DeMarrais, C. Gosden and C. Renfrew. Cambridge: McDonald Institute for Archaeological Research, 249–59.

Meskell, L., Nakamura, C., King, R., and Farid, S. 2008. Figured lifeworlds and depositional practices at Çatalhöyük. *Cambridge Archaeological Journal*, 182, 139–61.

Miller, D. 1987. *Material Culture and Mass Consumption*. Oxford: Blackwell.

Pels, P. 1999. *A Politics of Presence: Contacts between Missionaries and Waluguru in Late Colonial Tanganyika*. Reading: Harwood Academic Publishers.

Pels, P. 2003. Introduction: Magic and modernity. In *Magic and Modernity: Interfaces of Revelation and Concealment*, eds. B. Meyer and P. Pels. Stanford, Calif.: Stanford University Press, 1–38.

Pels, P. 2008. The modern fear of matter: Reflections on the Protestantism of Victorian science. *Material Religion*, 4(3), 264–83.

Pietz, W. 1985. The problem of the fetish, I. *Res*, 9, 5–17.

Pietz, W. 1987. The problem of the fetish, II: The Origin of the Fetish. *Res*, 13, 23–45.

Pietz, W. 1988. The problem of the fetish, IIIa: Bosman's Guinea and the Enlightenment theory of fetishism. *Res*, 16, 105–23.

Poovey, M. 1998. *A History of the Modern Fact: Problems of Knowledge in the Sciences of Wealth and Society.* Chicago: Chicago University Press.

Renfrew, C. 2001. Symbol before concept: Material engagement and the early development of society. In *Archaeological Theory Today*, ed. I. Hodder. Cambridge: Polity Press, 122–40.

Rowlands, M. 2004. The materiality of sacred power. In *Rethinking Materiality: The Engagement of Mind with the Material World*, eds. E. DeMarrais, C. Gosden and C. Renfrew. Cambridge: McDonald Institute for Archaeological Research, 197–203.

Sanjek, R. 1996. Household. In *Encyclopedia of Social and Cultural Anthropology*, eds. A. Barnard and J. Spencer. London: Routledge, 185–288.

Taussig, M. 2003. Viscerality, faith and skepticism: Another theory of magic. In *Magic and Modernity: Interfaces of Revelation and Concealment*, eds. B. Meyer and P. Pels. Stanford, Calif.: Stanford University Press, 272–306.

Trigger, B. 1989. *A History of Archaeological Thought.* Cambridge: Cambridge University Press.

10

The Neolithic cosmos of Çatalhöyük

Paul K. Wason

Ideas about the basic nature of the universe are often implicit in our thinking and thus, in the manner of water to a fish, hard to appreciate. But what we think about the size and shape of the cosmos and about the nature of causation in the world around us – what there is, who is there and how it 'works' – permeates whatever we may come to think about anything else. Our cosmology will affect how we live in the world in deep and varied ways.

By "cosmos" I mean the nature of reality in its full extent and depth. A people's understanding of the cosmos, their cosmology, is their basic picture of the world, their most general or fundamental understanding of the overall structure of the universe (Smith 1995).[1] This is very similar to what others have called "worldview."[2] Many of us view cosmology as a scientific matter. It is thanks to scientific research that the universe

[1] Hetherington defines cosmology as 'our understanding of the organization and evolution of the universe' (1993: 4), while Rappaport prefers to speak of 'cosmological axioms', which he defines as 'assumptions concerning the fundamental structure of the universe or, to put it differently . . . the paradigmatic relationships in accordance with which the cosmos is constructed' (1999: 264). These, he goes on to point out, are not the same as values, though axioms concerning fundamental reality will almost inevitably entail values.

[2] For example, in his classic monograph on the Crow, Robert Lowie begins the final chapter, titled 'World-View', 'The Crow universe was narrowly bounded' and goes on to describe how they orient themselves spatially (1935: 327). Robert Redfield defines worldview in this way: 'That outlook upon the universe that is characteristic of a people . . . a worldview differs from culture, ethos, mode of thought, and national character. It is the picture the members of a society have of the properties and characters upon their stage of action. Worldview attends especially to the way a man in a particular society sees himself in relation to all else. It is the properties of existence as distinguished from and related to the self. It is in short, a man's idea of the universe' (1952, quoted in Gill 2002: 15).

our minds now inhabit is profoundly different from that of any human even a century ago. It was only in the 20th century, to take just a few of the more transformative examples, that galaxies were discovered, that we realized the universe is more than a few million years old and expanding, that DNA is a key to inheritance and that there are inevitable – not just technical – limits to what it is possible to know. The 1856 discovery of a skull in Germany's Neander Valley, along with the work of people like Lyell and Darwin needed to appreciate it, set in motion an equally dramatic revision of how we understand our own coming into being.

All of this has transformed our cosmos. Where we came from does not fully determine what we are, of course, but where we *believe* we came from affects how we understand our capacities and so what we will try. Our own understanding of what the cosmos is and how it works is still adjusting to this dizzying array of discoveries, and very likely it influences what we imagine our ancestors thought about the nature of things as well.

But throughout history, ideas about what and who is out there, about agency and causation – why things happen – have more often been religious and philosophical ideas. They still are to a far greater degree than we sometimes appreciate. Consider the matter of how things work. Do we understand the universe to be a predetermined affair as in the widespread concept of *karma* or as in 18th-century deism and the closely related mechanistic science of the time? If we did really think this way, how would it affect what we do? We have all heard stories of people who refuse to wear seat belts, saying that if their time has come, it couldn't help, and if it has not come, it is not needed.

Or, to continue this thought, do we instead understand our world to be largely capricious and random, perhaps at the whim of some member of the Greek pantheon? The debate between Stephen Jay Gould and Simon Conway Morris over the Burgess Shale fossils is instructive concerning how our basic cosmological assumptions influence how we look at things. Do these materials demonstrate a radical contingency to history (Gould 1990), or is the history of life more structured, perhaps to the extent that the emergence of intelligence is closer to inevitable than accidental (Conway Morris 1998, 2003)? This is not an arcane squabble about what happened a half-billion years ago, but touches on (while, importantly, also growing out of) our deepest understandings of what kind of world this is, our cosmology.

Whether we believe we are in the hands of a benevolent deity or surrounded by petty ancestors vying for our attention and sacrifices will affect society in more ways than just seat belts. And Neolithic life would have been equally influenced by what people then considered the effective causes and agencies of the cosmos. Not that it is all simple and straightforward. First, people do not always live consistently with their beliefs. In addition, inferring a belief system, even at a general, broad-brush level, from configurations of material remains presents issues that, although familiar enough to archaeologists, are nevertheless difficult to break through.

For the moment I wish only to emphasize the 'fundamental' nature of the beliefs about reality that make up a people's cosmology. It seems inevitable that what we think about such matters really does influence how we approach everything from the minutia of our daily lives to grand, society-wide decisions. Yet many archaeologists, myself included, have tended to think otherwise, that 'causation' in human affairs goes one way, from the physical need to get food, for example, to after-the-fact 'ideological' justifications of how we got the food. Or perhaps (myself again included) we have been skeptical about getting anywhere with uncovering ancient thought and have ignored what we cannot discover. This is fair enough as far as it goes. We can learn more about a people's food-ways than about their cosmology, and thus the former figures more largely in our understanding of the past. But if we were to acknowledge that what people believe about the cosmos influences their actions, such as why they chose to locate their settlement in a given spot, yet turned around and tried to explain the settlement's location simply in terms of resource availability, we would be missing something. It is not that subsistence issues are unimportant, but rather that they cannot fully explain what people do. And it may be that fundamental cosmological perspectives affect subsistence activities as much as vice versa.

In the following sections, I explore what we can learn about the cosmos inhabited by the Neolithic people of Çatalhöyük. What can we infer about how they understood time, place and causation in the world? This is meant as a way of getting at some of the four core questions of this project while sidestepping, for the moment, issues concerning what religion is.

I believe it is fair to begin the conversation with a few points that are very common, cross-culturally, even if not independently demonstrated for cosmological perspectives at Çatalhöyük, such as that the inhabitants believed in spirit beings and held to a three-tiered cosmology at least at the core (Lewis-Williams and Pearce 2005). This, of course, is just a starting point. We have a tendency to think that religion and conceptions of cosmology can take any possible form, perhaps because they are all so irrational anyway. But while prescientific cosmologies are, in important ways, either wrong or incomplete (as our own cosmology probably is as well) this is not the same as irrational. Elements in a cosmology are likely to fit together nicely, and if they seem disjointed or contradictory, it is much more likely that we simply do not understand the underlying premises. Also, they will most likely have some grounding in empirically observed 'reality' (such as the sun moving across the sky) and in consistent patterns of how things appear to work (the prominence of a regular round of seasons could be seen as warrant for a cyclical view of time/history generally). Similarly, whatever our own, more specific questions might be, cosmologies the world around can well be expected to cover some of the same ground: helping to understand where the physical boundaries are, where humans fit in, how long things have been around, whether they are likely to change, what other kind of beings there might be and how things work.

If cosmologies are in part empirically grounded and systematic – however misleading even these rational tools can be – we can assume they can take only certain forms. However varied cosmologies seem to be on the surface, the possibility space is limited, as with culture generally (Cronk 1999), and it is likely that we will be able to discern some of the outlines of even ancient and otherwise distant ways of understanding the world. There will always be strong elements of local knowledge, and there is no denying that these unique ideas may constitute some of the most interesting and determinative elements of a cosmology. Yet I argue, along with other cognitive archaeologists (Mithen 1996; Donald 2005), that not everything will be unique and obscure.

For example, if a people believe in many deities or spirit beings (vs. one or none), what might we see? Perhaps a greater variety among images of beings in formal, ritual areas or a greater variety in forms of ritual worship. From materials like those available at a prehistoric site, would we be able to tell that Christianity is monotheistic, as its adherents have always said? Representations of a single divinity in three aspects could easily be seen as three distinct divinities. Would we be able to tell that those traditions in which many saints figure prominently represent the same religion as that represented by the more austere art and architecture of the Reformation? Very possibly not.

But from the point of view of exploring elements of ancient cosmology, this may not be the problem it seems. Variations of Christianity have been connected with widely differing cosmologies over its long history and vast geographical spread. It may well be that if we confuse some threads of similarity, we can at the same time discern some of the deeper variation among these cosmologies. So it may be that careful analysis will help us distinguish polytheistic, monotheistic and various other systems.

At Çatalhöyük there is much evidence to help us discern elements of cosmology that were present, and I have done no more than scratch the surface in this brief effort. It has long been argued that the wall paintings and installations can be interpreted in terms of cosmology (Mellaart 1967; Lewis-Williams and Pearce 2005), and the figurines have attracted widespread discussion from many angles (Gimbutas 1991; Cauvin 2000; Meskell 2008; Meskell et al. 2008; Nakamura and Meskell 2009). But we will see that the organization of mundane life, as in the orientation of houses, also gives an insight into cosmological perspective.

Time

Both our experience and our conception of time are of central importance to how we understand and live in the world. This is probably as true of most traditional cosmologies as it is in contemporary scientific cosmologies where time is part of the framework of the universe itself. Of the many possible 'dimensions' of time that we could explore, I will begin with aspects of change and endurance, conceptions of the past and perspectives on the future.

TIME, CHANGE AND ENDURANCE IN GENERAL

Archaeologists have increasingly come to tackle questions surrounding the understanding and perception of time (Lucas 2005). From studies of the anthropology and history of time (e.g., Le Goff 1982; Gosden 1994), it is clear that many different conceptions of time can exist and, importantly, coexist and have their different social roles.[3] Changing mechanisms for the measurement of time have affected how we understand and perceive time and the social process, and it is widely recognized that psychological perceptions of time, sacred time and mundane or physical time can constitute very different ways of looking at the world. Changes in how we perceive time have affected changes in how we understand our place. Indeed, it has been argued that the greatest change in how people of the West understand the cosmos has come not through evolution (appreciation for transience and change generally), relativity (which hasn't much affected everyday life yet) or appreciation for the size of the universe, but through the realization of its age, which situated humans in a very different context (not to mention making possible one of the greatest developments in world culture, the field of archaeology).

The personal experience of time is important for understanding how cosmology engages with religion. Some religious kinds of experience include transcendence, which may mean something beyond ordinary experience without necessarily implying a transcendent being. The experience of timelessness is one example. In altered states of consciousness, time and space and the categories of human and animal may break down and change. Lewis-Williams and Pearce (2005) have argued for altered states of consciousness at Çatalhöyük.

THE PAST

The material context of daily life at Çatalhöyük would have involved people in a strong notion of time passing, of duration and of the past. Living on a mound that grew higher with every generation would have led to some sense of the *longue durée*. Every time a new house was built or a refuse pit dug, the walls of earlier buildings would have been

---

[3] Gallois reminds us that 'each of our lives consists of the mediation and the running together of a series of different forms of time – the present, memories, hopes, our knowledge of death, our guesses as to what happens after death, our picture of nature, sleep and our view of time in others' lives, among others – and their resolution into a more manageable general conception of time, which we tend not to think of too much' (2007: 13). While the passage of physical time – for preindustrial peoples perhaps more universally marked by day and night and the lunar and annual cycles than by any briefer segmentations – is basic and common to all humans, these other senses of time are likely to be as much affected by other elements of cosmology as by the bedrock of physical time.

encountered, as well as the bodies and artifacts of earlier inhabitants. The bricks and mortar and the plasters for the walls were often made from earlier materials, so that small pieces of pottery and painted plaster from earlier times can be seen in the plasters, bricks and mortars of today. The flat landscape contrasted with the human-made mounds, the products of living in the same place over time.

Of course, this notion of time passing may not have been very deep, and it may not have been very specific. In hunter-gatherer societies, there is often little conception of time beyond a few generations (Woodburn 1980). But among complex hunter-gatherers and farmers, there is a delayed return for the input of labor, and as a result longer and more specific histories may be built. Throughout the Neolithic of the Middle East there seems to be a concern with ancestors in general (Goring-Morris 2000; Kuijt 2008).

One of the most striking of the findings from Mellaart's excavations was the prominence of burial beneath house floors, a pattern that is also common among houses excavated under the current project.[4] Many of these are primary burials (Andrews, Molleson and Boz 2005) in that they remain fully articulated and undisturbed. But secondary inhumations and variously disturbed burials are also found, as are separated skulls, which are sometimes found in houses inhabited much later than the burial from which the skull came.

Postburial treatment of human remains is quite common at Neolithic sites in the Middle East. For example, groups of skulls are also found beneath floors or, as at Çayönü, in a special building (Özdoğan and Özdoğan 1990). But at Çatalhöyük it is possible to argue that specific links were made to individual buried ancestors, since individual skulls are found, in one case plastered and in another person's burial, held by a woman (Hodder 2006). Very few people had their heads removed after death at Çatalhöyük (in contrast with other sites in the Pre-Pottery Neolithic in the Levant, where it appears to have been a more common practice), and there is evidence (from their layout, associated artifacts in graves and isotope studies) that they were specially treated individuals before the head was removed.

---

[4] Speaking as one who has tried working with the published records of the burials uncovered in the 1960s, it is impossible to overestimate what the careful excavation and analysis of the current project will contribute to our ability to study the Neolithic understanding of reality.

There is no evidence that people at Çatalhöyük envisioned eras or stages, what the world was like before the vulture made our ancestor or the leopard made the village, a golden age from which we have advanced or degenerated. But evidence from Göbekli in southeastern Anatolia, suggests large, dominant human males that give life to the natural world (Schmidt 2000), perhaps through their sexuality (Hodder and Meskell, Chapter 2). Whether these massive humans shown in the pillars at Göbekli are ancestors is less clear. Hodder (2007a) has argued that the location of houses on earlier burials is found very early in the development of settled life in the Middle East (see also Goring-Morris 2000; Kuijt 2008). It is tempting to read this evidence, burial below floors at Çatalhöyük and the pillars at Göbekli as indicating revered ancestors. This view is reinforced by certain specific finds. For example, at Çatalhöyük a skull has been found placed at the base of a post holding up a house. This certainly suggests ancestors as the base of the house.

But are these really ancestors, and if so, what do they mean for the people living among them? Testart (2008) has argued that severed skulls could be those of enemies taken in warring between groups. In this case the power derived from the skulls tells less of ancestors than of success in warring and warrior prowess. However, given that there is little evidence of wounds and fighting on the human remains at Çatalhöyük, and given that there is no evidence of a close packing of settlements competing for resources on the Çarşamba Fan on the Konya Plain, it seems most likely that ancestors were an important part of the Çatalhöyük conception of time, and it also seems most likely that, at Çatalhöyük at least, these were specific historical ancestors.

Hodder has pointed out that we still need an integrated program of dating for the skulls and headless skeletons at Çatalhöyük in order to see whether distant ancestors, or only the recent dead, were kept and passed down. But there is much to suggest that being close to the dead was of central importance at Çatalhöyük.

Kuijt wisely observes that memory and forgetting come together in complicated ways and also change over time. Concerning the dead, initially "memory and commemoration are experiential – personal and direct. As more time passes, however, memory is based on reference to the deceased and being deceased is characterized as being remote and anonymous" (2008: 174–5). This seems perfectly reasonable in general, and perhaps one major step in this process can be identified as a further generalization, what happens when there is no longer anyone among the living who knew the dead personally.

This much seems a good generalization based on how personal memory works and how social memory, being in a sense an abstraction beyond the personal, produces an additional tendency toward anonymity quite apart from the passing of time. But it does depend on, and not just influences, a people's cosmology. It could be that these practices at Çatalhöyük and other sites described by Kuijt are in part an attempt to slow or bypass this 'anonymizing' process, an attempt to retain the memory not just of ancestors, but of this specific ancestor.[5]

In any case, the finds at Çatalhöyük suggest that these Neolithic people held a view of reality in which the individual is of some importance in the universe. But the kind of commemoration we see does not necessarily imply ancestor worship in the sense of rites meant to connect with the spirits of people of the past; they could, in ritual, instead represent the 'spirit' of the present (if I might be excused for indulging the common practice of using the word 'spirit' in totally different ways in the same sentence).

This in turn suggests at least two things about the overarching view of the world that might have been held by the inhabitants of Çatalhöyük: first, that there was a sense of the personal and individual as something important and as something that persists well beyond the loss of the fleshy body among us (though connected to it via skeletal material) and, second, that their conception of the past itself is in part personal in that it is anchored by memories of specific individuals, albeit probably semi-anonymous 'social' individuals. There is a part of me that wants to say that this is trivially self-evident, for surely it is characteristic of all humans. But there is more to it than this. Yes, all humans can be expected

---

[5] On analogy with our own social memories focusing on specific people, these would not necessarily be individuals in exactly the same way living people are individuals. I write this in the month of Abraham Lincoln's 200th birthday, which is being celebrated with a variety of articles showing how at some level we re-create this thing called 'Lincoln' for our own use in each generation. He is a specific person about whom we know many things – the average American has access to far more information about him than did the average American when he was alive – but he is no longer the same. Through the process Kuijt describes, Lincoln has become in part an object on which people of each era project the 'personality' of their times. This is true despite the fact that some of our narratives about such people qualify as history in the most rigorous sense. It is likely enough that narratives of some sort accompanied each burial, perhaps themselves changing via the process Kuijt has described.

to recognize individuality, as do many other mammals and birds (some of whom mate for life), but as a feature of one's cosmology, there may be room for great differences in what an individual 'means' in the world and for society. And the tendency for humans to be represented differently in the symbolism of the Palaeolithic (something akin to the human form is found among figurines, many symbolic figures are thought to represent 'vulvas', etc.) than in the Neolithic (where we find more active human figures represented) might suggest there really was some change in the Neolithic.

But of course we *could* be seeing the worship of, or at least efforts to retain the proximity and goodwill of, active spirit agents of deceased ancestors. Can we say whether the cosmology of the inhabitants of Çatalhöyük included active personal ancestral spirits living among them? This seems to me much less clear. Burial under the floor would suggest an effort to maintain a physical proximity for some less physical or more mystical purpose. And as already noted, I consider it a plausible starting point to assume their cosmology included active spirit agents unless shown otherwise.

But when we look at what has actually been found during excavation, there seems to be a major social dimension to it, particularly concerning who is buried in which building and who is chosen for such special treatment as recovery of skulls. Based on information I could glean on burials from the Mellaart excavations, I earlier concluded that only a small portion of the people who lived at the site were actually buried beneath house floors (Wason 1994: 159–60). And from this I concluded that the practice has less to do with ideas on how the dead were to be treated in general than with something the still-living people needed or wanted from certain specific deceased individuals. It also appeared to be evidence of status distinctions.

Recent work, however, suggests that a much greater proportion of the total population was in fact buried under the floors of houses. Analysis of these finds is not yet complete, but it is currently estimated that the skeletal materials excavated in the current project total about 400 individuals. There are some uncertainties – concerning how much of the site has actually been excavated, as well as the widely varying estimates of the number of people inhabiting Çatalhöyük at any one time. But while some limited form of my earlier conclusion remains possible, it now seems that the number of burials being found is large enough to suggest we may be seeing a large portion of the site's total. Lori Hager and Başak Boz, who have excavated a large number of the burials and who have undertaken considerable human remains analysis, believe that when all the tallying is done we will find that most people who lived there were in fact buried beneath the floors (Hager and Boz, pers. comm.). It is possible that young men are underrepresented, but this is much more likely due to their having died away from the settlement than from a choice to bury them in a different way. The social dimension suggested earlier concerns the possibility that not all individuals were likely to have been buried in the same buildings in which they lived (the number of burials per house varying, in some cases, dramatically) and the unusual finds that likely carried extra symbolic meanings, such as foundation burials, and the intriguing tendency for child burials to include more associated artifacts than adult burials, which often included nothing by way of grave goods.

In any case, the Neolithic view of reality does appear to include ancestors as an important factor, and perhaps all individuals were important. But in addition, people seemed to take a special interest in specific individuals for specific purposes. Does this suggest a view of the 'afterlife' that involves a kind of differentiation, even hierarchy, that is not paralleled, or only modestly so, in social relations among the living?

If we cannot be so certain about there being an ancestor cult at Çatalhöyük, there are other implications of their burial practices that we can consider. One explanation for the close packing of houses at the site is that people wanted to live as close as possible to the dead. Some houses contain more burials than others (up to 62 beneath the floor of Building 1), and it is possible that later houses crowded around these ancestral houses. Within the houses it seems most likely that people slept on the whiter floors and platforms beneath which humans were buried. Sleeping only a few centimeters from corpses must have brought people very close to the dead, especially since it seems likely that some seepage of bodily fluids and odors may have been experienced.

There is much evidence that people understood the bodily anatomy of the dead extremely well, as the way in which body parts (mainly heads but also limbs and other body parts) have been removed indicates great care and precise anatomical knowledge, as well as a good memory of specifically where they had been buried. As new bodies were added to graves below platforms, earlier bodies would have been encountered and were often rearranged and resorted. Kuijt describes the implications of secondary burial as follows: 'Secondary mortuary practices facilitate a kind of perpetual rebirth and highlight that life is intergenerational and links past, present and future. Although the dead are no longer present, they do not belong to the past: rather they reside among the living in another place' (2008: 176). Or, possibly, the 'past' is not the same as what we think of it. Perhaps the past is more a part of the people at Çatalhöyük, or they see themselves as more a part of it than our own cosmology allows for us. They may think of the living as a possibly transient element and the past as more solid and stable, like the great mound they lived on.

In any case, people lived very close to the dead. They also lived in houses that repeated earlier layouts and earlier activity patterns. This repetition of the everyday over years, centuries and even millennia suggests a strong sense of living within tradition. And yet the specific digging down to obtain human body parts suggests more a concern with history than an unconscious repetition (Connerton 1989). It seems also that parts of animal bodies, especially horns, skulls, teeth, tusks and claws, were passed down from house to house, creating specific conscious histories – thus forming 'history houses' (see Chapter 7). A cattle skull and horn cores that were deposited at the same time as the lentils in a bin in Building 1 had a good chance of being older than they were by up to 80–150 years (Hodder 2007c). In Building 52 excavators found 11 wild cattle horns stacked above a cattle skull placed in a wall. It seems likely that such a quantity of horns was amassed over some period of time.

It is possible that over the period in which Çatalhöyük was occupied, the cumulative affect of their burial practices, the history houses and the weighty reality of the growing mound itself would have helped shape a sense of historical depth to life along with a connection with a 'place' that is semipersonal in the sense that it is in part a connection with *our* past, *our* ancestors, not just some abstract passage. It would have lent a tangibility to the continuity of life there, perhaps contributing to social inertia in a range of ways. This admittedly draws in another complex discussion, but it is my own sense that while Çatalhöyük may have begun in a bright flash of creativity, the 1,400 years of its habitation seem more like a quiet, steady glow of continuity.

THE FUTURE

And what of their ideas about the future? Is there any evidence of planning ahead, or do we have reason to believe that, as in the popular imagination, people in the deep past, unlike the modern scholars who write about them with creativity and intention, merely reacted to circumstances?

In fact, at Çatalhöyük there is much evidence of future thinking. The materiality of daily life would have involved people in an awareness of future events and consequences. In particular, there grew to be a clear understanding that the construction of mud-brick houses without stone foundations had its limitations. House walls were usually constructed on the stubs of previous walls, carefully following their alignments. Where walls were built over fill or midden, they slumped and leaned dramatically. There are many examples of slumping walls being strengthened, shored up, reinforced. So in the building of new houses over wall stubs, people realized they had a firmer foundation for the future, a means of guarding against future wall collapse.

There is much other evidence that the initial construction of houses was carefully planned, but also ritually sanctioned. For example, in the pre-floor packing for Building 1 in the North Area, the overall layout of platforms in the building was already being prepared; the whole layout was conceived very early on. The construction was also embedded in ritual. For example, there were three infant interments at the threshold into the main room, placed there in the construction phase of Building 1. There was another neonate in the construction deposits of Building 1, as well as some adults. The burial of four neonates during the construction of Building 1 is of particular interest, as no neonates were buried during its occupation (Hodder 2007c). The clearest example of a foundation burial is in Building 42 in the South Area. Cut through the foundation deposits of a platform, but sealed by the first floor plasters, was the grave of a woman holding the plastered skull of a man. Also in the grave was the very rare find of a leopard claw (Hodder 2006). This was a highly significant burial, found beneath a building that was partly built over rubble and refuse. It was a new foundation, and the inclusion of this very special foundation burial suggests an intentional break with past uses of this part of the site and engagement with a future of greater change. In other cases (e.g., Space 105, Level VII), there are probable feasting deposits of animal bones beneath walls, as if protecting the walls for the future life of the space and suggesting that community-oriented ritual activity was involved.

One enduring tradition at the site was to perform a series of procedures, possibly ritual in nature (as suggested by their relative uniformity and likely importance) upon the abandonment of a building. These concern change of use, starting and ending, for while the old dwelling was properly closed off and filled in, eventually something new would be built on top of it, perhaps to the same plan. That is, at Çatalhöyük the closing of a building was also the start of a new building as the upper walls of a building were dismantled, the interior fittings and furnishings removed, the house filled in and the new building constructed. In a number of cases in the current excavations (e.g., Building 2, but also in buildings in the 4040 Area, such as Building 49), the dismantling of plaster features inside a building is associated with feasting remains. There are concentrations of the meat-bearing parts of large animals, especially wild bulls, at a first stage in the dismantling and infilling process. This suggests that the abandonment was often seen as a social and symbolic event, as well as having practical components. In a sense, of course, this referred to the past in that most likely buildings were closed off carefully because of their previous importance as dwellings and resting places for ancestors, but it is also a looking to the future, for the same activities prepared the base for new construction.

Perhaps the clearest example of future thinking at Çatalhöyük is the deposition of obsidian and other artifacts (e.g., white pebbles) in small pits or caches below floors. A wide range of foods was stored in bins in the houses, for later consumption in the annual cycle. But the obsidian and other caches suggest longer-term considerations. In many houses there is at least one shallow scoop, somewhere near the oven/hearth and ladder entry. In these scoops are found up to 77 pieces of obsidian. These obsidian pieces are blanks or pre-forms for making a variety of tools. Associated with these caches is evidence of in situ obsidian working, and in one case at least, the flakes can be refitted onto a pre-form that is like those found in the caches. Some scoops are empty or contain only a few pieces. It seems clear that obsidian came as pre-forms from sources in Cappadocia (170 km, or 100 miles, away) and was taken into the house, where it was buried. People then dug down and excavated pieces when they needed them and worked them nearby, inside the house. Since the houses were inhabited for 70–100 years, and since there are very few obsidian caches in the houses, it seems likely that these obsidian stores were created to cater to long-term future use.

Nakamura (Chapter 11) discusses 'magic' caches of objects. It is likely that at least some of these were forward looking, to protect or harm people or houses in the future. A number of obsidian mirrors have been found on the site, especially in burials. While it is possible that these were used to apply facial coloring and jewelry, it is just as likely that they were involved in some way in relationships with the spirit world, including divining the future.

Obsidian caching occurs only in the lower levels on the site. Indeed, it seems that the overall focus on past and future at Çatalhöyük changes through the sequence and seems to decrease in the uppermost levels. Obsidian caches do not occur in the upper levels, but also the continuity of houses decreases (Düring 2006). By the time of the TP Area (see Team Poznan in Figure 1.6) on the East Mound, and by the time of the Chalcolithic occupation on the West Mound at Çatalhöyük, burial becomes rare in houses and may disappear entirely. Excavation in the TP Area has revealed considerable information about occupation at the end of the use of the Neolithic East Mound, and by this time the tradition of carefully filling in earlier houses and building new ones on top has largely disappeared. Instead walls are placed alongside earlier walls in a complex and collapsed stratigraphy. The house society in the earlier levels Çatalhöyük is associated with the passing down of rights within houses. It is thus intimately connected with the *longue durée*. As this system changes in the upper levels of the site (see Chapter 9), focus on past and future, at least as evidenced in the context of building activity, decreases.

In addition to these hints at planning in the sense of looking some way ahead, there are of course many indications of a seasonal round of activities that naturally required planning in a more routine sense (Fairbairn et al. 2005). It is probably the case that most people, both at that time and today, lived mainly in a world of routine cycles of days, months, seasons and years. There is little evidence of large-scale projects or of planning for large collective activities. Even the storage of food, though careful and overall fairly complex, was not done on anything like a grand scale even on a per household basis. It is likely that most households did not store enough grain for the family for the entire year, though this is not a failure to plan ahead so much as an indication that they continued to rely substantially on a diversity of foods, including wild foods (Atalay and Hastorf 2006: 301). But the elements reviewed here do suggest some areas in which longer than annual planning took place.

Space

SHAPE OF THE COSMOS AT LARGE

There is no information so far from Çatalhöyük that indicates how the inhabitants conceived the size and shape of the cosmos. There are no reliable clues as to how they understood the stars and their location in relation to their home, or whether they thought of the earth as endless or instead concretely bounded. I have not yet come across anything to indicate whether they saw the cosmos as growing, shrinking, static or some combination of these.

Suggestions have been made about the differing cosmological regions or divisions in the Çatalhöyük cosmos. As suggested earlier, it would seem reasonable to assume a three-tiered cosmos. Whether or not, as Lewis-Williams and Pearce (2005) argue,[6] this view is a product of our physical neural structure, it is a cross-culturally very common core understanding – sometimes elaborated,[7] sometimes, with effort, submerged, but a very

[6] Lewis-Williams and Pearce conclude their discussion of several chapters: 'In summary, we can say that both neuropsychology and world ethnography show that the near universality of belief in a tiered cosmos and in movement between the levels may be ascribed to the functioning of the human nervous system in a variety of altered states. The vortex leads through a tunnel or some such construal down to a nether level, while flight leads up to a realm in or above the sky. This conclusion does not mean that each and every member of a community experiences the full gamut of altered states.... Those who do not experience states at the full hallucinatory end of the consciousness spectrum manage to glimpse in their dreams [or other religious experiences] something of what the visionaries experience. That is their reassurance' (2005: 69).

This is a most interesting idea, and though traced through their work, it is not a very tight argument. It is based in part on their idea that religions at heart derive from the experience of altered states of consciousness and not, like so many other beliefs common among humans, from contact with some kind of reality outside of our heads. It also carries more weight for those who agree with Lewis-Williams here and in his other work (e.g., Clottes and Lewis-Williams 1998; Lewis-Williams 2002) that most if not all people of the Palaeolithic into the Neolithic had a religion somewhat like what we know ethnographically from around the world as shamanism. This has been heavily criticized, of course (e.g., Paul Bahn's reference to the spread of the idea as 'shamania'; see Wason 2007), but the idea that something known to be so common cross-culturally could have roots in our cognition is both plausible and potentially very important.

[7] And sometimes when a people's model of the cosmos seems to be elaborated, either it has a three-tiered cosmology at the core, or our understanding of the elaboration is wrong. For example, the ancient Mesoamericans are widely believed to have imagined a universe stacked in nine or more vertical layers, but Nielsen and Sellner Reunert have shown that this is due largely to the influence of post-Conquest European ideas (as in the Codex Vaticanus A). They conclude instead 'that a basic three-tiered model combined with a strong emphasis on the horizontal divisions of each layer is more likely to have been the dominant scheme before the Spanish invasion' (2009: 411).

reasonable starting place even before exploring concrete local evidence. And the special organization of the site consistently encourages this view. One can imagine the cosmos having been so ordered that people living on the surface went down (the ladder) into a lower world, with the dead residing further in that direction, beneath the floor. The notion that the dead, or at least the skulls of the dead, were taken upward into the sky by vultures or other birds is discussed by Hodder and Meskell in Chapter 2.

HOUSES, ENTRIES AND FLOOR PLANS

There is much evidence that at Çatalhöyük the lived world was ordered so as to have at least a general kind of astronomical significance. As a new house is dug at Çatalhöyük, the excavators almost always successfully predict roughly where everything will be. The hearth and oven are normally near the ladder entrance, and any obsidian caches are in the southern part of the house. This is where most domestic activities took place and most occupation residues are found. As one moves northward in a house, more and higher platforms are found. These are covered in a different kind of plaster (of a brighter white) than floor areas in the southern part and contain most of the burials. People of all ages are buried in the north, but only neonate and child burials occur in the southern part of the house. Most installations and paintings are found to the north. Large painted bulls normally occur on the northern wall of the main room. The rules that create these differences between the north and south parts of houses are not absolute – ovens can be moved to northern parts, and specific local contingencies can result in idiosyncratic arrangements – but the arrangement is consistent enough to justify the idea that they are rules. Importantly, this internal floor plan and design are also closely correlated with the cardinal directions (or with the movement of the sun) rather than with the plans of other buildings, suggesting that these rules relate to the people's understanding of wider cosmic order rather than being 'arbitrary' cultural convention.

Differences between west and east in the houses also occur, but here there is more leeway for variation. For example, in many houses there is a bench at the southern end of the central east platform. This bench is sometimes inset with bull horns. But in one case, Building 52 in the 4040 Area, the bench embedded with horns was set along the west wall of the main room. This building was unusual, as it had been made by knocking down a wall between two adjacent houses, and as a result an idiosyncratic arrangement might be expected. The splayed bear figure is often found on west walls in many main rooms, but not always. The central eastern platform is often the main burial platform, but in some houses, the main burial platform is that in the northwest. It seems that houses may either have a central east or a northwestern focus, with red painted walls and paintings on walls concentrated in one or other location (contrast Buildings 1 and 49 with Buildings 44, 56, 60 and 65). Large bucrania often occur on west walls of main rooms.

There is thus a strong north–south orientation of the houses at Çatalhöyük and a weaker east–west focus. But we can also consider movement around these spaces. How did the body move through the main room of the house (see Hodder 2007c), and how was the space experienced through the day?

As one enters the house, one moves down the ladder on the south wall. This is always orientated so that one enters the house moving eastward. At the bottom of the ladder, one often stands on a small platform in the southeast corner of the main room (Figure 10.1). It is difficult to move north from here, as there is often a bench, sometimes with cattle horns inset, barring movement northward. One is thus encouraged to move westward past the oven and into the south part of the main room. This area receives the most light (from the roof entry and from the oven and hearth) and is also where food is prepared as well as where neonates and children may be buried.

Sharon Moses (pers. comm.) argues that there may have been a conception that clockwise movement around the house mimicked the path of a person through life from birth to death. Thus, starting from the southeastern entry and from the southern area of production and birth, one could move past the bucrania (which may be associated with initiation and coming of age; see Chapter 2) on the west walls to the burial platforms on the north walls. Continuing in a clockwise manner, one ends up at the central east platform, unable to move farther south because of the bench separating the central east platform from the southeastern entry area. The central eastern platform in Building 1 has more adult burials than the northwestern platform in the same house. It often has important burials or is marked by red painting (e.g., Building 60).

It has often been assumed that there was little light in the Çatalhöyük houses, as there is no evidence of windows. All light would have thus come from the ladder entry hole in the roof, from which smoke from the fire also escaped. Construction of an experimental house on the site has shown that the small rectangle of sunlight that comes through the entry hole reflects off the white walls to create very good visibility in the main rooms of the houses. The reasoning behind this design with roof entry does remain somewhat enigmatic, at least for the many houses with outer walls facing open spaces; it is very unlikely to have been for any of the reasons typically suggested, such as defense. At the risk of using a stereotyped line of reasoning, I have myself found worthy of a joke or two – if we can't imagine what possible *real* good it could have done, it must be religious – it is nevertheless an interesting possibility that, just as the internal floor plan must have had deeper significance than merely strategic use of limited square footage, so descending into a house might well have represented a movement among important levels within the cosmos.

Recent work by visual artist Eva Bosch has revealed that during the day the rectangle of light from the entry hole moves across the southern part of the main room (Hodder 2007b). Certainly there is very important practical value in letting in as much light as possible, and it appears that the roof openings do provide more light, or more usable light, than would a floor-level doorway. But it might still have significance in inhabitants' understanding of the cosmos. The greater visibility in this part of the house may explain the concentration of activities in this area, from cooking and food preparation to grease extraction and bead making. But Bosch's work also shows that daily life was embedded in a strong diurnal pattern. In the early morning, as the sun rises in the east, a bright rectangle appears on the west wall of the house, at its southern end. During the day, the rectangle moves, like a clock, eastward across the floor of the southern end of the main room, past the oven and ladder, and finally climbs the eastern wall of the house and disappears.

This strong daily sequence, west to east, of light in the house reinforces the notion that activities in and movement around the house were also set within a framework that was cosmologically ordered. In daily practice, it is the south–north distinction that is most clear. The light always remains in the southern part of the house during the day, and the light comes from the oven and hearth in the south at night. It is thus of interest that, as already noted, the south–north axis is the strongest in terms of adherence to orientational rules. But the east–west distinction is also important as one enters, moves around the house and experiences the daily movement of light from west to east.

10.1. Building 65 in the South Area. South is at the bottom of the image. The oven and hearth in the south of the main room, as well as the ladder entry platform in the southeast of the main room, can be seen. There are white burial platforms in the north and east of the main room, and a storage room to the west of the main room. *Source:* Jason Quinlan and Çatalhöyük Research Project.

A PLACE TO LIVE

Why did people come to live together in a large settlement at Çatalhöyük, abandoning the smaller settlements that we know had been scattered around the region (Baird 2005)? Why was the settlement so concentrated? It was not to save building materials, since for the most part each house had independent walls. It was not likely to have been for defense, since there is no evidence of conflict and it was not particularly defensive anyway. There is insufficient evidence for specialization to argue that people came together to take advantage of or to participate in specialized functions. It doesn't seem likely that they gathered there because of resource concentration, since recent studies have demonstrated that they routinely traveled some distance for various resources. The specific location of Çatalhöyük was certainly resource rich, but it seems that at least some of the agricultural fields may have been well away from the site (Rosen and Roberts 2005), and sheep and goats were herded over considerable distances (Pearson et al. 2007).

Perhaps, then, there was some specific meaning to this particular location and site that drew people to it. Certainly it is possible to argue that, at Göbekli Tepe in the 9th millennium in southeastern Turkey, the site, located on a highly visible hill, came to be seen as a regional center (Schmidt 2000). Çatalhöyük differed, of course, in being at heart a settlement rather than a ceremonial center. But it is still possible it was chosen because of some special feature or features that made sense within the inhabitants' cosmology but that at this point elude us. The distinctive symbolism at Çatalhöyük was not duplicated elsewhere. Although the symbolism occurs in houses rather than in public spaces, it is possible that the symbolic repertoire at the site was seen as specifically tied to place.

Douglas Baird has initiated excavations at the site of Boncuklu, 7 km from Çatalhöyük and inhabited in the preceding millennium. Boncuklu was probably located in a marshland, and the fauna and botanical remains indicate some reliance on wetland resources. The same is true of the 9th millennium BC occupation at the shelter site of Pınarbaşı, especially in relation to wetland birds (Baird 2007). We know that Çatalhöyük was located in close proximity to marshland, with seasonal flooding from the Çarşamba Çay. Is it possible that the location of Çatalhöyük continues a special relationship between settlement and wetland resources in the region?

There were of course advantages, in terms of subsistence and work effort, of a location among rich wetland resources. And if one intended to settle somewhere but continued to use scattered resources, it may be that no alternative would have offered a preferable local mix of resources. This would not explain why people came together in a large settlement but may be one reason that, given a desire for such a settlement, it was located here in particular.

It is also possible that location at the edge of an alluvial fan gave access to a wide range of clays and marls that were needed in the mud-brick constructions and plastered walls and features on the site. But water often has symbolic dimensions. Lewis-Williams and Pearce (2005) argue that water has been a widespread symbol of the lower cosmological level (e.g., a shaman's journey might often be through water). This suggestion would imply that the people located their settlement in a place symbolically connected with the lower cosmological level, that also associated with death. This perhaps connects with the attention paid to ancestors as well as the earlier speculation concerning a parallel between entering a house and descending into another realm.

Russell and McGowan (2003) have argued that the cut and wear marks on the wing bones of a crane found at Çatalhöyük can be interpreted in terms of the use of the wing and its feathers as part of a costume. Waterbirds are shown in the art at Çatalhöyük, and they have a prominent role on the pillars at Göbekli. As Hodder and Meskell note (Chapter 2) many figurines at Çatalhöyük have birdlike features. They further argue that birds and waterbirds may have been involved in the travels of the dead, or at least in the ascent of skulls from their bodies. While the latter assertion is most closely tied to vultures, waterbirds also seem associated.

There is little else that would indicate that people collected at Çatalhöyük because of symbolic associations of water, but it does seem likely that the site drew people to it because of the symbolism embedded in this place. As Baird (2005) has noted, the period of occupation of Çatalhöyük is associated with a disappearance of sites from the alluvial fan on which the site is located. People were drawn into (and perhaps also repulsed from) this special place.

Humans and other beings

What kinds of beings are there in this Çatalhöyük universe, and how do humans fit in with the rest? The project's Question 3 (see Chapter 1) is important here: "Do human forms take on a central role in the spirit world in the early Holocene, and, if so, does this centrality lead to new conceptions of human agency that themselves provide the possibility for the domestication of plants and animals?"

Behind this question, or somewhere nearby anyway, is the question of the causation of the move to agriculture. Could it be that it really was a kind of 'invention' or rather a 'decision or plan' and not a random accident, most of whose consequences were unintended? Could it be, indeed, that there is some teleological element to human history, that people sometimes did things to cause the results that actually happened? In our age of environmental problems, unintended consequences are heavy on our minds, but we should not forget that sometimes there are intended consequences that do come about, and that Neolithic humans were humans with intentions and some kind of self-understanding as agents, however different perhaps from our own.

Maybe there is an importance to 'scale' when one is thinking along these lines. The long-standing academic divide between the importance of inexorable and one might say anonymous processes, and lone geniuses in history, has persisted in part because even for well-documented historical periods the concrete evidence is ambiguous. For example, Thomas Edison is often used as the stereotypical inventive genius. And he did actually intend to 'invent' a practically effective incandescent lightbulb and he really did succeed. But the story, as often told, emphasizes instead the tedious trial and error as a lengthy, though persistent wallowing around in a not very systematic or directed search for the right materials. So it is not an either–or dichotomy, and any one event may have elements of intention and chance. And if the transforming individual view of recent history is overdone, it may be, conversely, that we sometimes overemphasize process and trends in archaeological contexts where these are far easier to discern than creative individuals.

Is it possible to tell, in an archaeological context, whether an event, change or even trend was the product of conscious human intentionality or a by-product of other efforts? And is it possible to detect changes in human self-conception and what in archaeology is usually referred to as agency? In one sense 'agency detection' is what archaeology is all about. These stones were broken by human agents, for a purpose that we may or may not be able to discern, and not naturally broken such as by frost erosion. But while there are occasional problems with 'geofacts' rather than real artifacts cluttering the search for the first stone tools or the entry of humans into the New World, the Neolithic is somewhat less of an issue and we rightly demand of ourselves a more nuanced effort.

To think ahead in any but the most minimal sense would assume some sense of history or at least to think outside of the present 'way things are'. It is sometimes argued that a *sense of history* is not found until the Greeks.

But in several chapters in this volume it is argued that history making was a key facet of life for the people of Çatalhöyük. We have also seen in this chapter that there is evidence that the inhabitants at the site had a clear sense of planning and of the future, even if this evidence is for a different scale.

All this indicates a definite intentionality. Following Cauvin (2000), Hodder (2006) has argued that a new sense of human agency emerged at the start of the Holocene in the Middle East, best encapsulated in the giant stelae at Göbekli. These large pillars have a human form, and these human forms dominate the wild animals engraved on them. Similarly, in the upper levels at Çatalhöyük, paintings depict humans teasing and baiting wild animals. This type of domination of wild animals can be seen as a prerequisite for the unequal relationship with animals that is involved in their domestication.

It has been suggested (Hamilton 1996, 2006) that there were significant changes in the figurines produced over time, with an increase in human representation from Level VI. Hamilton also detected a trend in changing gender representation, from male figurines predominating in the early levels to females becoming more common in later levels, the primary transition again being around Level VI. Speaking regionally, the early emphasis on male imagery might make sense in light of the heavy emphasis on male imagery at earlier sites like Göbekli Tepe. To the extent that this is true it could suggest a 'yes' answer to at least part of our Question 3, as noted earlier. However, a major reanalysis of the figurine materials from the site that emphasizes primarily materials from the current excavation has not confirmed all these trends. Meskell et al. (2008) suggest instead that they were at least in part a result of the differences in excavation approaches between the 1960s and today.

We still have these other lines of evidence for a strong conception of human individuality (as already noted) and agency. It seems likely that other beings, and not just humans, also were seen as having intentionality. Dead humans, ancestors, may have protected, cared for or threatened the living and perhaps the house. The placing of human skulls at the base of the posts of a house (Hodder 2006) suggests a notion that the skulls had some agency. The area of the house in which the adult dead were buried was always well treated, carefully kept clean and plastered in a fine white plaster and sometimes surrounded by protective decoration. The central place given to a range of wild animals in the symbolism at Çatalhöyük and elsewhere in the Neolithic of the Middle East is discussed in Chapter 2. In Building 77, the horns of two large bulls and the horns and skull of a wild sheep entirely surround the burial platform; they seem to embrace and protect the ancestors buried there (Chapter 12).

Material things too seemed to have agency. Already mentioned is the use of painting to surround or protect or mark out the dead. The use of 'magic' objects is discussed by Nakamura in Chapter 11. In the sequence of buildings labeled 44, 56, 65 a whole pot was in each building inset into the floor at the bottom of the ladder (in some way related to entry into the house). Blades of obsidian were stuck into the plaster around the edge of the main burial platform in this sequence. Animal bones, teeth and claws were placed in walls or worn on the body, and these too may have been seen as having some protective or memorial agency.

It can be argued that notions of agency increased in many spheres in the Neolithic of the Middle East – human, animal (spirit), material. One interesting question, from the point of view of a Neolithic understanding of reality, concerns whether this notion of agency as the ability to have an effect on the world assumes some dualism between mind and matter, self and other. During the seminar discussions of the Templeton group at Çatalhöyük, Harvey Whitehouse suggested that people are intuitively dualists, and that we can reasonably assume that people at the site could imagine their spirit being separated from their body or that a nonmaterial thing like 'mind' could influence a material thing like a 'body'. Although some scholars today consider dualism in general and the idea of a mind influencing a body to be simply wrong, it is nevertheless the case that dualism in this sense has been a very widespread belief among humans. Without evidence to the contrary it would seem more likely that the people of Çatalhöyük believed in an invisible realm of agents, spirit beings, than not. Ancestors, of course, would seem to be prominent among such beings.

At Çatalhöyük there is much evidence at least for dyadic oppositions of various kinds. I have already referred to the distinctions between north and south, east and west in the house. Even classic structures such as wild versus domestic can plausibly be argued. Nearly all the art and symbolism at Çatalhöyük focus on what we would identify as wild animals. The animals that we, in our own dualist classifications, identify as domestic (sheep and goats) are rarely shown in the art and play little role in installations. Dogs seem to have been treated in a special way (used in special deposits but not consumed), most likely representing the special link between dogs and humans found so widely historically and today. The depositional processes used for domestic sheep and goats (extensive processing for meat, marrow and grease extraction) differ substantially from those used for wild animals (special processing for large-scale consumption of wild cattle or consumption off-site of predators such as bears and leopards).

Yet there is less evidence that the inhabitants at Çatalhöyük were dualists in the sense of distinguishing spirit from matter. There is much to suggest that, as noted earlier, ancestors, animals and things could have agency in the sense of having effects in the world. Much of the symbolism at Çatalhöyük may have been pragmatic, aimed at achieving specific aims, getting things done. The 'theory of mind' employed at Çatalhöyük may have extended to inanimate things. In their lived reality people knew that their house walls would lean over and collapse if not looked after and that they would slump if not built on the hard foundations of earlier walls. But it is quite possible that they did not separate practical and spiritual ways of making sure that the house did not fall down or face other calamities. There is evidence that they believed ancestors could affect the world in which they lived, and of course ancestors were different from the living. But in what ways were they considered different? Was there a clear division between living and dead, flesh and spirit, visible and invisible and so on?

Conclusions

As preliminary as this study is, I believe we can, even now, say a few things about how the Neolithic inhabitants of Çatalhöyük pictured the world around them, its dimensions and durations, the ways things worked and how people conceived themselves.

They appear to have had a sense of history, recognizing the existence of a past that was important for their present. Their conception of their past may not have fully recognized the time depth of the site (some 1,400 years of continuous occupation) as we measure it, but it was substantive, aided by a range of physical reminders: remains of ancestors, houses rebuilt in the same place and the large mound itself. This history had a human and even personal element. At least it is the case that much of *our* evidence of their historical perspective concerns human activity and mainly activity concerned with specific individual ancestors.

Some conception of the individual was also an important element of how the people of Çatalhöyük saw the world and themselves as part of it. While we must use such words with care, given the fact that our own view of the individual and the related concept of the self is constructed of relatively recent cultural elements (Taylor 1990), the attention to specific individual ancestors is certainly a significant feature of their world.

At this site there are many indications of a complex of seasonal rounds of activities that naturally required planning, perhaps complexified by the size of the population. It is probably the case that residents, like most people even today, lived much of their time in a world of routine 'natural' cycles of days, months, seasons and years. But while there is no evidence of large-scale projects (e.g., community-wide infrastructure development representing long-range planning) or planning for large collective activities, there are substantial indications of planning at a longer than annual scale. These include activities connected with building cycles, some of which might qualify as periodic rituals (house closings, deposition of human remains at the start of a new foundation) and caching of obsidian blanks for use over a large part of the lifetime of a house.

There are a number of elements of the house and its design that suggest connections with a cosmological ordering. Connections with a multitiered cosmology (which we began by assuming, rather than demonstrating) might include descent into the house from above and location of the dead beneath the area of the living. The typical floor plan was fairly uniform internally and in relation to the cardinal directions, suggesting that, as is quite common among peoples worldwide, the cosmos was ordered in relation to some natural feature such as the movement of the sun or directions as perhaps measured some other way.

The settlement grew by agglomeration rather than evidencing any kind of overarching design or planning, and no community/non-household/specialized structures have as yet been discerned. Its growth correlates with the abandonment of a number of small settlements in the region, suggesting that it attracted people. It is probable that the site was chosen for some combination of reasons of convenience (local resources) and cosmological associations. It is not clear what the latter were, but one suggestion is that they have to do with the symbolic associations between water and the lower level(s) of a multitiered cosmology. This would correlate with the significant attention paid to burials, ancestors and what might be symbolism of violence and death in the murals and relief artwork.

Unlike the inhabitants of some "peasant" villages familiar to us today, people at Çatalhöyük traveled some to secure resources. The extensive trade network postulated by Mellaart was always a stretch and has not been confirmed, but they likely had some contact with other peoples outside the immediate region, as is typical of hunter-gatherers, for they continued to seek resources from some distance, obsidian perhaps being the most distant regular stop. But while their mindset may not have been at the parochial end of the scale, beyond this, I was unable to find evidence of what they actually did think about the extent of the world and its various parts.

What did the people of Çatalhöyük think of themselves and of what it is to be human more broadly? To achieve some focus in addressing this area of cosmology, I returned to the project's Question 3: Do human forms take on a central role in the spirit world in the early Holocene, and, if so, does this centrality lead to new conceptions of human agency that themselves provide the possibility for the domestication of plants and animals? It is actually a very complex question, but what I found tends toward the 'yes' side of the equation on the parts of it I was able to address.

As has been noted in other Neolithic contexts, figurines and other symbolic media give a much greater emphasis to human or human-like representations than is found in Palaeolithic works. What part of this corpus actually refers to the spirit world is not clear at this point. But it is probably somewhat less than interpretations of the 1960s excavations would suggest, or at least the connection is less direct in the sense that figurines are not as obviously goddesses, for example, as some have supposed. The order of causation was not at all clear either from these materials, but in some ways that might have been expected from a focus on one site, and that not at the very beginning of the changes in question. A new phase of this research project will include a serious engagement with regional trends, which should prove very interesting.

Human representations are found throughout the media – figurines and murals especially. The suggestion that humans are represented more commonly among figurines in later periods has been disputed, and that is not surprising given how much more evidence there is for stasis at the site than developments that sustain the creative burst with which the site began. As with the earlier Göbekli Tepe, humans are represented as teasing, baiting and generally dominating animals, including big dangerous ones like the wild bull, which was eventually domesticated.

So there is evidence for humans self-conceived as individuals and as agents in the world. Agency seems to have been attributed to others besides humans, including dead ancestors and some other animals. Even objects had a kind of causal efficacy through magical thinking, which is a view of causation and purpose in the universe quite different from that involved in thinking about how to work with fellow agent-beings, the latter often being the core of religious thinking.

There is much evidence for dualistic thinking but not necessarily for body–spirit dualism as we tend to think of it. However, if the dead could be conceived of as agents in the world, though no longer physical in the same sense as before, it is possible that they had some notion of a spirit being. Similarly with causation and agency. People recognized themselves as effective agents in a range of contexts and dead ancestors as well. They also seem to have thought in magical terms in which objects or formulas had a power of their own. These are all very important for understanding the world their minds inhabited, how they looked out at others and the world around them.

REFERENCES

Andrews, P., Molleson, T., and Boz, B. 2005. The human burials at Çatalhöyük. In *Inhabiting Çatalhöyük: Reports from the 1995–1999 Seasons*, ed. I. Hodder. Cambridge: McDonald Institute and British Institute of Archaeology at Ankara Monograph, 261–78.

Atalay, S., and Hastorf, C. A. 2006. Food, meals, and daily activities: Food habitus at Neolithic Çatalhöyük. *American Antiquity*, 71(2), 283–319.

Baird, D. 2005. The history of settlement and social landscapes in the Early Holocene in the Çatalhöyük area. In *Çatalhöyük Perspectives: Reports from the 1995–1999 Seasons*, ed. I. Hodder. Cambridge: McDonald Institute and British Institute of Archaeology at Ankara Monograph, 55–74.

Baird, D. 2007. Pinarbaşi: From Epipalaeolithic camp site to sedentarising village in central Anatolia. In *The Neolithic in Turkey: New Excavtions and New Discoveries*, eds. M. Özdoğan and N. Başgelen. Istanbul: Arkeoloji ve Sanat Yayınları, 285–311.

Cauvin, J. 2000. *The Birth of the Gods and the Origins of Agriculture*. Cambridge: Cambridge University Press.

Clottes, J., and Lewis-Williams, D. 1998. *The Shamans of Prehistory: Trance and Magic in the Painted Caves*. New York: Abrams.

Connerton, P. 1989. *How Societies Remember*. Cambridge: Cambridge University Press.

Conway Morris, S. 1998. *The Crucible of Creation: The Burgess Shale and the Rise of Animals*. Oxford: Oxford University Press.

Conway Morris, S. 2003. *Life's Solution: Inevitable Humans in a Lonely Universe*. Cambridge: Cambridge University Press.

Cronk, L. 1999. *That Complex Whole: Culture and the Evolution of Human Behavior*. Boulder, Colo.: Westview Press.

Donald, M. 2005. *Origins of the Modern Mind: Three Stages in the Evolution of Culture and Cognition*. Cambridge, Mass.: Harvard University Press.

Düring, B. S. 2006. *Constructing Communities: Clustered Neighbourhood Settlements of the Central Anatolian Neolithic, ca. 8500–5500 Cal. BC*. Leiden: Nederlands Instituut voor het Nabije Oosten.

Fairbairn, A., Asouti, E., Russell, N., and Swogger, J. G. 2005. Seasonality. In *Çatalhöyük Perspectives: Reports from the 1995–1999 Seasons*, ed. I. Hodder. Cambridge: McDonald Institute and British Institute of Archaeology at Ankara Monograph, 93–108.

Gallois, W. 2007. *Time, Religion and History*. Harlow: Pearson Education Ltd.

Gill, J. H. 2002. *Native American Worldviews: An Introduction*. Amherst, Mass.: Humanity Books.

Gimbutas, M. 1991. *The Civilization of the Goddess*. San Francisco: Harper.

Goring-Morris, A. N. 2000. The quick and the dead: The social context of aceramic Neolithic mortuary practices as seen from Kfar HaHoresh. In *Life in the Neolithic Farming Communities: Social Organization, Identity, and Differentiation*, ed. I. Kuijt. New York: Kluwer Academic, 103–36.

Gosden, C. 1994. *Social Being and Time*. Hoboken, N.J.: Wiley.

Gould, S. J. 1990. *Wonderful Life: The Burgess Shale and the Nature of History*. New York: Norton.

Hamilton, N. 1996. Figurines, clay balls, small finds, and burials. In *On the Surface: Çatalhöyük, 1993–95*, ed. I. Hodder. Cambridge: McDonald Institute for Archaeological Research and British Institute of Archaeology at Ankara Monograph, 215–63.

Hamilton, N. 2006. The figurines. In *Changing Materialities at Çatalhöyük: Reports from the 1995–1999 Seasons*, ed. I. Hodder. Cambridge: McDonald Institute for Archaeological Research and British Institute of Archaeology at Ankara Monograph, 187–213.

Hetherington, N. S. 1993. Introduction: Different cultures, different cosmologies. In *Cosmology: Historical, Literary, Philosophical, Religious and Scientific Perspectives*, ed. N. S. Hetherington. New York: Garland, 3–8.

Hodder, I. 2006. *The Leopard's Tale: Revealing the Mysteries of Çatalhöyük*. London: Thames and Hudson.

Hodder, I. 2007a. Çatalhöyük in the context of the Middle East Neolithic. *Annual Review of Anthropology*, 36, 105–20.

Hodder, I. 2007b. *Çatalhöyük 2007 Archive Report*. http://www.catalhoyuk. com/downloads/Archive_Report_2007.pdf (accessed January 3, 2010).

Hodder, I., ed. 2007c. *Excavating Çatalhöyük: Reports from the 1995–1999 Seasons*. Cambridge: McDonald Institute for Archaeological Research / British Institute of Archaeology at Ankara Monograph.

Kuijt, I. 2008. The regeneration of life: Neolithic structures of symbolic remembering and forgetting. *Current Anthropology*, 49(2), 171–97.

Le Goff, J. 1982. *Time, Work and Culture in the Middle Ages*. Chicago: University of Chicago Press.

Lewis-Williams, D. 2002. *The Mind in the Cave: Consciousness and the Origins of Art*. London: Thames and Hudson.

Lewis-Williams, D., and Pearce, D. 2005. *Inside the Neolithic Mind: Consciousness, Cosmos and the Realm of the Gods*. London: Thames and Hudson.

Lowie, R. H. 1935. *The Crow Indians*. New York: Holt, Rinehart and Winston.

Lucas, G. 2005. *The Archaeology of Time*. London: Routledge.

Mellaart, J. 1967. *Çatal Hüyük: A Neolithic Town in Anatolia*. London: Thames and Hudson.

Meskell, L. 2008. The nature of the beast: Curating animals and ancestors at Çatalhöyük. *World Archaeology*, 40(3), 373–89.

Meskell, L., Nakamura, C., King, R., and Farid, S. 2008. Figured lifeworlds and depositional practices at Çatalhöyük. *Cambridge Archaeological Journal*, 18(2), 139–61.

Mithen, S. 1996. *The Prehistory of the Mind: The Cognitive Origins of Art, Religion and Science*. London: Thames and Hudson.

Nakamura, C., and Meskell, L. 2009. Articulate bodies: Forms and figures at Çatalhöyük. *Journal of Archaeological Method and Theory*, 16(3), 205–30.

Nielsen, J., and Sellner Reunert, T. 2009. Dante's heritage: Questioning the multi-layered model of the Mesoamerican universe. *Antiquity*, 83, 399–413.

Özdoğan, M., and Özdoğan, A. 1990. Çayönü: A conspectus of recent work. *Paléorient*, 15, 65–74.

Pearson, J., Buitenhuis, H., Hedges, M. L., Russell, N., and Twiss, K. C. 2007. New light on early caprine herding strategies from isotope analysis: A case study from Neolithic Anatolia. *Journal of Archaeological Science*, 34, 2170–9.

Rappaport, Roy A. 1999. *Ritual and Religion in the Making of Humanity*. Cambridge: Cambridge University Press.

Redfield, R. 1952. The primitive world view. *Proceedings of the American Philosophical Society*, 96, 30–6.

Rosen, A., and Roberts, N. 2005. The nature of Çatalhöyük: People and their changing environments on the Konya Plain. In *Çatalhöyük Perspectives: Reports from the 1995–1999 Seasons*, ed. I. Hodder. Cambridge: McDonald Institute and British Institute of Archaeology at Ankara Monograph, 39–54.

Russell, N., and McGowan, K. J. 2003. Dance of the cranes: Crane symbolism at Çatalhöyük and beyond. *Antiquity*, 77, 445–55.

Schmidt, K. 2000. Göbekli Tepe, Southeastern Turkey. *Paléorient*, 26, 45–54.

Smith, J. Z. 1995. *The Harper Collins Dictionary of Religion*. San Francisco: Harper.

Taylor, C. 1990. *Sources of the Self: The Making of the Modern Identity*. Cambridge, Mass.: Harvard University Press.

Testart, A. 2008. Des cranes et des vautours ou la guerre oubliée. *Paléorient*, 34(1), 33–58.

Wason, P. K. 1994. *The Archaeology of Rank*. Cambridge: Cambridge University Press.

Wason, P. K. 2007. Art: Rock art and shamanism. In *Encyclopedia of Human–Animal Relations: A Global Exploration of Our Connections with Animals*, ed. M. Bekoff. Westport, Conn.: Greenwood Press, 99–103.

Whitehouse, H. 2004. *Modes of Religiosity: A Cognitive Theory of Religious Transmission*. Latham, Md.: AltaMira Press.

Woodburn, J. 1980. Hunters and gatherers today and reconstruction of the past. In *Soviet and Western Anthropology*, ed. E. Gellner. London: Duckworth, 95–117.

11

Magical deposits at Çatalhöyük: A matter of time and place?

Carolyn Nakamura

When is magic? That is, when does an act or thing become magical if it does so at all? Derek Collins (2000) poses this astute question in his recent discussion of Greek magic,[1] and the question seems requisite for any study of magic in the Neolithic as well. Asking *when* as opposed to *what* complicates any perfunctory characterization of magic that reinstates simplistic distinctions of symbolic versus pragmatic, ritual versus everyday and natural versus supernatural. Asking *when* underscores the nuances of context and attributes to prehistoric persons a complex range of motivations, strategies and desires that may have imbued certain moments and activities with a sense of what we might call 'the magical'. Asking *when* is infinitely more apt for examining the potential indicators of spirituality at Çatalhöyük, a site where discrete forms of religion and magic remain distinctly beyond archaeological perception. Similarly, it also seems appropriate to ask: *where* is magic at Çatalhöyük? If practices and things become magical at particular moments, they do so in particular spaces. If there is any 'evidence' of magic at Çatalhöyük, it will reveal itself, not as a ready-made or petrified cultural form, but more furtively at specific times and places.

It is impossible to deny that the Neolithic community of Çatalhöyük engaged some kind of concern with a world or force beyond that of the living human population. The plastering, circulation and installation of human and animal skulls, and the depiction of humans and animals in wall

[1] Following Goodman's approach to art (1976), Collins focuses on the 'when' rather than the 'what' of magic in order to sidestep the myopia of philological debates that focus on specific terms and definitions of Greek magic at the expense of illuminating the 'conceptions of causality and agency implied by the magical practices and objects themselves' (2000: 20).

painting and modeled media, suggest that certain animals and the dead were likely imbued with some kind of power in the socioreligious sphere. Moreover, the specific and sustained attention given to some houses, which sometimes persisted over several generations, indicates that the house itself played a central role in spiritual life at Çatalhöyük (Hodder 2005b, 2006b). In the past, some have treated the archaeology of certain evocative things – namely, figurines, burials, wall paintings and plastered sculptures – and their interpretation somewhat carelessly, giving them borrowed life through compelling, yet ultimately prefabricated narratives of spirituality, religion and art (Gimbutas 1974; Mellaart 1967). Certainly, this tendency in part reflected the interpretive habits and ideals of those times, but we are now dealing with a remarkably transformed archaeological record and set of standards. Accordingly, not only have the questions concerning religion and spirituality changed, but so also have the ways in which we can investigate them archaeologically.

Leaving the difficult discussion of what constitutes the religious or spiritual at Çatalhöyük to the other contributors to this volume, I will instead focus on what might constitute the magical domain at Çatalhöyük. These two themes are, no doubt, related; and indeed, before one can look for magic, one must first have a somewhat clear idea of the material forms and practices that religion encompasses. After briefly discussing the archaeology of the religious domain, I will discuss a few possible magical valences at Çatalhöyük, focusing on certain materials and their qualities, mixed deposits and their specific locations and temporalities.

From religion to magic

Discussions and debates concerning the nature of religious and magical practice during the Middle Eastern Neolithic have only recently begun again in earnest (Cauvin and Watkins 2000; Gebel et al. 2002; Lewis-Williams 2004; Mithen 1998; Watkins 2004). Not surprisingly, most discussions focus on the symbolic and ritualistic as opposed to the more practical and instrumental aspects of Neolithic life.

While such contributions reopen a much needed conversation about religion in the Neolithic, Webb Keane rightly reminds us that there are certain consequences of parsing archaeological evidence into things that are useful (instrumental) and things that are symbolic (Chapter 8; also see

Pels, Chapter 9, and his discussion of the 'fallacy of religion'); foremost is that the practical side of human activity becomes tacitly regarded as distinctly *not* symbolic:

> This point is important because other analytical consequences follow. The putative distinction between instrumental and symbolic is the basis on which most of the theories of religion in Çatalhöyük have been based. (Keane, Chapter 8)

The symbolic materials at Çatalhöyük are uniquely evocative in their overall aesthetic, concentration and constitution, and thus are the obvious focus of discussions and theories of religion at the site. However, there is also increasing archaeological evidence from recent excavations that challenges the notion of the symbolic realm as the sole arbiter of religious practice and belief (Hodder 1996, 2005a,b, 2006a,b). Implicitly questioning the conventional distinction between instrumental and symbolic realms, Tristan Carter (2007) has argued against treating the 'social' and 'technological' as distinct qualities and categories of meaning in the obsidian industries. For instance, the caching of obsidian blanks in houses at Çatalhöyük may have served multiple purposes and intentions: for saving the material for later retrieval, for its incorporation into the house structure (Carter 2007) or indeed for making a kind of dedicatory or magical offering.

In a different way, the figurine materials also argue against the separation of the instrumental from the symbolic in spiritual life. Figurines, once regarded by Mellaart and Gimbutas as objects of reverence or worship – idols or mother goddesses – now seem to encompass a ritualized, yet more everyday and disposable kind of practice (Meskell et al. 2008). Significantly, the current excavations have rarely found figurines from primary contexts and almost never from caches (the one possible exception being 14522.X8 from Building 65, discussed later in this chapter) or platforms. Rather, these objects are most ubiquitous in midden and infill. In contrast to obsidian, there seems to be less concern for the material itself – its hiding, keeping or incorporation within the house – than for the 'instrumental' process of its creation, fulfillment of a purpose, wish or whim and final disposal, most often in domestic trash or room fill. Lynn Meskell and I have repeatedly argued that figurine practices seemed valuable *as a means to various ends*; they encompassed a range of practices that consistently did not include the object itself being treated with the kind of care seen with other materials (Meskell et al. 2008; Meskell and Nakamura 2005; Nakamura and Meskell 2004, 2006). Notably, some have suggested that figurine practices are most evocative of wish-vehicles (Hodder 2006b; Voigt 2000). However, this kind of quotidian use does not preclude the possibility that figurines were involved in spiritual or ritual activities.

Marking a shift toward attending to the diverse modes of religious life, particularly centered around the house, some of the contributors to the current volume explore pragmatic, material-semiotic approaches to investigating the religious dimension at Çatalhöyük (e.g., Keane, Pels, Shults). Such approaches are particularly appropriate for prehistory, since they salvage materiality from its epiphenomenal status (especially in discussions of religion) and do not require or falsely sustain misleading divisions of sociality into discrete and purified realms.

While these scholars focus on different aspects of religion, they underscore a few cardinal aspects of the religious domain that provide a useful starting point for a discussion of magic at Çatalhöyük. Leron Shults (Chapter 3) situates religion/spirituality in terms of the ultimate limits of human engagement. He emphasizes that the religious addresses the boundary conditions of the world, or the world-constructing boundaries of a person's imaginative cultural engagement. In a similar vein, Peter Pels (Chapter 9) speaks of religion in terms of the experience of transcendence, but his unique contribution aims at articulating the transcendent in terms of the systematic study of temporalities and their overlap. These notions therefore identify and recommend the limits and temporalities of experience as practical anchors for examining religious life in the Neolithic. Shifting his focus toward human action and agency, Webb Keane further observes, 'Much of what seems to fit received categories of religion lies at one end of a continuum of forms of attention and hierarchies of value that range from relatively unmarked to marked' (Chapter 8). The idea of 'markedness of attention' here highlights various degrees of activity and effort concentrated on a certain task, material and/or moment, and draws our analytical attention to how people effectively dealt with the boundary conditions of the world they inhabited.

Needless to say, all of these points also could be applied to a discussion of magic. Magical practices also basically deal with boundaries, limits, temporal dislocations/conflations and certain kinds of 'marked' attention. Indeed, some might wonder if it is helpful or appropriate to distinguish between magical and religious activities at Çatalhöyük and the Neolithic more broadly. While it is quite likely that magic and religion were, in some sense, inseparable during this time, most would still maintain a certain difference between the two. Most explicitly, Peter Pels considers magic to be the most everyday form of religious activity: protection and wish fulfillment (Chapter 9). Ian Hodder also speaks of certain practices he interprets as protective and apotropaic as being magical (2006b). Furthermore, there seems to be a general acceptance of acts of defacement/fragmentation, deposits of 'odd' objects, the disposability and localized burning of 'symbolic' materials and the hidden placement of objects (or bodies) in liminal spaces *as archaeological indexes* for magical protection and/or wish fulfillment. While many or all of these actions may indeed be part of a magical idiom at Çatalhöyük, their articulation as such requires further consideration both indexically and contextually. Only after such considered attention can we move closer to addressing the question of how we might speak of magic as something qualitatively different from religion archaeologically.

Broadly speaking, the analytical category of magic has proved to be a rather slippery concept that seems to come clearly into view only when it serves to oppose or subvert something else. Consider one of the most 'probative' examples of magical thought: the superstition. A tradition becomes superstitious when there is no legitimate basis for belief in it anymore. Or rather, the basis for belief has fallen out of favor or is thought to stem from a distant past or remote place. Superstitions, in a sense, are merely a trace rather than a full-fledged dogma, doctrine or belief. There is some sense that they work – that they *do something* – and one may believe in this efficacy, but one can never explain why they work. Even if an explanation exists, it has no relevance to whether one believes in the efficacy of the gesture or not; it simply does. So superstitions become such only when they are invoked in the presence of a more favored explanatory or causal doctrine.

The elusive figure of magic seems to require a structured ground (like science, religion or rational thought) for it to 'stand out' against and thus make itself known. Notably, magic as a topic of scholarly interest shares an intimate history with the development of anthropology as a discipline. Early works by Victorian scholars, James Frazer and Edward Tylor, effectively established magical practice and thought as a defining characteristic of the Other, as a set of techniques that from a rational observer's perspective couldn't possibly work (Graeber 2001: 240). And since then, magic has yielded substantial explanatory power when deployed for debating ideas and practices that seem to confound rational thought (see debate prompted by Evans-Pritchard's 1937 ethnography of the Azande; MacIntyre 1970; Winch 1964) or as a foil for religion and science (Frazer [1890] 1957; Tylor [1871] 1977) or modernity (Benevides 1998; Styers 2004; Taylor 1989).

While notable scholars, such as Claude Lévi-Strauss, Edmund Leach and many since, have astutely argued against absolute distinctions between magic, science and religion, it is, perhaps, its very capacity to provide contrast if not opposition to its kindred fields that characterizes magic in its most lucid and persistent form. Moreover, while magic often needs to push against something – a dominant order or structure – in order to be discernible, it also, rather cunningly, appears to *belong* to the very system it labors to subvert; it has been the constant companion to modernity (Pels 2003), and at various points in history has been both an ally and agitator of religion and science (Tambiah 1990).

Perhaps this is because there is something about ordered systems and rule structures that begs to be transgressed, broken or done 'otherwise'. Perhaps, as Michael Taussig (1999) imagines, such systems bear within them the very possibility of (and even demand for) events of momentary breakdown. In this picture, magic need not be an adversary or alternative to religion. Rather, it might be more complicit: a necessary, integral supplement (loophole, escape route?) that ensures the smooth functioning and persistence of religion. Following Georges Bataille, Taussig emphasizes that transgression

> is not a rejection of rules that give human culture much of its form and density.... On the contrary, the transgressed rule is brought into ever greater relief, its power more fulsome as there is created, by means of its violation, an unresolvable negation of the negation whose sole aim and density is not resolution of contradiction but its exacerbation. (1999: 141)

Admittedly, Taussig is speaking of the more immoderate Dionysian or Rabelaisian enactments of becoming other through carnivalesque excess; but this notion of transgression still holds in less extreme conditions, which sustain more subtle interactions and, nevertheless, are no less 'exacerbating'.[2]

But transgression also points to another issue. If we recall the familiar Marxist critique of religion in which human beings are creators, religion becomes a prototype for all forms of alienation since it requires humans to project our creative capacities and agencies onto imaginary forces and beings, to which we then bow down and ask favors (Graeber 2001: 239). Here, people see their own creations as controlling them (see also Godelier 1999). Religion is therefore fetishistic in the way it locates the source of human sociality and creativity outside human action. In contrast, magic in Graeber's assessment is never fetishistic, since

> magic is about *realizing one's intentions* (whatever those may be) by acting on the world. It is not a matter of people's intentions and creative capacities being projected out into it and appearing to those people in strange, alienated forms. If anything, it's just the opposite. (2001: 240; added emphasis)

To transgress religious structures (the state of alienation) means to take back the source of human creative power, if only for a moment. Magic seeks to effect direct action – through intentional speech acts (Malinowski 1935; Tambiah 1990) or acts of doing (Mauss [1950] 2001) – action that does not necessarily require an intermediary source. So magic can provide an important pathway or outlet for human agency and creativity in contexts in which religious or other social forms structure and constrain human action and belief.

Examining magical practices, then, provides a way to get at human intentionality. While it is impossible to comprehend the precise meanings that motivated the selection of certain materials and performances in the Neolithic case, it may be possible to locate specific moments and spaces that became the focus for creative human intention and action. Such acts often engender a collision of worlds – of the familiar and unfamiliar, of the 'sacred' and 'secular', of the everyday and exotic. In this way, the study of the magical may also reveal aspects of the relations of human intentionality and power to the religious or other social forms.

---

[2] Hodder seizes upon a similar idea in his discussion of dangerous animal parts at the site. Following Georges Bataille and Maurice Bloch, he suggests that the symbolic incorporation of danger and violence can create moments of transcendence (Hodder 2006b: 203).

Articulating magic at Çatalhöyük

Given the real constraints of performing an archaeological analysis of magic in prehistory, we must admit a few hermeneutic concessions and assumptions. First, it is necessary to impose a very minimal 'definition' of magic from the outset, one that situates magic in relation to something else, in this case the religious. Second, we must imagine that it shares a distinct intimacy with such religious forms. Whether magic worked within, alongside or against such forms, it seems reasonable to assume both addressed similar concerns, albeit in different ways. I would suggest a heuristic positioning of magic as a kind of instrumental agency that contrasts or 'transgresses' certain normative religious patterns and ideals.[3] While this move, admittedly, recalls the kind of enchanted discourse that reconstructs magic as religion's other, it does so in a way that acknowledges how magic also belongs to religion (see Pels 2003). Moreover, this positioning has the benefit of rendering magic archaeologically legible; it allows us to focus on certain practices, spaces, materials, assemblages and temporalities that might assume more magical (contrasting) than religious (conforming) aspects. Needless to say, the departure into magic from religion at this Neolithic juncture is a highly uncertain venture. However, after pursuing this line of questioning, we should be in a better position to say whether the magical was something distinct from the religious in the Neolithic, and perhaps enrich or challenge some of the commonly accepted archaeological indices for magic noted earlier.

Commencing from this framework then, we must first establish a ground from which magic arises – namely, the religious domain as a 'normative' sphere of belief and practice. What experiential limits, spatiotemporal frames and forms of 'marked attention' constituted the religious domain at Çatalhöyük? Archaeologically, the most suggestive evidence stems from a particular focus on the dead, ancestors and wild animals (particularly bulls, but also vultures, leopards and possibly bears), all asserting a strong presence in the house (Hodder 2006b). Furthermore, we might

---

[3] Certainly, this working definition draws from the influential ideas of Malinowksi ([1948] 1992) and Mauss ([1950] 2001), whose ideas on magic as a practical act, performed as a means to an end (Malinowski [1948] 1992:70), in isolation and secrecy, often against certain organized orders (Mauss [1950] 2001: 28–9), have come to define our most common notions of the magical. These ideas generally expand and modify earlier ideas on magic (and its distinction from religion) proposed by Frazer and Tylor.

note the practical emphasis on clay and plaster. These materials were abundant and pervasive in daily life. Most utilitarian objects, including building materials, pottery and clay balls, derive from clay. Plaster covers walls, floors, platforms and features, including installations of wild sheep and cattle bucrania, and often builds up over dozens of layers. The house encapsulated the processes of both life and death. Both humans and houses were buried (houses were 'buried' under other houses or midden), and the particular remains of both could be retrieved, while other materials (obsidian, clay balls, remains of meals) and animal parts (mandibles, scapulae, horn cores, claws) were cached or incorporated into buildings during various stages of their life cycles (see Hodder 2005a). These events, and their consistent occurrence across the site and over time, suggest a baseline for normative ritual practices at Çatalhöyük; moreover, most of these practices are thought to have engaged some sense of exploring the limits of human experience, including life and death, wild versus domestic power and the visible and invisible.

Considered across space and time, the material record underscores a few significant themes. On the most basic level, the worlds of *clay* preoccupied daily life at Çatalhöyük. While clay-based materials and activities clearly dominated the domestic sphere, certain forms such as plaster, with its particular qualities and capacities to smooth, hide, brighten, build up or, indeed, to reflesh and enflesh (Meskell 2008), were likely imbued with symbolic power. The malleable, reusable, combinable and transformational capacities of clay more generally might also have registered on the symbolic level. As Gaston Bachelard has poetically imagined:

> Clay, too, for many people will become a theme of endless reveries. Man will wonder endlessly from what mud, from what clay he is made. For *in order to create, some kind of clay is always needed*, some plastic matter, some ambiguous matter in which earth and water can come together and unite. (1983: 111; added emphasis)

Although clay was ubiquitous at the site, its abundance would not preclude it from being attributed some kind of symbolic force. Clay was the material par excellence of human creation and adaptation. Its accommodating properties allowed humans more control over their relations with the natural world and may have been associated with ideas of creation, abundance and self-preservation. The various modalities of clay (utilitarian and symbolic) sit squarely with Hodder's ideas of entangled practical, symbolic and ritual spheres centered on the house (2006b). Additionally, the *house* itself (made of clay) located the primary domain for religious practice, and the repeated acts of burial, memory and retrieval of certain human and animal body parts likely constituted what Keane (Chapter 8) terms 'highly marked' forms of attention.

Hodder has interpreted much of this activity in terms of a genealogical concern for ancestors and generational continuity. In terms of space, then, we might identify the inside of the house, ovens and horizons between successive rebuilds as 'spaces' marked by religious attention. The site, since Mellaart's time, is well known for its bull imagery – installations of bucrania in rooms – which would have been an imposing presence in the house. But recent excavations also point to distinct patterns of foundation or construction/closure deposits consisting of neonate burials and animal bone deposits (particularly scapulae) (Hodder 2006b). Furthermore, there also seems to be an attention to the specific merging of houses, humans and wild animals. This idea appears in many registers, including the wall paintings with humans interacting with wild animals, burials of individuals with entire animals (e.g., F.1702) or animal claws or tusks (see units 8814, 10829, 11306, 16503), animal and human bodies (and parts) incorporated into house features and structures (both hidden and circulated) and the incorporation of pottery – a distinctly human index – with placed 'feasting' deposits (Russell and Martin 2005). However, this incorporation does not seem to occur at the bodily level, as there are no clear examples of animal–human hybrids at the site (although see Hodder 2006b; Russell and McGowan 2003). In terms of time, these practices suggest a concern for creating a link between the past and present – what Hodder terms 'the invention of history' (2006: ch. 6). Acts of retrieving human skulls and sculpture required remembering the past (the exact locations of such materials and individuals) in a specific rather than general way (Hodder 2006: 147). While the concern for a secure future may be implicit in such memorial acts, the instrumental focus of these conservative practices lies in creating material links to the past, to what was known and/or remembered.

So the house itself, the integrated matrix of house–ancestor–wild animal, powerful body parts (skulls, horns, teeth, claws, mandibles and scapulae) and memorial practices that hinge on revelation through concealment, seemed to locate a somewhat standard set of practices that gesture toward something transcendent or spiritual incorporated into daily life. There is a sense here that such practices focused on creating and maintaining certain foundational relationships – namely, those between group and house, humans and wild animals, present and past. And there is a strong emphasis on marking endings and beginnings and on ovens and heat installations. In other contexts, where the religious domain is more specifically delineated (by textual sources), many of these practices could well be interpreted as magical (Nakamura 2004, 2005). Returning to this point later, I would first like to consider practices that might be slightly more set apart from the religious sphere at Çatalhöyük.

If we follow the idea that magic served in some way to contrast certain normal practices, our attention might be drawn to certain deposits that include some unusual materials that are not common to the daily life and practices of the site. Setting out with these vague ideas in mind, I first queried the Çatalhöyük database for 'clusters', an excavation unit category reserved for a group of homogeneous or heterogeneous materials that appear to be associated in space and time.

Sorting through around 250 cluster deposits, I found that a few interesting patterns stood out. First, a number of deposits included an odd object or two in a larger group of other materials; these assemblages often contained a single piece of obsidian, pottery, flint and/or stone (see Table 11.1). Second, other deposits show the repeated combination of certain materials like obsidian, antler, pottery fragments, crystal, pigment, special stones or ax heads, deposited either with other unusual finds (human skull, baby leg, fossil) or with other more common materials (animal bone, stones, ground stone, figurines). Finally, most of these deposits were found in buildings (see Tables 11.1 and 11.2; Figures 11.1 and 11.2).

These deposits raise a few compelling, if somewhat expected, possibilities. One is that certain rare and possibly exotic materials that appear in mixed deposits, such as crystal (speleothems) and pigment, might have been imbued with some kind of special power or significance. Another is that certain materials *in combination* might have had some kind of power or significance (Figure 11.3). Finally, consideration of the list of deposit descriptions in Table 11.1 suggests the frequent occurrence of these deposits in liminal spaces and moments – points of closure or transition (transformation) in the life cycle of the house such as infill deposits, floor abandonment, construction, retrieval pit or bench construction.

Table 11.1. Mixed deposits

	Unit	Area	Space	Building	Feature	Level range	Materials	Deposit description
1	1212	North	187	1	–	VII–VI	Animal bone, obsidian, shell, tooth	Infill deposit in south part of B.1
2	4210	South	117	2	–	IX	Obsidian +1 flint	Obsidian cache
3	4401	South	163	6	–	VIII	Badger mandible, tooth pendant, stone +1 flint, +1 obsidian, green rubbing stones, ax point	Scoop deposit, located under oven near south wall of building
4	4915	South	173	6	–	VIII	Clay ball, animal bone, stone, obsidian	Floor deposit in eastern side of space
5	4989	South	178	23	–	X	Mostly obsidian flakes and cores +2 burned bone +1 stone	Floor deposit associated with sequence of hearths and ovens
6	5021	South	170	17	538	IX	Animal bone (badger paw), obsidian, flint, figurine, ground stone, pottery	Fire installation in south corner
7	5022	South	170	17	–	IX	Human skull, ground stone, obsidian, clay object, animal bone	Postretrieval pit deposit, northwest corner
8	10281	4040	94	52	–	VI, V	Animal bone, shell bead, stone	Horn cores, west wall
9	10666	South	120	44	1325	?	Stone, animal bone, clay object, obsidian	Scoop deposit, rubble from oven
10	10845	South	112	50	–	VII	Scapulae (2: 1 M, 1 F) +1 obsidian	In between wall packing deposit
11	12400	IST	–	–	1980	?	Obsidian and flint	Cache in clay box
12	12401	IST	283 (252)	63	–	IV–V	Stone, figurine, pottery, obsidian	Infill deposit
13	12485	IST	301	–	–	IV, V	Animal bone (dog skull, bucrania) +1 figurine, obsidian, flint	Infill deposit in northern area
14	12516	South	257	53	–	VI	Ground stone and mud brick with 2 obsidian flakes	Possible construction deposit in northeast corner of northeast platform
15	12806	South	122	56	–	III	Phytoliths, worked bone, obsidian +1 flint	Floor deposit

(*continued*)

Table 11.1 (*continued*)

	Unit	Area	Space	Building	Feature	Levels	Materials	Deposit description
16	12807	South	122	56	–	III	Animal bone, stone, obsidian, flint	Floor deposit
17	13212	4040	227	58	2250	IV, III	Clay object and obsidian	Pit/scoop deposit
18	13342	South	123	56	–	III	Stone, pigment, crystal, ax head	Infill deposit (see Figure 11.3)
19	13359	South	297	65	–	V, VI	Obsidian blades +1 bone awl +1 rounded pebble	Northeast of space near pilaster (see Figure 11.5)
20	13365	South	298	65	–	V, VI	Stone, bone, obsidian, crystal, pigment	Infill deposit between wall and bin
21	13370	South	299	65	–	V, VI	Stones, bones, bone tool, crystal, phytolith, obsidian, ax head	Infill deposit behind oven back wall
22	13491	4040	278	60	2369	V, VI	Obsidian	Brick deposit
23	13640	4040	100	49	1493	VII–VI	Bucrania, grinding stone, animal bone, seeds	Postretrieval pit deposit, northeast corner
24	13937	IST	284	63	2313	IV, V	Scapula +1 pottery	Basin deposit
25	14009	South	297	65	2098	V, VI	Pebbles, bone, obsidian, bone tools, crystal	Placed deposit in bench
26	14019	South	297	65	–	V,VI	Animal bone, stone, pottery, clay object, figurine, obsidian, pigment, crystal	Construction/ abandonment deposit; platform leveling/makeup?
27	14078	South	299	65	2090	V, VI	Stone, fossils, crystal, rub stones	Stone packing layer within oven, with added materials
28	14522	South	297	65	2086	V, VI	Animal bone, figurine, baby leg, stone, obsidian, crystal	Platform deposit; construction/ abandonment deposit
29	14929	4040	322	55	–	Un-assigned	Cluster of stone +1 bone tool	Construction/ abandonment deposit floor deposit
30	16554	South	328	75	–	V	Animal bone (scapula, mandible, skull, ribs) and stones	Pit deposit
31	17094	South	299	–	–	V, VI	Animal bone	Bone cluster (external area)
32	17097	South	299	–	–	V, VI	Animal bone, obsidian	Floor deposit

Table 11.2. *Deer antler deposits*

	Unit	Area	Space	Building	Feature	Level range	Materials	Deposit description
1	Un-known	TP	326	74	–	III	Antler + pigment	Infill deposit in western part of space
2	1052	South	106	MEL House 16	–	VII	Antler, bead, obsidian, figurine	Undifferentiated building fill (near west wall)
3	1350	North	185	1	17	VII, VI	Animal bone	Pit cluster
4	1889	South	117	2	257	IX	Clay balls, ceramics, animal bone, worked bone, antler, obsidian, figurine, ground stone +1 flint	Domestic dump deliberately placed over bin
5	2268	BACH	88	–	–	VII,VI	Stone, antler, cattle skull, figurines, obsidian, bricks	Abandonment deposit in room
6	3037	North	153	–	–	VII, VI	Animal bone (antlers and horn core)	Infill deposit
7	4677	South	172	18	516	X	Antler	Bin wall deposit
8	4717	South	198	–	–	X	Antler, scapula, animal bone	Horizon deposit?
9	6250	BACH	88	–	165	VII, VI	Antler, obsidian, bone tool, ochre	Platform deposit
10	10292	4040	93	52	2003	VI, V	Animal bone, antler tool, stone, obsidian	Floor deposit/pit cluster
11	10499	South	202	42	1515	V, IV	Antler tools, obsidian +1 flint	Burial tool cache
12	10602	South	–	44	–	Un-assigned	Antler	Building horizon deposit?
13	10835	South	112	50	1709	VII	Flint and animal bone (antler)	Burial deposit
14	11317	South	202	42	1515	VI, V	Obsidian, flint, antler (animal bone)	Burial deposit/cache
15	11897	IST	–	–	–	?	Animal bone (antler), stone, obsidian and pottery	Infill deposit/feast?
16	11904	4040	93	52	2004	VI, V	Antler, pig mandible, cattle hoof, goat bones and horns, worked bone, food remains +1 obsidian arrowhead; topped by 1 stalactite/crystal, 1 boar mandible	Bin in southeast corner
17	11923	4040	93	52	2004	VI, V	Animal bone, mandible, antler	Feasting deposit/bin deposit

(*continued*)

Table 11.2 (*continued*)

	Unit	Area	Space	Building	Feature	Level range	Materials	Deposit description
18	11965	4040	93	52	2040	VI, V	Stones, obsidian, sheep bones, antlers	Box/basket deposit, southeast corner
19	11969	4040	94	52	–	VI, V	Animal bone (antler, mandible, skull)	Abandonment deposit? Placed on top of bucranium set into wall niche
20	13352	South	121	65	–	III–IV	Antler, horn cores +1 obsidian blade, scapulae, stone tools, figurine?, obsidian, flint	Placed infill deposits
21	13571	TP	318	–	–	III, II	Antler (1), worked stone (4)	In 'niche' of eastern wall of 'passage'
22	13932	IST	284	63	1997	IV, V	Antler, stone, pottery, animal bone, obsidian	Cache; construction/ abandonment deposit (bench 1997)
23	14460	4040	335	49	4006	VI–V	Stones, animal bone, antler, obsidian, flint, worked bone	Midden deposit under platform, southeast corner)
24	15803	TP	326	74	–	III, II	Antler, skull, maxilla, bone tools, worked stone, clay objects, pigment, obsidian	Infill of eastern part of building, also filling doorway in southern wall
25	16459	4040	337	77	–	VII–V	Antler, horn core	Burned infill deposit?/from collapse? (near southern wall)
26	16488	4040	337	77	3092	VII–V	Antler, stones, goat horn core, scapula	Bin deposit
27	16489	4040	336	77	–	VII–V	Antler, mandible, tortoise shell	Infill deposit in front of alcove in northern wall (above a possible stone/ grindstone/stone tool abandonment deposit)
28	16492	4040	336	77	–	VII–V	Bone tool, clay balls, scapula, skull, antlers, figurine, green stone axes, grindstone	Abandonment deposit? In front of southwest platform and in center of space
29	16523	South	332	75	–	V	Antler (1), flint (1), bone points, scapula	Dump in southwest corner

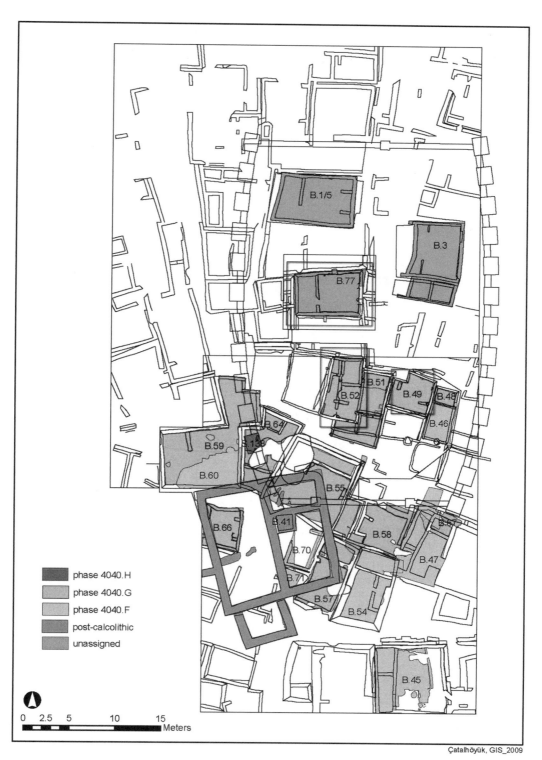

phase 4040.H
phase 4040.G
phase 4040.F
post-calcolithic
unassigned

0 2.5 5   10   15
                        Meters

Çatalhöyük, GIS_2009

11.1. Plan of 4040 Area with new Hodder phasing. *Source:* Çatalhöyük Research Project.

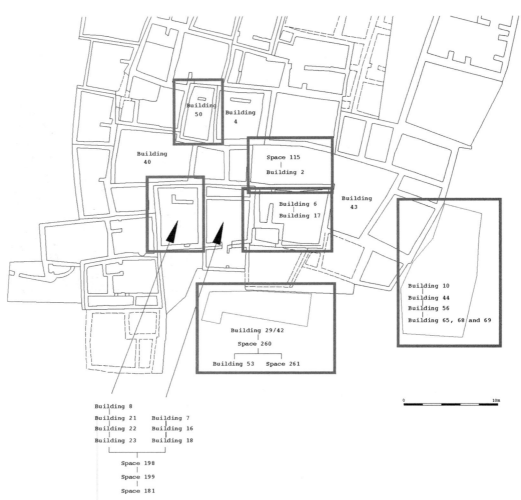

11.2. Plan of South Area. Buildings with mixed or antler deposits are outlined in black. *Source*: C. Nakamura and Çatalhöyük Research Project.

MAGICAL MATERIALITIES

While magic often seeks out isolated and hidden spaces, perhaps it does so only to contain the force of its performance. On a sensory level, magic acts to captivate, agitate and even derange normative modes of perception; at such moments, one would perceive a distinct disruption

11.3. (13342) Cluster found in Space 122 of Building 56: yellow pigment (right), ax head (top), stone (middle) and crystal/speleothem (left). *Source*: Jason Quinlan and Çatalhöyük Research Project.

in the expected. Against the earthen, smooth surfaces of clay and plaster and enduring presence of human and animal bone, certain materials such as crystal and pigment would have stood out for their different qualities, such as color, appearance or hardness (along similar lines, some stones and pebbles from deposits also might have been selected for their color, shape or general quality). None of these materials are commonly found at the site.

Crystal forms are associated with caves as they derive from speleothems, namely, stalactites and dogtooth spar (Gürcan 2008). Indeed, their color, hardness and appealing natural form would have provided a notable interruption in the clay materiality that dominated daily life. Furthermore, these materials might have drawn upon their respective associations with caves and other distant locales. Regardless, their presence would assert a quality of the exotic, different or otherworldly into the house. Such interruptions may have yielded a kind of power that was guarded (hence their occurrence in hidden contexts such as construction deposits or within a bench or placed between walls; see Table 11.1) and not widely known or available to the general population. Their procurement may also have been shrouded in secrecy. It is perhaps significant that most of the deposits containing crystal occur in the South Area, and almost exclusively in Building 65 (13365, 13370, 14009, 14019, 14078, 14522); this building belongs to one of the history house sequences (65, 56, 44 and possibly 10; see Regan 2006), and all of these deposits seem to mark off transitional (and therefore liminal) moments when certain rooms or features go in and out of use. Given that crystal seems to be associated almost exclusively with Building 65 (the one exception being the crystal block found in association with a bin in the burned Building 52), there may be some particular association of this material with this house. Intriguingly, Mellaart (1967) also reported finding broken stalactites in 'special' buildings.

The rare occurrence of pigment in these deposits (13342, 13365, 14019, 15803 and TP), either in or next to B.65, is also intriguing. Clumps of pigment sometimes occur with skeletons in burials (F.200, F.760, F.3010, F.6000) and have rarely been found in any other context. The deposits with pigment listed in Table 11.1 occur in between a wall and bin or oven, or near a wall. Karen Wright (pers. comm.) has suggested that the prevalence of grindstones (to grind pigment for the paint) in B.65 may indicate that this was a house of wall painters. This suggestion, while inconclusive, is provocative and does not rule out a magical use for pigment. In fact, the act of painting itself may have evoked something of the magical, as many wall paintings were visible only intermittently (Hodder 2006: 190) and were plastered over and repainted numerous times, suggesting a powerful, temporally bounded, performative act.

It is not only rare and exotic materials that might have held particular power. Many scholars have suggested that obsidian, which is relatively ubiquitous at the site, had both a symbolic and an economic vitality at Çatalhöyük (Carter 2007; Conolly 2003; Hodder 2005b, 2006b). Like the more uncommon materials already mentioned, obsidian dramatically contrasts with the compliant qualities of clay. Obsidian is hard, darkly luminous and dangerous; it requires significant skill to bring out its sharp and mortal potential, yet it can also be made reflective (as mirrors; see Mellaart 1962), and its ubiquitous presence underfoot even creates a distinct sonority within the house (see Carter 2007). Notably, obsidian is one of the few materials consistently cached in houses. All of the cached obsidian pieces are pre-forms (Carter 2007), that is, material that is on its way to becoming something else. Carter notes that some have interpreted these caches as either capital (Mellaart 1963) or symbolically powerful assemblages (Conolly 2003; Hodder 2006b) and further implies that these hoards might in fact exploit both of these valences, as they were meant to become incorporated *as part of* the building (Carter 2007). Obsidian was obviously valued for a variety of reasons, and it is possible that certain forms of the material – not the finished pieces or the debitage scrap, but the *intermediary* pre-forms with the potential of becoming something else – were deemed powerful in such a way that needed to be contained and/or incorporated into the house. In this case, particular materials and forms might have been viewed as 'magically' powerful because of certain properties and qualities they yielded.

Whereas obsidian was fairly ubiquitous across the site, another less common material also occurs with significant frequency in mixed deposits and liminal contexts: deer antler (Table 11.2). Russell and Martin (2005) have observed that deer in general are not very common on-site, although their remains are more abundant in the early levels (pre-XII.B). After this point, only the antlers and skins occur on the mound, suggesting that deer were not being eaten in significant amounts. Deer antler takes the form of tools (picks, pressure flakers, soft hammers, hafts/handles), ornaments, pendants, pre-forms and waste material (Russell 2007, 2008). While antler, as a raw material, does not provide the stark contrast to the clay- and bone-dominated townscape, it is a relatively rare material at the site. Russell and Martin suggest that there may have been taboos against eating deer on-site, and given the particular treatment and occurrence of deer parts on-site, deer likely encompassed a very different set of meanings from cattle (2005).

In depositional (and possibly ritual) terms, deer antler is particularly marked by its occurrence in certain placed and infill deposits in buildings. Antler often occurs with other materials in contexts that appear to be marking room and bin closure or transition events, alcove/niche/doorway areas and certain individuals in burial contexts (Table 11.2). So antler, like obsidian, had multiple uses and valences; with a natural hardness and pointedness, it was visually and perhaps symbolically dramatic, but it also could be transformed into a variety of tools, thereby participating in numerous productive activities.

Strikingly, while antler deposits occur in many different buildings, they seem particularly 'thematic' in two buildings in particular: Buildings 52 and 77 (Table 11.2; Figure 11.4). Both buildings, dating to levels ranging from VII to V and located in the 4040 Area, were 'burned', perhaps intentionally (Cessford 2005; Hodder 2008; Twiss et al. 2008). In particular, antlers and antler tools in these buildings were associated with bins, corners and gestures of closure or 'abandonment'.

Symbolically, antler is a highly evocative material, as it can signify continuity, specifically through the trope of cyclic rejuvenation. Visually, deer antlers are also evocative of roots and fire, and may also symbolize tradition, aggressive masculinity, sacrifice and so on. Unlike horns, which continually grow and form over a lifetime, antlers shed and regrow annually; they issue from the same foundation, yet instantiate continual change in life through a repeated cycle of death and rebirth. Notably, antlers do not regrow exact copies of what came before; they are similar, but never the same. It is possible that the Çatalhöyük inhabitants, like other cultures, may have attributed to deer antler a kind of intrinsic regenerative power: that of life (continuity) through constant transformation (growth, death, rebirth). This kind of self-rejuvenating power of the antler would contrast with (but not necessarily oppose) the more steadfast and accumulative power of the horn, which visually, and perhaps symbolically, dominated the house and religious domain.

Finally, with respect to the presence of deer on-site, there is some indication that these animals and some of their body parts were prized, aesthetically and/or symbolically. Worked animal teeth often occur as beads. Most of these beads stem from badger (Russell 2008), dog (F.2050 in B.44 in the South) and boar (F.1710) teeth. However, deer teeth and *fake* deer teeth forms made from long bones also occur in this bead form (see 5169.X2-13 from F.563 in B.17 and 10829.X5, 7, 15 from F.1710). Deer teeth are the only bead forms that appear to be copied, and this act of copying may indicate special significance given to deer teeth or to deer in general.

While we may only speculate as to the symbolic meanings of these various materials, examining their particular materialities along with their contexts of use and deposition does provide some suggestive possiblities. One quality common to obsidian, antler and teeth is that they are natural, hard, pointed or sharp materials that can evoke a sense of danger, power and perhaps defense. Hodder and Meskell (Chapter 2) underscore the

11.4. (16492) Cluster on floor of Building 77 with deer antler in front of southwest platform, sealed by building collapse/demolition. *Source*: Jason Quinlan and Çatalhöyük Research Project.

potential association of teeth and claws at the site with male prowess, the construction of memory and piercing of the flesh. In addition, I would suggest that these materials, as indices of the wild and its power, might have been used defensively for apotropaic protection – as the 'defense that goes on the offensive', to use a Derridian turn of phrase (Derrida 1994). This kind of apotropaic logic appropriates certain materials and animal parts that have the power to wound, pierce and kill, since these objects, when displayed defensively, can effectively ward off potential aggressors. Given the focus on discrete animal heads (horns, mandibles, and teeth in particular) and claws and paws, it is possible that humans viewed these body parts as the very source and condensation of animal power. This idea finds support in the marked concern for removing both heads and 'hands' from actual animal bodies (seen in cattle bucrania, bird talons and claws, bear paws, etc.) and their representations in plastered sculptures (Mellaart 1962, 1963). Notably, the display of teeth and claws is a relatively consistent *defensive* behavior among mammals in response to threat stimuli such as predators or attack situations (Blanchard and Blanchard 2000). The removal, displacement and fetishization of horns, teeth and claws, then, could have rendered a powerfully concentrated symbol in the part separated from the whole (Albrecht 1999). It was as if all the force of wild animal power and vitality came to reside in these castrated parts, but with the caveat that such power was no longer bound to a wild, dangerous animal agency; rather its power in such castrated forms could be appropriated and redirected defensively.

Similarly or mimetically, then, other sharp or sharpened materials such as teeth, antler and obsidian at various times might have operated within this kind of 'domesticating' apotropaic logic. Fitting to such a task, we often find such materials in liminal and perhaps dangerous spaces: in burials, in corners and in between spaces, and in building and feature transition horizons. I will return to these themes of space and time later on, but for the moment I wish to briefly address the power of association and assemblages.

MAGICAL COMBINATIONS

While certain materials may take on magical qualities at Çatalhöyük, we know that these same materials were not always or exclusively magical. Obsidian and antler, for instance, also provided the raw material for crafting blades, points, hammers and other tools. At times, a piece of obsidian was simply a blade, just as an antler was a hammer, or a tooth an ornament. Magical qualities therefore emanated not only from the materials themselves, but also from a particular associative constitution in time and space.[4] Tables 11.1 and 11.2 list nearly 60 deposits of various groups of materials, some of which may testify to a magical act or event. Common materials occurring in combination include obsidian, animal bone (especially scapulae and mandibles), figurines, pottery fragments,

---

[4] This idea departs significantly from Mauss's notion of 'magical milieu', which emphasizes the intentional *marking-off* or bounding of magical spaces and times (generally with formal entry and exit rites and taboos) that oppose a 'normal' milieu (Mauss [1950] 2001: 61, 123). Rather, what I am proposing is more of a *happening* of magic that occurs in the assembly of certain materials, agencies, locales and moments. Human marking, in the sense of Keane's idea of 'markedness of attention' (Chapter 8), is certainly part of such events, but it does not require the rigid bounding and separation of normal vs. abnormal modes or categories.

11.5. (13359) Cluster of objects located on an upper floor of Building 65, possibly placed near a pilaster at the central west wall of the structure prior to abandonment: one bone point, six pieces of obsidian and a small rounded stone. *Source*: Jason Quinlan and Çatalhöyük Research Project.

flint, ground stone, worked bone, colored stones and pebbles, as well as ax heads. Such collections also occur in waste deposits, so in themselves these materials together do not likely signify a magical operation. What catches the eye, however, is when one piece of a different material appears in a collection of another kind of material. For example, excavators have found instances of a single piece of flint in an obsidian cache (e.g., 4210), and one bone tool amid a cluster of stone (e.g., 14929). The intrusion of a non-everyday object also marks certain deposits as something different. Some of the more provocative groupings include the following:

[4401] a badger mandible, tooth pendant, green rubbing stones, an ax point and one piece each of obsidian and flint deposited in a scoop under an oven in B.6;

[5019/5022] a human skull, ground stone, obsidian, clay object and animal bone deposited in a postretrieval pit in the northwest corner of B.17; and

[14522] animal bone, figurine, baby leg, stone, obsidian and crystal deposited in the southeast corner of B.65 under pre-construction makeup of a platform.

Groupings of numerous different objects engage our associative capacities in a much different way than do those that contain the same one or two materials. Were such collections intentionally placed? If so, then why this selection of objects and for what purpose? Again, there is something in the juxtaposition or play of contrasts that captures our attention. In some cases, the collections seem to represent materials from various aspects of life: eating, working, crafting (animal bone, obsidian, grindstones, tools); these have been interpreted as commemorative (Russell 2008; Twiss et al. 2005) or perhaps dedicatory deposits (Hodder 2006b).

However, in other cases, some materials seem to evoke more metonymic or symbolic relations. For instance, mandibles and scapulae, animal parts not known for their meat, occur frequently in mixed deposits (see also Wilson 1999). Ax heads, flint, figurines, horns and human bones in addition to the materials already discussed also regularly appear. Certain materials also seem to co-occur more than others, and it would be interesting to investigate these relationships more closely in future studies. Regardless of the specific relationships, in a general way these groupings suggest a collision of various worlds: domestic, exotic, destructive, creative, animal and human. Alternatively, it is possible that these object collections sought to capitalize not on the power of their specific connections, but rather on the presentation of radical indeterminacy. Placing familiar objects in unusual combinations asserts a kind of derangement of normative modes of perception. Positioned between the known and unknown, these deposits might have been regarded as objects 'out of place'. As such, they would constitute an event that disrupted the consensus (Nakamura 2005). And I am similarly struck by the way in which these material assemblages effectively accomplished the equivalent of what Deleuze regarded as the force of painting (and what I regard as the force of magic): a presentation that conjures a force that exceeds the totality of the complex relations and ideas that produce it (2003). What is magical may be scrutinized, picked apart and analyzed, but to little avail;

for while there may be rules to follow, it is its performance and effect, not its comprehension, that yields social power.

MAGICAL MOMENTS AND PLACES

Certain materials and assemblages seem to reveal a unique form of human attention, one that we might qualify as magical. Yet perhaps the most compelling evidence of magic at Çatalhöyük is to be found in a particular marking of space and time. The deposits listed in Tables 11.1 and 11.2 range from clusters of objects scattered on a common floor surface to objects sealed in inside features. Excavators sometimes refer to many of these deposits as 'abandonment/closure' and/or 'foundation' deposits, given their locations in specific places and transitional moments. The acts of building and rebuilding/reuse were highly ritualized practices at Çatalhöyük. In addition to these deposits, there is a distinct pattern of systematic clearing, leveling, infilling and rebuilding of houses at the site. Some history houses such as the B.65–56–44–(10) sequence display a remarkable degree of consistency in such practices, from the way in which features and structures are closed and remade to the locations and kinds of deposits incorporated into the house (Regan 2006, 2007). Given the centrality of the house in social life, such processes were likely incorporated into the religious domain. However, given the hidden (and perhaps dedicatory and/or apotropaic) nature of these deposits, it is appealing to imagine that they operated on a register slightly different from the more exposed, public trappings of a community-building spirituality.

Hodder (2006b) and Pels (2003) have noted the vital economy of revelation and concealment that fuels certain memorial and spiritual practices at the site. But the retrieving of human skulls, sculpture and architectural materials from previous foundations underscores the memory and revelatory side of the process. What of those deposits that were not meant to be 'retrieved'? While perhaps not forgotten, these events were not meant to be remembered, if remembering meant to be revealed and propelled back into the living human domain. The kind of work they accomplished, be it dedication, sacrifice, protection, recognition, constitution or all of the above, mapped out a different kind of economy. For one thing, the nonrevelatory logic of these deposits is one of accumulation rather than recycling. Furthermore, these deposits marked the boundaries of certain 'forms of life' (i.e., features, rooms and houses). At moments of building, retrieval, closing or transformation, they marked as significant not only the features or houses, but certain *liminal moments*; and one wonders if such 'marking' attributed agency not only to specific objects (such as ovens, bins, platforms and houses), as Keane and Pels describe (Chapters 8 and 9), but also to particular moments in time as well – to the transitional, liminal and sheer potential in processes of becoming.

On a practical level, placed deposits mediated a direct relationship with the house itself. They marked and therefore recognized a certain kind of life or power, both in the features or spaces they inhabited and in the moments of their transformation. Such liminal zones are highly charged by their ambiguous potential, as they inhabit that indeterminate area in between two existential states. Transitional moments and spaces, then, instantiate the very essence of becoming. And in such localized moments lie gainful opportunities to intervene in and affect a future outcome.

Conclusion: Magical orders

Things that remain hidden articulate a different kind of concern for the future than those that are found and retrieved. In a sense, the former become timeless as they remain 'on hold', never meant to fulfill that sovereign moment of revelation at a specific future moment. The marking of liminal locales in such a way, with collections of durable, often fragmented objects from all spheres of life, suggests a kind of magical harnessing of power. Namely, the intentional juxtaposition of the transitory (the liminal) with an enduring materiality composes an act of sublime transgression. To mark the 'in between' places is to focus on *connection* rather than discrete objects, places and times. It is the denial (indeed, the violation) of the boundary or limit par excellence, while in the very same movement, it announces – no less than enhances – its absolute power and significance. If humans create and seek out boundaries and limits in order to make sense of their world (the realm of religion), they also retain the primordial right to occasionally reset and transform them. Perhaps the magical, then, is simply this instrumental memory of noting and performing a certain prior (or other) truth that has been all but forgotten, yet persists in some absent-minded bodily or material form. And the cunning assertion that such acts put forth is that order and sense are founded upon their very transgression and dissolution; magic keeps open the possibility of things being otherwise under the guise of a conservative form of memory.

While it may never be possible to pin down the precise significance of certain evocative finds and deposits at Çatalhöyük, as a form of human marking they do underscore the idea that magic does not necessarily reside in certain materials and their attendant agencies or in certain humans and their skills. Sometimes it seems to encompass a more indeterminate kind of agency, one conjured through the conscription of a specific time, locale, group of materials and their attendant 'agencies' in order to accomplish an instrumental and perhaps transcendent act of observation or recognition.

Certainly, at Çatalhöyük this kind of power might have been privileged and guarded capital, and the particular concentration of 'magical' materials and deposits in some houses is intriguing. One might wonder if certain groups had differential 'access' to magical technologies and how this might correlate to the distribution of religious or spiritual capital across the site. As noted earlier, Buildings 52 and 77 and building sequence 65–56–44–(10) seem especially marked by the presence of these kinds of 'unusual' deposits, but in unique ways. In future work, the general category of clusters must be studied in more detail in order to flesh out significant differences between less marked and highly marked deposits, and further consideration of these houses and their remains might shed some light on the more specific social valences of magic and spirituality at the site.

REFERENCES

Albrecht, T. 1999. Apotropaic reading: Freud's "Medusa's Head." *Literature and Psychology*, 45(4), 1–30.

Bachelard, G. 1983. *Water and Dreams: An Essay on the Imagination of Matter.* Dallas: Dallas Institute of Humanities and Culture.

Benevides, G. 1998. Modernity. In *Critical Terms for Religious Studies*, ed. M. C. Taylor. Chicago: University of Chicago Press, 186–204.

Blanchard, D. C., and Blanchard, R. J. 2000. Defensive behaviors. In *Encyclopedia of Stress*, ed. G. Fink. San Diego, Calif.: Academic Press, 652–56.

Carter, T. 2007. Of blanks and burials: Hoarding obsidian at Neolithic Çatalhöyük. In *Technical Systems and Near Eastern PPN Communities*, eds. L. Astruc, D. Binder and F. Briols. Antibes: Éditions APDCA, 343–55.

Cauvin, J., and Watkins, T. 2000. *The Birth of the Gods and the Origins of Agriculture.* Cambridge: Cambridge University Press.

Cessford, C. 2005. Fire, burning and pyrotechnology at Çatalhöyük. In *Çatalhöyük Perspectives: Themes from the 1995–1999 Seasons*, ed. I. Hodder. Cambridge: McDonald Institute and British Institute of Archaeology Monograph, 171–82.

Collins, D. 2000. Nature, cause and agency in Greek magic. *Transactions of the American Philosophical Society*, 133, 17–49.

Conolly, J. 2003. The Çatalhöyük obsidian hoards: A contextual analysis of technology. In *Lithic Studies for the New Millennium*, eds. N. Moloney and M. Shott. London: Archtype Books, 55–78.

Deleuze, G. 2003. *Francis Bacon: The Logic of Sensation*. Minneapolis: University of Minnesota Press.

Derrida, J. 1994. *Specters of Marx, the State of the Debt, the Work of Mourning and the New International*. London: Routledge.

Frazer, J. G. [1890] 1994. *The Golden Bough: A Study in Magic and Religion*. Oxford: Oxford University Press.

Gebel, H. G., Hermansen, B. D., and Jensen, C. H. 2002. *Magic Practices and Ritual in the Near Eastern Neolithic: Proceedings of a Workshop held at the 2nd International Congress on the Archaeology of the Ancient Near East (ICAANE), Copenhagen University, May 2000*. Berlin: Ex Oriente.

Gimbutas, M. 1974. *The Gods and Goddesses of Old Europe, 7000–3500 B.C.: Myths, Legends and Cult Images*. London: Thames and Hudson.

Godelier, M. 1999. *The Enigma of the Gift*. Cambridge: Polity Press.

Goodman, N. 1976. *Languages of Art: An Approach to a Theory of Symbols*. Indianapolis: Hackett.

Graeber, D. 2001. *Toward an Anthropological Theory of Value: The False Coin of Our Own Dreams*. New York: Palgrave.

Gürcan, G. 2008. Speleothem project. *Çatalhöyük Archive Report*, 2008 (http://www.catalhoyuk.com/archive_reports/).

Hodder, I. ed. 1996. *On the Surface: Catalhoyuk, 1993–95*. Cambridge: McDonald Institute and British Institute of Archaeology at Ankara Monograph.

Hodder, I. ed. 2005a. *Inhabiting Çatalhöyük: Reports from the 1995–1999 Seasons*. Cambridge: McDonald Institute and British Institute of Archaeology at Ankara Monograph.

Hodder, I. 2005b. Peopling Çatalhöyük and its landscape. In *Inhabiting Çatalhöyük: Reports from the 1995–1999 Seasons*, ed. I. Hodder. Cambridge: McDonald Institute and British Institute of Archaeology at Ankara Monograph, 1–30.

Hodder, I. ed. 2006a. *Changing Materialities at Çatalhöyük: Reports from the 1995–1999 Seasons*. Cambridge: McDonald Institute and British Institute of Archaeology at Ankara Monograph.

Hodder, I. 2006b. *The Leopard's Tale: Revealing the Mysteries of Çatalhöyük*. London: Thames and Hudson.

Hodder, I. 2008. Season review: Hitting the jackpot at Çatalhöyük. *Çatalhöyük Archive Report 2008* (http://www.catalhoyuk.com/archive_reports/).

Hodder, I., and Meskell, L. M. In press. A 'curious and sometimes a trifle macabre artistry': Some aspects of the symbolism of the Neolithic in Anatolia. *Current Anthropology.*

Lewis-Williams, D. 2004. Constructing a cosmos: Architecture, power and domestication at Çatalhöyük. *Journal of Social Archaeology*, 4(1), 28–51.

MacIntyre, A. 1970. Is understanding religion compatible with believing? In *Rationality*, ed. B. R. Wilson. Evanston, Ill.: Harper & Row, 62–78.

Malinowski, B. 1935. *Coral Gardens and Their Magic: A Study of the Methods of Tilling the Soil and of Agricultural Rites in the Trobriand Islands.* New York: American Book Co.

Malinowski, B. [1948] 1992. *Magic, Science and Religion.* Prospect Heights, Ill.: Waveland Press.

Mauss, M. [1950] 2001. *A General Theory of Magic.* New York: Routledge Classics.

Mellaart, J. 1962. Excavations at Çatal Hüyük. *Anatolian Studies*, 12, 41–66.

Mellaart, J. 1963. Excavations at Çatal Hüyük, 1962, second preliminary report. *Anatolian Studies*, 13, 43–104.

Mellaart, J. 1967. *Çatal Hüyük: A Neolithic Town in Anatolia.* London: Thames and Hudson.

Meskell, L. 2008. The nature of the beast: Curating animals and ancestors at Çatalhöyük. *World Archaeology*, 40(3), 373–89.

Meskell, L., and Nakamura, C. 2005. Figurines. *Çatalhöyük Archive Report 2005* (http://www.catalhoyuk.com/archive_reports/).

Meskell, L., Nakamura, C., King, R., and Farid, S. 2008. Figured lifeworlds and depositional practices at Çatalhöyük. *Cambridge Archaeological Journal*, 18(2), 139–61.

Mithen, S. 1998. The supernatural beings of prehistory and the external storage of religious ideas. In *Cognition and Material Culture: The Archaeology of Symbolic Storage*, eds. C. Renfrew and C. Scarre. Cambridge: McDonald Institute for Archaeological Research, 97–106.

Nakamura, C. 2004. Dedicating magic: Neo-Assyrian apotropaic figurines and the protection of Assur. *World Archaeology*, 36(1), 11–25.

Nakamura, C. 2005. Mastering matters: Magical sense and apotropaic figurine worlds in Neo-Assyria. In *Archaeologies of Materiality*, ed. L. Meskell. Oxford: Blackwell, 18–45.

Nakamura, C., and Meskell, L. 2004. Figurines and miniature clay objects. *Çatalhöyük Archive Report 2004* (http://catal.arch.cam.ac.uk/catal/archive_reps.html).

Nakamura, C., and Meskell, L. 2006. Figurines. *Çatalhöyük Archive Report 2006* (http://www.catalhoyuk.com/archive_reports/).

Pels, P. 2003. Magic and modernity. In *Magic and Modernity: Interfaces of Revelation and Concealment*, eds. B. Meyer and P. Pels. Stanford, Calif.: Stanford University Press, 1–38.

Regan, R. 2006. Buildings 56 & 65. *Çatalhöyük Archive Report 2006* (http://www.catalhoyuk.com/archive_reports/).

Regan, R. 2007. Building 65, Space 319, Space 305, Building 68, Space 314, Building 75 and Spaces 329, 332 & 333. *Çatalhöyük Archive Report 2007* (http://www.catalhoyuk.com/archive_reports/).

Russell, N. 2007. Çatalhöyük worked bone. *Çatalhöyük Archive Report 2007* (http://www.catalhoyuk.com/archive_reports/).

Russell, N. 2008. Çatalhöyük worked bone. *Çatalhöyük Archive Report 2008* (http://www.catalhoyuk.com/archive_reports/).

Russell, N., and Martin, L. 2005. Çatalhöyük mammal remains. In *Inhabiting Çatalhöyük: Reports from the 1995–1999 Seasons*, ed. I. Hodder. Cambridge: McDonald Institute and British Institute of Archaeology at Ankara Monograph, 33–98.

Russell, N., and McGowan, K. J. 2003. Dance of the cranes: Crane symbolism at Çatalhöyük and beyond. *Antiquity*, 77, 445–55.

Styers, R. 2004. *Making Magic: Religion, Magic, and Science in the Modern World*. New York: Oxford University Press.

Tambiah, S. J. 1990. *Magic, Science, Religion and the Scope of Rationality*. Cambridge: Cambridge University Press.

Taussig, M. 1999. *Defacement: Public Secrecy and the Labor of the Negative*. Stanford, Calif.: Stanford University Press.

Taylor, C. 1989. *Sources of the Self: The Making of the Modern Identity*. Cambridge, Mass.: Harvard University Press.

Twiss, K. C., Bogaard, A., Bogdan, D., Carter, T., Charles, M. P., Farid, S., Russell, N., Stevanovic, M., Yalman, E. N., and Yeomans, L. 2008. Arson or accident? The burning of a Neolithic house at Çatalhöyük. *Journal of Field Archaeology*, 33(1), 41–57.

Twiss, K. C., Martin, L., Pawlowska, K., and Russell, N. 2005. Animal bone. *Çatalhöyük Archive Report 2005* (http://www.catalhoyuk.com/archive_reports/).

Tylor, E. B. [1871] 1977. *Primitive Culture: Researches into the Development of Mythology, Philosophy, Religion, Language, Art and Custom*, vol. 1. New York: Gordon Press.

Voigt, M. 2000. Çatal Höyük in context: Ritual at early Neolithic sites in central and eastern Turkey. In *Life in Neolithic Farming Communities: Social Organization, Identity, and Differentiation*, ed. I. Kuijt. New York: Kluwer Academic/Plenum Publishers, 253–93.

Watkins, T. 2004. Architecture and 'theatres of memory' in the Neolithic of Southwest Asia. In *Rethinking Materiality: The Engagement of Mind with the*

Material World, eds. E. DeMarrais, C. Gosden and C. Renfrew. Cambridge: McDonald Institute for Archaeological Research, 97–106.

Wilson, R. 1999. Displayed or concealed? Cross-cultural evidence for symbolic and ritual activity depositing Iron Age animal bones. *Oxford Journal of Archaeology*, 18(3), 297–305.

Winch, P. 1964. Understanding a primitive society. *American Philosophical Quarterly*, 1(4), 307–24.

12

Conclusions and evaluation

Ian Hodder

What has been achieved by this experiment in interdisciplinary dialogue on an archaeological site? Archaeologists are so often forced to work in relative isolation as they excavate and analyze, being able to engage in wider debate only in summary conference papers, workshops and the literature. The Templeton project has now been extended for a further three years, with a larger group of scholars and with new forms of more intense collaboration and investigation. But we can for the moment take stock and ask whether the initial phase, reported on in this volume, of sustained interaction by a group of scholars with a set of archaeological data produced any added value for archaeology. And have the different disciplines themselves gained anything from their brush with the archaeological process?

In attempting to provide a summary and evaluation of the main conclusions and results I will organize my comments initially in relation to the four questions asked by the project. I will refer to the project participants who produced chapters for this volume, but also to others who contributed to the project listed in Chapter 1 but who did not write chapters.

1. How can archaeologists recognize the spiritual, religious and transcendent in early time periods?

As is clear from the preceding chapters, there was much discussion of this first question during the dialogues enabled by the project. The group of scholars engaged at first hand with the materials from the site and asked questions of the archaeologists. Detailed discussions in the laboratories at the site, regarding obsidian, pottery and figurines or plants, animal bones and human remains, led to reflexive dialogue about the degree to which a separate spiritual or religious part of life could be discerned, especially in these early time periods.

At theoretical and comparative levels, problems immediately arose when we asked the question of whether it was helpful to talk of a separate arena of life at Çatalhöyük that could be called religious. Some members of the group felt strongly that sociological and anthropological debate has demonstrated the difficulties of defining a separate religious sphere in certain forms of society. In Chapter 6 Bloch bluntly states that 'I am confident that there was no religion in Çatalhöyük'. In an early meeting of the group of scholars, the sociologist of religion Robert Bellah argued that 'religion' was a relatively recent concept and that 'transcendent' was a term that was given very specific meanings in different religions. The scholars from religious studies and philosophy took a postfoundational approach and argued for diversity. Both Shults and van Huyssteen in Chapters 3 and 4 argued for religion as an emergent property of complex human systems. Their accounts of religion remained nuanced and contextual. Yet they saw value in continued use of the term 'religion' as a general category.

Van Huyssteen does not see a clearly demarcated religious domain in the Neolithic at Çatalhöyük (Chapter 4). The neurological capacity for different forms of consciousness is linked by him to the human ability to symbolize. Human spiritual and religious experience can be understood as an emergent consequence of the symbolic capacity in humans. Religion is about playing out specific and embodied worldviews within this universal framework. LeRon Shults (Chapter 3) suggests that religious theorists no longer deal with an opposition between matter and spirit. Referring to emergent complexity theory, he sees spirituality as an emergent form of self-awareness. The spiritual is associated with the experience of ultimate boundaries or boundedness. Spirituality at Çatalhöyük is not a separate domain. The hiding and revealing process (e.g., hiding and revealing paintings or obsidian caches or human skulls) suggests a concern with ultimate boundaries. The ridges and boundaries on the floors and platforms that define everyday activity in the house are linked to the dead buried beneath the floors, and in this way they are linked to the ultimate – perhaps the ancestors.

The anthropologists, such as Maurice Bloch, Webb Keane and Peter Pels, were wary of the value of the term 'religion', which they saw as inextricably linked to particular developed social and institutional forms and particular modes of power. But they nevertheless were keen to develop an account of phenomena that others might categorize as religious. Thus in Chapter 6 Bloch discusses houses, roles, corporate groups and the transcendental at Çatalhöyük rather than religion. In that chapter and elsewhere (Bloch 2008) he has also suggested an approach to religion that sees it as deriving from, and continuous with, the general human capacity to imagine other worlds (Bloch 2008; see also Chapter 6). In these ways his position, at the general level, is close to that of Shults and van Huyssteen. Bloch (2008) describes humans and chimpanzees as having complex social worlds. Chimpanzees engage in much Machiavellian politicking: they have what Bloch terms a *transactional* social. But they do not have the *transcendental* social – that is, roles that continue on beyond the individual. It is the ability to imagine a social structure that endures, and to treat elders as honored previous holders of roles, and indeed to treat ancestors as holders of roles, that separates humans from chimpanzees. This exposition by Bloch is highly relevant to Çatalhöyük and to the origins of settled life in towns, because the evidence strongly suggests that a key concern at this time period was indeed the endurance of roles, of structure and of the centrality of ancestors (see Chapters 7 and 9). The transcendental imaginings that are seen in the art and symbolism suggest a social world concerned with establishing the longer-term social relations that are at the heart of agricultural and settled town life. But more generally, we can see the possibility of religion as an emergent property of the human capacity to imagine – as seen in Upper Palaeolithic art well before the agricultural revolution (see van Huyssteen 2006).

One example of the assumptions that often, unhelpfully, travel with the term 'religion' is that religion is always about belief. As Pels and Keane pointed out in our discussions, Talal Asad (1993) has argued that historically anthropologists had come to understand religion as propositional, yet some religion is about proper practice rather than being propositional. Anthropologists now accept that much religion is not about propositions. However, even ritual practice involves some sense of belief. Belief and meaning do not need to be separate and propositional. They can be embodied and embedded. A different though comparable distinction is made by Whitehouse in his discussion of modes of religiosity (Whitehouse and Hodder, Chapter 5).

Webb Keane (Chapter 8) is another anthropologist wary of using the term 'religion' and seeking to find other, general and comparative ways of describing what others mean by religious phenomena. He argues that what looks to us like religion emerges from convergences between different kinds of practice that are not necessarily 'religious' in their own right, but become so when they are combined. He suggests that there is evidence at Çatalhöyük of the general processes of 'marking' and 'absence'. Marking is a way of setting some things as apart, special, different, difficult. The most obvious examples at Çatalhöyük are the kills of dangerous, wild animals, the associated feasts and the display of the resulting bucrania. One source of the difficulty associated with such marking is absence. Absence refers to the ways in which some practices produce an experience that there is something beyond experience that is still relevant. This something beyond is not just gone; it impinges on us somehow. An example at Çatalhöyük is provided by the wild boar mandibles buried in the walls – absent (hidden) but still there and relevant to the lived practices of feasts and wild animal kills. Another example is the human bodies buried beneath the floors that remain relevant to social life so that the graves are reopened and skulls removed and circulated. Obsidian and stalagmites deposited in caches and graves also produce the effect of absence. Practices that produce the effect of absence display people's control or power over absence and presence, and the transitions between them. Marking and absence work against the background of habit – the routine flow of daily life. In the Çatalhöyük house, marking, absence and habit all come together and affect one another. Life may be a continuum between unconscious routine and conscious acts or events, but certain practices sharpen the differences between the extremes of that continuum, to social effect.

The approach outlined by Keane, and the related perspective of Pels in Chapter 9, seem very useful for archaeological discussion. The marking, hiding and making absent of things have long been a focus of archaeological interest in the religious, whether it be Renfrew's (1985) account of things that attract attention and so mark, or Bradley's (1990) discussion of ritual conspicuous deposition of metal objects (hidden or made absent) in rivers and bogs, or Tilley's (1997) description of the marking of the landscape with rock art that symbolizes absent or distant animals or boats, or the common notion that objects that are carried over longer distances often have special significance or value that is manipulated socially

(Sherratt 1981). In relation to Çatalhöyük the approach is very productive, partly because the marking and the absence can be set within the context of habitual routines. Because of the embedding of symbolism and ritual in domestic life at the site it is unhelpful to talk of a separate religious sphere, and yet it is clear that we need a way to talk of religious experience at the site, however much it is embedded in daily life. Thus the ridges on the house floors mark differences between activity areas. Bull horn pilasters mark the edges of platforms under which people are buried, as in Building 77 (Figure 2.7), so that the platform is marked in relation to daily activities on the floors and so that the human bones buried beneath the platform are both made present (by the bull horn marking) and hidden or made absent. The whole social process in the house can be described as one in which absences are marked, and the beyond is constructed in the midst of the practices of daily life.

It is clear that there were rules at Çatalhöyük about what could be done in different areas of the house. Adults were buried in the northern part of the house but not in the southern part. Pottery that was used to cook food in the southern part of the house was never placed in a grave. Different types of matting were placed on different types of platform. There was social control over what could be done in different parts of the house, and over the transitions between those spaces. The practices that produced the effects of absence displayed people's control or power. The bull horns marked the dead beneath the platform and made them present. The obsidian cached below the floor could from time to time be dug up and used. The skulls of the ancestor could from time to time be dug up, used and redeposited to found a new house. In all these ways the control over absence and presence, and the transitions between them, were integrally linked to social power – perhaps between elders and youngers or between history houses and other houses.

But it is important to recognize that the ways in which marking and absence are manipulated and experienced vary through time and in different contexts. How people experience absence and the beyond varies. Harvey Whitehouse in his contribution to the discussions and to this volume talks of these different ways of experiencing as 'modes of religiosity'. Most rituals are either high or low arousal. All low-frequency rituals are high intensity (Whitehouse terms these *imagistic*) so that the experiences are burned into people's minds. People then reflect on what happened over long periods of time. Low-intensity, high-frequency ritual (termed *doctrinal*) is more closely associated with the transmission of doctrine and knowledge, and it often involves persuasive leaders. At first sight, Çatalhöyük would seem to fit into the high-frequency, low-intensity category since the same images, symbols and practices are repeated over and over again in the houses. But there also seem to be cases of low-frequency, high-arousal events such as the feasts associated with wild bulls. Whitehouse and Hodder explore the value of this model for Çatalhöyük in Chapter 5. There seem to be good grounds for arguing that 1,400 years of occupation at the site saw a gradual shift from a more imagistic to a more doctrinal mode. Much the same argument could be made for the Neolithic of Anatolia and the Middle East more generally. The Pre-Pottery Neolithic B often seems associated with high-arousal and remarkable events such as the deposition of human figures at 'Ain Ghazal (Rollefson 2000), the plastering of skulls at Jericho and other sites (Bonogofsky 2005) or the impressive carved stone stele with dangerous, wild animals at Göbekli. And yet by the Pottery Neolithic throughout the area there is less evidence of obvious and distinctive ritual practices and a wider dissemination of symbolism into pottery decoration and stamp seals. Evaluation of this claim for a broader shift in modes of religiosity at this time will have to await further research, but the overall effect of the approach offered by Whitehouse is to shift archaeologists from identifying religion as a separate sphere to focusing on practices, effects and experiences.

Another approach to identifying different religious modes is Nakamura's contrast between magic and religion (Chapter 11). It is difficult to provide stable distinctions between religion and magic, but the latter term is often used to describe practical acts that lie outside or alongside religious schemes. While it is difficult to draw lines between magic, science and religion, it is often the contrasts with the other two terms that define magic. Magic is part of religion but it also transgresses. The normal religious themes at Çatalhöyük (the clay plastered bucrania, burial and dangerous, wild things in the clay house) can be contrasted with unusual clusters of objects. These clusters include obsidian, antler, pottery fragments, crystal, pigment, special stones or ax heads, stalactites, a baby leg, fossils and so on. Deposits of such objects often occur in liminal spaces and times – for example, in the construction or abandonment deposits in a house. They can be termed 'magical' in that they seem linked to particular practices that stand against the usual religious repertoire and can be seen as having a more direct instrumental character.

In summary, there was disagreement among members of the group about whether the term 'religious' should be used at all in the context of discussion about the types of society associated with Çatalhöyük, but there was agreement that a more applicable approach focused on marking or dealing with 'the beyond' – defined as absence, ultimate boundaries or the transcendental. There was also general agreement that in small-scale societies, and at Çatalhöyük in particular, this focus on 'the beyond' was embedded within forms of social and material life and did not constitute a separate institutional sphere. In evolutionary terms there was also general acceptance of the view that religion was an emergent property of other human capacities, instantiated in particular times and places.

2. Are changes in spiritual life and religious ritual a necessary prelude to the social and economic changes that lead to 'civilization'?

As noted in Chapter 1, this question can be seen as having two components. The first concerns the evidence from the Middle East as a whole and deals with the factors associated with the formation of settled villages from the 11th millennium BC onward. The second concerns the factors associated with the domestication of cattle at Çatalhöyük itself in the 7th millennium BC.

In relation to the first, more general question there was much discussion in our dialogues of the overall evidence for the adoption of farming in the Middle East, and in particular of the new evidence from Göbekli Tepe. There was much fascination with this site, not only with the richness of its symbolism but also with the evidence that such elaboration and complexity could occur so early, before fully domesticated plants and animals. The site seems to invite the speculation that communities first came together around large-scale and intense rituals before they intensified their subsistence economies to such an extent that genetic change occurred in crops and flocks. But it is important to recognize that genetic change in the process of domesticating plants and animals was preceded by the intensive collecting, cultivating and herding (Fuller 2007) of genetically wild species. Some degree of settled agglomerations, sometimes associated with ritual structures, occurs from the Natufian onward in the southern Levant (see Chapter 1). Göbekli Tepe is a remarkable site, and it raises in a very stark fashion the possibility of a very early role for symbolism and ritual in the formation of settled agricultural life. But it is itself only part of a larger and gradual process.

Certainly at the theoretical level, the scholars involved in the project accepted that a close tie was to be expected between spiritual and religious life and increasing social and economic complexity. In our general discussions, Bellah argued that different forms of religion are appropriate to different contexts (so that it is not possible to have Moses in Aboriginal Australia). Shults (Chapter 3) argued that changes in symbolic thought probably were a prelude to the major changes that led to complex 'civilizations'. Girard also suggested that the idea of living together came before the city – the idea of togetherness preceded the concrete realization. It came to be widely agreed among the group that picking apart causal chains was fraught with difficulties and that the most likely answer to the general question is that religious life and socioeconomic life were and are inextricably linked.

As noted in Chapter 1 there is possible evidence that at the more specific level at Çatalhöyük, there were changes in the symbolic manipulation of cattle before biological evidence of domestication of cattle. We await the new evidence from the site to see at what point cattle were domesticated – in the upper levels of the East Mound or only in the later West Mound. But there is certainly a decrease in the availability or use of wild cattle in the upper levels of the Neolithic East Mound, and also in the upper levels we see new forms of symbolic relationship between humans and animals, with, for example, domesticated animals being buried with humans in the TP Area.

But how did the religious and the economic interact in relation to cattle at Çatalhöyük? In terms of the framework presented by Keane in Chapter 8 and summarized in this chapter, cattle were marked at Çatalhöyük by killing, feasting and display, and thus were singled out as a focus of attention and interest. This could have been a factor in the domestication process: various ways of marking cattle as foci of special attention drew attention to what humans could do to them. Thus the symbolic and religious marking might have accelerated whatever incipient domestication was already going on. By way of contrast, sheep and goats had already been domesticated at the start of the site. They were thus less useful in the production of absence – and indeed they play little to no role in the symbolism and religious practices at the site. Indeed, one might ask why cattle were domesticated so late at Çatalhöyük and elsewhere in the Middle East. After, all sheep and goats had been domesticated for one to two millennia before cattle were domesticated. At Çatalhöyük it remains possible that the cattle were specifically 'kept' wild so that they could play their role in the production of absence, the imagining and manipulation of the beyond. The 'history houses' in the main early to middle levels of the site depended on this social construction of difference and otherness in transcendental experience.

Our overall conclusion, then, is that there is much both general and specific data to support the notion that changes in spiritual life and religious ritual are a prelude to or accompany the social and economic changes that lead to 'civilization'. But the question also asked whether they were a necessary prelude and accompaniment. Discussion of this aspect of the question also tended to lead to an affirmative. It was recognized that settled agricultural life involved a whole series of new structures and constraints on social and economic life. Longer-term relationships had to be set up to deal with the delayed returns from the investments of labor. There had to be ways of dealing with disputes in the large villages and towns. There had to be mechanisms for the passing down of property. All these changes involved new conceptions of humans in relation to each other, in relation to the environment and its resources. The new structures had to be imagined in a spiritual realm alongside their envisioning in practice.

Some additional support for the overall conclusions at Çatalhöyük has been provided in the past few years in the excavations conducted by Dr. Douglas Baird and Dr. Trevor Watkins at the nearby sites of Boncuklu and Pınarbaşı (Baird 2007, 2008). These sites stretch back to the 13th millennium BC, and they show, especially at Boncuklu, the very early development of many of the special features of Çatalhöyük. Boncuklu has the division of houses into south and north parts, burials beneath floors and elaborate installations on walls. And yet the site is small and low density. So it is clear that all the elaborate ritual and symbolism does not suddenly appear at Çatalhöyük as the result of agglomeration. Rather, the symbolism already exists prior to the aggregation on the Konya Plain at Çatalhöyük. The earlier small dispersed settlements were abandoned as people moved into the big center. But the inhabitants brought with them a symbolic and religious world through which they envisaged and built the town.

3. Do human forms take on a central role in the spirit world in the early Holocene, and, if so, does this centrality lead to new conceptions of human agency that themselves provide the possibility for the domestication of plants and animals?

For many members of the group this seemed a largely historical question to be answered by reference to archaeological data and thus less amenable to broad anthropological and theological debate. As with the second question, it seemed likely to all that the domestication of plants and animals involved changed conceptions of the world and that these changed conceptions would be embedded within other realms of thought. In particular, the domestication of animals would have involved new conceptions of the relationships between humans and animals, which must have been linked to other changes in thought at the time. Members of the group accepted the archaeological evidence that in contrast to the cave paintings and other symbolism of the Upper Palaeolithic in Europe, the imagery from Göbekli Tepe and Çatalhöyük indicated a domination of wild animals. Such a notion of human agents as able symbolically to dominate wild animals would have been helpful as the process of actual domination of animals in terms of their domestication got under way.

With respect to Webb Keane's account of religion in terms of marking and absence, it is possible to explore how such processes have historical consequences. In Chapter 8, Keane argues that marking and absence single out certain things as good candidates for attributing agency to them. Whether people are claiming agency for themselves – for example, by killing dangerous animals – or displacing it onto others – for example, by treating birds as spirits – they are objectifying agency. By objectifying agency, people can reflect on it. This makes it possible for them to transform habit into purposeful actions. It allows people to act in inventive, or morally responsible, or simply audacious new ways. If the Neolithic can be seen as a revolution in human abilities and efforts to intervene in the world, then self-consciousness about agency itself, meta-agency, is a crucial part of the process.

4. Do violence and death act as the foci of transcendent religious experience during the transitions of the early Holocene in the Middle East, and are such themes central to the creation of social life in the first large agglomerations of people?

As noted in Chapter 1, it proved important to separate the discussion of violence from that of death.

(a) In our discussions, LeRon Shults (Chapter 3) wanted to understand the violent imagery at Göbekli Tepe, Çatalhöyük and other sites in terms of the intensification it produced. He argued that in such moments of intense or heightened experience there was an awareness of the need for a new understanding of the self in relation to others. The participant was thus released to find a place in the world in a new way. The productive aspects of violence, rather than negative connotations, were a general theme in our debates. Indeed, the very term 'violence' might be unhelpful, as it may be other aspects of what we perceive as violent scenes that may be more salient. Thus a leopard claw may be kept because it indexes a powerful animal or because it endures rather than because it represents death and violence.

René Girard's initial response to the apparently violent imagery at Çatalhöyük involved a full interpretation of the symbolism at Çatalhöyük. For him religion is a way of managing and evacuating the violence generated inside the human community (Girard 1988). Most archaic religions show a narrative that involves going through violence to resolution. At Çatalhöyük there is often a pairing: two cranes, two skulls or two confronting leopards in deadlock. The other key symbol is the reverse of this: a group of people surrounding an exaggerated animal. The bull is about to be killed and taken into the house. The people will kill and be reconciled. This is a matter not of worshipping violence, but of peace produced through violence. There is a destructuring in the deadlock and a resolution into a new structure if the bull is treated right.

Maurice Bloch also noted that violence would have been a central theme in Çatalhöyük. His approach was more sociological (see Bloch 2008) and based on the general assessment by the group that Çatalhöyük was some form of 'house society' in which rights and resources were passed down in 'houses' (see Chapters 6–9). He argued that in such contexts there would have been the violence of wrenching women from their birth 'house' and forcing them to live in a marital 'house'. More generally it was recognized that there would be much conflict over resources in the dense town. And yet there is much evidence coming out of the human remains laboratory that the people at Çatalhöyük lived nonviolent lives. There were few indications of the cuts, wounds, parry fractures and crushed skulls that are so common on many other sites. So how had the potential for violence been so well managed at Çatalhöyük? Bloch argued that symbolic violence was a necessary part of the movement into another world. He saw most human societies as understanding that there is a permanent framework to social life that transcends the natural transformative processes of birth, growth, reproduction, aging and death. The violence and symbolic killing take people beyond process into permanent entities such as descent groups. By leaving this life, it is possible to see oneself and others as part of something permanent and life transcending. For Bloch (1992; see also Chapter 6), mastering the virility of wild bulls in rituals and depictions in the house 'reanimated' the transcendental social and thus contributed to the continuity of the house.

The moments of danger and/or violence involved movements away from the here and now; they involved transcendent experiences in which the social group could be transformed and made permanent. So it seems that there could indeed be a link between the violence in the imagery at Çatalhöyük and the lack of violence on human bodies. Social violence was dealt with by living within a symbolic, transcendent world of violence in which conflicts were resolved and social structures made permanent.

The view that the violent imagery at Çatalhöyük and other sites had a key role in creating the social and the long term as people first settled down and formed complex societies is summarized in Figure 12.1. In this diagram, on the central horizontal axis, the person is made social through violence and death, either through initiation and other rituals or in the daily interactions with bull horns and other animal parts present or made absent in the house. In the lower part of the diagram, this social process is linked to the transcendental and the spiritual as persons experience something beyond themselves that is integral to their lives. Spiritual power is gained by individuals in these experiences, but also is controlled by elders or history houses. In the upper part of the diagram these spiritual powers are related to social powers. The social manipulation of rituals and symbols of violence gives power to elders and history houses. There is also evidence that the power of wild animals was used to provide or protect. Thus in Figure 2.7 the bull horns surround and protect the ancestors buried beneath the platform, and in one case wild goat horns were found over, perhaps protecting, a bin containing lentils (Building 1; Hodder 2006).

This is a very different conception of the symbolism and ritual associated with the origins of agriculture and settled villages from that normally outlined (e.g., Cauvin 1994; Mellaart 1967). It has become commonplace to argue that the early farmers would have emphasized ideas of fertility, nurturing and abundance (Hodder and Meskell, Chapter 2). People associate this time period with images of women, often interpreted as pregnant or fertile, and much attention is paid to the few female figurines that have been found. But in fact male and phallic imagery is common, linked to images of wild male animals at Göbekli Tepe and Çatalhöyük. Social rules and roles seem to have been established in these first communities largely through a conception of the world in which violence and dangerous wild animals played a central part, as outlined in Figure 12.1.

In Chapter 8 Webb Keane discusses violence and death based on a Sumbanese example. He argues that there is a bundle of many different things that killing large dangerous animals does. The process is not unitary, and violence might not be the most important aspect. One aspect that he stresses because it is consistent with other things going on at Çatalhöyük is that killing big animals is a dramatic display of the control over the transition from life to death, visible to invisible, presence to absence. Thus, once again, social power is created through violence and death.

(b) There is wide agreement in this volume that death played an important social role in the building of house-based social groups at Çatalhöyük. It is clear that while all houses were very similar in size and elaboration at the site, some houses were larger, more elaborate and lasted longer than others. These more elaborate houses often contained more burials than other houses and indeed seem to have been used as repositories of the dead from other houses. Thus some physical sun-dried mud-brick houses became 'houses' of people held together by the circulation of human remains. Because these 'houses' also seem to have amassed animal parts, curated and passed down as memorials of feasts and animal kills, and because they also contained other symbolic elaboration such as

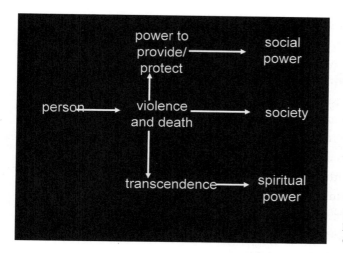

12.1. An interpretation of the role of violence in the social and religious process at Çatalhöyük. *Source:* Ian Hodder.

reliefs and paintings, these houses have been termed 'history houses' by Peter Pels.

This focus on history houses, and on the wider category of house societies to which they belong, might seem to be an unnecessary tangent in a volume about religion. But in fact this would be a misunderstanding of the role of the house at Çatalhöyük. In house-based societies, houses *are* religion. As we have seen, the play of presence and absence that is the religious process at Çatalhöyük takes place in the floor platforms, ridges, accoutrements and burials of the house. In particular, the heads of wild animals and humans are passed down from generation to generation within individual houses and between houses. Following Bloch, we can say that the virility of wild bulls installed in the material house reanimated the social house. The passing down of the objects of the house and the remembering and reliving of earlier houses constituted the social through the religious.

In Chapter 7 Peter Pels and I conducted a quantitative analysis of the houses at Çatalhöyük in order to explore the differences between history houses and other houses. We could find little difference between these two house types in terms of access to resources. So how was it possible for some houses to gain social and spiritual power through the amassing of skulls and wild bull horns and human burials while others did not? In Chapter 8 Keane discusses history houses in a way that is consistent with Pels but is historical. He suggests that bull horns and other objects accumulate over a career. The marks in a house (horns, paintings, etc.) are historical – they are traces of events. Some houses never get marks or burials, and they might be categorically different from those that do (e.g., branch or cadet lines). But the differences among houses with marks may be historical in nature, not categorical. Over generations, some houses acquired more events than others. Houses with 60 burials probably are categorically different from those with none. But houses with many bucrania or paintings are also houses that have persisted long enough to acquire more marks. As archaeologists we catch them at a late stage in the career of accumulating marks. The quantity of marks is in part a function of time. This explanation begs the question of why some houses persist longer than others. Perhaps many contingent factors are involved. But it remains possible that the more persistent and long-lasting houses were those that most effectively manipulated marks and absences, those that came to be recognized as good at protecting the dead and most capable of reanimating the traces of kills and feasts.

In addition to the four questions considered by the project, other questions and themes came to play a significant part in our discussions, and they play a central role in many of the chapters in this volume. Two additional themes are of particular note: temporal change during the occupation of Çatalhöyük and the role of cosmology at the site.

As noted in particular in Chapter 1, by Peter Pels in Chapter 9 and by Whitehouse and Hodder in Chapter 5, there is much evidence for change through time at Çatalhöyük. The explanations for these changes may include climate and environmental change (Roberts and Rosen 2009) – for example related to the sudden climatic event at 6200 BC (Thomas et al. 2007). There are undoubted social changes, with houses becoming larger and being more quickly and less exactly replaced in the upper levels of the Neolithic East Mound (Düring 2006). There are also changes in spiritual life and, in the upper levels and on the ensuing West Mound, burial gradually shifts and is less frequently found beneath house floors. Other changes in ritual and symbolism were also discussed. For example, much of the symbolism in the lower and middle parts of the mound involves indexing or 'presencing' wild animals and their associated wild animal spirits or 'gods'. Thus the actual body parts of wild animals were placed in the fabric of houses. But in the upper levels, religion seems to become more discursive in that the actual body parts of animals are less prevalent and the actual remains of ancestors are less common in houses. Instead, a discourse on religious themes emerges in the form of narrative wall paintings and codified stamp seals and more elaborately decorated and imaged pottery. This shift is closely related to that from a more 'imagistic' to a more 'doctrinal' mode of religiosity, as suggested by Whitehouse and Hodder in Chapter 5.

Other productive discussions took place regarding the cosmology of Çatalhöyük. Much can be said about the arrangement of space at the site in relation to the cardinal points, and we discussed ideas presented by Eva Bosch (2008) regarding the ways in which shafts of light traveled through the house on a daily basis (see Wason, Chapter 10). This notion of directionality and movement in the house can also be extended to the notion of circular movement around the house in a clockwise direction, and retracing the cycle of a human life from birth (in the south area with entrance, light, child burial) to middle age (bull heads and other signs of vitality) to old age and death (burial of adults in the eastern part of the house). The cosmology of Çatalhöyük can also be discussed in terms of notions of time and planning. There is much evidence of recall and remembrance and memory construction, but also of future thinking and planning as houses were laid out and plans made about the future uses of spaces.

Concluding summary

What has been achieved? As I have outlined so far and will summarize in this section, considerable success can be claimed in answering the four questions. But in addition, fresh new ideas have emerged from the interaction of an interdisciplinary group of scholars with archaeologists at a site in the process of being excavated. These new insights concern Çatalhöyük, but many are also relevant to understanding the formation of settled agricultural village life in the Middle East. The conception of religion as culturally variable but as involving processes of boundary marking and the production of absence is widely applicable in archaeology, as are comparative theories about modes of religiosity. Religion can be seen as an emergent quality deriving from aspects of human nature and the human condition. Radical new perspectives have been presented that are relevant to the Neolithic of the Middle East as a whole and in which violent imagery takes precedence over images of nurturing female fertility. The identification of history houses at Çatalhöyük is relevant to many sites at earlier and later times in the Middle East and Anatolia.

Fresh new ideas have emerged, but has there been substantive success in answering the four questions set by the project?

1. HOW CAN ARCHAEOLOGISTS RECOGNIZE THE SPIRITUAL, RELIGIOUS AND TRANSCENDENT IN EARLY TIME PERIODS?

There was general agreement across the spectrum of contributors to the discussions that it is undoubtedly possible for archaeologists to identify religion, even if there was disagreement about the value of the term itself in the context of societies such as at Çatalhöyük. But they also agreed that it is not helpful to designate a separate religious sphere in such societies as Çatalhöyük. The contribution of the project to the first question has been to show that the understanding of religion in archaeology needs to be embedded in particular understandings of the ways in which people marked out certain boundaries, and dwelled on absence and the beyond in relation to the routine and habitual practices of self and community.

2. ARE CHANGES IN SPIRITUAL LIFE AND RELIGIOUS RITUAL A NECESSARY PRELUDE TO THE SOCIAL AND ECONOMIC CHANGES THAT LEAD TO 'CIVILIZATION'?

In looking at the Middle East as a whole it was agreed that changes in spiritual life and religion are inextricably linked to settled agglomerated life and agriculture. This is because the substantial social and economic changes that are involved depend on shifts in perspective and imagination that are worked through in the religious and spiritual dimensions. In the specific case of Çatalhöyük, the appearance of domesticated cattle is preceded by or associated with changes in symbolism and religious ritual that lead to new conceptions of the relationships between humans and animals.

3. DO HUMAN FORMS TAKE ON A CENTRAL ROLE IN THE SPIRIT WORLD IN THE EARLY HOLOCENE, AND, IF SO, DOES THIS CENTRALITY LEAD TO NEW CONCEPTIONS OF HUMAN AGENCY THAT THEMSELVES PROVIDE THE POSSIBILITY FOR THE DOMESTICATION OF PLANTS AND ANIMALS?

In the Neolithic of the Middle East as well as at Çatalhöyük itself, representations of the human form reach a new centrality that does indeed suggest a new conception of human agency, less reciprocal and more dominant in the world of animals and animal spirits. Both at Göbekli Tepe in southeast Anatolia and at Çatalhöyük, humans come to dominate animals and animal spirits.

4. DO VIOLENCE AND DEATH ACT AS THE FOCI OF TRANSCENDENT RELIGIOUS EXPERIENCE DURING THE TRANSITIONS OF THE EARLY HOLOCENE IN THE MIDDLE EAST, AND ARE SUCH THEMES CENTRAL TO THE CREATION OF SOCIAL LIFE IN THE FIRST LARGE AGGLOMERATIONS OF PEOPLE?

In terms of (a) violence, the focus has been to explain new evidence that suggests that violent imagery, rather than imagery of birth and rebirth, is associated with the first large agglomerations and then with agriculture. Through violent imagery and practice the person was drawn into a social world in which long-term transcendent social institutions were increasingly prevalent. In terms of (b) death, there is much evidence that dead ancestors came to be central in the formation of social units centered around houses at Çatalhöyük. Perhaps the greatest advance made by the project has been in the definition of 'history houses'. These are long lineages of houses that were rebuilt in the same place and in which human burials, body parts and animal parts were amassed and handed down. Within a relatively egalitarian society, the status of those living in these history houses was based not on the control of production but on the control of the religious rituals and transcendent events that became the hallmark of the history houses, and of Çatalhöyük as a whole.

Evaluation

In this chapter I have so far focused on the impact of the interdisciplinary project on archaeology – on the archaeology of Çatalhöyük and the Neolithic of Anatolia and the Middle East. But what of the impact on the participating group of scholars and their own disciplines? In this final section I wish to report on personal comments from the group of scholars on what they may or may not have learned from this brush with the archaeological process. As the disciplines increasingly specialize and diverge, exciting bridges are often built in conference halls and workshops. But has anything different been gained from in-depth exposure to the trenches and laboratories at Çatalhöyük? What is the result (for each of the contributors' disciplines and for each of their individual research agendas and project) that comes from the time and effort spent on-site and in discussion with the archaeological experts? This final section may be more personal in tone, but it also points to general theoretical implications of this experiment in interdisciplinary engagement in the process of doing archaeology.

One response of all the group participants was to note the community aspect of archaeological research, at least at Çatalhöyük, where it has been possible to bring 120 researchers from diverse backgrounds to work at the site each summer. Statements made about an archaeological site have to be checked against data from excavators, faunal laboratory specialists, phytolith specialists, radiocarbon determinations and isotope readings. There is thus a dense material matrix that makes certain statements possible and constrains what can be said. The result is collective. Team work characterizes what archaeologists do in comparison with the solitary nature of research in many related fields, including much ethnography.

As Webb Keane reported to me, 'One reason I was first drawn to this project was that I was intrigued by the fascinating evidentiary problems posed by archaeological work. In Çatalhöyük, the materials seemed both rich and recalcitrant. It has been surprising to see how sophisticated the new technologies in archaeology have become.' At the start of the three-year project, most scholars came expecting to be able to apply their own disciplines and personally developed theoretical perspectives to the site. The scholars often went through a process of surprise that the archaeological data were sufficiently robust to resist the facile imposition of off-the-shelf theory. But they then settled down to work with the data and tried to adapt ready-made hypotheses to the site itself. As Peter Pels writes in Chapter 9, 'I was struck by the numerous occasions at which I turned out to be mistaken or premature in my conclusions in the face of analytical insights already provided by the archaeologists working at the site.'

In Chapter 6 Bloch worries at the start about being a 'blundering ignorant amateur'. Given the huge battery of archaeological techniques and the immense range of information now available to archaeologists, does the anthropologist outsider have anything to offer? Bloch argues that he brings general theoretical knowledge as well as specific knowledge of a couple of contemporary societies and cultures in Madagascar. Since these societies in Madagascar have their own histories, quite different from that of Çatalhöyük, any attempt to draw analogies he feels must be based on linking arguments that involve 'chains of causation that ultimately go back to general characteristic of our species.' In archaeology this approach is most clearly associated with behavioral archaeology (Schiffer 2000) and with evolutionary archaeology and human behavioral ecology (Bird and O'Connell 2006). Bloch argues for a universalism grounded in very basic aspects of what it means to be human. Of course, archaeologists also build their own theory and they are no longer as dependent as they used to be on anthropology as a source of theory. But general anthropological theory remains of value to archaeology because much cultural or social anthropology approaches theory from a perspective not available to archaeologists. This is not a better or privileged perspective; it is just different. Cultural anthropologists bring a general theoretical perspective derived from detailed in-depth studies of societies. Archaeologists can never attain this type of detailed knowledge. But as we shall see the great advantage that archaeologists have is time depth. So the perspectives are just different.

The theologians in the group of scholars also went through a process of surprise at the dense network of data available to archaeologists before they settled into a learning and adaptation mode. I quote here at length a comment from LeRon Shults:

> My experience of visiting the site was a bit of a roller coaster. It began on a high. Or, better, before it began I was on a high. Anticipating the first visit I was quite excited about seeing in person what I had explored on the Internet and in books. Perhaps I had seen too many Indiana Jones movies (my favorite as a boy), and my expectations were slightly unrealistic. The first day was exciting as we walked through the ditches and got the big story. But by the second and third days, I was getting a bit aggravated. The scientists kept focusing on the empirical material, and were fascinated by the smallest thing, down to the tiniest piece of preserved poop. As a philosopher and theologian, my mind kept wanting to go to the big, ever bigger, indefinitely bigger, picture. I felt deeply agitated and annoyed – far from my intellectual home turf and off balance. Then on the fourth day, I realized this was the whole point. For me to be forced to focus on the empirical material as well as to invite the scientists at the site into exploratory discussions about cross-disciplinary interpretations. I realized it only as I became accustomed to being at the site, as I relaxed and began talking informally with the scientists during meals, etc. In the time between visits, as I worked on

my essay, I often remembered the concrete details of the site, usually connected to a personal conversation with a scientist. During later visits I was much more relaxed, had a better sense of what to expect, and was even eager to hear about the latest discoveries of preserved poop – what insights would they disclose? I am still a philosopher and theologian, and my mind still intuitively moves toward abstraction. But the ongoing experience at the site has given me a fresh appreciation for, and even enjoyment of, dwelling a little longer in concretion.

One example of how general theory came to be accommodated to the site is in relation to house societies. Throughout this volume reference has been made to the notion that Çatalhöyük is a version of a category of society first defined by Lévi-Strauss as *sociétés à maisons* (Bloch, Chapter 6). But in many ways, the houses at Çatalhöyük differ very much from the large, even massive houses most commonly associated with the term in medieval Europe and Japan or in the traditional societies of the northwest American coast. In addition, the social system at Çatalhöyük is very egalitarian in contrast to many of the historical or ethnographic examples. So it has proved preferable to talk instead of history houses, institutions that have some of the characteristics of house societies, such as the passing down of objects, without all the baggage of full-scale complex societies with specific forms of exchange and political power (Carsten and Hugh-Jones 1997; Joyce and Gillsepie 2000).

Perhaps the greatest contribution the archaeological data make to broader theory and the other disciplines is in terms of time depth. Pels reports that 'without the Çatalhöyük experience I would not have gained such a strong sense of the need to further explore relationships between things and time, or materiality and temporality.' As Keane notes, 'In working with the team, I have become increasingly interested in the perspectives offered by grappling with deep time, compared to the very shallow histories with which most cultural anthropologists work. This in turn has led me to reconsider the problem of comparison in cultural anthropology (as well as across the subdisciplines). The word has a bad reputation among many cultural anthropologists today, yet comparison is surely implicit in everything we do. The problem is that, too often, comparison is the work that refuses to speak its name. Done unwittingly, it is likely to be done badly. It may take collaborations like these to shake us out of our old preconceptions and ask ourselves how to go about this business in more explicit, thoughtful, and inventive ways.'

Harvey Whitehouse made a related comment: 'One of the things that has surprised and excited me about Çatalhöyük is the extent to which it is possible to uncover patterned relationships between things like the frequency, scale, and emotionality of feasting events on the one hand and cosmological themes of hiding and revealing on the other – in other words, even though there is much we will never know about the details of prehistoric cosmologies we can still recover much salient information about ancient religious life that can in principle be compared with patterns found in thousands of other cultures, past and present. I had not imagined that would be possible to the extent it really is until we started discussing the evidence in detail. Even if Chapter 5 just takes a few baby steps it points to future methods of research of a much more systematic and sophisticated kind, all the more so as large volumes of data become available electronically.' As a result it becomes possible to envisage contributions to studies of long-term change. The transformation to a more discursive kind of religiosity at Çatalhöyük paves the way for the doctrinal mode long before the advent of advanced inscribing practices. Such a contribution to the debates (stemming from work by authors such as Goody (1986)) on what comes first (both causally and chronologically) – literacy or the doctrinal mode – is an example of one way in which the archaeology at Çatalhöyük changes our 'grand theorizing'.

Another example of the value of a long-term perspective concerns general theories about social and economic change. Many theories, from Marxist to evolutionary and systemic, argue for close links between changes in economy, society, symbolism, ritual and religion. The data from Göbekli and Çatalhöyük, and from other sites in the earlier Neolithic of the Middle East, provide ample evidence for economic and social changes in the early Holocene as large villages are formed and plants and animals are cultivated and then domesticated. And yet throughout these millennia from 10,000 to 6000 BC there is a paucity of images that deal with crops, animal husbandry, nurturing fertility and the like. At Çatalhöyük there is no symbolic elaboration on pottery or on grain storage bins, and domesticated sheep and goats appear seldom if at all in the art. It is as if the changes that we now focus on as so foundational in the emergence of 'civilization' were hardly noticed at all. They seem to have had little social significance and play no role in the symbolic and religious spheres. As we have seen, religion was thoroughly involved in the creation of new social forms during this period. These preoccupations with the religious and with the formation of new forms of social grouping during these millennia ignored other changes, perhaps more significant, that would in time utterly transform what it meant to be human. It may be that this process of distraction is of relevance today. Whatever the explanation of this phenomenon, answers will depend on a long-term perspective.

REFERENCES

Asad, T. 1993. *Genealogies of Religion: Discipline and Reasons of Power in Christianity and Islam*. Baltimore: Johns Hopkins University Press.

Baird, D. 2007. Pınarbaşı: From Epipalaeolithic camp site to sedentarising village in central Anatolia. In *The Neolithic in Turkey: New Excavations and New Discoveries*, eds. M. Özdoğan and N. Başgelen. Istanbul: Arkeoloji ve Snatat Yayınları, 285–311.

Baird, D. 2008. The Boncuklu project: The origins of sedentism, cultivation and herding in central Anatolia. *Anatolian Archaeology*, 14, 11–14.

Bird, D. W., and O'Connell, J. F. 2006. Behavioural ecology and archaeology. *Journal of Archaeological Research*, 14(2), 143–88.

Bloch, M. 1992. *Prey into Hunter: The Politics of Religious Experience*. Cambridge: Cambridge University Press.

Bloch, M. 2008. Why religion is nothing special but is central. *Philosophical Transactions of the Royal Society*, June 2008, 2055–62.

Bonogofsky, M. 2005. A bioarchaeological study of plastered skulls from Anatolia: New discoveries and interpretations. *International Journal of Osteoarchaeology*, 15, 124–35.

Bosch, E. 2008. The sun clock and light and shadow inside the replica house. *Çatalhöyük Archive Report 2008*, 282–3.

Bradley, R. 1990. *The Passage of Arms*. Cambridge: Cambridge University Press.

Carsten, J., and Hugh-Jones, S., eds. 1997. *About the House*. Cambridge: Cambridge University Press.

Cauvin, J. 1994. *Naissance des divinités, naissance de l'agriculture*. Paris: CNRS.

Düring, B. S. 2006. *Constructing Communities: Clustered Neighbourhood Settlements of the Central Anatolian Neolithic, ca. 8500–5500 Cal. BC*. Leiden: Nederlands Instituut voor het Nabije Oosten.

Fuller, D. 2007. Contrasting patterns in crop domestication and domestication rates: Recent archaeobotanical insights from the Old World. *Annals of Botany*, 100, 903–24.

Girard, R. 1988. *Violence and the Sacred*. London: Athlone Press.

Goody, J. 1986. *The Logic of Writing and the Organization of Society*. Cambridge: Cambridge University Press.

Hodder, I. 2006. *The Leopard's Tale: Revealing the Mysteries of Çatalhöyük.* London: Thames and Hudson.

Joyce, R., and Gillespie, S. D., eds. 2000. *Beyond Kinship: Social and Material Reproduction in House Societies.* Philadelphia: University of Pennsylvania Press.

Mellaart, J. 1967. *Çatal Hüyük: A Neolithic Town in Anatolia.* London: Thames and Hudson.

Renfrew, C. 1985. *The Archaeology of Cult.* Los Angeles: University of California Press.

Roberts, N., and Rosen, A. 2009. Diversity and complexity in early farming communities of Southwest Asia: New insights into the economic and environmental basis of Neolithic Çatalhöyük. *Current Anthropology*, 50(3), 393–402.

Rollefson, G. 2000. Ritual and social structure at Neolithic 'Ain Ghazal. In *Life in Neolithic Farming Communities*, ed. I. Kuijt. New York: Kluwer, 163–90.

Schiffer, M. B., ed. 2000. *Social Theory and Archaeology.* Salt Lake City: University of Utah Press.

Sherratt, A. 1981. Plough and pastoralism: Aspects of the secondary products revolution. In *Pattern of the Past: Studies in Honour of David Clarke*, eds. I. Hodder, G. Isaac and N. Hammond. Cambridge: Cambridge University Press, 261–305.

Thomas, E. R., Wolff, E. W., Mulvaney, R., Steffensen, J. P., Johnsen, S. J., Arrowsmith, C., White, J. W. C., Vaughn, B., and Popp, T. 2007. The 8.2 ka event from Greenland ice cores. *Quaternary Science Reviews*, 26, 70–81.

Tilley, C. 1997. *Phenomenology of Landscape.* London: Berg.

van Huyssteen, J. Wentzel. 2006. *Alone in the World? Human Uniqueness in Science and Theology.* Grand Rapids, Mich.: Eerdmans.

Index